The Irish Act of Union

A Study in High Politics
1798–1801

The Irish Act of Union

A Study in High Politics
1798–1801

PATRICK M. GEOGHEGAN

GILL & MACMILLAN

Gill & Macmillan Ltd
Goldenbridge
Dublin 8
with associated companies throughout the world
www.gillmacmillan.ie
© Patrick M. Geoghegan 1999
0 7171 2883 0
Index compiled by Helen Litton
Print origination by Carole Lynch
Printed by ColourBooks Ltd, Dublin

This book is typeset in Ehrhardt 11pt/12pt.

A CIP catalogue record for this book is available
from the British Library.

1 3 5 4 2

Contents

Preface

The enemy of the human race.
(The French national convention on William Pitt, 1793)

*I approach you with the greater confidence from a thorough conviction of
your wisdom, spirit, and zeal for the public service . . .* this *is the period,
for you are the minister.*
(Theobald Wolfe Tone to William Pitt, 10 August 1788)

The act of union has dominated Irish nationalism for almost two centuries. Symbolically, as much as anything else, it is the defining event of modern Irish history, the focal point for the swirling issues of nationalism and political identity. The union brought into effect the United Kingdom of Great Britain and Ireland, and was a genuine, if flawed, attempt at creating a new Anglo-Irish relationship. Nevertheless it failed, chiefly because of the protracted circumstances of its birth. Already tainted by the whiff of corruption that had accompanied its passing, the union was fatally damaged by the government's inability to accompany it with catholic emancipation. It endured, rather than flourished, after 1801, a mere shell of what had originally been envisaged. As a unifying security mechanism the act of union was stillborn.

This book examines two key areas, which although inextricably linked have previously been separated by historians: the Irish act of union and the resignation of Prime Minister William Pitt. Irish historians who have covered the union have tended to end their descriptions in 1800; other historians, however, usually start at that point when examining the fall of the ministry; only biographies span both areas, and these, by their very nature, have a narrow axis. Both accounts become clearer when they are seen as two parts of the same story. High politics has perhaps become an unjustly neglected pursuit; here it helps explain three important historical questions — why the union was introduced, how it was passed, and why the government collapsed in 1801. If Pitt's resignation was a cynical manoeuvre to withdraw from office, with the catholic question as a pretext, as many observers and historians have alleged, then a cloud is placed over the integrity of the government's position on catholic emancipation during the passing of the union. Conversely, if Pitt and his key ministers felt obliged to resign over the failure to accompany the union with emancipation, then this issue helps clarify some of the questions surrounding why and how the union was passed. If May 1798 is the correct starting point for a study of Pitt's resignation, then this book also shows why March 1801 marks the natural conclusion for any study of the act of union.

It is the central contention of this work that the union cannot be properly understood unless the influence it had on the government's collapse in 1801 is known, and that, likewise, Pitt's resignation is incomprehensible unless the centrality of the catholic question is fully recognised. Had catholic emancipation been granted in 1801, no Irish history of the period would have ended in 1800 with the passing of the union. Yet the failure to grant emancipation in 1801 is at least of equal significance. Pitt's resignation is regularly described by historians as 'a mystery'. But many of the problems with the crisis dissolve once 1798, and Ireland, is taken as the starting point, and not British foreign policy in 1800.

Until now, the only extensive modern study of the measure has been G.C. Bolton's *The passing of the Irish act of union*, published in 1966. A towering work, the book concentrated on how the union was passed, and avoided an analysis of why the act was introduced. Bolton also neglected to examine the consequences of the union, and the collapse of Pitt's ministry. Indeed, he mistakenly attributed the breakdown of relations with the king in 1801 to a different matter entirely from the catholic question.

This confusion over Pitt's resignation has been prevalent. It was not understood at the time, and amongst historians the only constant has been the absence of consensus. Even today the resignation remains one of the most controversial areas of British political history. John Ehrman, Pitt's most recent and authoritative biographer, enlisted the earlier analysis of Richard Pares and concluded that 'the occasion has remained one of the "special mysteries" of the age'. The problem that faced the nineteenth-century audience, and was subsequently to face historians, resulted from an inability to understand Pitt's behaviour, stemming in part from a flawed understanding of the Irish dimension. The examination of the collapse of the government in the second section of this book, coming as it does after an examination of the Irish union, avoids this problem, and attempts to provide the most comprehensive account yet of Pitt's resignation. Only by placing the events of 1800 and early 1801 in their proper domestic and foreign policy context is it possible to remove the ambiguity that has cloaked the affair, and attempt a definitive explanation.

One controversial area that appeared to be laid to rest by Bolton's research was the question of corruption. Allegations of impropriety and illegality were never far away during the passing of the union, and they remained popular, if never proven, afterwards. Bolton demonstrated that the generous patronage employed by the government to facilitate the measure was acceptable by the conventions of the time and, although perhaps ethically dubious, was not illegal. This had been the chief criticism levelled at the union by those who challenged its legality. Jonah Barrington, Henry Grattan and Daniel O'Connell all accused the government of having bribed the parliament to vote for its own abolition, a charge that was readily accepted by most subsequent historians, including the great nineteenth-century scholar W.E.H. Lecky. The case for corruption, however, rested on mere supposition and hearsay, and the lack of any concrete evidence eventually ensured that Bolton's analysis became the accepted academic conclusion.

This consensus has been shattered by the discovery of 'lost' secret service papers, which are now deposited in the Public Record Office in Kew. These accounts provide proof that covert illegal funds were used by the government to help fund its union campaign. This book is the first full account of the union to make use of these papers, documents that show the extreme lengths to which the government was prepared to go to ensure compliance. The role of the alien office is particularly significant. While it was long disregarded as an unimportant subsection of the home office, much recent scholarship has proven that in reality it acted as a fully efficient secret service network for the British government during the 1790s. The passing of the union, therefore, cannot be seen in a purely Irish context; rather it was part of an increasingly organised and ruthless British response to the war on the continent.

Linking the domestic and foreign crises, the first part of this book examines how and why the act of union was passed, from May 1798 to August 1800. Throughout these chapters the catholic question is a recurring theme, and it unites both parts of the book. The question of emancipating the catholics was a problematic one for the government and it searched for many ways to address, or avoid, the problem. The political paralysis that followed the union was also in evidence during its passing as the government attempted to placate all sides, and secure the measure on the cheap. In the second part of the book the focus shifts, temporarily, away from Ireland as the mounting problems facing Pitt's ministry in 1800 are examined. The catholic question is thereby placed in its proper context: a government and a prime minister slowly coming apart from their growing difficulties, until both collapse in January 1801. Chapter 7, dealing with the chronology of Pitt's resignation, is in many respects the pivotal chapter. The events between the end of January and the end of March 1801 generated a crisis that had severe repercussions for Britain, and brought to a head everything that had been happening in Irish affairs over the previous three years. Catholic emancipation, which had been tantalisingly close, was again prevented, the lord lieutenant and his chief secretary resigned, and for a time it appeared that the union itself would be compromised by unwelcome revelations.

The thesis from which this book has developed was subtitled 'a study in high politics'. But, if anything, the turbulent events of 1798–1801 are a study in character. From Prime Minister William Pitt, through to Lord Lieutenant Cornwallis and his chief secretary, Viscount Castlereagh, to the hardened opponents of union such as William Plunket and Henry Grattan, the struggle was as much a conflict of individuals as ideologies. Between 1798 and 1801, as the union lurched from victory to defeat, and back again, with alarming regularity, and as political machinations threatened to destabilise it completely, the contest became a test of character for those involved. As fissile temperaments cracked under the strain, the culmination of the struggle was as much rooted in psychological as political matters.

This book has two functions. It explains why the act of union was introduced and how it was passed, before examining the effects of this policy on the stability of the British government. Foreign policy difficulties and other domestic problems in Britain are not ignored as they provide a valuable context, but it is the union that created the momentum that brought down Pitt's ministry, and it is the catholic question that provides a constant theme. The prime minister, William Pitt, is also central to everything. It was he who directed the union strategy in its initial stages, struggled to find a solution to the catholic question, and was ultimately broken by his inability to do so. His resignation in 1801 brought to an end the delicate attempts to create a stable Anglo–Irish connection. The measure, itself, left a legacy of broken promises and bitter memories. Far from Pitt's intention of resolving the problems in the Anglo–Irish relationship, the union became the source, and focal point, for future discord and rancour. In the end, the union collapsed under the weight of its own expectations.

Acknowledgments

This book is based on my 1997 Ph.D. thesis, 'The Irish act of union, the catholic question, and the collapse of Pitt's ministry: a study in high politics, 1798–1801', and many of the debts incurred with writing that are transferred to here. I was very fortunate in University College Dublin to have not one but two excellent supervisors. Once again, I would like to thank both for their constant support and advice. Mr James McGuire was the original inspiration for my thesis with his final-year documents course, and was the main reason why I wanted to do my postgraduate degree in UCD. In the second year of my research Professor Thomas Bartlett became Professor of Modern Irish History and kindly agreed to supervise my thesis with Mr McGuire. Together they made invaluable suggestions, and added immeasurably to the tone, nature and quality of the thesis. I must also thank the Combined Departments of History for their help during my time in UCD. In particular I would like to mention Dr Michael Laffan and Dr David Doyle for their support, and especially Professor Mary Daly, who was my tutor in first year and a guiding influence. I would also like to thank the department for honouring me with the Desmond Williams Travelling Scholarship, which enabled me to carry out extensive research in English archives.

John Ehrman, the authoritative biographer of Pitt, kindly read my thesis, and his comments and extraordinary generosity are greatly appreciated. Professor John Derry, of the University of Newcastle, was also kind enough to read my work and I would like to thank him for his warm support. During my research I was very impressed with the assistance shown to me by the various libraries and record offices. I would like to thank Dr A.P.W. Malcomson and his staff at the Public Record Office of Northern Ireland for their exceptional attention, and likewise the staff at the National Library of Ireland, University College Dublin, Trinity College Dublin, Cambridge University Library and the Royal Irish Academy.

Since completing my thesis I have been involved with the Royal Irish Academy's *Dictionary of Irish Biography*, a momentous project, and what will surely be a vital contribution to Irish history, and I would like to thank the RIA for permission to use some of my research in this book. I would also like to pay tribute to my publishers, for developing this work, and especially Mr Fergal Tobin for his unflagging enthusiasm and support, Ms Deirdre Rennison Kunz and my copy-editor, Ms Angela Rohan.

This book would not have been possible but for the constant help of my friends and family. It is not possible to mention them all by name but they may be assured that their contribution will never be forgotten. Nevertheless a special mention is necessary for Mrs Mary Connellan and my Uncle Tommy, for their generous hospitality in Dublin and London, and also for the spirit of Room 3040 in Trinity College Dublin. Finally, as with my thesis, I would like to dedicate this work to the memory of my Uncle Pat, whose love and encouragement will always be remembered; and also to my mother, for her unceasing support.

1

The search for security: the Anglo-Irish relationship

DECEMBER 1783–JULY 1798

I should say that without a union *Ireland will not be connected with Great Britain in twenty years time.*
(Lord Lieutenant Rutland to Prime Minister Pitt, 16 June 1784)[1]

The great question remains: what is it that in truth will give satisfaction and ensure permanent tranquillity to Ireland? . . . We may keep the parliament but lose the people.
(Prime Minister Pitt to Chief Secretary Orde, 19 September 1784)[2]

The union was an act of arrogance. It was arrogantly conceived, and executed with the ruthless inefficiency that characterised much of government activity in the period. The outbreak of rebellion on the night of 23 May 1798 forced William Pitt, somewhat reluctantly, to direct his attentions to Ireland. A union between the two kingdoms had been something long desired in high political circles in Britain.[3] In particular, Pitt, who had been prime minister since December 1783, saw in union the only practicable solution to the difficult problems posed by the neighbouring island. Legislative independence in 1782 had clouded the Anglo-Irish relationship. Afterwards, the failure of attempts to redefine and re-establish the relationship, such as the commercial propositions of 1784–5, only increased fears about the permanency of the connection between the two kingdoms. Events over the next decade convinced Pitt that an independent Irish legislature could never guarantee security for Britain or tranquillity for Ireland: only union offered a framework within which these related aspirations could be addressed. Joining the Irish and British legislatures made possible the eventual inclusion of the Roman Catholics in parliament, and thereby offered a mechanism for gaining their support. More importantly, union offered the means for Pitt to restructure the relationship between Britain and Ireland in a way that would enhance the security and strength of the empire.[4] The civil emancipation of the catholics, the removal of their remaining political and legal restrictions, was certainly a calculation in this strategy, but union represented more than a means to secure this end. Union was not an expedient response to rebellion, nor was it designed to achieve emancipation. For Pitt, union was grounded in imperial, not Irish, considerations. Its adoption and execution encapsulated government conduct and concerns in the late 1790s, and reflected a growing confidence, bordering on recklessness, in the way the war with revolutionary France, and empire, were being pursued.

The French revolution of 1789 had contaminated previous certainties about the state and the individual. It had a pervasive, and sometimes pernicious, influence on events in Ireland, and inaugurated a gradual shifting in political radicalism. In one sense it made the Irish rebellion of 1798 possible, helping to transform the United Irishmen into a separatist organisation and imbuing political debate with a new ideological fervour. The threat of the French contagion terrified the British government, especially once war broke out between the countries in 1793. It dominated its attitude towards Ireland, and defined its attempts to blend repressiveness and conciliation in both islands.

With Ireland in the spring of 1798 heading towards open rebellion, Dublin castle adopted rigorous countermeasures to terminate the crisis. Thomas Bartlett, during the bicentenary commemoration of the rebellion, offered a new interpretation about the confused and turbulent events in the first half of 1798. Re-evaluating both when and where the rebellion occurred, he suggests that the castle acted as if it were already fighting a rebellion prior to the night of 23 May. And if the official rising was limited to a few counties on the east coast of Ireland, then it was probably due to the mass arrests the government had authorised, with prisoners located in almost equal measure throughout the country.[5]

The rebellion in 1798 enabled Pitt to transform his aspiration for a union into government policy. It afforded a rare opportunity for the king's government[6] to press the merits of the question. King George III recognised this when he advised Pitt on 13 June that no time should be lost in manipulating the crisis in Ireland 'for frightening the supporters of the castle into a union'.[7] In turn, the threat presented to the security of the empire by events in Ireland created a new urgency about union. It had become no longer merely desirable but strategically necessary for the defence of the two islands. The rebellion in 1798 made Irish problems assume a significance that the pressures of war intensified.

The 'true reason' for the union, Pitt privately asserted in the autumn of 1798, was 'that the old Irish system neither can last in its present shape, nor be corrected by anything in Ireland'.[8] The 'old Irish system' had been severely tested and found wanting on many occasions in the previous ten years, most crucially during the regency crisis of 1788–9. All the hidden strains in the Anglo-Irish relationship, which had been heightened by the settlement of 1782, were brought to the surface. At a time of confusion and uncertainty the Irish parliament had revealed that it could not be trusted. In the aftermath of this, Pitt was forced to re-examine the frustrating problem of Ireland. Closer bonds through economic union had been rejected in 1785. That had been an attempt by Pitt to join the two countries commercially, economically and defensively, so that 'England and Ireland [would become] one country in effect, though for local concerns under different legislatures . . . The two countries will be to the most essential purposes united.'[9] Adam Smith, a major influence on the young Pitt (although this should not be exaggerated),[10] had recommended a union between Ireland and Britain to benefit Irish trade and make the inhabitants 'one people'.[11] Over time, Pitt began to accept that only a full legislative union, and not any regulation in the commercial relationship, could bring the security and the new reciprocal Anglo-Irish relationship that he craved.

In the 1790s the threat facing Britain from the continent forced the king's government to consider methods for enlisting the help of the Irish catholics. As work on the relationship between military and religious questions at this time has revealed, the support of the catholics was seen as an essential part of any wartime strategy.[12] Bartlett makes a powerful case that 'it was above all the pressure of war that forced the catholic question onto the political agenda, and kept it there'.[13] In the winter of 1792 the worsening situation in Europe, notably the threat posed by revolutionary France, made Pitt and Henry Dundas, home secretary at the time, seek to 'connect all lovers of order and good government in a union of resistors to all the abettors of anarchy and misrule'.[14] They did not see any reason to exclude the Roman Catholics from this alliance.

Securing the support of the Irish catholics required certain concessions, the most controversial of which was the right to sit in parliament. Whitehall consistently maintained that this was too dangerous a concession within the existing political framework. Observers then, and since, have dismissed such fears. Oliver MacDonagh suggests that the few catholics who would have suc-ceeded in entering parliament would have been more servile than their protestant counterparts.[15] Whether government fears were justified or not, and MacDonagh accepts that it could not have predicted with certainty the effects of emancipation, it continued to regard emancipation as a threat to the connection with Britain. Faced with this problem Pitt began to turn over in his mind the idea of a legislative union followed by catholic emancipation. This was suggested in November 1792 to Westmorland, the Irish lord lieu-tenant, who revealed that the protestants would prefer a union to conceding the franchise, and that likewise the catholics would prefer a union rather than continue as they were. The viceroy advised Pitt that it was worth considering 'how the violence of both parties might be turned on this occasion to the advantage of England'.[16] The idea of a legislative union followed by the civil emancipation of the catholics was one, Pitt admitted, that had 'long been in my mind'.[17] He revealed to the lord lieutenant his opinion that

> the admission of catholics to a share of the suffrage could not then be dangerous — the protestant interest in point of power, property and church establishment would be secure because the decided majority of the supreme legislature would necessarily be protestant.

This opinion was not enthusiastically received by Westmorland. Early in 1793 he enquired of Pitt if he meant 'to force the protestants to a union',[18] not convinced that such a course was sound policy. He advised Pitt to 'choose between the catholic or the protestant interest', refusing to be drawn into a discussion about union.

France's declaration of war in 1793 led Pitt, gradually, to strengthen his ministry through a coalition with the Portland section of the whigs. As part of this arrangement Earl Fitzwilliam was sent to Ireland as lord lieutenant in 1795. His precipitous actions upon arrival created a dangerous predicament for the government. Believing that he had cabinet approval for supporting a catholic relief bill, Fitzwilliam inflamed feelings on all sides in the country, alienating protestant supporters of government by his peremptory dismissals from office, and at the same time raising the expectations of the catholics without being able to deliver emancipation. Fitzwilliam was quickly recalled but the Anglo–Irish connection had been severely strained.

George III lost no time in informing Pitt of his opposition to further catholic relief. The king had been reminded, from a hint by the Irish lord chancellor, the earl of Clare, through Lord Chancellor Loughborough, of his coronation oath. In a strongly worded statement on the subject he warned his prime minister that the government would have to think carefully before encouraging any emancipation proposals, 'propositions which cannot fail, sooner or later, to separate the two kingdoms'.[19] The question was not one that any cabinet could ever have responsibility for deciding. In an assertion of his royal authority the king informed Pitt that

> the subject is beyond the decision of any cabinet of ministers — that, could they form an opinion in favour of such a measure, it would be highly dangerous without previous [word illegible] with the leading men of every order in the state.

The second Earl Camden, a close friend of the prime minister, was sent to Ireland as Fitzwilliam's replacement. He inherited an unstable situation that only increased the attractiveness of union in London. Two years earlier Camden himself had advised his step-nephew Robert Stewart, the future Viscount Castlereagh, that 'Ireland must be our province if she will not be persuaded to a union, and if she would, she ought and would enjoy complete and reciprocal benefits with this country.'[20] But while Camden believed in the merits of a union, he did not feel that catholics should be allowed to sit in a united parliament. He accepted that he was, quite possibly, 'a very prejudiced Englishman'.[21]

In 1797, with unrest brewing in Ireland, Camden wrote to Lord Grenville, the foreign secretary, urging the government to lose no time 'in relieving ourselves from the very inconvenient terms upon which the two countries are at this time'.[22] This recommendation was followed up more explicitly in a letter to the prime minister a few months later in which he described the worsening state of the country. In it he argued against the hasty concession of catholic emancipation as it would only lead to calls for reform and

> if both of these points are conceded do you not lose the best, the only chance of adopting the measure which can alone render this country and England so united, as that it should be an advantage to it instead of being a point dreadfully vulnerable in all future wars — I mean a union?[23]

Like Westmorland, Camden declined to speak further and refused responsibility for overseeing such a measure.

Historians have disagreed over where blame for the 1798 rebellion should be placed. Popular judgments have censured Pitt. Thomas Pakenham has argued that it followed the failure of the prime minister to have any policy for Ireland.[24] It is true that after the failure of the commercial propositions, and the regency crisis, in the 1780s, Ireland had become 'that unlucky subject' for Pitt.[25] He admitted to Camden in 1795 that the country occupied little of his thoughts.[26] In an often quoted letter on Irish affairs in 1798 John Beresford, the first commissioner for revenue, expressed his delight at finding the prime minister 'thinking on the subject of Ireland'.[27] Yet while historians from G.C. Bolton to John Ehrman are correct in highlighting Pitt's lack of interest in Irish affairs, there has been a mistaken tendency to conclude that Ireland occupied *none* of his thoughts. Before the outbreak of a rebellion Pitt did not studiously avoid Irish affairs.

The welfare of the empire was never far from Pitt's thoughts. Concerns with protecting and strengthening it always forced Ireland into his considerations, despite his obvious discomfort. There was always the outline of an Irish strategy in Pitt's mind. Marquess Wellesley confirmed this in 1801, when discussing the catholic question with Grenville. Wellesley was an enthusiastic supporter of emancipation and believed it a necessary corollary of the union: 'this, as you may remember, was my opinion long ago, when I pressed the necessity of the union at Holwood [Pitt's home] and elsewhere in various debates and discussions'.[28] These 'debates and discussions' could only have taken place prior to November 1797, as in that month Wellesley (then earl of Mornington) departed for India to become governor-general.[29] The informal meetings, which probably involved Pitt, Dundas, Grenville and Wellesley, reveal much thinking on the subject of Ireland in the lead-up to the rebellion.

Baker street, London, provides an intriguing clue about the growing momentum for union prior to the rebellion. Valentine Lawless (later second Baron Cloncurry) attended a dinner at the home of John Macnamara, sometime between 1795 and 1797, where he later claimed he heard Pitt speak on the 'contemplated project' of a union.[30] Disturbed by this intelligence,

Lawless wrote a spirited pamphlet against the measure, a pre-emptive strike in the propaganda war, that was published in Dublin in 1797, entitled 'Thoughts on the projected union'. While it is not clear how speculative Pitt's discussion was, and it is unlikely that he would have used a dinner party for anything more serious, it is nevertheless indicative of a certain thinking about an Irish solution.

Further, and more decisive, evidence is that an envoy was sent to Ireland, in the second half of 1797, to discuss the union question with the lord lieutenant. This secret mission, underlining Pitt's commitment to a solution for Ireland, has hitherto gone unnoticed by historians.[31] The person given this delicate task, Robert Smith, was an interesting choice. Smith, who had become the first Baron Carrington of Bulcot Lodge in the peerage of Ireland the previous year, was a close friend of Pitt who had helped arrange the prime minister's disorganised financial affairs in 1786.[32] In a letter to Pitt on 10 October 1797, sent via Smith, Camden revealed a desire to be allowed to retire from his position as lord lieutenant. He insisted that such a request was not grounded in any desire to be 'pressed' into staying on in Ireland, nor was he demanding a return to England where he felt he could really be of service.[33] The reasons Camden gave for his request were numerous: the absence from friends, the confusion of his affairs in England, the great expense he was incurring in Ireland, and the poor health of his wife; all were given as contributing to his desire to leave the country. Upon such a return, Camden hoped that he would not 'absolutely retire to *the woods*' but be given some office of responsibility at Pitt's discretion. Camden was prepared to stay in Ireland 'with cheerfulness' for as long as his services were 'really required'. The continuance of the war with France, however, was considered a barrier to the realisation of these 'private considerations'. Significantly, Camden also saw the war as an obstacle to 'the discussion, and certainly the settlement, of those subjects which Lord Carrington touched upon when he first came to Ireland and upon which I understood you to have desired him to converse with me'. Union was not by name mentioned in the letter although it is clear from the content that this was the important subject under discussion. Camden did not want to take up much of Pitt's time on the matter more than the prime minister 'can or ought to allow to any subject upon which it is not necessary immediately to decide', a guiding principle for Pitt. Nevertheless Camden was convinced that the unnamed question of a union was 'one which must be taken up whenever the war is at an end for it is impossible the two kingdoms can remain on the footing upon which they respectively subsist at present'.[34]

This letter serves as a counterpoint to the charges that Pitt was forced into a union by events, and that his thinking about it, and Ireland, began with the rebellion. Rather it is clear that the prime minister, in the course of his time in office, had considered various ideas for best utilising Ireland for the empire. At some point between 1783 and 1797, and it is impossible to date it precisely, Pitt decided that a legislative union was the only pragmatic long-term solution for the difficulties posed by Ireland. In the search for a new imperial security, Pitt realised that union offered the only hope of realising it. Throughout his life Pitt was firmly convinced that 'innovations were at all times dangerous, and should never be attempted but when necessity called for them'.[35] War with France made union both a desirable and a dangerous change, but the Irish rebellion made any thoughts of postponing the measure until peacetime redundant. Political necessity determined the pace.

Perspectives on the union have tended to reflect the preoccupations of its chroniclers. Interpretations have been dominated by peculiarly local concerns, Irish accounts emphasising the importance of the catholic question, British accounts preferring to dwell on the rebellion of 1798 and the war with France. Neither position has fully convinced in explaining Pitt's lengthy fascination with union, and both ignore the prime minister's ambitious strategy for the empire that was central to his thinking on Ireland, even at the time of the commercial propositions. Pitt saw union as a framework to restructure the empire. Ireland's diminishing status from kingdom to colony was obvious to observers. The union was to be the vehicle for reversing this dependency, and the dangerous notions of independence, to give both Ireland and Britain a harmony of interest[36] within the empire.

The union represented an imperial design. The intention was not to perpetuate the inequality between Britain and Ireland but to create a united kingdom that would be at the heart of the empire. Ireland was to be elevated from being a dependent periphery country to become a component of the dominant centre. The commercial propositions had been an earlier, failed attempt, forcing Pitt to accept that the jealousies, and the differences, between the two countries could be resolved only through a union. Catholic emancipation was important because it alone could make Ireland stable. Ireland in 1798 was a periphery kingdom where the protestant ascendancy had shown itself to be too resistant to change and incapable of running the country; and where the catholic masses represented a dangerous threat to Britain at war. Union was to elevate Ireland to the centre of empire building. A new security was to be created through uniting the parliaments.

The opponents of the union were to view the union less kindly. It was to be seen as a cynical alliance designed to tie Ireland to Britain, and destroy the privileges that had been won in 1782. This was the fear of a sizeable number who opposed the measure, and in many respects they were correct. Declan Kiberd summarises the two perspectives on the union: to some it was 'a benign offer of membership in one of the greatest organisations in human history'; to others it was 'the most insidious of all oppressive tactics'.[37] Not surprisingly, each perspective reflected differing attitudes towards Britain's motives for the measure. An examination of the union proceedings, and Pitt's preoccupations, between 1798 and 1801 reveals much evidence for both interpretations:[38] they were by no means incompatible. Patrick O'Farrell's claim that the union was 'an urgent and naked assertion of British power', and Erich Strauss's analysis that it 'was designed to perpetuate Irish subjugation', are not completely wrong, merely misleading.[39] Pitt's proud design for the Irish people was to raise their status within the empire after humbling them first by destroying their parliament. The guardians of the Irish 'nation' (that is, the Anglo-Irish ascendancy) were quite prepared to accept a greater role within the empire. But they were to cling proudly to their legislative independence, as they had in 1785, and refuse Pitt's prescription for them. Thus the union struggle was to become dominated by the conflict between these two immovable forces. The Irish catholics, for their part, had never shared in the benefits of legislative independence. Their response would be grounded in a desire to end their political exclusion, but it was recognised that they would prefer emancipation without a union to emancipation with. For some catholics, even the promise of full relief was not sufficient reason to support the measure. During the attempts to pass the union it proved impossible to determine conclusively what was right and what was wrong; ultimately the dividing line proved to be the channel.

A 'certain imperiousness' had crept into the conduct of Pitt's ministry by 1798.[40] Fifteen years of dominance in parliament had given Pitt an undisputed ascendancy in the country that the secession of the Foxite whigs in 1797 only reinforced.[41] An essay on Pitt in 1798 declared him to be 'in many points of view the most conspicuous prime minister which modern Europe has ever beheld'.[42] An informed observer in 1801 referred to his 'absolute power', and blamed it on so many years without 'a single check of adversity'.[43] This supremacy was particularly noticeable in the pursuit of foreign policy objectives. Secret service activity, and the disposal of 'Pitt's gold', worked in tandem with diplomatic efforts to combat revolutionary France. The hauteur discernible in domestic policy, where vigorous repression tactics sought to maintain order against conspiracy,[44] was carried through into covert foreign activity. The function of the alien office in directing secret service activity has been well documented by Elizabeth Sparrow,[45] and the lead role of William Wickham has also been examined by some historians.[46] The conduct of the king's government towards Russia encapsulates these operations. There, Sir Charles Whitworth, the British ambassador, directed secret service funds to bribe both Tsar Paul I's mistress, and his valet, to arrange favourable terms for Britain in the commercial treaty of 1797 between Britain and Russia.[47] The following year Lord Grenville authorised 40,000 roubles (worth about £1,500 sterling in 1800) to bribe the valet Kutaisov, again, this time to bring Russia into the coalition against France.[48] No consideration was given to Burke's civil list act that restricted secret service expenditure, just as it was conveniently ignored when similar funds were used in Ireland to assist the union.

This ruthlessness in foreign policy was typical, and in this department as in all others, Pitt's dominance was intelligible. There was a consensus in 1794 that 'Mr Pitt has hitherto been absolute, and other members [of the cabinet] have had no more to do than to give their opinions and submit to his, unless Lord Grenville chooses to make a stand'.[49] Even then Pitt found ways of circumventing his foreign secretary and demonstrating his superiority.

During the Lille peace negotiations with France in 1797 Pitt conducted a complex, and highly devious, intrigue to withhold information from his own cabinet. His friend and protégé, George Canning, under-secretary at the foreign office, was his willing agent, editing reports before showing them to his immediate superior. This was even while Malmesbury, the chief British negotiator, was already sending two dispatches, one for the cabinet and one for Grenville and Pitt.[50] The prime minister, alone, had a control over all information. No wonder Canning was to remark in awe that Pitt 'is really master now'.[51]

The government had begun to reflect the character of the prime minister. Writing a number of years later, a contemporary of Pitt accused him of 'a love of power and of glory', and recorded that 'pride was the harshest feature that disfigured him to the public eye'.[52] Nowhere was this proud nature more evident than in the duel Pitt fought on 27 May 1798, an incident that scandalised polite society. Two days previously, in what should have been an innocuous debate on a bill for the manning of the navy, Pitt had reacted intemperately to opposition from a whig member, George Tierney. In a vicious attack Pitt accused Tierney of acting 'from a desire to obstruct the defence of the country'.[53] There was an immediate uproar and Tierney called the prime minister to order, appealing to the chair for protection. The speaker, Henry Addington, sought an explanation but the prime minister affected a lofty disdain. He obstinately maintained his accusation, even repeating it to the house.[54] Tierney stormed out of the house 'evidently in great wrath' and the next day requested satisfaction out of parliament.[55]

And so Putney Heath was the scene of a remarkable afternoon meeting between the tall, thin frame of Pitt and the rather more prosperous figure of Tierney. The duel was taken seriously with Pitt making his will before he set out. Both men fired at twelve paces, missing, and on the second attempt Pitt fired into the air. Neither man was injured and both retired with honour satisfied.[56] Pitt, indeed, was well satisfied with the incident. Reaction to the duel was immediate and almost unanimously critical of the prime minister. The king was horrified by his minister's conduct in an affair that had been of his own making. But there was to be further evidence of Pitt's proud nature. His friend William Wilberforce, sharing his fellow countrymen's shock, and particularly offended that the duel had taken place on Whit Sunday, decided to put a motion down in parliament condemning duelling. Pitt's high response was to warn Wilberforce that any such attempt would be regarded as an attack on him personally, forcing his resignation, and his friend duly withdrew.[57] George Pretyman, Pitt's friend, tutor at Cambridge, bishop of Lincoln and biographer, considered the duel to have been the only event 'over which I should gladly throw a veil, condemned as it must be by all'.[58] The unbending and haughty manner of the prime minister throughout this affair reflected a growing hubris that would be further visible during the union.

'Cannot crushing the rebellion be followed by an act appointing commissioners to treat for a union?'[59] It was the king's opinion that Pitt could take a long time to think about something, but that once his mind was made up he moved very fast.[60] The prime minister at times was notoriously indecisive and quickly discouraged by defeat; on other occasions, he was capable of acting with great single-mindedness and precision.[61] With reports reaching England of the outbreak of rebellion in Ireland, Pitt moved swiftly. Despite the duel, and the mounting pressures that had been responsible for Pitt's outburst in the first place, the prime minister showed a remarkable clarity for business. The day after he received the news, 28 May (his thirty-ninth birthday), Pitt wrote to Lord Camden about a union.[62] There has been some confusion amongst historians about the exact date on which he decided to adopt a union. W.E.H. Lecky considered the first reference to union to have been 4 June.[63] John Holland Rose dates the first reference much later, to 13 June, while G.C. Bolton in his towering work on the union points to 2 June. Both Bartlett and Ehrman, however, correctly adopt 28 May as the key date.[64]

The question Pitt posed on 28 May 1798 revealed a number of levels in his thinking. The most obvious was that it showed the immediate leaning of the prime minister towards a legislative union as a solution to the crisis. Earlier in the year he had criticised the proposed absentee tax for being a move towards 'cutting off the little that now remains of union between the two countries, which ought on the contrary to be drawn closer on every practicable occasion'.[65] Rebellion persuaded Pitt to act decisively to keep Ireland and Britain together. The long-considered union was now adopted as policy. Pitt's enquiry was also important for what it revealed about the manner in which the union was to be agreed. The appointment of commissioners had preceded the act of union between England and Scotland in Queen Anne's reign. During the Irish union proceedings there was a certain amount of confusion amongst the proponents of the measure about whether it would be in the form of a treaty, negotiated by commissioners, or whether the articles would be decided by government.

Union with Scotland had been considered necessary by England at the start of the eighteenth century for a number of reasons. It had suggested itself as the only solution to the problems that had seen Scotland drift further away from the crown while it also secured the succession to the throne, which had become a difficult issue.[66] In 1705 the Scottish parliament voted to appoint commissioners to negotiate a treaty of union.[67] The commissioners were chosen from both countries and they sat from 16 April 1706 to 22 July.[68] Neither set of commissioners met during the negotiations, sitting in separate rooms, and communicating only through writing. Twenty-five articles were prepared, fifteen of which concerned economic matters. The commissioners had been forbidden to treat of ecclesiastical matters, these areas being left for separate acts in 1707.[69] The articles of union were debated in the Scottish parliament from 3 October 1706 to 16 January 1707 where they were ratified with minor alterations. These were then adopted and ratified by the English parliament. From the outset of the Irish union, however, it was clear that the king's ministers wished to retain control over key details of the measure.

There was an underlying assumption that only government could handle the complexities of union. Thus the ambivalence in their attitudes between, on the one hand, wanting to follow the Scottish precedent and, on the other, wanting to determine the content themselves.

In the first ten days of June 1798 Pitt carefully discussed the matter of a union with key advisers. Lord Grenville was quickly included in the deliberations, probably on 2 June.[70] The foreign secretary appears to have informed his brother, the marquess of Buckingham, a former lord lieutenant of Ireland, of the scheme, for on 3 June he urged for a union, 'which can never be if not now'.[71] The Scottish union of 1707 was seen as the basis for the proposed Irish one. Lord Auckland, joint postmaster-general, and a regular adviser on Irish affairs, was informed of the proposed union on 4 June.[72] Pitt revealed that he and Grenville had been having 'a good deal of discussion', culminating in 'a paper', on the subject of following up the rising with a union. Both men were confident that they saw 'daylight' on almost everything except what related to trade and revenue. It was hoped that Auckland would contribute to these remaining parts.

'The paper' that Grenville wrote on union, with the assistance of Pitt, has proved elusive for historians. There is sufficient internal evidence, however, to suggest that it is the undated 'Points to be considered with a view to an incorporating union of Great Britain and Ireland'.[73] This nine-page-long document contained various suggestions for the structure of the union, which was to be 'on the plan of the Scotch union'. The first point was that the king's authority 'ecclesiastical, civil and military' would continue to be exercised by a lord lieutenant resident in Ireland. Acknowledging the commercial points as the most difficult of the measure, Grenville highlighted the difficulties in regulating duties. If the duties of import and export were made the same for both countries then the burden would be too great for Ireland. Conversely, if the port and internal duties remained on their existing terms then it would make it impossible to achieve the abolition of import duties from Ireland to England. This regulation was seen as being of great importance; in the margin Pitt noted that 'something approaching to this is indispensable to the scheme'. The commercial propositions were considered useful for details on economic points. It was implicitly understood that commissioners from both countries would be appointed. It seems, however, that their responsibility would extend only to working out the specific details after the broad terms were agreed by government. For example, the finalising of the commercial points, in particular those that related to debt and contributions, was to be left for the commissioners to negotiate. Grenville acknowledged that their task would be a difficult and long one. 'The interest of both kingdoms, and the success of the measure itself' required that once the idea was 'on float it should proceed with the utmost possible expedition'.

There was also an examination of the composition of the united parliament in the paper. The population of Ireland, at 4 million, was compared with that of Scotland in 1707, at 1.5 million, suggesting an addition of 40 Irish peers to the house of lords and 120 MPs to the commons. Comparing the population of Ireland to the then population of Scotland, however, implied a much greater Irish addition. Based on the most recent population census, which revealed the population ratio between Scotland and Ireland to be four to ten, there should be an addition of 108 peers and 223 commoners to the united parliament. This was considered too great an increase that would dangerously alter the nature of both houses of parliament. Grenville therefore concluded that the 1707 proportions had to be used; Pitt was in full agreement, writing 'certainly' on the margin. The peers might be chosen on the basis of the Scottish union, which Grenville considered the best option, or else the king could nominate them, allowing existing Irish peers 'in the interim' to sit in the commons. The advantage of this method was that it was the one currently being used, and 'one of the great objections to any new system' was the danger that if it was thought more advantageous to the Irish peerage than the existing mode was to the Scottish, the latter might demand to be placed on a similar footing. With either method of selecting peers it was suggested that the Irish bishops might choose amongst four to eight of their number or alternatively leave the matter to the king's discretion. If 150 MPs, half the existing number in the Irish parliament, was not thought too large a number they could be returned 'in the present mode of election, only choosing one at each election instead of two'. The chief advantage of this method was seen as its simplicity: the avoidance of anything that could be used to promote calls for radical parliamentary reform was considered vital. Grenville concluded the paper by noting that 'any attempt to establish anything like a uniform system, or theories of population, contributions etc. must, it is presumed, lead to confusion in both countries'.[74]

Catholic emancipation appears to have been a component of the scheme. On the issue of parliamentary representation in the united parliament, Grenville outlined the idea of 'giving to catholics as well as protestants the right of eligibility, under *effective* qualification laws of property, in both kingdoms'. This is the only reference in the paper to the catholic question but it is a highly significant, if somewhat ambiguous, sentence. It is, perhaps, the most revealing insight into the union thinking of Pitt and Grenville at this time. The absence of any notations by Pitt after the sentence suggests that the prime minister shared his foreign secretary's thoughts on the matter. The sentence implies that catholics in both Ireland *and* Britain were to be allowed seats in the united parliament. It is possible that Grenville intended the sentence to refer to giving catholics in both kingdoms the right to *vote* for MPs, rather than granting them the right actually to sit in parliament, but such a meaning would have been out of context in the paper. Pitt was to admit a few months later that he had been in favour of including emancipation with the union at this time.[75] This being the case it seems clear that the union was regarded as the mechanism for solving the religious problems in Ireland by removing the outstanding restriction against the majority inhabitants.

For others the union was seen as the means of closing the door on catholic emancipation for ever. King George III enthusiastically approved of the moves towards a legislative union. But while the king was informed early on about the union, the religious component of his leading ministers' scheme was not revealed to him. Perhaps suspicious of their leanings the king took the opportunity from the outset to reiterate his beliefs on the subject. Union was to be on a strictly protestant basis with no concessions to the catholics. The lord lieutenant, the king informed his minister, must

> understand that no indulgence can be granted to the catholics further than has, I am afraid unadvisedly, [been] done in former sessions, and that he must by a steady conduct affect in future the union of that kingdom with this.[76]

The division on the catholic question between the king and certain of his ministers was to become an important part of the union business. It was to define the nature of the work and determine many of the conflicts surrounding it; it was also to decide its limits.

The biggest difficulty that faced the measure in its early days came not from any opposition to the idea but from an unforeseen crisis involving the head of the government. At the start of June, Pitt suffered from one of his recurring bouts of ill health, which prevented him from going to the commons for the last month of the parliamentary session. Wilberforce recorded on 2 June that Pitt was 'seriously ill', while *The Morning Chronicle* two days later reported that the minister could scarcely cross the room from weakness. At the end of the month, another opposition paper, *The Courier*, even reported that Pitt had gone insane.[77] This last report was quickly denied but it was not considered altogether implausible given the medical history of Pitt's family. Lord Rosebery, in his biography of Pitt, asserted that, although he was not insane, the minister's health was 'seriously impaired' at this time.[78] The minister's indisposition did not go unnoticed by the king. George III expressed his concern in a letter to Pitt on the union on 10 June. He hoped that because Pitt had not mentioned his health there had been some improvement.[79] The minister's recovery was swift but not complete. He assured his mother in early July that his strength was recovering daily.[80] Over the next months Pitt worked at gaining 'a stock of health', for occasions 'when it will be more wanted than here'.[81] Less optimistic, though, was Auckland, who saw Pitt in August and reported him 'much shaken in his constitution'.[82] The attack was probably caused by a combination of stress and overwork. Pitt's health was once diagnosed as varying depending on 'the change of seasons and of situation'.[83] Certainly the combination of a rebellion in Ireland, the conflict with France, a legislative union in contemplation, and the unfortunate incident of the duel, provided enough 'subjects of anxiety and interest' to precipitate a health crisis. Pitt's health always affected the efficiency of government, and was to become an increasingly important factor over the next three years, particularly in the lead-up to the collapse of his ministry.

If, from the end of May, Pitt was clear in his determination that a union was necessary, he was also aware that Camden could not be the man to oversee its passage. The end of Camden's viceroyalty has been often overlooked by historians. The conventional interpretation that Camden resigned because he did not wish to remain in the position has been accepted by, amongst others, Bartlett, Bolton, Ehrman and Hyde.[84] A closer examination of the matter reveals that in reality Camden was considered unsuitable, and even if he had not been ambivalent on remaining, would have been removed for the sake of high policy. Before the details of the union could be finalised a decision had to be made about the holder of the office of lord lieutenant. A number of factors combined to rule Camden out of continuing in office.

On the surface what first appeared to rule Camden out was the viceroy himself. He had expressed a clear desire to return to England in 1797, and in the first half of 1798 had grown even more restless. People began to comment on how he appeared to have tired of the country.[85] The apparent truth of this assertion was borne out by the increasingly negative tone of his correspondence. In March he recommended that a military character was necessary to save the country, a theme that was to become ever more prevalent.[86] The respected general, and former governor of India, Lord Cornwallis, was Camden's preferred choice of successor, with Sylvester Douglas as his chief secretary.[87] When the rebellion did break out, these recommendations became more and more frequent and forceful. Others too saw Cornwallis as a more appropriate viceroy. Behind the scenes Lord Carlisle, himself a former lord lieutenant, recommended that the 'best soldier' would make the best viceroy. Cornwallis occurred to him too as the best qualified.[88] Camden had no idea of the precariousness of his position. Apart from his own unwillingness to oversee a legislative union other issues made him less acceptable. In particular his opposition to full catholic relief stood against him. Pitt had no wish to close the door on catholic concessions accompanying union and, as the paper of June reveals, it was believed that a union would allow a solution to the religious divisions in Ireland. This made Camden an inappropriate viceroy. He had, on many occasions, made his opposition to catholic emancipation clear.

The final factor which weighed against Camden's continuance in office was his self-confessed problems in handling the rebellion. Pitt wanted the rebellion to be put down with as much restraint as possible shown. He was particularly eager to avoid atrocities against innocent parties. Wilberforce recounted how, during a discussion of the rebellion in the lords, Clare confirmed Beresford's admission that atrocities had been committed during the rebellion with a nonchalant, 'Well suppose it were so.' Pitt's response left an enduring impression on his friend, who recounted that the prime minister 'turned round to me with that high indignant stare which sometimes marked his countenance, and stalked out of the house'.[89] This strong desire for restraint was tested early in the rebellion by Camden's admission, on 29 May, that it was 'scarcely possible to restrain the violence of my own friends and advisors within any justifiable bounds'.[90] The viceroy also urged the necessity of sending immediate reinforcements to the country. On receiving the letter, Pitt promptly replied assuring Camden that even before his letter had reached him he had arranged for five thousand men to be dispatched to Ireland. Two conditions were stressed. The first was that they were to be used only for the duration of the temporary crisis. The second, which Pitt insisted was of 'even more importance', was that the forces were to be used consistent with Camden's principles and feelings but that he was to 'resist with as much firmness the intemperance of your friends, as you do the desperate efforts of the enemy'.[91] The prime minister strongly advised the viceroy to follow his instructions, cautioning him that if he did so all would be well.

On 1 June Camden received Pitt's enquiry of 28 May about the possibility of following up the rebellion with a union. After considering the matter he warned against catholic emancipation and parliamentary reform being conceded as this would throw away the best opportunity for passing it. A legislative union, he agreed, was the only measure which could bind the two countries, and prevent Ireland from remaining 'a point dreadfully vulnerable in all future wars'.[92] Remaining consistent with his earlier statements Camden repeated his conviction that he did not feel he could be 'the instrument to carry the measure into effect'. A 'deeper statesman', or a general of acknowledged ability, was instead recommended to take control in Ireland. Camden advised taking full advantage of the alarm that existed amongst the leading figures to press the measure successfully. If the government were to decide that the union was too bold a measure, it would be rash to concede full catholic relief. The lord lieutenant believed that emancipation should be prepared cautiously and receive approval from the pope. Again, in line with earlier statements, Camden noted his own belief that he could not bring in a union. He did, however, believe that with Cornwallis's aid he could save the country from 'immediate destruction'. As time passed, the force of Camden's assertions did not wane, but in fact grew stronger. Less than a week later, on 6 June, he recommended an efficient military man being placed at the head of the government or the army; he himself was 'perfectly inadequate to the task'.[93] Cornwallis, if he retained his energy, was his preferred choice. The situation had become so perilous that 'his inclination to the catholic cause ought not to weigh against him'. The duke of York, the king's son, was another he believed to be a suitable candidate.

With everything seemingly weighted in favour of Cornwallis the decision was taken, on 9 or 10 June, to replace Camden with the former governor of India and current master-general of the ordnance. Pitt had long acknowledged Cornwallis's abilities. Indeed in 1791 during a restructuring of the cabinet, he had decided upon Cornwallis as home secretary. Henry Dundas, who quickly proved his abilities, was initially considered only as locum tenens until Cornwallis returned from India.[94] In 1797 Cornwallis had been urged by Camden, and the government, to go to Ireland, but had refused, apparently because catholic emancipation was not forthcoming.[95]

Charles Cornwallis, the second Earl Cornwallis, had served the crown with distinction in other, similar crises. In 1776 he had been sent to America, and had been the lieutenant-general who had eventually surrendered at Yorktown in 1781 after a number of initial victories.[96] After this loyal service Pitt believed that he was the only person capable of restoring political and military order to India. With Ireland at a critical juncture in 1798 it was only natural that the government should once more turn to the figure who had served so well elsewhere in the empire. Bartlett correctly sees the appointment of Cornwallis as constituting 'an indication that the British cabinet was, at a minimum, maintaining an open mind on the catholic question'.[97] Pitt's mind was indeed favourable towards the catholics.[98] However, Cornwallis himself does not appear to have been aware of any shift in government policy towards the catholics. He accepted the post in 1798, not because the circumstances behind his refusal in 1797 had changed, but because the events in Ireland made his going a matter of great importance for the empire. This was a more significant consideration for Cornwallis than his personal sympathies towards the catholics, as events were later to confirm.

The king was kept informed of the range of issues under discussion. In a letter to Pitt on 10 June George III warned that the reinforcements sent would be of no avail unless a military lord lieutenant, he named Cornwallis, was sent immediately.[99] Thomas Pelham was his preference for chief secretary. Camden's handling of the rebellion had not impressed the king. He was critical of the way the viceroy had become 'too much agitated', and believed him to have fallen under the control of the Irish privy councillors. These he blamed for the mistakes which he thought would drive the rebels to fight. As examined earlier, two important instructions for Cornwallis were emphasised by the king. The first was that no indulgence was to be conceded to the catholics further than what had been granted in the past. The second was that Cornwallis was to oversee the legislative union of Ireland with Great Britain.[100] Three days later the king repeated his concerns to Pitt. Further concessions were not to be granted to the catholics as 'no country can be governed where there is more than one established religion'.[101] The king was clear that while the catholics could, perhaps, be tolerated, they could not be trusted.

Valuable progress was made on the union on 10 June. Dundas had 'a very satisfactory conversation' with Cornwallis about taking up the post of lord lieutenant in Ireland. Camden's letter of 6 June arrived on this day. Somewhat disingenuously, Pitt was to claim that the sounding out of Cornwallis began on receipt of that letter. The speed and content of communications between Dundas, Grenville, George III and Pitt on the issue of replacing Camden suggest, however, that the decision was made before, and not as a consequence of, the letter of 6 June. The change was probably seriously considered as soon as the union was adopted as policy. Pitt went to London on 11 June, chiefly to see Cornwallis.[102] The meeting was successful and Cornwallis accepted the commission to go to Ireland.[103] It remained to tell Camden of the change. Pitt approached the delicate matter on 11 June when he informed his friend that the only way his recommendation of having a military man at the head of the government or army could be effectively achieved was through uniting the positions of commander-in-chief and lord lieutenant. Cornwallis,

Pitt reassured the viceroy, would undertake the task with sentiments perfectly in line with Camden's own, a lie but a polite one, the 'new arrangement' taking effect 'with the least possible delay'.

Restraint remained an important consideration for Pitt. He expressed a wish, 'in common with yourself and with us all', that in Camden's last days in office he would not 'preclude the hopes of clemency towards those who may submit'. The aim was to help achieve a permanent settlement, that would secure the connection between Ireland and Great Britain. This, Pitt was convinced, could be achieved only through a union. Lecky examined the charges made against the government, at the time and afterwards, that the rebellion had been manipulated to pass the union. He concluded that the rebellion was not sparked just to assist a desired government policy, but he did feel it could not be denied that 'a desire to carry a legislative union had a considerable influence in dictating the policy which in fact produced the rebellion, and that there were politicians who were prepared to pursue that policy even at the risk of rebellion'.[104] While there was no conspiracy involved this analysis does have an element of truth.[105] The king and his government were quite happy to use the confusion and panic created by the rebellion to implement a union. Cornwallis was later to confide that difficult circumstances could help Pitt the same way 'that the rebellion assisted the union'.[106]

Ian R. Christie has commented that in the reign of George III 'cabinet practice is notoriously elusive'.[107] Pitt's ministry was not quite a 'government of departments', although he was the key figure in all departments. As Spencer Perceval recalled in 1809 'each of his colleagues must have felt that Mr Pitt could do without him, though he could not do without Mr Pitt'.[108] Ministers, especially those in the inner circle, had influence covering a range of areas, even in matters outside their departments.[109] The duke of Portland, who had succeeded Dundas at the home office at the formation of the coalition in 1794, was not one of the main figures in the government. Although he was theoretically in charge of Irish affairs, many of the decisions regarding the union, particularly in the early stages, were made by others. In the early union deliberations certain individuals were kept more informed than others about the union policy, and on how committed the inner circle of ministers were to it.[110] The cabinet appear to have been informed individually of the thinking in favour of a union but not on how committed Pitt and the king were to its adoption as policy. Lord Chancellor Loughborough expressed his support for the idea on 13 June but seemed unaware of the extent of Pitt's determination on the matter. He merely advised that 'it would be very rash to make any suggestion from here' on the question.[111] Instead, he recommended patience in waiting for the idea to originate in Ireland. In his dispatches to Portland up to September, Cornwallis, when referring to 'the pursuit of that great question', always defined it, not in terms of a union, but rather as 'how this country can be governed and preserved, and rendered a source of strength and power, instead of remaining a useless and almost intolerable burden to Great Britain'.[112] Union, when it was referred to, was mentioned only as an option.

While Portland would have been aware that a union was being considered it seems that it was left quite late before the home secretary became an instrument of policy, perhaps as late as September.[113] In that month Cornwallis, in what appears to be an attempt by the viceroy to defuse any tension that might have resulted from the home secretary's exclusion from the inner circle determining policy, wrote apologising that,

> if I have not appeared to give my sentiments to your grace with the utmost freedom, and to speak with the most perfect openness of heart on the subject both of men and measures in this country . . . [it was because I was not] able to give you opinions which I had not formed, or to explain things which I was not sure that I understood.[114]

Pitt 'felt most at home in high policy'.[115] It would not have been unusual for him to have retained control of the union strategy in its earliest stages. The existence of an inner cabinet of Pitt, Dundas and Grenville, and their involvement in matters theoretically outside of their domain, was recognised at the time.[116] A desire to control all aspects of policy was an integral part of Pitt's character. As Dundas noted, there was also a disposition in his friend to fasten his eyes on 'the object immediately in contemplation',[117] an enthusiasm that Pitt brought initially to the union.

The removal of Camden was one to which Portland only reluctantly gave his consent. He did not consider the change necessary, believing that there would not be a viceroy better than Camden. Nevertheless, despite reservations, he made out Cornwallis's patent of office immediately.[118] The same day, 12 June, Pitt informed other figures in the government of the change. In each case it was stated in terms of 'repeated representations from Lord Camden recently and strongly renewed'; part of the reasoning but not the complete story.[119] The appointment was declared to be effective immediately.

The decision to relieve Camden reached the viceroy on 15 June. He immediately wrote to William Elliot, the Irish under-secretary for the military department, who was in London, remarking on how he was prepared 'to sacrifice every personal consideration to an object which is so extremely material to the salvation of the empire'.[120] He wished that some 'mark of confidence' should be given to him so that no 'false construction' could be placed on his removal. This optimistic hope was also sent to Pitt, Pitt's brother Chatham, and Pelham. In the correspondence with Pelham the outgoing viceroy, in addition to the sentiments expressed in the letter to Elliot, revealed his regret at leaving Ireland. He insisted that he would have been happy to have remained in Ireland to quell the rising, 'but personal feelings ought to yield to public duties'.[121] He reiterated his conviction that a military man was needed in Ireland. If this had not been deemed necessary he claimed he would have liked to have assisted in the introduction of a union.

In an undated letter, but which was probably written on 15 June, Camden asserted that Ireland needed a military lord lieutenant, sentiments in line with his letters of 6 and 7 June. He felt it would be acting 'traitorously to my country' if he allowed personal feelings to interfere in his public duty. His preference, he admitted, would have been for a military character to have joined with him to quell the rebellion. As this was regarded as being less advantageous than uniting the two offices he therefore resigned with cheerfulness.[122] Perhaps unsurprisingly, Camden was keen to maintain his reputation after the change. Fearing allegations that he had been afraid to fight out the rebellion (he had after all sent his family to England at its start) Camden wished that the duties that he had performed 'honourably and effectively' should be rewarded. His own preference, he claimed, was to retire to the country but this, of course, would not be creditable to the state.[123] In a postscript, Camden noted that he had informed the lord chancellor, Clare, and the speaker of the house of commons, John Foster, about the change. Both expressed their regret at the news and were anxious that there should be no changes made to the system of government by the new viceroy. As for Pitt's expressed desire for clemency in his letter of 11 June, Camden warned that if Cornwallis was immediately to pursue 'mild measures' it would mark the outgoing administration with 'much more harshness than it deserves, and it will not be advantageous to the country'.[124]

The speed of the change in the Irish administration startled Camden. He admitted to Pitt that his feelings had been 'somewhat hurt' by the affair. Even though he accepted that his retirement from the post was based on his own repeated advice, he felt his reputation should have been more consulted, and that Pitt should have waited for him to reply to his letter before taking his decision. Since this had not occurred and the decision had been taken, he willingly consented but hoped his retirement would not be 'misunderstood'. Again some 'mark of approbation' was felt to be necessary, some employment where his services could be utilised. The leaving of the country, which he had long requested, had now become 'a very painful duty'.[125] Camden had not wanted responsibility for a union, but neither had he really wanted to leave. What shocked him more than anything was the advanced state of government thinking on a union. He still believed that a military figure could have complemented his administration with the question of a union reserved for a later consideration. Unable to comprehend Pitt's strategy for Ireland Camden was left bewildered as a military figure swiftly replaced him.

The substitution of Camden for Cornwallis is usually seen as only a minor part of the whole union business. In actual fact, the complexities of the matter reveal much about the deeper thinking behind the union, and the workings of government. It would have been possible to appoint Cornwallis as commander-in-chief with Camden as lord lieutenant, the outgoing viceroy's own preference, if that had been seen as desirable. It was not. In any case the combination of civil and martial law required a martial figure to supervise; a division of offices was impractical. The 1798 rebellion had forced a decision about union. Once this was made Camden's position became untenable. The viceroy was temperamentally unsuited to the delicate work required to pass the union. His views on the catholic question and the harshness of some of his policies set him against the more conciliatory opinions of Pitt, who wanted a legislative union to ameliorate the religious and other problems in the country. Camden was an embarrassing reminder of the old Anglo-Irish relationship, evidenced by his willingness to alienate the catholic masses in putting down the rebellion. He was not the man who could mark the change that Pitt wished the union to represent. In addition Camden's dependence on the repressive inner 'cabinet', a group of advisers that had established an almost hypnotic dominance over successive viceroys since Westmorland's day, made him appear unable to run the country without their approval. He was deemed incompetent in handling the rebellion and incapable of overseeing the union, and it was this reasoning, and not his apparent unwillingness in early June 1798 to stay, that compelled the king's government to appoint Cornwallis. Camden was a liability and his replacement by a conciliatory figure, who was capable of managing both the military dimension and the political one (being a sympathetic figure to the catholics while at the same time willing to put the interests of the empire first), was not surprising. Neither Edward Cooke, the under-secretary for the civil department, nor Viscount Castlereagh, the acting chief secretary, approved of the change.[126] But Castlereagh was later to accept that there had been no alternative given General Gerard Lake's inability to handle the situation, and since Camden's friends had driven Sir Ralph Abercromby from his post.[127]

The change of viceroy was followed by a sharp change in policy. Cornwallis arrived in Ireland on 20 June and his desire for restraint and clemency immediately set him at odds with the so-called Irish 'cabinet', which included John Foster (the speaker of the house of commons), the archbishop of Cashel, Beresford and Clare. The rebellion had sent shock waves through Irish protestant society. The gentry and political elite were traumatised by the violence, and the expectation of violence, to the point of paranoia. With the spectre of republicanism imagined to be lurking everywhere, reason was guillotined and replaced by a furious rage that masked the anarchy, and clouded the senses. Fear and panic inflamed tempers and religious animosities to the extent that some protestants began to consider the destruction of the catholics as the only solution. They were reported to discuss this 'with great composure as the only cure for the present, and the only sure preventative for the future'.[128] Cornwallis could not conceal his disgust when he discovered that this frenzy also gripped the viceroy's traditional advisers and he discarded them without hesitation. Their disapproval of his conduct did not bother him in the slightest. Castlereagh had warned him that the Irish 'cabinet' had proven inconvenient and embarrassing prior to his arrival, and he took great pleasure in setting them aside completely.[129]

The break had the potential to become a crisis for the new viceroy. The figures Cornwallis was isolating himself from were powerful and influential, even with, or perhaps because of, their prejudices and paranoia. The speaker, John Foster, became alienated from the new viceroy within a matter of days. Accustomed to a position of respect in the Irish administration Foster was horrified to find himself ignored and his advice shunned.[130] This soon turned to bitterness and as time passed he reflected critically on Cornwallis's 'speculative nonsense of conciliation'.[131] The lord lieutenant's isolation from the old clique made his position fragile until Lord Chancellor Clare threw his support behind Cornwallis's policy of clemency. This timely intervention, together with Castlereagh's support, consolidated the viceroy's position against the attempts to factionalise the administration, even before it had properly started.[132] The importance of Clare's intervention has been accepted by historians,[133] the motivation behind it less so. The lord chancellor's behaviour is usually attributed to his awareness that conciliation and clemency were necessary for the well-being of Ireland.[134] Given Clare's involvement with an Irish 'cabinet' that had urged harsh measures on Camden this appears somewhat improbable. A more likely explanation is that Clare was aware of the plan for a legislative union and that this encouraged him to throw his support behind conciliatory measures which he might otherwise have had some personal difficulties supporting. Auckland involved him in the secret at some point in June 1798, probably before 20 June.[135] Buckingham asserted in September 1798 that Cornwallis knew the lord chancellor's opinions on union 'before he came to Ireland'.[136] As Clare did not believe that Foster would support the union, a measure he himself was in favour of, it is more than plausible that the lord chancellor came to Cornwallis's assistance on the issue of the state prisoners rather than risk making the new lord lieutenant's position untenable, and thereby damage the union cause.[137]

Cornwallis was aware of the proposed measure for Ireland before he departed from England.[138] The castle secretaries were soon informed of the scheme, as were Robert Hobart, a former chief secretary, and Buckingham, with Beresford also consulted. The lord chancellor was one of the first to be informed of the measure of which he has been incorrectly described as being 'the mainspring'.[139] Auckland informed him of the idea in June, more than likely encouraged by Pitt to sound him out unofficially. Clare responded enthusiastically to the suggestion of a measure which, he said, he had urged Pitt to adopt in 1793 and 1797, as 'nothing short of it can save the country'.[140] The main difficulty which faced the union, according to the lord chancellor, was the 'national love of jobbing'. Opposing the measure, he believed, would be the catholics, the northern republicans, Foster and the protestant archbishop of Cashel. The power of borough compensation was astutely noted by Clare, who recognised that it would alleviate the qualms of many owners who might otherwise oppose. On the whole, he believed that success with the union was quite attainable.[141]

Within the lord lieutenant's administration there was also much thinking on the union. Cooke, who Camden believed understood Ireland better than anyone,[142] and who was once called 'the man who really governs the kingdom',[143] supported the idea, but correctly gauged that if the government was serious about the measure it must be 'written-up, spoken-up, intrigued-up, drunk-up, sung-up and bribed-up'.[144] John Beresford also wrote to Pitt to commend the union scheme. His presence was likewise requested in England in the autumn to 'give some useful hints',[145] with his commercial expertise particularly valued. Despite the attempts at secrecy, the arrival of Buckingham, in late June, with his regiment, widened the numbers of those aware of the measure. Gossip about the impending change circulated, and the numbers of those who knew of it multiplied.

It was never likely that Cornwallis would have fallen under the sway of the Irish 'cabinet'. The violent tempers of the old friends of government in Ireland set them firmly apart from him. He did not derive much satisfaction from his position as lord lieutenant, believing the life of viceroy to come close to his idea of 'perfect misery'.[146] His objective was the consolidation of the empire, and he felt if that could be achieved he would be sufficiently rewarded for his exertions. The lord lieutenant was convinced that the combination of the temper of the Irish protestants and the ferocity of the troops served only to disrupt all plans for conciliation.[147] He was particularly critical of the Irish militia. This was perhaps in part the prejudice of the officer against non-regular troops, but was also because of their unreliable, and disgraceful, behaviour. In a dispatch to the home secretary he denounced them as being useless against the enemy and ferocious and cruel against any parties that came under their power. Disgusted, he concluded that 'in short, murder appears to be their favourite pastime'.[148]

Terror was combated with counter-terror. Burning, rape and murder were favoured tools, as the military lost all shape and discipline, engaging in acts of brutality that exceeded the violence of the rebels.[149] On neither side was any discretion used, or quarter given. The behaviour of Lord Kingsborough was representative. At Carrick he 'flogged a man and during the punishment threw salt on his back', and boasted of having slept with a number of women in return for having spared their relatives' lives. Torture was readily employed to extract information, and oftentimes for no reason at all.[150]

The strategy Cornwallis adopted was a steady mixture of conciliation and force: the leaders of the rebellion were to be punished, the followers pardoned. The conflict was one of 'plunder and massacre', not one of open conflict, and Cornwallis believed his approach was the only one which could terminate it successfully.[151] Control of the military had been seriously tested in the early days of the rebellion and Camden had been unable, or unwilling, to stop the injustices and atrocities. Considered the ablest general in the army, Cornwallis recognised that the restoration of discipline and authority was imperative. One of his first official actions was the issuing of 'the most posi-tive orders against the infliction of punishment under any pretence whatever, not authorised by the orders of a general officer in pursuance of a sentence of a general court martial'.[152] Bartlett has recognised that Cornwallis was not 'unduly lenient'.[153] Of the 400 cases he determined by March 1799 he permitted the execution of 81 of the 131 sentenced to death.[154] Significantly, these figures were released by the chief secretary in 1799 to defend Cornwallis against the charge of having been too soft during the rebellion. A battle-hardened general, Cornwallis was never going to shirk from executing those he considered to merit it. The earl of Clare in 1801 praised the viceroy for his humanity that had been 'equal to his courage'.[155] He revealed that Cornwallis had never resorted 'to acts of violence but under the most pressing necessity' and that he had 'never permitted an individual to suffer without the most minute investigation of his case'. Compared to what preceded him, and what others were urging at the time, the lord lieutenant did indeed follow a lenient strategy.

'Ireland in its present state will pull down England: she is a ship on fire.'[156] Lord Carlisle's observation defined the problem presented by Ireland in 1798. Carlisle himself saw only two possible solutions for the king's government. It could either cast off the ship or extinguish the fire. Upon hearing of the Irish rebellion in May 1798 Pitt instantly recognised the threat posed to the empire. His response to the 'ship on fire' in May was more far-reaching than even Carlisle could anticipate a few months later. The prime minister decided to bring Ireland into a complete union with Britain, and end the political uncertainty of the past decades. John Beresford, in August, was to regret 'the great misfortune' of Ireland that

> for many years ministers have never thought of her except when she became extremely troublesome to them, when by some temporary expedient they have patched up a temporary quiet, and left things to chance until another crisis called upon them again to think. The mischief which has been done is great, and how it will be set right, God only knows.[157]

Years previously Lord Charlemont, speaking of Pitt's father, had declared that it was

> easier for a camel to go through the eye of a needle, or for a rich man to enter heaven than for a politician to lay aside disguise, or for a minister *here* to think as we would wish with regard to our affairs.[158]

In 1798 Irish affairs had very much a priority in government thinking, with the conclusion that 'the only remedy is union, union, union'.[159] It was an ambitious strategy, and characteristic of Pitt that he should attempt it despite the numerous difficulties. Union demanded a number of things, including an amelioration of the problems in Ireland, and particularly a solution to the religious animosities. Firmly entwined with the desire for union was an aspiration to involve all of the Irish people within the new arrangement. The union was to be no less than an attempt to redefine the Anglo–Irish relationship within an imperial context. Pitt identified, early on, that to be successful the union had to be more than just a political amalgamation, it had to unite the peoples of both countries. Therefore the importance Pitt and Cornwallis attached to restraint should not be underestimated. It reveals significant aspects of their thinking on Ireland. The viceroy was genuinely sympathetic to the catholics, and anxious to see justice for their claims. Pitt's position was more rooted in matters of state. Tranquillity in Ireland was necessary because it offered the only hope of future security, through joining the two kingdoms in a union of interest and affection. Pitt's commitments to union and restraint were related; both were components of the same strategy for Ireland. Previous attempts to secure the connection, based upon the existing system, had failed. Therefore the system was to be changed completely. For the security and future prosperity of the empire Pitt had decided to keep the people but lose the parliament.

2

Preparing for a union: men and measures

AUGUST 1798–DECEMBER 1798

I think that the salvation of Ireland . . . does not depend
upon measures but upon men.
(Lord Fitzwilliam to William Ponsonby, 1797)[1]

Ireland has too long been governed by expedient.
(Lord Redesdale to George Rose, 1804)[2]

The challenge for government, in the second half of 1798, was to find a way of reconciling various interests to the union. As the introduction in parliament approached, it became necessary to define comprehensively the terms, and limits, of the measure. This proved difficult, not least because doing so revealed the central obstacle to its passing. To be successful the union had to achieve majority support in Ireland, both within parliament and outside of it; therefore it had to appeal to both public and private interest, and catholic and protestant interests. The catholic question made such a consensus unlikely, being the most contentious of those issues requiring definition. The future status of the Irish catholics within a united kingdom would determine who would support the union, and how enthusiastically. Other factors, too, were important: the support of key figures in the political elite remained to be enlisted, the method for introducing the union had yet to be settled. Central to the entire process was the enigmatic figure of Pitt. A few years previously he had been cautioned to avoid taking a position on a matter until it was unavoidable. Now key decisions were necessary and Pitt was obliged to resolve how far the union would go on a number of issues; in doing so he defined it.

ENDING THE INSURRECTION

As the rebellion raged throughout the summer of 1798, Cornwallis continued his controversial strategy of combining leniency with effective military action. In July he devised a plan, with Clare's approval, for issuing a general pardon throughout the country. It was to exclude only those guilty of 'cool and deliberate murder', and leave leaders liable to banishment for life.[3] This was never issued, because of caution in London, but in its place a bill of pardon less favourable to rebels was produced.[4] *The Morning Chronicle* in August expressed its support for Cornwallis's approach. It remarked how

> the conduct of Marquess Cornwallis in Ireland has justified the hopes which his appointment had raised. He has emancipated the government of Ireland from the dominion of a party, by whom it was occupied as a kind of freehold. He has liberated the people from a ruinous system, and an unpopular administration. In the contest between good and evil, the former seems to have prevailed. This victory will outweigh the triumphs of a hundred battles.[5]

In short, within a few weeks of arriving in Ireland, Cornwallis had rescued the government from the cliquish elite that had previously controlled it.

An incident in October 1798 revealed much about the new lord lieutenant and his direction. Anxious to avoid injustices, Cornwallis spent four hours each day reading the minutes of court martials.[6] He could not have failed to notice one particularly blatant miscarriage. On 13 October a court martial had been held for a yeoman, Hugh Whollaghan, for the murder of Thomas Dogherty, the permanent court martial presided over by Lord Enniskillen and six officers. The facts of the case were not denied, Whollaghan's only defence being the assertion that Dogherty was 'a rebel'. Hearsay evidence was even admitted in the defendant's favour. The sentence read that the court did find that Whollaghan had shot Dogherty, 'a rebel', but despite this it acquitted him 'of any malicious or wilful intention of murder'.[7] Cornwallis was furious with the verdict and was determined that justice should be done and be seen to be done. He instructed his military secretary, Captain Taylor, to write to Lieutenant-General Craig, who was in command of the Dublin district, stating, in very direct terms, his displeasure. Craig was informed 'that his excellency entirely disapproves of the sentence of the above court martial, acquitting Hugh Whollaghan of a cruel and deliberate murder, of which, by the clearest evidence, he appears to have been guilty'.[8] Cornwallis would not tolerate such behaviour, which threatened the policies of conciliation he was attempting to pursue. Only one course of action was strong enough. He ordered the permanent court martial to be 'immediately dissolved', and directed that Whollaghan should 'be dismissed from the corps of yeomanry in which he served, and that he shall not be received into any other corps of yeomanry in the kingdom'.[9] This judgment was to be read to the president and members of the court martial in open session. In addition the court martial was to be re-formed with none of those who served on the

Whollaghan case to be admitted as members. It was strong language, which caused no small measure of offence to Enniskillen, who was to prove trouble-some later, but the point was made: such behaviour was unacceptable. At the cost of making further enemies Cornwallis had firmly established the tone and conduct of his administration.

The question of a union was forced to rest in Ireland for as long as the military threat existed. Cornwallis's chief consideration was military affairs and he left most political matters to his staff in Dublin castle.[10] The commander-in-chief was preoccupied with attempting to extinguish the vio-lence from the enemy rebels, and his own forces. The 'mischievous' effect of the military outrages on the running of the country was fully recognised.[11] Cornwallis despised the 'wretched situation' in which he found himself placed, best exemplified, he believed, by the joy expressed by all when a priest was put to death.[12] Taming the military proved to be an arduous task. To restore discipline and calm amongst the soldiers Cornwallis felt obliged to issue a general order at the end of August. This called on generals, and all the commanding officers of regiments, to put an immediate end to the licentious conduct of the troops. The ordinary Irish subjects were to be protected from being robbed or ill-treated. Officers became responsible for the conduct of soldiers. If any soldier was caught 'either in the act of robbery or with the articles of plunder in their possession, they shall be instantly tried, and immedi-ate execution shall follow their conviction'.[13] Cornwallis was not just concerned with defending the protestant ascendancy, he was equally concerned with protecting the Irish catholics.

On 22 August General Humbert and three French frigates reached Killala bay.[14] The rebellion had now assumed the much darker appearance of a foreign invasion, suggesting a terrifying portent of the future for the increasingly paranoid loyalists. Fearing that the landing in the west of Ireland represented part of an advance guard, Cornwallis went cautiously to meet the threat. The French were encouraged by an initial victory at Castlebar on 27 August, when the loyalist militia panicked and fled, in an infamous rout that became known as 'the races of Castlebar'. Anxious to take direct command, Cornwallis moved quickly to intercept the French army, and on 8 September faced Humbert at Ballinamuck. The French surrendered and their Irish collaborators were slaughtered. As Marianne Elliott states, 'neither side emerged with credit'.[15]

The bloodshed at Ballinamuck all but quenched the insurrection. Unaware of the unravelling of the United Irishmen's plans, Theobald Wolfe Tone set sail from Brest on 16 September with a fleet carrying 3,000 French soldiers. However, in a demonstration of the increasing dominance of the British navy, he was captured at sea in October and brought to Dublin in chains. His trial for treason on 10 November marked one, final riposte for the late rebellion. Dressed in his ceremonial French officer's uniform, he pleaded guilty to the charges, and delivered a stirring oration in defence of his actions:

> I have laboured in consequence to create a people in Ireland by raising three millions of my countrymen to the rank of citizens . . . I have attempted to

establish the independence of my country; I have failed in the attempt; my life is in consequence forfeited and I submit: the court will do their duty and I shall endeavour to do mine.

Denied the right of death by firing squad, he was sentenced to execution by hanging, but cheated the noose by cutting his own throat on 15 November. Embarrassment was avoided by his impending death: a legal appeal was being prepared on the grounds that he should have been tried at the admiralty court since he was captured at sea, with even the lord chancellor admitting that the government had got itself into 'a little scrape' by its carelessness. Clare's relief did not extend to showing any magnanimity towards Tone; he gruesomely recommended carrying out the sentence before the prisoner died, even if the hanging would sever the head from the body in the process.[16] Tone died from his wound on 19 November, the 1798 rebellion reaching its apotheosis in the moment of his death.

BEGINNING THE NEGOTIATIONS

From June to September Cornwallis had been chiefly occupied with quelling the 'growing evil' of anarchy.[17] With the country gradually brought under control, and the French threat neutralised, he turned his thoughts to the consolidation of the country within the empire through a union. This was the 'great measure' on which he considered the safety of Britain and Ireland to depend.[18] As the country quietened, two things became apparent to Cornwallis. The first was that a perseverance with the old system would only lead to a deterioration in the situation and ultimately separate the two countries. The second was that the principal figures in Ireland, by their prejudices and passions, had revealed an unpardonable ignorance about the country.[19] One of the few and perhaps the only individual outside of his secretaries and his friend Major-General Sir Charles Ross that Cornwallis felt it was worth discussing the situation with was Clare, 'the most right-headed man in the country'.[20] The lord lieutenant was impressed with the lord chancellor's apparent willingness to discuss the words 'papist and moderation'.[21] As Clare's visit to London later in the year was to show, the lord chancellor was quite capable of appearing reasonable and temperate when he chose. Nevertheless his moderation even at this time did not extend to agreeing with the admission of catholics to parliament.

In July Cornwallis discussed with Pitt the best moment at which to bring forward, or at least sound out opinion on, the 'great point of ultimate settlement'.[22] While the one or two 'cautious people' he had broached the subject with warned that the time was not right for it, Cornwallis stated his commitment to a union as the only measure that could save the country and he vowed 'never [to] lose sight of it'. It was possible to frighten the country into a union, Cornwallis acknowledged, but frightened or not, the ascendancy would never consent to emancipation being a part of union. It had also become clear to the viceroy that the hatred of the catholics towards the government would have to be softened.[23]

Tensions between Cornwallis and Portland, which had originated years before during the American war, began to reassert themselves within months of his arrival as viceroy. Portland was less inclined to clemency than the lord lieutenant and tempers flared when the home secretary revealed that he would rather execute the traitors than banish them to America. Cornwallis complained to Pitt and expressed himself to be a 'little hurt' by the attitude.[24] The prime minister stood over the lord lieutenant's actions. He reassured him that he would lose no opportunity to contradict 'any false imputations of the transaction with the state prisoners'.[25] These strains repeatedly threatened the co-ordination of the government strategy. It was reported in December 1798 that Cornwallis and Portland were not even on speaking terms, 'though the correspondence is properly in that office'.[26] Pitt was often forced to mediate and had occasion to overrule the home secretary from sending harsh criticisms to the viceroy,[27] something that Cornwallis soon bitterly realised.

Lord warden of the Cinque Ports, Pitt often sought refuge in the splendour of Walmer castle. A favourite place in times of ill health, there he indulged in his love of landscape gardening,[28] a significant aspect of his character.[29] Recovering from his illness, in August the prime minister declared himself 'very impatient to hear something more on the subject of union'.[30] Between June and August he had written notes on the union which, at one point, he had given to Auckland for examination. This burst of activity had culminated in a 'much longer paper' on the subject.[31] All the time Pitt was working with his small circle of advisers. Sylvester Douglas, for example, made a compilation on the union, with particular reference to the earlier one with Scotland.[32] Waiting for news Pitt weighed up different aspects of the union, but was prevented from writing them down because of 'the attractions of the sea-side'.[33] There was a fear that he would lose interest in the matter, and increasingly he became pessimistic about the outcome. A week later, in the middle of August, the minister's natural optimism was restored, and he was cheerful about the way Ireland would go, although Grenville was less sanguine. There was still impatience about the leisurely pace of news from Ireland. Pitt eventually received two papers on union, one from Cooke that he considered 'extremely worth reading', and one from another source that he considered less so.[34]

The shift in thinking on union between June and August is revealing. The two points that Pitt admitted occupied most of his thoughts on Ireland were tithes and contribution. A suggestion by Cooke to reduce the proposed number of Irish MPs in the united parliament from 150 to 100 was agreed by Pitt. He feared, however, that selecting 100 might create problems that would 'stir too much the principles of parliamentary reform'.[35] In its place Pitt recommended an alternative method for choosing the 100. One member could be chosen from each of the 33 counties (Pitt mistakenly added an extra county to the kingdom) and a further member from the 17 'most considerable cities or towns'. The final 50 seats could be chosen from the existing 100 places, 'two places choosing one member either *jointly* or *alternately*'. Pitt was unsure whether compensation would be required for seats that were abolished, or lost value, and if so how much would be required. On the question of peers Pitt believed that 30 might be sufficient, including 6 bishops.

The religious dimension of the union remained delicate. Pitt believed that some security was necessary for the protestant establishment along the lines of 'that provided for the church of England by the articles of union with Scotland'. But he did not accept that this precluded the inclusion of the catholic religion in the state. The prime minister considered Cooke's point on an oath for the united parliament to be 'exactly what I wish', supposing the existing oath 'to be satisfactory to the better part of the catholics, which should be ascertained'. Pitt was taking care not to rule out the catholics from involvement in the united parliament. He wondered that if the existing oath 'as settled by the Irish act 33 Geo. III, c.21' was 'sufficient for office, why require a different one for parliament? And why are corporation officers to be exclusively protestants, when those of the state may be catholics?' The difficult question of tithes, that Pitt now considered on his horse-rides, was one he believed had to be addressed in the union. By giving 'a competent provision' to 'a reasonable number of catholic clergy' the issue could be made less contentious. Through such a provision the clergy could be 'enlisted on the side of government'; Pitt accepted that 'their influence cannot be at once destroyed'.

THE CATHOLIC CONJECTURE

Delicately poised between duty to their followers and obligation to the state were the catholic hierarchy. The first eight months of 1798 magnified the stresses they laboured against, as they attempted to maintain their fragile relationship with the British government and simultaneously avoid alienating the Irish catholic population. It was a challenge that had been complicated by the French revolution, and the subsequent treatment of the catholic religion by the revolutionaries, including the recent imprisonment of Pope Pius VI. The hierarchy's attempts to steer a moderate course throughout the rebellion period were buffeted by the destruction of churches that took place, and rocked by the doubts of the castle, who continued to view the bishops and priests with suspicion.

The subtle nuances in the catholic hierarchy's leadership were best epitomised by the behaviour of the archbishop of Dublin, John Thomas Troy. Although a strong advocate of loyalty to the state, he had also courted controversy, especially in 1793 with his *Pastoral on the duties of Christian citizens*, where he had referred to the catholics as 'an enslaved people' and provoked outrage by his use of the word 'citizens' in the title.[36] Troy's overriding concern was to disassociate the rebellion from catholicism, preparing various addresses and pastorals proclaiming the church's loyalty while simultaneously attempting to ensure that loyalty throughout the country. On 27 May he published short instructions that were uncompromising in their attack on the rebels and promising excommunication unless they desisted. As a result Troy found himself assailed from all sides, regarded with suspicion by the government, mistrust by many of his own clergy, and hostility by the rebels; in July Castlereagh placed him under government protection for his own safety.[37]

The reaction of the hierarchy was based on more than expediency, it was infused with ingrained memories. In many cases education in France had intensified subsequent revulsion for the revolution, and some even had first-hand experience of the terror. Maynooth college, which had been established in 1795, chose as its second president the elderly priest Dr Peter Flood, who had narrowly escaped death during the September massacres in Paris in 1792. Imbued with a horror of revolutionary violence, upon his accession in 1798 he supported the expulsion of students believed to be conspiring with the United Irishmen. In June, Flood was relieved to receive government assurances that Maynooth would not lose its grant.[38] As president he would go on to become an ardent proponent of the union, described by Castlereagh as 'a very worthy and respectable man' and 'a zealous supporter of the great measure in contemplation'.[39]

THE LEADERSHIP QUESTION

Before the rebellion many people had enthusiastically recommended uniting the offices of lord lieutenant and commander-in-chief. They soon repented their hasty judgment. Cornwallis was a cantankerous old man with an almost quixotic sense of his own character. His rigid code of honour and under-standing of his line of conduct was absolute. Scornful of all public opinion and sentiment, he had a single-minded determination and instinctive aware-ness of what the occasion required. He was judged harshly by his opponents, and it is necessary to assess how successful he was at achieving his objectives. On assuming the office of lord lieutenant Cornwallis was expected to exercise his leadership function in four areas: he was to quell the rebellion cleanly and expeditiously; he was to restore military discipline and end atrocities; he was to make government palatable to the catholics and enlist their support for future endeavours; and, finally, he was to implement a legislative union. Ironically, the very autocratic manner that made Cornwallis so successful in terminating the rebellion, and restoring order to the country, not surpris-ingly proved to be a liability in the political world. His unbending self-righteousness, his unwillingness to accommodate brittle egos, made him detested by the political elite in Ireland. The isolation of Foster and the old clique of politicians was no doubt correct from a practical point of view, but in political terms it was at best unwise, at worst suicidal. Incidents such as the Whollaghan court martial were admirable in moral terms, and helped restore confidence in the judicial system, but the price was high. Cornwallis's high-handed and dismissive treatment of people used to unquestioned respect was a disastrous attitude for someone leading an administration that was attempting to persuade the political nation to extinguish itself. There is little evidence for Senior's bold assertion that Cornwallis was 'a man of con-siderable tact'.[40] As for enlisting the support of the Roman Catholics here Cornwallis had little room for manoeuvre, so long as emancipation and union were kept separate issues. He did his best, and it was not his fault that, although sympathetic to him personally, the catholics preferred to remain aloof from government. Unwilling to embarrass the cabinet, Cornwallis avoided making the catholics aware of his favourable opinions towards them.[41] E.L. Muson has defined leadership as 'the ability to handle men so as to achieve the most with the least friction and the greatest co-operation . . . Leadership is the creative and directive force of morale.'[42] It was by this standard that Cornwallis failed.

Thus it was that in the first seven months of Cornwallis's viceroyalty he experienced an unprecedented barrage of criticism. There were three chief grounds for complaint. The first was his seeming incapacity, or unwillingness, to communicate with London. The cabinet was impatient for news about Ireland, and Portland, in particular, became infuriated with the infrequency and style of the lord lieutenant's dispatches, which he complained were written in the form of private letters.[43] The second complaint was that Cornwallis was too lenient in military matters, with his restraint taken for weakness. The decisive final complaint was that Cornwallis had set aside the old Irish cabinet and had alienated many figures, most crucially Foster, whose support would make the passage of the union much easier. These last two charges cast serious doubts over Cornwallis's leadership, as his enemies gathered and his position became threatened.

The viceroy's sharpest critic was Buckingham. Although he was generally regarded as oversensitive, and something of an embarrassment, his family connections made him a serious adversary. Buckingham shared Cornwallis's desire for a union, catholic relief, and clemency, but a clash of wills sparked off a running feud. It was not helped when Cornwallis assigned command of a Bucks detachment to someone else. The snub wounded Buckingham's pride to the extent that he wished to lay the whole matter before the king.[44] He maintained that he would not be 'degraded by any man', and considered the behaviour 'the *dénouement* of my cursed Irish journey, in which I certainly looked to much misery, but not to oppression and humiliation'.[45] Influenced, no doubt, by this private grudge Buckingham began to dissect all of Cornwallis's actions, and was venomous in his criticisms of what the viceroy did, or did not do. Writing to his brother, Lord Grenville, the foreign secretary, sometimes more than once a day, his initial complaints were directed at the 'no-government' which resulted from Cornwallis's absences in the field.[46] Even on the battlefield his leadership was attacked and there were numerous complaints against the commander-in-chief for being 'so completely and repeatedly out-generalled'.[47]

For Buckingham, it was only the presence of the troops which kept Ireland subdued, not the 'imbecility of Lord Cornwallis's government'.[48] He considered the lord lieutenant's unpopularity to be a threat to the union, turning people who would otherwise be supporters of the government into opponents. Cornwallis's casting aside of the old Irish cabinet Buckingham blamed for alienating many. Nor did he have much confidence in the acting chief secretary, Castlereagh, who he felt was not up to the task of governing in Cornwallis's place.[49]

Claims were made that there did not exist 'one grain of confidence' in the viceroy's abilities. Buckingham blamed Cornwallis for having 'thrown away the greatest game that ever was put into the hands of man'.[50] The opposition to the lord lieutenant was 'increased, increasing, and not likely to be diminished'.[51] Whitehall did not appreciate Cornwallis's reluctance to keep them informed, and this failing was confirmed in his dealings in Ireland as well. There his lack of 'all communication' had even more disastrous consequences, alienating many individuals from the government.[52] Buckingham's animosity towards Cornwallis grew to the extent that by December he proclaimed the lord lieutenant, whom he sarcastically referred to as 'the great pillar of our Irish salvation', the 'most contemptible personage I ever knew'.[53] The lord lieutenant attempted to remain aloof from these attacks. He refused to become involved in a war of words, merely remarking to a friend that 'the Marquess of B. has behaved very ill to me, but much worse to his country'.[54] But the charges made by Buckingham were confirmed by others. Both Hobart and Carysfort had problems with the lord lieutenant, which they reported on visits to London in the autumn of 1798.[55]

Within Dublin castle there were also some serious doubts. Edward Cooke, whose opinion was highly respected, shared in the criticisms of the viceroy and blamed his lack of involvement in the running of the country for rising discontent.[56] The under-secretary confirmed that the unwillingness to communicate ran to the heart of the administration. Even Castlereagh, the acting chief secretary, was rarely consulted and 'much mischief' was predicted. As Cornwallis seemed firmly set in his ways Cooke held out little hope of changing him.[57] The opposition to Cornwallis on personal grounds was verified by Cooke. It had reached the stage where any measure proposed by the lord lieutenant was likely to be opposed by the yeomanry and the orange party, purely because it was his measure. A dinner at the lord mayor's was cited where, on the proposal of a toast to Cornwallis and the prosperity of Ireland, 'not a man drank the whole, but only the latter clause'. Cooke warned, unsuccessfully as it turned out, about the lack of consultation, and the 'fatal' absence of an Irish cabinet. Despondent, he admitted that many of the charges against Cornwallis were true.[58]

Further confirmation of these failings came from the king's advocate-general, Dr Patrick Duigenan, the narrow-minded MP for Armagh, who informed Castlereagh that the 'unaccountable conduct' of Cornwallis had made the lord lieutenant

> not only an object of disgust, but also of abhorrence, to every loyal man I have conversed with since my return from England, [and] had induced many persons to oppose a union, who, if uninfluenced by resentment against the Marquess Cornwallis, would have given no opposition if they did not support that measure.[59]

Even those generally favourable to Cornwallis accepted the lord lieutenant's shortcomings. The acting chief secretary wrote that he and William Elliot, the under-secretary for the military department, had been 'confirmed in the opinion we entertained that Ld. C. is rather inattentive to parliamentary management'. Castlereagh was not sure whether to attribute this weakness to Cornwallis's military temperament or habits formed in India. But he feared this inattentiveness would prove mischievous and lead the lord lieutenant to underestimate the embarrassment and difficulties that might occur in parliament.[60]

DEFINING THE UNION

Obstinately pursuing his own path Cornwallis attempted to prepare the way for union. He was surprised to find himself in complete agreement with the lord chancellor on almost all issues, the principal difference revolving around catholic relief. Clare's character, he believed, had been 'much misrepresented in England'. It was in sharp contrast to the 'absurdly violent' attitudes of almost all the other key political figures on the island. There had always been a plan for the key figures in Ireland to visit England at some point to discuss the union. As the deliberations in London could only go so far, it was decided that the Irish advisers should visit in the autumn. The most important individual, and the first one they wished to consult, was Clare. Cornwallis devised the pretext in August of a trip to Bath, ostensibly for the lord chancellor's health, to enable him to visit London and discuss the measure there for a few days, without arousing suspicion.[61] Clare willingly gave his consent to this proposal.[62]

One of the recurring themes throughout this time was the presence of the large military force in Ireland. It was seen by many as an instrument of intimidation, and government was well aware of its power. Castlereagh was in no doubt as to the necessity of maintaining the troops in Ireland, 'not merely as securing the British interest in this country, but as marking distinctly that it is to her interposition we are altogether indebted for our safety'.[63] The persuasive power of the military was tacitly acknowledged. The absence of such a tangible representation of British power and authority would 'tend to make the public mind impracticable and render even our best friends less disposed to a different settlement of the country, without which it is in vain to hope for any permanent tranquillity'.

One of the most crucial aspects of the entire union endeavour was how the settlement would affect the catholics. Pitt and his government had a choice between a union on a strictly protestant basis, excluding the catholics from the united parliament, or a union which would allow them to be safely included amongst the representation. George III had immediately insisted the union was to be of the former kind. Despite Cornwallis's sympathies towards the catholics, the king had wished him to understand that no further concessions were to be granted to them.[64] Within the cabinet there was more flexibility, particularly amongst Pitt, Grenville and Dundas. Bartlett has recognised that 'Pitt had been, or claimed to have been' favourable to the catholics some months before November 1798.[65] Certainly the evidence of Grenville's paper on the union, which he wrote with Pitt in the first days of June, confirms this.[66] There was a definite willingness in the primary stages to facilitate the catholics within the union terms. Soon, however, caution replaced the initial enthusiasm for emancipation. Dundas alone retained his belief in its necessity[67] while Grenville's early sentiments gave way to a moderate scepticism. Why he changed in his determination is unclear. Peter Jupp suggests that it was due to Clare's visit in the autumn of 1798.[68] Grenville himself admitted that he had been initially convinced of the propriety of full relief, but had been persuaded against this by the rebellion.[69] The position of the prime minister was the most interesting. It was cloaked in ambiguity as Pitt preferred to maintain a certain vagueness around the union details. This was not because of indecisiveness or weakness; paradoxically Pitt saw the union in clearer terms when it was undefined. Then, it contained numerous possibilities for strengthening the empire. It has been argued that Pitt decided in 1798 to implement his Irish policy in stages, with a union first followed by emancipation. What is more likely is that he wished to delay a decision as long as possible before being forced to determine the status of the catholics within the united kingdom. Even then a judgment on the possibility of emancipation following the union in the long term was to be safely postponed for a later consideration.[70]

In Ireland Cornwallis was less vacillating. He remained convinced that the union should be accompanied by full catholic relief. But, as he encountered stiff opposition to further catholic concessions from all the leading figures in Ireland, including Clare, he began to realise how difficult this would be. Significantly, Cornwallis believed the union was still necessary, even if it was to be on a protestant basis.[71] To safeguard the rights of the catholics, Cornwallis decided to resist firmly any clause in the union that would make the exclusion of the catholics a fundamental part of the measure. Until the catholics were given full political rights, which Cornwallis accepted could be safely conceded only in a united parliament, there would be no peace or stability in Ireland.[72]

Observers in England were heartened in September to find Irish affairs occupying so much of Pitt's time.[73] The work on the union revealed his pronounced preference for British, over Irish, contributions. In that month deliberations on the union were at an advanced stage although they were not sent officially to Dublin. On 26 September Castlereagh was leaked the suggestions for the leading union articles that had been developed in London.[74] These bore a marked resemblance to Pitt's paper of August. There was a provision for tithes, and queries as to borough compensation, and parliamentary commissioners: 'if any to be appointed such, and who?' This valuable information was sent *'only for your lordship's eye,* in the strictest confidence and in any letter which you may write to this country, I am sure you will never make any allusion to them'.[75] The first Irish advisers arrived in England in October with a draft copy of the articles eventually sent to Ireland the next month.

A decision on the catholic question had to be made in the autumn. Recognising this, Cornwallis submitted his analysis to Pitt in early October, as Clare prepared to depart for England. He guessed at what the determination would be, and was not optimistic that his broader idea for a union would be adopted. The king's government, he unhappily predicted, would turn its back on a union with the Irish nation and instead make it only with a party in Ireland. Cornwallis was not blind to the supposed defects of the catholics. He accepted that they would not

> be immediately converted into good subjects, yet I am sanguine enough to hope, after the most plausible and most popular of their grievances is removed (and especially if it could be accompanied by some regulation about tithes), that we should get time to breathe, and at least check the rapid progress of discontent and disaffection.[76]

Leaving these thoughts with Pitt, Cornwallis relinquished responsibility for the matter. His pessimism was reflected by his pressing strongly the 'most constant recommendation' that whatever was determined would not be made irrevocable.[77] Castlereagh's preference was to avoid touching upon the catholic question until a decision was made regarding catholic and protestant claims. Otherwise, he felt, the danger would outweigh the advantages.[78] Buckingham, on the other hand, was convinced that the catholics should be made to understand that the union was proposed for their benefit to achieve the maximum advantage from their numbers. The catholic question was the most important consideration for Buckingham, and he admitted that the whole of his mind turned upon it.[79]

The lord chancellor's visit to England in October 1798 brought the question to a head. On his arrival in England, Clare met with Pitt, the British lord chancellor, Loughborough, and Portland. Immediately, a debate on the catholic question flared. The Irish lord chancellor lamented the 'critical state of our damnable country'[80] and presented his argument that the rebellion had shown the failings of previous policies towards the catholics.[81] The union, he insisted, had to be formed on a strictly protestant basis with no promise of emancipation. Clare was shocked to find the ministers 'as full of their popish projects as ever' but was heartened to find that Pitt seemed firm about excluding the catholics.[82] Aware of Cornwallis's willingness to acquiesce on this point Clare used this knowledge to strengthen his persuasive case.

The prospect of concerted opposition to emancipation had indeed led Cornwallis, in October, to concede that a union must be a protestant one. But he had done so reluctantly, fearing the ultimate result of such a narrow policy. As the situation in Ireland worsened, the lord lieutenant decided to make one last, desperate, effort to influence policy. He did not believe that a union between Great Britain and the Irish protestants could be of any great benefit to the empire. Excluding the catholics from the measure was an easier point to carry, he accepted, but it weakened its purpose in attempting to stabilise the country. Cornwallis feared that the union would come to serve as a permanent barrier to the rights of the catholics rather than securing 'permanent tranquillity' for Ireland, which could be achieved only by admitting them to parliament.[83] Therefore on 17 October the viceroy sent William Elliot, a strong proponent of emancipation, over to London to counterbalance Clare's arguments. Cornwallis would have liked to have sent Castlereagh with him, and regretted that he could not spare him.[84] In a letter to the prime minister, dispatched with Elliot, Cornwallis warned that a union with the Irish protestants might serve as 'a temporary respite' from the problems in Ireland but he doubted whether the catholics would wait patiently for their emancipation from the united parliament. He claimed that it was 'a desperate measure for the British government to make an irrevocable alliance with a small party in Ireland, to wage war against the catholics and presbyterians'.[85] Cornwallis was fighting for the 'time to breathe' he had wanted.

Examining the situation in broad terms, Cornwallis noted how the presbyterians and catholics composed about nine-tenths of the population. 'Attempting to reason the future from the past', the lord lieutenant pointed out that one could not be optimistic about the outcome of a union hostile towards the catholics, particularly as the opposition in Britain would attempt a 'mischievous intervention'. Further, on a pragmatic level, the union afforded the king's government the only opportunity of deriving credit from the granting of emancipation which could otherwise, within a short time, be forced anyhow.[86]

This dramatic intervention was explosive. Up until then the discussion had been leading 'towards a union strictly protestant'.[87] Clare was shown the lord lieutenant's letter and was horrified by this startling contribution to the debate. He believed that 'some untoward devil must have taken his station in my accursed country . . . Nothing more unfortunate and ill-timed could have happened than the letter of Lord Cornwallis'.[88] The lord chancellor clearly realised that the best way of pressing his case was by employing reason not prejudice. He forcibly urged the necessity of a protestant union while at the same time confessing that he himself feared nothing 'from the catholics having everything'.[89] Alas, he argued, it was impossible to carry this point in Ireland. Indeed he assured his listeners that the protestants of Ireland would happily make it 'a fundamental part of the union that nothing further should be done for the catholics hereafter'.[90] This was rejected. George Canning, the young protégé of Pitt who shared many of his views, insisted that the question should be reserved, with 'a full demonstration of what is right upon it at a proper season'. This had the great advantage of boosting the probable success of the measure. The discussion was concluded by 'drunkenness at Bellamy's'.[91]

That Canning, one of Pitt's closest friends, believed the question should be postponed for a future date is suggestive. In 1798 Pitt was still viewing the union in broad terms. The key objective was security; everything else was secondary to this, including emancipation. The prime minister wished to introduce a union first and then, from a position of strength, decide upon what was necessary for the empire. The introduction of a legislative union, uncomplicated by emancipation, left the matter open for future consideration, after a peace, and after the king's mind had been worked upon. Camden at the end of October said that Pitt was 'inclined most strongly to the union on a protestant basis'.[92] A more accurate account had been provided by Elliot three days previously: Clare's arguments had 'operated powerfully on Mr Pitt's mind' and he 'says that his judgement is not yet formed on the subject'.[93] William Wilberforce, who would have known Pitt's sentiments, became doubtful about the measure when he found out that emancipation was to be excluded, as

> this destroys what was in my mind, the grand presumptive benefit of the union, viz. — the enabling you without danger to make the Roman Catholics such concessions as might make them feel themselves good subjects.[94]

Pitt believed that catholic relief before a union would solve nothing. This was because the union itself was the central security measure; emancipation was not.

Supporting, and certainly influencing, the prime minister was his foreign secretary. Grenville had been a believer in the necessity of emancipation but in the aftermath of the rebellion had changed his opinion. He then adopted Clare's position that no alteration should be made to the catholic laws as part of the union, fearing that it would be seen as an encouragement to rebellion, 'instead of showing that every endeavour to disunite Great Britain and Ireland only makes them "cling close and closer" to each other'.[95] The matter, he too believed, should be reserved, to be decided at a later date. The loss of Grenville from the catholic cause was a serious blow. Pitt had begun to rely heavily on his cousin's judgment, much to the disappointment of Dundas, who as the secretary of state for war was beginning to break with Grenville on matters of policy. The triumvirate of Pitt, Grenville and Dundas, which had acted as an inner cabinet for many years, was slowly dis-integrating.[96] If Grenville had remained firm on emancipation, supported by Dundas, then Pitt would have been unlikely to have yielded the point. Dundas became embittered by Pitt's lack of conviction and criticised his weakness in following the opinion of the last person he had conversed with, 'which has often, too often, led him to give up his better judgement to the persevering importunity of Lord Grenville'.[97]

Dundas, 'the thane', was the only minister who was fully convinced that catholic emancipation should be included in the union. He believed that the king would have to make up his mind on the matter of full relief, sooner rather than later, and was apprehensive that someone was agitating the king's mind upon the subject. The catholic question for him was 'the plainest of all political truths', but one that required delicate handling.[98] With his experience of the religious situation in Scotland, Dundas was more aware than most of the possibility of another non-Anglican region in the empire. Unfortunately for the catholics, Dundas was in Scotland when Clare arrived in England. Cornwallis was later to curse this absence, believing that had Dundas been in London, 'he might perhaps have been able to carry the point of establishing the union on a broad and comprehensive line, but things have now gone too far to admit of a change'.[99]

By the time Dundas returned to London the matter had been decided. Catholic emancipation was not to be included within the union terms. Nevertheless Dundas was keen to reassure Elliot that the subject was not permanently closed. Dundas believed that the union should be on the broadest possible basis, provided Cornwallis continued to think that such an idea was feasible. While elsewhere, people were losing faith in the lord lieutenant, Dundas asserted that he retained 'that *enthusiastic* confidence in Lord Cornwallis which he has always entertained'.[100] It appears that Pitt shared his friend's sentiments. Dundas informed Elliot that the opinions of the lord lieutenant, on the catholic question, would still influence the final determination, as Cornwallis's 'sentiments will ultimately have much weight in Mr Pitt's determination'.[101] The union was to be on protestant lines, but the catholic question would remain open for a future discussion if this was considered desirable. At this time Elliot noted that there was 'some dryness between Dundas and Pitt' on the question of leaving the catholics out of the measure, but he did not believe it would last.[102]

The result of these talks was soon sent back to Ireland. Elliot wrote to Castlereagh on 24 October to confirm that the union, and catholic emancipation, were to be treated as separate issues. Two reasons were cited for the decision. The first was the desire to avoid a debate in Britain and Ireland on the religious laws at that time. Then there was the unwillingness to risk alienating the Irish protestants, particularly since the rebellion had already inflamed their prejudices.[103] Camden confirmed this a few days later pointing out how Pitt had become 'inclined most strongly to the union on a protestant basis'.[104] The decision to pursue the union on narrow lines enabled Pitt, through Auckland, to give Foster the assurances he required, namely that the union would support the 'exclusive system' the speaker wished to maintain.[105]

The only encouragement that the prime minister could give Cornwallis concerned the oaths section of the draft treaty and the difficult question of tithes. All the Irish politicians, whom Pitt had seen by the middle of November, had expressed support for some arrangement respecting tithes. The heads of the treaty of union which Portland sent to the lord lieutenant on 12 November insisted that MPs must take the existing oaths but that these oaths were subject to such alterations as the united parliament wished to decide on.[106] In this way the catholic question was kept open for a future discussion. Pitt informed the lord lieutenant that this arrangement was the only footing on which the question could be dealt with at that time.[107]

The disappointment was not disguised in Ireland. Yet there was little alternative but for Cornwallis to accept the situation. The absence of a clause preventing the future agitation of the catholic question at least left the matter open for the future 'wisdom and liberality of the united parliament'.[108] The point had been conceded. Cornwallis recognised the impossibility of changing the narrow principle of the union, given that 'the principal persons in this country have received assurances from the English ministers which cannot be retracted'.[109] It was reluctantly noted, this time by the chief secretary, that Pitt had pledged himself to the lord chancellor and others 'not to propose any change of the test laws [nor for] bringing the subject forward'.[110] It appeared that the catholics would support the union, as an improvement to their existing situation, and because the protestants seemed to be against it.[111] Cornwallis was instructed to consult with leading individuals in the country whose support Pitt believed the success of the measure depended upon.[112]

The prospect of a union on protestant lines caused serious problems for some members of Cornwallis's administration. The under-secretary to the military department, at the time the lord lieutenant's envoy in England, was very sympathetic to the catholic claims and had debated the points at length with Pitt. The prime minister had not been convinced. William Elliot, he informed the viceroy, had not satisfied him 'of the practicability of such a measure at this time [n]or of the propriety of attempting it'.[113] Not only was Pitt sceptical of the practical side of achieving emancipation, he was now unsure about the merits of the issue. Elliot quickly became disheartened by the decision to press for a union on strict protestant terms. Ministers were beginning to waver in their determination for a union, faced with the weight of the growing opposition, leading Elliot to suspect that the measure might even be allowed to drop, and, as 'Mr Pitt has chosen to make the attempt upon the *narrow* basis, my regret at the dereliction of it will be much diminished'.[114] So disenchanted was 'the castle spectre' that he decided to resign. He informed Castlereagh that if the union was 'persevered in the plan proposed I am afraid it will be impossible for me to continue without much embarrassment to myself and injustice towards those with whom I am to act'.[115]

Those aware of Elliot's background would not have been surprised. He had been a regular of Edmund Burke's 'intimate coterie at Beaconsfield' in the 1790s, and after Burke had written a public letter to him suggesting the line he should take, he had become a committed supporter of catholic emancipation.[116] Despite his reservations the under-secretary gradually came round to the belief that a union, even on a narrow basis, was better than the existing system, and would prove beneficial to the empire. Elliot hoped the catholics would see it this way, although he privately accepted that they had justifiable grounds of complaint.[117]

Pitt's weakness was much criticised. Elliot felt that a little more firmness in London might have enabled the catholic claims to be incorporated into the union. Instead, the prime minister's 'lamentable facility yielded the point to *prejudice*, without I suspect, acquiring a support in any degree equivalent to the sacrifice'.[118] Some have dismissed Elliot's criticisms as being 'wide off the mark'.[119] But Elliot had discussed the catholic question with Pitt in detail and had not been given any indication that the prime minister intended the union to pave the way for emancipation. Instead Pitt had chosen to define the union in a way that would alienate the least, and placate those with whom he was talking at the time.

A few days reflection did not alter Elliot's determination to resign. He and Castlereagh had struck up a deep friendship, which the under-secretary admitted had given him 'an interest in Ireland I never expected to acquire'.[120] Given the 'critical conjuncture', Elliot expressed a preference for remaining in office, but, as he was certain that the catholic question would be brought forward at some stage in the union discussion, and as he could not 'reconcile the exclusion of the catholics to any principle, either of justice or of sound policy, [and as] it is quite impossible for me to vote against a proposition for the admission of their claims',[121] he felt obliged to resign. His integrity would not allow him to stay away from the commons when the question was being debated; that would only create a dangerous precedent for others to follow on different occasions, and parliamentary discipline would be essential once the union was introduced. Elliot decided to write to the lord lieutenant that day, 28 November, or the next, to request permission to withdraw. He apologised for the tardiness of his decision but defended it on the grounds that he had been waiting to confirm by what religious principle the union was to be proposed. The deciding point was the pledge given to Clare, which he was hurt that he had not even been aware of until Cornwallis and Castlereagh had revealed it. Elliot did, indeed, submit his resignation but was persuaded to withdraw it when both the lord lieutenant and the chief secretary made it clear that the door was not closed permanently on the catholics.[122] That a senior member of the castle administration came so close to resigning over this question has been brushed over by historians but its significance should not be ignored.[123] It illustrates just how high tensions were running at this time, and the growing threat posed by the catholic question.

THE UNION DIPLOMACY
One of the most prominent charges against Cornwallis was the alienation of Foster from government. The difficulties had begun almost immediately after the lord lieutenant arrived in Ireland on 20 June. The setting aside of the Irish cabinet, in which the speaker was a key figure, and the viceroy's plans for conciliation, had not met with Foster's approval. Nevertheless it was still believed that the speaker might be brought over to the union side. Neither Cornwallis nor Castlereagh sounded him out on the subject, although the acting chief secretary did recommend inviting him over to England in early October when Clare was travelling.[124] This was agreed, but there was some confusion in London in October as to whether the speaker had actually been invited. Portland warned Pitt that the speaker's presence was vital for deliberations, convinced that 'every moment it is delayed will add to his objections which I suspect he will be likely to make to a union and increase the difficulties we shall meet'.[125] Foster, however, had indeed been written to, both by Auckland, who had taken the opportunity to sound him out about a union, and by Pitt. The speaker replied to these letters separately on 21 October.

Foster's letter to the prime minister was polite but brief. He thanked Pitt for the 'flattering sentiments' that he had expressed, but politely declined a

journey to England. He trusted his letter to Auckland would explain his sentiments.[126] It was later reported that Foster declined this invitation to England
because the offer came through Cornwallis, who had sent a messenger to the
speaker with the letter.[127] Foster was more forthcoming in his letter to
Auckland. He admitted he found the union question to be 'a momentous one
indeed', but one that he had never turned in his mind. He confessed that he
did not see the danger which required such an expedient, considering union
to be nothing more than just that.[128] The rebellion would not have occurred,
Foster argued, if the king's government had not given concessions to
the catholics in Ireland. It was these that had encouraged them to imagine
themselves a distinct body. The correct response, he advised, was not an
unnecessary union. Instead, a steady support for the Irish protestants would
restore the country to tranquillity. At a time when Britain was standing
against jacobin principles, 'the new-fangled and hazardous doctrine of
innovations', it was not safe to risk the security of the country by abolishing
the legislature.[129] The speaker did not feel that the lord lieutenant had handled
the rebellion correctly. Pardoning would not serve to feed the rebels and,
human nature being what it was, people would not starve voluntarily. His
alternative policy would have been to start great public works to teach the
rebels to respect the government.

The speaker's support was recognised as critical by Clare and Buckingham,
'without it nothing can be done'.[130] Despite Foster's hostility towards
Cornwallis, both men shared a hope that Pitt could still engage his help.[131] It
was alleged that the main cause of his opposition was jealousy on the part of
Foster, who was understood to be envious that he did not stand well with Pitt.
The prime minister did not give up on securing the speaker's eventual
support for the union. But the letter which Foster sent to Auckland on
21 October was not one which the minister found easy to answer. The speaker
did not accept the cornerstone of Pitt's thinking on the union, namely that
the Irish system needed to be changed from outside. Nevertheless Pitt was
optimistic that the speaker could be persuaded to acquiesce in the measure if
the right things were emphasised. Auckland was instructed to send Foster, in
a confidential communication, the abstract of the plan for union which Pitt
had prepared. It was to be firmly stated to the speaker that Britain would
assist, in men and money, the 'support of such an exclusive system as he aims
at'.[132] This 'exclusive system' was the protestant system, the inclusion of the
catholics in the political system being considered too dangerous. Pitt's readi-
ness to reassure the speaker on that point shows the leaning of the prime
minister away from the catholics at this time.

Attempts were also being made in Ireland to secure Foster's support.
Cooke entered into discussions with the speaker and he discovered that his
position appeared to be that

> he is ever willing to do his utmost for the public good, but when he finds
> himself treated in a manner so different from that in which he has been

treated by every government for twenty years, he should feel himself cen-
surable for assuming the part, or for exposing himself to the imputation of,
a confidential adviser, when he is so completely excluded from confidence.[133]

Cooke accepted that this was a fair assessment but he did not rule out the
possibility of softening Foster's position. The under-secretary found the
speaker 'open but opinionative' and felt that by 'kindness and confidence he
may even be worked to reciprocal feelings'.[134] Foster was considered vain, and
Cooke noted his pleasure in displaying his own knowledge and abilities.
Nevertheless, despite his optimism, Cooke warned that Foster was not 'a
friend to a union — he does not see the use of it to the country'.[135]

The speaker eventually consented to go to England and he travelled over
in the first week of November. At last Cornwallis got round to discussing the
union with him, shortly before his departure, on the morning of 6 November.
The lord lieutenant found that Foster was obstinately against the measure but
nonetheless thought that Pitt would find the speaker 'more placable on the
subject' than he might have thought. The meeting for Cornwallis was
perfectly cordial and he reported how he gave 'an amicable explanation' to his
'supposed grievances after which we shook hands and parted very good
friends'.[136] How imagined these grievances were is not clear; two months previously Foster had castigated the lord lieutenant at a dinner for being 'a
damned silly fellow'.[137]

A draft treaty for a union was completed in November 1798 and sent to the
castle.[138] The difficult issue of Irish representation in the united parliament
was resolved by deciding that there would be one hundred Irish MPs and
thirty-two peers.[139] The peers were to comprise twenty-six temporal and six
spiritual lords. The 'commoners' were to be selected using the existing
system except that each place would return one member instead of two.
Under article four all the members of the united parliament would be
required to 'take the oaths now required by law in Great Britain', thereby
excluding the catholics from the terms of the measure.[140] The following
article made the 'continuance of the present church establishment in each
kingdom to be a fundamental article'. A proposal was included, though, to
deal with the tithe problem in Ireland. Financially, Ireland was to be liable for
one-sixth of all the annual expenses within the united kingdom.

The inclusion of 'one hundred wild Irish'[141] in the commons satisfied no
one. The Irish considered it too small a number. In Britain, Lord Sheffield
argued that seventy-five was sufficient, and cautioned that country gentlemen
would be unwilling to enter parliament if they would be greeted by 'one hundred Paddies'. If this was to be a term of the union, Sheffield warned that he
could not support such a dangerous innovation.[142] Despite this representation
no change was made to the article. While all these points were being debated
it was decided not to include a mention of the union in the king's speech and
the draft reference was deleted.[143] This decision received the consent of the
king. George III readily approved of the necessity of the union but was more

uneasy about its passage than his prime minister, who he felt was a little too sanguine.[144]

The union was being discussed in detail when Foster arrived in London. Pitt found the speaker 'perfectly cordial and communicative'. Although opposed to the measure in his 'general opinion', Foster was nevertheless prepared 'to discuss the point fairly', a differentiation that impressed the prime minister.[145] The speaker was eager to keep his conversation with Pitt private. Therefore Pitt only informed Cornwallis of his impressions of the discussions, feeling 'not at liberty to make any but this confidential use of it'.[146] It is unlikely that Foster would have appreciated this distinction.

Pitt showed Foster the draft sketch of the plan for union that Portland had transmitted to the lord lieutenant a few days previously. The speaker admitted that he did not foresee any difficulty in the execution of the measure. This satisfied Pitt, who was optimistic that Foster would not attempt to obstruct it. He even maintained a hope that the speaker's support could be enlisted, if the union could 'be made palatable to him personally'. It was here that Pitt made a grave miscalculation. He instructed Cornwallis to hold out to the speaker the prospect of a British peerage and, if possible, some ostensible situation, together with the provision for life that Foster would be entitled to on quitting the chair.[147] Camden was responsible for this assessment of the speaker's venality. In his observations on the union the former lord lieutenant had confidently predicted that 'an English peerage and a respectable provision would make a great impression upon his opinions'.[148] This was apparently the advice of 'a person much in the speaker's confidence' to Pelham.

Other members of the old Irish cabinet were invited to London in November. The chancellor of the exchequer, John Parnell, and John Beresford joined Foster and Clare in the discussions. Pitt's reading of the talks was that both Parnell and Beresford, the latter in particular, were against a union being proposed at that time. As with Foster, the prime minister remained optimistic that they would acquiesce and support the measure once it was adopted as government policy. The doubts of Beresford and Parnell, it seemed to Pitt, centred on the necessity of consulting leading individuals, and public opinion, in Ireland.[149] Until then, they did not believe the measure should be announced as a decided one.

Not everyone misjudged Foster and Parnell as badly as Pitt. Elliot, who was still in London at this time, reported to Castlereagh that the speaker was 'still adverse to a union, and, from all I hear, I think it dubious whether he will not entirely oppose it'.[150] Parnell, likewise, while talking 'very loosely' on the matter also appeared to be 'unfriendly to the measure'. Further discussions reinforced this assessment. Elliot believed that despite Pitt's meetings with Foster and Parnell nothing 'decisive' or 'conclusive' had been formed.[151] Given both Parnell's and Foster's subsequent opposition to the union, and Beresford's support, it seems strange that Pitt could have been so mistaken about their opinions. Bartlett, and A.P.W. Malcomson, Foster's outstanding biographer, show little sympathy to the minister, the former especially critical

inferring that Pitt treated the speaker with contempt.[152] There is some truth
in this. Pitt did after all keep Foster waiting before eventually seeing him. And
Wilberforce was possibly reflecting the prime minister's disdain when he
mockingly referred to Foster as 'Mr Spaker'.[153] In his defence the prime
minister was not at his best in meetings of that sort. Ehrman has recognised
this weakness in Pitt's character by noting that while he was 'a prime connector in the range of business, he was scarcely a connector of people'.[154]
Given that Parnell was prevaricating on the subject, speaking 'very loosely', it
is perhaps not surprising that Pitt was unable to comprehend his position.
But there was more to this than mere shyness. The supercilious manner
ingrained in Pitt's character combined fatally with an obvious lack of respect
for the Irish visitors. Indeed he had invited Foster over in the first place only
because Clare had recommended it and 'seems to think [it] may be of great
importance'.[155] Foster was no more than an inconvenience, and because this
was so blatant it was all the more wounding to his pride.

The consequences of the prime minister's arrogance were soon revealed.
The support of Parnell and Foster proved to be much more elusive than
anticipated. Parnell wrote to Cornwallis at the beginning of December
informing him that if a union could solve the problems of Ireland with no
other loss than a loss of vanity then 'it would be a most desirable object'.[156]
He feared, however, that it would rather serve to disunite and injure Ireland.
As for the speaker's support, Pitt had made a serious misjudgment about
securing it through patronage. In fact, given Foster's request that the discussion with Pitt should remain confidential, it is conceivable that Cornwallis
alienated the speaker further by attempting a clumsy seduction. Whatever
about Foster's venality, and post-union events would seem to confirm it, the
bungling manner in which government attempted to obtain his support was
never likely to succeed.

The failure to secure Foster for the union cause was a serious setback.
Figures as diverse as Grenville, Buckingham and Cooke all blamed
Cornwallis. Lords Sheffield and Clare, together with Euseby Cleaver, the
Roman Catholic bishop of Ferns, concurred with this belief.[157] Malcomson
interprets Cornwallis's behaviour as being more stupidity than animosity.[158]
But it would be unfair to single out the lord lieutenant for blame; Pitt was
equally culpable. The meetings between Foster and Pitt were tragicomic in
the scale of pride, incompetence and misunderstanding involved. If the depth
of Foster's opposition was determined by pique at the way he was treated then
Pitt must share the blame with Cornwallis. Neither treated the speaker with
any respect or finesse. Where Pitt was presumptuous Cornwallis was merely
blundering in his inability to accommodate the speaker. Their mistakes were
to have important consequences for the union. Yet Cornwallis was partly
correct when he claimed that securing the support of Foster would have been
at too high a price, and this would not have been a peerage but the defining of
the union in a manner that neither Pitt nor Cornwallis could countenance. In a
cogent defence of his actions Cornwallis stated that he had carefully avoided

giving offence to any person or group and that, as a result, 'no person of consequence is hostile to my government, except the speaker'.[159] The lord lieutenant showed that he was well aware of the prohibitive cost attached to Foster's support:

> I know not one method by which I could have secured his political friendship unless I had placed myself entirely under his guidance and persevered in a system which I disapproved, and which I was convinced from experience must end in the utter ruin of the country.

Cornwallis insisted that he had neglected no opportunity of showing his disposition to oblige the speaker personally. His own feelings, he assured the prime minister, would never prevent the adoption of any means that might be useful to the empire.

The incompatibility of Foster's and Cornwallis's prescriptions for Ireland made a break unavoidable. One believed wholeheartedly in the maintenance and continuance of the old system in Ireland. The other was convinced that the country could not be saved unless this system was discarded. Little convergence was possible. It was these differing aspirations for Ireland that led Cornwallis to cut himself off from the cabal that both Castlereagh and George III believed had ruined Camden. While Cornwallis's abrupt manner did not help, it is difficult to see how Foster could have been persuaded to support the union. Clare, from the beginning, emphasised the speaker's likely opposition to a union and Foster's own sentiments never wavered from his October letters rejecting the need for a union. The speaker was never likely to support a union, on any terms, and although the strength and intensity of his opposition was dictated by events, a passive opposition was the most that could ever have been hoped for.

Early in November Clare decided to return to Ireland. Grenville was 'vexed' to see him go, anxious to discuss the union in private with him. Matters in Ireland were reported as 'pressing' and Grenville readily accepted this: 'I can well enough understand that his absence dissolves the little government that did exist.'[160] Clare had been unwilling to damn Cornwallis to Pitt, and the foreign secretary regretted that he probably would have been equally reticent with him about 'the real state of affairs' in Ireland.[161] The exclusion of the catholics ensured that Clare left happy, confidently predicting the success of the union. For Grenville the only doubt concerned the execution of the measure. He was sceptical about the validity of appointing commissioners, the original intention. That had been useful in 1707 between England and Scotland, 'two really independent kingdoms', but Ireland was different. A treaty could not take place when 'the kingdoms are inseparably annexed to each other, and the legislatures only are independent'.[162]

Despite his failings the lord lieutenant still possessed a clear perspective on the approaching contest. In December, as Castlereagh prepared to join the cast of Irish figures in England, Cornwallis wrote to the home secretary warning about the likelihood that some of the king's Irish servants might oppose the union. He urged Portland to 'leave no means untried to impress these gentle-men more favourably before their return to this kingdom'.[163] It was only at this time that Cornwallis began consulting with many of the leading individuals in the country. He wrote to the archbishop of Cashel, Charles Agar, and informed him of 'the unfortunate situation of this country [which] has induced his majesty's ministers to think seriously of a union between the two kingdoms'. It was hoped that the archbishop would consider the matter dis-passionately and sacrifice — what the viceroy believed was — a small amount of vanity to secure much more substantial benefits.[164]

CASTLE INTRIGUES
Running parallel to the union discussions in 1798 was a smaller, but still significant, debate. It concerned who was to occupy the position of chief sec-retary. The holder of the office would have an important role in the union proceedings, especially given Cornwallis's inattentiveness to political matters. Castlereagh's eventual confirmation in the position was not quite as clear-cut as some have regarded it. The appointment of Castlereagh being believed to be either straightforward or unworthy of comment, it has been widely ignored, even by his own biographers.[165] In reality the events, like Camden's replacement, revealed important considerations of the time.

The problems began in March 1798 when Camden's chief secretary, Thomas Pelham, became 'dangerously ill'.[166] He was reported to be spitting blood and at one point was considered to be in 'extreme danger'. On 16 March Camden wrote to Pitt reporting that Pelham was so sick his recovery was barely possible, even then it would take many weeks and possibly months. Camden insisted upon the necessity of a replacement secretary. The only person he claimed was capable of the task was his step-nephew, Castlereagh, who was reported to be unwilling to accept the position, 'but will do anything I wish, and what he considers to be his duty to the country'.[167] Camden had recommended his nephew previously but it had been rejected on the grounds that he was an Irishman. Camden felt that this objection had been superseded by the perilous state of the country.[168] Both he and Castlereagh had apparently first considered Elliot for the position but his health was considered too delicate for the task.[169] Absolute discretion with respect to the change was requested in case Pelham recovered, and would no doubt be sensitive about the unseemly haste of his substitution.

The request reached London a few days later. Few Irishmen since the glorious revolution had previously held the post of chief secretary, and the break from tradition did not rest easily with Portland, Pitt or George III. On 19 March Portland cautiously presented the lord lieutenant's dispatches to the king.[170] Other members of the government were reported to be strongly in favour of the appointment and Pitt was expected to submit the request to the king as well. With some reluctance, the decision was taken to appoint Castlereagh as acting chief secretary. When it was decided to replace Camden with Cornwallis in June 1798 the king was very eager to see Pelham return as secretary.[171] Cornwallis expressed a similar preference, or, if this was not possible, Grenville's middle brother, Thomas Grenville.[172] Pelham, however, accepted the request to return to his office.[173] George III rejoiced at the news and praised Pitt for having 'saved Ireland by engaging Mr Pelham in the present state of that kingdom to return there as soon as his health will permit'.[174]

Upon his arrival in Ireland, Cornwallis found Castlereagh to be much more capable than perhaps he had expected. Like many others, he found the man to be cool and aloof: 'so cold that nothing can touch him'.[175] Nonetheless he recognised Castlereagh's 'abilities, temper and judgement', which he hailed for being the 'greatest use'.[176] The new lord lieutenant respected his acting chief secretary's 'sincere and unprejudiced attachment to the general interests of the British empire'. More tellingly, in Cornwallis's private correspondence he praised Castlereagh as 'a very uncommon young man'.[177] By the end of July the 'decided preference' shown to Castlereagh was being commented on, with approval from many quarters.[178] This did not mean that Castlereagh had established himself in the post on a permanent basis. He was still regarded as a locum tenens. Pitt was sceptical of an Irishman remaining as secretary after Camden left Ireland. Gradually, the behaviour of Castlereagh, his 'perfect impartiality', and line of conduct, had 'taken off that prejudice in Pitt's mind'.[179] Pitt, indeed, was soon entrusting the acting chief secretary with all the confidential details of government during Cornwallis's absences from Dublin.[180]

It was still hoped that Pelham's health would recover sufficiently for him to resume his station. The home secretary hoped that Pelham would return to take up his responsibilities, or even share them with Clare if his constitution would not permit the full workload. The lord chancellor was also seen as an appropriate long-term alternative.[181] Meanwhile Cornwallis maintained a wish for Thomas Grenville to assist him as chief secretary. He asked his friend, Major-General Ross, to sound out Grenville about the possibility of him taking up the post.[182] Pitt was anxious to protect Castlereagh's reputation in the matter of the change and he suggested that the resignation should emanate from the acting chief secretary when it became necessary.[183] Pelham was still being considered, but Castlereagh was assured in late September by a friend in London that Pelham would use his influence with ministers to have the acting chief secretary appointed permanently if his health did not recover.[184]

In October it appeared certain that Pelham would return. To facilitate this he wished for Parnell to be given a peerage and Castlereagh to take over as chancellor of the exchequer. The acting chief secretary refused, not wishing to gain at Parnell's expense.[185] It was expected that Pelham would set out for Ireland in the last week of October. The only potential delay was that Pelham considered remaining a short time longer, if Foster was coming over, to receive updated instructions before departing.[186] In the end Pelham's health did not recover sufficiently and Cornwallis wrote requesting that Castlereagh's appointment be made permanent. The king gave his verbal consent on 31 October, despite being 'most extremely sorry for it'.[187] Portland remained sceptical of an Irish secretary and shared the king's misgivings.[188]

The behaviour of the lord lieutenant infuriated the Grenville family. The foreign secretary was to record how Cornwallis 'employed Pitt, and through him, me, and also General Ross, separately, to press Tom to accept the thankless office of his secretary'.[189] What particularly irked was Cornwallis deciding, without first consulting Thomas Grenville, that if Pelham declined to return he wished to have Castlereagh. Grenville considered the whole affair to be 'of a piece with all the rest!'[190] Pelham, by declining the post, did, in the end, ensure Castlereagh's continuation in office. Upon hearing of Pelham's resignation Cornwallis followed up his request for Castlereagh a few days after his initial communication to Pitt.[191] The same day the lord lieutenant made the request to Portland. The lord lieutenant reassured the home secretary that Castlereagh was perfectly suited for the post,[192] despite being Irish-born, as he was 'so very unlike an Irishman'.[193]

Castlereagh was aware of the overtures to Thomas Grenville, but whether he was fully aware of the precariousness of his position is unlikely. Camden was always enthusiastically cheerful in his letters to his nephew informing him of the support he had in London, and particularly from Pitt.[194] Nevertheless Pitt did offer the post of chief secretary to Thomas Grenville, if Pelham was not returning.[195] Thomas Grenville declined, awaiting further information, and this tardiness, combined with Cornwallis's respect for Castlereagh, probably decided the issue in the latter's favour. How committed Cornwallis was to securing the services of Thomas Grenville is uncertain. Whether he really wanted him in November over Castlereagh, or whether the Grenvilles misinterpreted him, is equally unclear. Needless to say the confusion only increased the foreign secretary's suspicions of the viceroy. When Castlereagh visited London in December Cornwallis presented his chief secretary as someone possessing his 'entire confidence, and who is perfectly well acquainted with my thoughts on every subject that concerns our present situation'.[196]

While Pelham's illness is in no doubt he was nonetheless reported to be 'very well and in great form' in December.[197] And curiously, after the failure of the union in January 1799 Cooke lamented the change of viceroy in 1798 and that 'the necessity of making Pelham vacate early [was] insisted upon!'[198] Nor was Pelham unanimously seen as the best person for chief secretary. Buckingham believed that Pelham's return would do more harm than good 'for he is sunk in character here very much'.[199] Clare, whom he referred to as the 'one person', was quoted as hoping 'to God' that Pelham would not resume his duties.[200] The evidence for all of this intrigue is not conclusive. If Pelham had wanted to return he would, it seems clear, have been restored to office. How much his return was genuinely desired by all is less certain. Portland and George III wished his return but it is possible that Pelham did not wish to put Castlereagh out and declined on those grounds.[201] Pelham had received good reports about him, not only from Camden, but from his friend Elliot, who recommended the acting chief secretary over anyone else. The performance of Castlereagh, despite the prejudices against him, impressed his predecessor.[202] Furthermore Pelham was somewhat sceptical about the necessity of a union and he, or others, might have considered this a serious liability.[203]

THE END OF THE YEAR

There was soon unease about some of the union details sent to Ireland. At the end of November Portland wrote to Cornwallis to express concern on a few points. On no account was the number of Irish MPs to exceed one hundred. Secondly, the government was to preserve the rights of election of every county, city and place that currently sent members. These two conditions were stressed and 'in neither of which any alteration will be admitted'.[204] The home secretary also wanted the lord lieutenant to gauge feelings in Ireland on the mode for returning members. Two alternatives for selecting MPs were given to supplement the one proposed in the draft of 12 November. Instead of returning one member from each county instead of two, the counties and eighteen of 'the most considerable places' could choose one each for the united parliament with the remaining one hundred places choosing fifty by ballot. Alternatively, delegates could be chosen to select the final fifty seats.[205]

The suggestions of Portland were noticeably ungenerous. The number of thirty-two peers and one hundred MPs was settled but Cornwallis was urged to try to obtain smaller representations if possible.[206] Realising that it would be difficult enough to persuade the Irish to accept the highest figure on offer Cornwallis had none of this. He replied to Portland in December, politely dismissing any notions of lowering the numbers by suggesting that 'perhaps it may be as well to fix the representation of the peers at thirty-two'.[207] 'By taking the highest numbers proposed' it was hoped that government could moderate some of the other demands 'which will be very great'. Cornwallis's advice eventually triumphed over Portland in cabinet and the home secretary was forced to concede defeat.[208]

As it became obvious that legislative independence was under threat a propaganda war was waged for the hearts and minds of the Irish people. An early victory was won for the unionists by the publication of an anonymous pamphlet, actually by Edward Cooke, that feigned to be an impartial examination of the issue. In it, union was compared to 'a partnership in trade'.[209] The pamphlet was significant for its accommodating tone towards the catholics. Highly intelligent, and with an elegant prose style, Cooke included an inventive account of why the present system could not remain; 'admitting the catholics to seats in the legislature, and retaining the present parliamentary constitution, would be like inviting a man to dinner, and on his acceptance of the invitation shutting the door in his face'.[210] The implicit suggestion was that union would enable the only acceptable solution — catholic emancipation. The question of a false national pride was also addressed. Ireland owed much to Great Britain and 'if her dignity and pride do not suffer by receiving such assistance and protection, how can they be injured if she makes herself a part of that nation'.[211] The conclusion of the pamphlet was a sophisticated rationale for the measure. Ireland was faced with a stark choice — either separation or union. One was deluged in blood; the other involved 'making her power the power of Great Britain'.[212] By early December the pamphlet was 'very universally read',[213] prompting a printing frenzy in response.

A notable success for the opponents of union was the resolution of the Irish bar on Sunday, 9 December 'that the measure of a legislative union of this kingdom and Great Britain is an innovation, which it would be highly dangerous and improper to propose, at the present juncture, to this country'.[214] The bar had previously met to discuss the union on 9 September and William Saurin had moved, then, that the union 'was an innovation, dangerous and improper to propose at the present juncture'.[215] In December the merits of the union were more fiercely debated with one participant employing the classical allusion that was to become one of the great clichés of the business, 'timeo Danaos et dona ferentis'.[216] Goold rejected the unwelcome gift and declared that Pitt could 'gild the pill as he pleases, I will not swallow it'. Another speaker painted the union in sweeping nationalistic colours: 'no bribe should tempt a nation to renounce their honour and abdicate their independence'.[217]

The meeting of the bar intensified apprehensions in the capital about its future. Dublin was always perceived as the main source of opposition to the measure and its inhabitants were 'excited' by the debate, which encouraged 'the fears of decay incident to a metropolis'.[218] Their probable stance was confirmed towards the end of the month when it was reported that 'a project so hostile to the selfish views of so many inhabitants of this capital must induce much opposition and clamour'.[219] There was an undisputed belief that 'the voice of a capital is a voice of great vociferation, and carries with it an almost irresistible force and persuasion'.[220] Little was done to reassure the people that Dublin would not suffer materially from losing its status as the centre of Irish government.

The response of the Irish catholics to the separation of the union and emancipation was difficult to gauge. Despite the decisions made against them, they appeared to remain hopeful about the ultimate benefit of the union, with leading catholics reported to be in favour of the measure in early December.[221] Cornwallis was happy at the sentiments of Archbishop Troy, and 'my' Lords Fingall and Kenmare.[222] Nevertheless he remained dubious that the union would solve the problems of Ireland if they were excluded from its terms. He did not accept that their inclusion would pose any great difficulty.[223] This disappointment grew as the catholics' correct behaviour made the lord lieutenant regret all the more the 'narrow principle' upon which the union plan was formed.[224] The viceroy was also becoming even more disgusted with the 'corrupt country' he was trying to save. The union question was not being judged on its merits, but only in terms of promoting 'private objects of ambition or avarice'.[225]

Optimism that the catholics would support the union soon proved misguided. As opposition to the union grew in the capital so too did the cynicism of the catholics. Cornwallis discovered that the catholics were even considering joining with the protestants to defeat the measure if they thought it would separate the two countries, such being the extent of their sense of alienation from the king's government. Matching this was the lord lieutenant's own darkening outlook. He began to feel that all was lost: 'I think that from the folly, obstinacy, and gross corruption which pervade every corner of this island, that it is impossible that it can be saved from destruction'.[226] Cornwallis did all in his power to avoid making the protestant principle of the union irrevocable. This included playing down any negative aspects of the catholics' position in his official reports. To Portland, the viceroy merely warned of the growing appearance that their attitudes were hardening against the union.[227]

The perceived importance of the catholic body increased the closer the union came to being introduced in parliament. Cooke, who had at one stage bitterly opposed concessions to the catholics (and had been one of those singled out for dismissal by Fitzwilliam), was gradually won over to supporting catholic emancipation, under Castlereagh's influence.[228] The undersecretary for the civil department warned Auckland, at the start of the new year, that if the protestants did not throw their support behind a union Britain would be 'obliged hereafter to take up other interests against them — this has effect'.[229] Cooke recognised that conceding the principle of emancipation could ensure victory in the union debate for the government, a strategy he himself recommended.[230]

As opposition mounted, it became necessary to steady nerves in London. The overconfidence of the ministers was replaced by panic and they began to waver; it was decided that the chief secretary should visit England. Portland wrote to Castlereagh in the last week of November requesting his 'immediate presence' in London.[231] The arrival of the chief secretary early in December had a stabilising effect and his reassurances steeled the ministers to press on with the measure.[232] The formal decision to implement a legislative union was taken at a cabinet meeting on 21 December. The minute taken at this meeting read:

> that the lord lieutenant of Ireland should be instructed to state without delay to all persons with whom he may have communication on this subject, that his majesty's government is decided to pass the measure of a union as essential to the well-being of both countries, and particularly to the security and peace of Ireland as dependent on its connection with Great Britain; that this subject will now be urged to the utmost, and will, even in the case (if it should happen) of any present failure, be renewed on every occasion till it succeed; and that the conduct of individuals on this subject will be considered as the test of their disposition to support the king's government.[233]

Revealingly, the last line initially read 'a test of their attachment to the English government' but this was soon amended to the broader, less Anglocentric 'king's government'.

By the close of 1798 it was apparent that the full range of government patronage would have to be employed to assist the passage of the union. The lord lieutenant was sent an assurance by the home secretary, in the 'most explicit and unqualified terms', that

> every one of the king's servants, as well as myself, will consider themselves indissolubly obliged to use their best endeavours to fulfil whatever engagements your excellency may find it necessary, or deem it expedient, to enter into.[234]

This promise of patronage did not go far enough. On two decisive areas the government disregarded just how important self-interest would be. The first of these was borough compensation. Many borough owners were unwilling to vote away their seats, which they regarded as valuable property. There was a manifest desire amongst government to avoid 'resorting to the embarrassing principle of avowed compensation'.[235] The second point was more the fault of rumour than anything else. It became widely reported towards the end of December that no one was to lose their positions as a result of their vote in parliament. It was disclosed that this was the position of the administration, Cornwallis's name being quoted as the source.[236] Although this was eventually revealed to be inaccurate the damage, by then, was done. The ministers in London were repeatedly warned that they had to remain resolute and steadfast in their determination to secure a union. The administration in Ireland was convinced that only a clear understanding that the union would be persisted with until it succeeded would 'give the measure a chance of success'.[237] Attempts were also made, unsuccessfully, to persuade the prince of Wales to declare publicly in favour of the union.[238]

An ominous shadow hung over the government in Ireland as 1798 drew to a close. The initial stabilising influence of Cornwallis was gone, and he was now perceived as a burdensome weight on the administration. Gathering a majority in parliament became more difficult as the 'protestant gentry' refused to trust the lord lieutenant — worse, 'they abhor him'.[239] No civil officer of the crown was reported to have had 'the slightest intercourse' with Cornwallis and some military figures claimed that 'as an officer he has lost every faculty of explaining himself, so that we literally have no government'.[240] One analysis was particularly piercing: 'mankind are made of flesh and blood, and there is but one way of managing them, even for their advantage'.[241] John Pollock, a Co. Meath farmer whose patron was Downshire, did not believe Cornwallis could procure a union; 'he may *force* it indeed, but what may be the consequences? I have seen since last May a good deal of bloodshed and I tremble at the thought . . .' The opposition cause was to be greatly assisted by the return of Foster in early January. The speaker's language was soon reported to be 'very hostile'.[242] The mood of the country was bleak. Despite this the administration in Ireland remained confident about the probable success of the union. Castlereagh bravely declared that with 'a purpose so manly, our friends cannot hesitate to stand by us'.[243] The castle maintained that the union would succeed in parliament, despite growing opposition. The new year was to show whether this confidence was misplaced.

3

Ruthless inefficiency:
failure in parliament
JANUARY 1799

The year 1799 was to be unusually cold and miserable.[1] The uncertainty in the weather was reflected politically with a tense and volatile atmosphere at the start of the new year. Opposition to the union in Dublin grew in intensity and feeling, as Cornwallis searched for a formula to harden wavering support, and prevent desertions from the unionist camp. It was clear to him that the success of the measure depended upon raising the full powers of government. Unless it was understood that the union would succeed, and would be resolutely pursued until it did succeed, then it would be impossible to prevent desertions from the government side.[2] As for the state of public opinion in the rest of the country, the castle had 'remarkably little idea'.[3] Meanwhile Foster and Parnell refused to speak to Castlereagh, the protestants ignored the catholics, Buckingham abused his superiors, and no one would speak to Cornwallis. The beginning of the year was dominated by the parliamentary debates in both countries. The real struggle was in the Irish house of commons, where the opposition used the earliest opportunity to attack the principle of union. In Britain success was more assured and Pitt used the set-piece debates to outline his views on the subject. The parliamentary debates would define many of the questions about how the union would be pursued and provide clear examples of what could be expected in the future. Henry Dundas once said, on a different subject, that 'I begin to think whatever appears most improbable is the most likely to happen.'[4] The events in the month of January 1799 would demonstrate the wider wisdom of this aphorism, and provide a severe test for the lord lieutenant and his young chief secretary, eventually forcing a restructuring of the entire union strategy.

Everything depended upon perceptions of government's strength. As long as the government preserved an air of authority and confidence the numbers supporting the union would be maintained; an illusion of victory would be self-perpetuating as 'much depends in this country at all times on first

impressions'.[5] Any signs of weakness or confusion would lead to a haemor-
rhaging of the pro-union numbers. To reinforce the administration's authority
the chief secretary brought with him from London a declaration that the
union would be persevered with by the king's government until it succeeded.[6]
There was, crucially, to be no alteration in government policy towards the
catholics. This astonished Buckingham, who believed the separation of issues
'*cannot be in fact*, though it may in appearance; because unless the catholics
understand distinctly that the door is left open . . . at some convenient and
fitting opportunity, be assured that the measure cannot pass'.[7] With such an
ungenerous attitude the catholics proved unwilling to rush to government's
support. In fact their previous neutrality was believed to be moving to opposition.[8] The 'fury upon the subject' in Dublin was dying down, however, and
union was gradually being seen as becoming a parliamentary 'not a mob-
concern' — 'if they will give us this much, all will go smoothly'.[9]

The rumours that no office holders would suffer if they opposed the union
were having disastrous consequences. The matter was allowed to drift for too
long, and it was only as the opening of parliament approached that an adequate
response was taken; in the process the authority of Cornwallis's administration
was severely damaged. The lord lieutenant was baffled as to how they should
handle the problem, believing it to be 'a question of considerable delicacy'.[10]
Dismissals would reassert the government's authority, but this was seen as
going against a previous assurance that the administration would not precipitate the decision of parliament or the country, nor would it attempt to force
public sentiment. This principle was eventually sacrificed as it became clear
that something needed to be done urgently. Given the extent of the problem
Cornwallis decided that it would be inappropriate to make immediate
examples of minor office holders like John Claudius Beresford, the son of the
first commissioner of the revenue. A bigger example was required.

The first 'exercise of ministerial authority' was to be directed at the chancellor of the exchequer, Sir John Parnell. By his conduct and attitude he had shown
himself to be unacceptably hostile to the union, and was the ideal victim to be
chosen to intimidate others. Parnell had not yet returned from his consultations
with the government in England, and had deliberately missed his meeting of
10 January with Castlereagh. This slight convinced the lord lieutenant to relieve
him of his office, and from there proceed to 'the inferior members of the administration'.[11] Waiting for Parnell to reach Ireland, it was not until the evening
of 15 January that Cornwallis had the satisfying opportunity of dismissing the
chancellor. The following day Isaac Corry was chosen as his successor at the
exchequer.[12] Parnell had placed too much faith in the stories that no office
holders were to be punished, and had convinced himself that his position was
secure, whatever his actions. He was stunned by his dismissal and it was later
reported that he bitterly regretted his conduct.[13] This led Buckingham to feel,
with some justification, that his support could have been obtained if better
managed. Instead, Parnell had stood against the government through a combination of misplaced confidence and the heady influence of the speaker.[14]

A second casualty was the prime serjeant, James Fitzgerald, who was dismissed from his office, and replaced by St George Daly. Dubbed the silver-tongued serjeant, Fitzgerald had made public his opposition to union the previous month. His sacking only increased his reputation for probity, and in the following months the bar continued to show him precedence in court, as if he were still prime serjeant. This ignited the fury of Clare, who even dismissed one court case because the barristers had made a point of showing deference to Fitzgerald.

A different interpretation of Fitzgerald's conduct, however, was presented by Mary Anne Clarke in 1813. In the 1800s Clarke was the mistress of the duke of York, and used the relationship to secure military patronage which she then sold for money and other favours. Both Fitzgerald and his son, William (who as Vesey Fitzgerald would be defeated by Daniel O'Connell in 1828), were implicated in the scandal when it broke in 1809. They avoided prosecution, however, when William provided valuable evidence for the government, securing his father's letters to Clarke (his mistress) in the process: James Fitzgerald denied any inappropriate behaviour and suggested that it was merely an affair, a familiarity he shared not only with the king's son but with his own.

In an embittered public letter to William in 1813, Clarke reserved particular scorn for his 'worthy father'.[15] Taking it for granted that the union had passed by 'the powerful engines of bribery and corruption', she refused to accept that the prime serjeant had acted disinterestedly. She alleged that prior to his dismissal he had been offered a judicial appointment, and a peerage for his wife, in return for his support but that he had held out for the inclusion of a financial settlement. The letter ended with a flourishing attack on William, whose 'father owed his advancement in life, not to merit, but to the dirty arts of political intrigue; whose aunt is a common street-walker, and whose cousin was hanged for horse stealing'.[16] While there is no evidence for the government's supposed offer to Fitzgerald (and ignoring the lurid family history) it is nonetheless interesting that the honourable character of 1799 emerges as a self-interested scoundrel ten years later.

Oblivious to the planned sackings, Foster landed in Ireland in the second week of January, and like Parnell chose to snub Castlereagh.[17] He refused to call on him, an insulting gesture that added to the pressure facing the young chief secretary. Only twenty-nine years old, Castlereagh laboured against many burdens, including the suspicion that nepotism had played too great a role in his rise. The caricature of the poet Shelley, almost twenty years after the union, might have found many admirers in 1799:

> I met Murder on the way —
> He had a mask like Castlereagh —
> Very smooth he looked, yet grim;
> Seven bloodhounds followed him.[18]

He was reviled by the liberals for his betrayal of earlier whig sentiments, and his part in putting down the 1798 rebellion, and his unpopular work was not made any easier by the failings of his lord lieutenant. Buckingham, that impartial observer, urged a 'real minister' to replace Castlereagh in November, at a time when it appeared that Thomas Grenville might be on his way over.[19] A change was seen as necessary because of Cornwallis's indolence, and Castlereagh, even 'if he had the abilities of an angel, cannot *do* all that a minister must *do* in that station'.

Much was expected of Castlereagh. He had to soothe any hurt feelings caused by Cornwallis's manner and at the same time gather a secure majority in parliament in favour of the union. This required delicate man-management skills that were not helped by Castlereagh's icy temperament. The most common adjective used to describe Castlereagh throughout his life was 'cold', and although friends attested to his warmth in private, much like Pitt's friends, his aloof manner was not well calculated to appeal to Irish figures.[20] The diarist Charles Greville penned a portrait of Castlereagh, the day after his death in 1822, in which he suggested that 'perhaps he owed his influence and authority as much to his character as to his abilities. His appearance was dignified and imposing; he was affable in his manner and agreeable in society.'[21] His greatest ability was believed to have been his 'cool and determined courage which gave an appearance of resolution and confidence to all his actions'. Castlereagh, indeed, had remarkable self-control, and despite numerous provocations, only once visibly lost his temper during the union. His biographers have generally been sympathetic to his conduct at this time. John Derry suggests that Castlereagh's character is 'more complex and attractive than legend suggests'.[22] He quotes with approval the judgment of the earl of Ripon regarding 'the suavity and dignity of his manners, his habitual patience and self-command, his considerable tolerance of difference of opinion in others . . . whilst his firmness when he knew he was right'.[23] Other accounts have recognised the flaws. C.J. Bartlett believes that 'there was in Castlereagh's conduct at this time a little too much of the impetuosity and over-confidence of youth'.[24] Bolton praises Castlereagh's dealings with the catholics and protestants as displaying a 'rare virtuosity',[25] but Thomas Bartlett dismisses as 'fatuous' the chief secretary's attempts to portray union as all things to all creeds: 'such transparent dishonesty fooled only the gullible or those willing to be hoodwinked'.[26] Cornwallis himself was to note to a friend the superiority of his military secretary, Littlehales, over Castlereagh in 'the private management of mankind'.[27]

The chief secretary was required to be the chief defender and promoter of the union in parliament. As the bar were largely against the union, and since they composed most of the debating talent in parliament, it was even more important that he could champion the measure and rally the government benches with his oratory. Castlereagh was not a good speaker. Worse, he was 'prolix, monotonous and never eloquent, except perhaps for a few minutes when provoked into a passion by something which had fallen in debate'; and this from someone sympathetic to him.[28] Henry Brougham recalled 'the hopeless confusion and obscurity of his speech' and wrote of 'the poverty of his discourse'.[29] Compensating was a 'considerable fund of common sense', and his courage, for 'he was a bold and fearless man . . . brave politically as well as personally'.[30] His endurance was to be sorely tested in the coming session.

'Within these last six weeks a system of black corruption has been carried on within the walls of the castle which would disgrace the annals of the worst period of the history of either country.'[31] There was some substance to this allegation flung at Castlereagh on the first day of the parliament. The instruction of the cabinet at the end of 1798 that the castle could use whatever means were at its disposal[32] had shown a decided willingness to have the union 'written-up, spoken-up, intrigued-up, drunk-up, sung-up and bribed-up'.[33] The king's government had grown accustomed to a certain informality of procedure in the pursuit of its objectives.[34] The ruthlessness cloaked within its foreign policy was here applied to Ireland, with the involvement of William Wickham as the common denominator. Ostensibly a mere under-secretary at the home office, in reality Wickham was one of the most powerful figures in Europe. From his important position in the alien office, the department that co-ordinated and controlled British secret service activity, Wickham was the financier of intelligence operations, and directed espionage on the continent.[35] Roger Wells has commented that 'secrecy, intrigue and conspiracy are the hallmarks of politics in the nineties [1790s]'.[36]

On 7 January 1799 Wickham sent Castlereagh £5,000 in Bank of England notes, with the bills cut in half and sent by two separate messengers.[37] This sum was to be held 'at the disposal of the lord lieutenant' and a larger sum was also promised.[38] Castlereagh received the money on 10 January and assured the home office that it could depend on it 'being carefully applied'.[39] This sum came through regular channels, most likely the treasury, and was not part of the covert secret service fund that was used later in the year to assist the union. Wendy Hinde speculates that the money may have been used to persuade 'impecunious young barristers' to write union articles in newspapers.[40]

The government was still attempting to create its imperial policy on the cheap. The ungenerous spirit evident in the terms towards the Irish was reflected in the meanness displayed in other areas of persuasion. The unwillingness to compensate borough owners may have been to avoid embarrassment, but equally may just have been a desire to save the estimated million pounds necessary. Less expensive forms of encouragement were available, such as the promise of peerages and the other kinds of patronage; and, as always, intimidation cost nothing. After all, what had the castle been promised but that 'every one of the king's servants . . . will consider themselves indissolubly obliged to use their best endeavours to fulfil whatever engagements your excellency may find it necessary, or deem it expedient, to enter into'.[41]

The contest of wills soon became a competition for numbers. Both the speaker and the chief secretary gathered lists of their supporters for the opening of parliament and each was confident that he had a majority. Castlereagh's confidence was matched initially by Buckingham, who observed that 'nothing except Lord Cornwallis's imbecility' could prevent the union from succeeding.[42] A greater cause for concern was government's insistence that the union and catholic questions were to be treated as separate matters. The under-secretary for the civil department, Edward Cooke, shared his superiors' confidence that the measure would succeed. He estimated the opposition at around 100, as opposed to Buckingham's more pessimistic figure of 120.[43] Both men maintained that the support of the catholics would decide the question. In addition the under-secretary recognised the crucial support of key borough patrons. As long as Lords Ely, Downshire and Abercorn were in favour of the measure he was confident that it would succeed. Against this, the 'underhand' work of the 'old friends of government' gave great cause for concern. 'Tricks' by Downshire, and Ely in particular, Cooke feared, would put the success of the union in jeopardy.[44]

The support of the three aforementioned lords could not be relied on, as Bolton has shown. Each controlled a number of parliamentary votes, estimated to be sixteen in total, and their defection would be a fatal blow to the measure.[45] Of the three, Downshire's support was the least certain. He warned Castlereagh, at the close of 1798, that he did not believe that union was desirable at that time.[46] It was feared that personal feelings were influencing the patron's decision given his unbridled hatred of Castlereagh, who not only had stood against him for parliament in 1790, but whose family represented a threat to his northern hegemony.[47] Pitt attempted to reassure Downshire, who resided in England, that there was nothing to fear from a union. The meeting was not a success and Pitt decided to stress that 'in all events the union will be persisted with'.[48] A promise of support on the union question was not forthcoming, and Downshire left, 'apparently undecided and embarrassed'.[49]

Doubts about the union were also entertained by Ely. His opinions were noted to be 'verbatim' those of Foster and the other opponents of union.[50] In November 1798 Ely had supported the union with enthusiasm. One month and a visit to England later, and his eagerness cooled. London was once more exerting its fatal charms. On 7 January he was able to inform both Castlereagh and Portland that the union was 'a mad scheme', and professed that he had not heard any valid arguments in its favour.[51] This was discouraging news for Cornwallis and Castlereagh and they quickly informed the cabinet that they expected persistent attempts to alter his opinions; the lord lieutenant even bluntly explained to Ely that he would not be allowed 'to shuffle on this occasion'.[52] Camden, noted for his misjudgments, discussed the matter with Ely and confirmed that he was 'biased against the measure' but was, at the same time, 'open to conviction'.[53] If there was an expected amendment to the king's address then Ely declared that he was undecided about his response.

There was an immediate reaction to this wavering. No opportunity was lost in attempting to persuade Ely that a union was still necessary. Pitt returned to London specifically to meet and negotiate with him, and pledged the patron that all 'his objects would be attended to'.[54] Such an assurance convinced both Pitt and Camden that Ely's members would oppose any hostile amendment, and would not object to a discussion of the union measure in principle. In a second conversation with Ely on 16 January the prime minister again used all his powers of persuasion. Pitt's assessment of the meeting was characteristically optimistic. He was convinced that Ely set out for Ireland on 17 January 'quite unprejudiced' about the union, and it was hoped that he would support the measure as he was 'apparently very well disposed'.[55] Before he left, the lord lieutenant sent Ely a message warning that if he opposed the union, a so-called mild measure, then it would be taken as 'an absolute separation on the part of your lordship and your friends from all connection with his majesty's government'.[56]

The support of Lord Abercorn was the only one that proved to be solid. Even then, Abercorn informed Castlereagh that although he and his 'friends' would support the union measure, one of his members, George Knox, a commissioner of the revenue, had permission to oppose it. Abercorn would not tolerate any retribution against Knox for this stance. No attempts were to be made to remove him, and the borough owner warned that 'if a hair of his head is touched, every vote whom he [Abercorn] can influence should oppose'.[57] This was a particularly embarrassing predicament for government, but was resolved without any unpleasantness when Knox took the decision out of their hands by resigning his office.[58]

The mode of proceeding with the union in the Irish and British parliaments had been decided in December. The measure was to be recommended in both countries on 22 January and approved in a general way. A day would then be fixed for discussing the subject, probably 5 February, and a joint address of the two houses in each kingdom would then 'express their disposition to promote so desirable an object on suitable terms'.[59] Commissioners would be appointed in each kingdom the same day 'to confer together, and prepare a plan for each kingdom to be submitted to his majesty and, if his majesty shall think proper, to be laid before parliament'. As it would be impossible for the Irish commissioners to visit England in February or March, because of the parliamentary schedule, it was suggested that a delegation of the British commissioners should visit Ireland and confer with a subcommittee of their Irish counterparts. Those chosen would be experts in 'details of Irish and English trade, particularly the former' and it was believed that 'more progress might be made towards a conclusion by a fortnight or three weeks of such discussion taking place upon the spot, than in as many months of formal conferences between large bodies of commissioners, sitting in England'.[60]

Five days before the Irish parliament was to meet, a new plan was devised in Whitehall and sent to Dublin. There had always been some uncertainty as to the desirability or necessity of parliamentary commissioners, and confusion as to the correct procedure for appointing them. The original idea of selecting them immediately after the address was therefore changed, 'until the principle upon which the measure is to be entered into have been discussed and agreed upon', as this was considered the fairest method and 'most conformable to common practice of analogous situations of a public or private nature'.[61] Rather than give the commissioners too much scope to influence the terms, most of which had been agreed in private anyhow, parliament would instead lay down certain preliminary guidelines, in the form of resolutions. The first meeting of the commissioners would mark out the details of these particulars, but would not decide the particulars themselves. These resolutions would be introduced in both parliaments, but not concurrently. 'Decency' required that a fortnight elapsed before they could be introduced in the Irish commons, so the earlier schedule of 5 February was continued with. The British parliament was a different case that required no such interval. As soon as the king's message was debated resolutions would be proposed, thus expediting the process.[62]

The first day of the Irish parliament, 22 January, remained a crucial meeting, requiring full parliamentary strength. Castlereagh chose to provoke a discussion on the union rather than have the battle brought to government.[63] The removal of Parnell, and rumours of the impending dismissal of other office holders, almost succeeded in the desired effect, and intimidated some waverers and 'stray sheep' into returning to the fold.[64] But it was too late to prevent the bulk of the deserters from leaving the government side. The union was seen to be sinking and there were 'very many rats'.[65] The numbers were uncertain right until the opening of the parliament. Castlereagh believed the government could muster between 160 and 170 of the 300 MPs. This was if they all attended, the critical question, and as this was not certain the chief secretary was nervous about the considerable numbers of undecided.

Any mention of union had been carefully excluded from the king's speech. Instead a hope was expressed that 'some permanent adjustment' might extend the advantages of Britain to Ireland and maintain and improve 'a connection essential to their common security, and [a means] of consolidating as far as possible into one firm and lasting fabric the strength, the power, and the resources of the British empire'.[66] The opposition had been torn between two tactics. The first was to avoid a conflict on the address, although it implicitly urged a union, and wait for the union to be proposed separately. The second had been to move an amendment to the address and attack the union head-on. It was this option that the chief secretary correctly guessed had been adopted. The opposition tactics became apparent when Lord Tyrone, attempting to move the traditional address of thanks, was interrupted by George Ponsonby. Given precedence by the speaker, Ponsonby promptly challenged the validity of the chief secretary's parliamentary seat, which, he argued, Castlereagh had vacated upon accepting that office. There followed two hours of debate, which was resolved only when the attorney-general pointed out that the relevant act had been passed after Castlereagh had been confirmed in his office, and had not been intended to be retroactive.

With this resolved, Tyrone was able to continue in proposing his address of thanks. He observed that the king's speech only pledged the house to a discussion of a union, it did not determine the house on the question. This was not sufficient for the opponents of the measure, and Parnell challenged the chief secretary to accept that the address implicitly hinted at a legislative union. Castlereagh admitted that this was so wherein Ponsonby immediately proposed an amendment to maintain

> the undoubted birthright of the people of Ireland to have a free and independent legislature, as it was asserted by the parliament of this kingdom in 1782 and acknowledged and ratified by his majesty and the parliament of Great Britain.[67]

There followed a long and frequently furious debate. The speeches became more bitter as the debate progressed, the violence of some of them shocking the normally unflappable John Beresford, who reported that 'you would have thought you were in a Polish Diet. Direct treason spoken, resistance to the law declared, encouraged, and recommended. I never heard such vulgarity and barbarism.'[68]

The speeches were notable for their eloquence and even Castlereagh distinguished himself. Jonah Barrington, an anti-unionist MP and hostile witness, admitted that his speech 'far exceeded the powers he was supposed to possess'.[69] It was fortunate for the chief secretary that he was speaking confidently for he was subjected to alarming vitriol. William Plunket lost no opportunity of pouring scorn on his opponent's youth and inexperience, and sarcastically dismissed the chief secretary as an 'unspotted veteran', an 'unassuming stripling', and a 'green and sapless twig',[70] the last a snide reference to Castlereagh's apparent inability to have children. Barrington recorded that as Plunket attacked the competence of parliament to destroy itself the 'effect was indescribable, and Lord Castlereagh, whom he personally assailed, seemed to shrink from the encounter'.[71] One passage, in particular, was notable for the intensity of its impassioned rhetoric. Plunket declared that

> for my part I will resist it to the last gasp of my existence and with the last drop of my blood. And when I feel the hour of my dissolution approaching, I will, like the father of Hannibal, take my children to the altar and swear them to eternal hostility against the invaders of their country's freedom.[72]

All the 'furious expressions' of opposition were 'applauded with clamour', but the best government speeches were 'not cheered at all'.[73] Most of the government benches were 'half empty, and the members affecting carelessness and inattention'.

As deserters from the unionist side grew, government fell back on direct methods of persuasion. One MP, Frederick Trench, spoke initially in favour of the amendment as being the lesser of two evils. He believed a decision on the union to be 'premature', asserting that until the wishes of the people were revealed to be in favour of union then parliament 'has no right to make a radical change in the constitution'.[74] An informal discussion with Cooke prompted Trench to make a second speech, just after midnight, in which he admitted that he had been mistaken in his earlier beliefs and that he was now in favour of the address to allow the matter to be discussed at a future time. He was 'not ashamed to avow his error', and considered it more honourable to admit it than continue. It was widely held at the time that the under-secretary had discussed terms with the member, with the approval of the chief secretary. Whatever the truth of this, and subsequent events would appear to confirm the story, two years later Trench became Lord Ashtown.[75] Barrington was to record the remarkable story of Luke Fox, one of Ely's members, who apparently tried to hide during the division, and when discovered claimed to have vacated his seat under the place act. The next day Castlereagh, it was rumoured, bought him out.[76] Reports of corruption were rampant. The *Dublin Evening Post* on 26 January, quoted in the commons two days later, attacked the 'corrupt minister and his corrupt phalanx'.[77] In Britain Lady Bessborough, the sister of a cabinet minister, wrote to her friend Granville Leveson-Gower, a minor government official, and told him that their people in Ireland had 'certainly managed very ill there. Not that I believe that *corruption* and bribery were wanting: there was as much as you could wish for.'[78]

The opening debate lasted for twenty-one uninterrupted hours during which over eighty MPs contributed, the most eloquent of whom were said to be against the union.[79] A division was finally called at 1.30 p.m. on 23 January, when Ponsonby's amendment was narrowly defeated by 106 votes to 105. The address was then carried by 107 votes to 105.[80] The margin of victory was so close as to constitute a defeat for the government. Castlereagh accepted that the measure would have to be postponed until 'the house and the nation appeared to understand its merits' when he promised it would be brought forward once again.[81] The 'tricks' of Downshire and Ely were confirmed. Only two of Downshire's and three of Ely's members had turned up for the debates.[82] Worse, one of Downshire's members had even voted against the government on the following night. Shaken, Castlereagh wrote to Portland, 'I am truly sorry it was not more favourable.'[83] In the house of lords alone was there some success with the address passing by 51 to 17.[84]

There was further bad news for the government on 24 January. The paragraph hinting at a legislative union was deleted from the address in the commons by 109 to 104 votes.[85] Sensing outright victory the committed anti-unionists then tried to bind the house irrevocably against a union. This resolution of William Ponsonby, elder brother of George, was quickly challenged by several MPs who, while they had joined Ponsonby in opposition to the address, were not natural allies. These members, including J.C. Beresford, refused to bind the house on an issue that although they opposed it then, might become desirable at some future point. Aware that the resolution could not command a majority Ponsonby withdrew his motion.[86] Regarding the union Castlereagh announced that 'he would be a silly minister indeed who would bring forward such a measure on this day'.[87] On 28 January the parliament was adjourned until 5 February. The defeat of the government was marked by much celebration in Dublin; bonfires were lit, unionists' windows were smashed, and the mob celebrated Foster's journey home.[88] The weather was to be an unlikely ally of the government on the first night, with rain preventing much of the rioting from spreading.[89] Cornwallis was forced to send out the troops to protect the streets; Clare dispersed one mob with a blunderbuss.[90]

The indecisiveness and uncertainty of government had shattered all confidence.[91] Buckingham continued in his campaign to remove the lord lieutenant. The union he still considered as attainable, once the eighty-three MPs who had not voted were worked on, 'but it is insanity to attempt to carry this or any other point so long as this mill-stone hangs upon the shoulders of government'.[92] He was convinced that Cornwallis would prevent any success with the measure, having 'disgusted every man in the country, friend or foe, and having shown, in the common management of the question and of the men through whom he was to work, the most absolute incapacity'.[93] Blame for the lord lieutenant was also forthcoming from other influential sources. Cooke accused him of mismanaging the business and requested to be relieved of his position — 'I am disgusted here.'[94] The conduct of the cabinet in London had not been much better in the eyes of the under-secretary. It had managed Ireland 'with so much ignorance . . . that I am perfectly sick'.[95]

It was necessary to regroup and recover support. The question of further dismissals was still a delicate one. The particular dilemma of J.C. Beresford was resolved on 25 January when he resigned voluntarily.[96] The most serious problem was what to do with the speaker. Cornwallis placed the matter before the cabinet to determine, believing that it was not one which required an immediate decision. Pitt considered further dismissals, including Foster's son, to be necessary. On hearing of the Irish parliamentary defeat on 26 January he wrote to the lord lieutenant that 'it seems very desirable (if government is strong enough to do it without too much immediate hazard) to mark by dismissal the sense entertained of the conduct of those persons in office who opposed'.[97] No exception was to be made of the speaker's son as 'no government can stand on safe and respectable ground which does not show that it feels itself independent of him [the speaker]'. For lesser office holders more restraint was advised. This was also the line that Portland adopted.[98]

As rumours circulated Dublin that Cornwallis had protected the rebels in order to promote a union,[99] the lord lieutenant's position came under threat. It was believed that he would soon go the way of Fitzwilliam for failing with the union, because of what Cooke called his 'conceit and mulishness'.[100] Cooke laid the blame firmly on Cornwallis's shoulders. The unionists had been without a leader — they had 'nobody, worse than nobody I suspect'.[101] The under-secretary accused Cornwallis of having carelessly sabotaged the measure by alienating Foster, 'the person most necessary for the service'. The lord lieutenant was also blamed for losing the support of many of the gentlemen of the country. These criticisms were shared by Lord Grenville, who was even thinking of recalling the viceroy but found 'the question of his removal [to be] . . . a very difficult one indeed'.[102] He caustically regretted the appointment of Cornwallis, his share in which, he confessed, he would deplore to the hour of his death. Since his arrival in Ireland the lord lieutenant had shown not 'one trait of that character which I thought he had displayed in former situations of great difficulty'. The situation required 'a mixture of civil and military talents' not 'some old woman in a red riband that has not a grain of either'.[103] Nevertheless, as Bolton notes, replacing Cornwallis risked subjecting the Irish administration to much unwelcome confusion.[104] It is also unclear if Pitt shared in all the criticisms. Finally, the absence of any suitable replacement with the necessary military and civil experience made change an expedient that Grenville was not quite prepared to recommend. And so, although the credibility of Cornwallis, and to a lesser extent Castlereagh, had been compromised they were allowed to remain in office rather than precipitate a lengthy and painful reorganisation of the Irish administration.

Cornwallis was to reveal the next year that he was fully aware of the criticisms directed at him. At this time he chose to ignore them, pressing on in his attempts to prevent further mischief. He was weighed down by an increasing sense of fatalism; he despaired that 'I am doomed to waste the remainder of my life, and sacrifice the little reputation which the too partial opinion of the world had allowed me, in this wretched country, where nothing can prosper.'[105] A serious threat was revealed to him by Lord Kenmare, a leading catholic, on 25 January. On the day parliament had opened, the Ponsonbys had allegedly sent the catholics an assurance that if they presented a petition against the union a motion would be made, as soon as the union business was disposed of, in favour of catholic emancipation. The invitation, Kenmare revealed, had not been accepted by the catholics, although moves were afoot, soon after the government's defeat, to have them join the agitation against the union by promising that emancipation would still be brought forward.[106] The attempts to construct an alliance between the anti-unionists and the catholic body were potentially devastating for the government. Such a conjunction would have sounded the death knell for the measure. Both Cooke and Cornwallis cautioned that such a plan was being devised in the immediate aftermath of the union defeat.[107] All appeared lost on 26 January when it was mistakenly reported that such an alliance had been forged. Buckingham claimed that the Ponsonbys had persuaded Foster to offer the catholics full political rights in return for opposing a union, another example of the uncertain atmosphere, and the power of rumour.[108]

The lord lieutenant was under no illusions that the catholics would prefer equality without a union to equality with it. It was recognised that 'in the latter case they must ever be content with inferiority; in the former, they would probably by degrees gain ascendancy'.[109] The support of the catholics was not sufficient to pass the union but their opposition was enough to prevent it; public opinion in the period could not be disregarded. Therefore Cornwallis and Castlereagh felt it was imperative that the catholic question was not raised by opposition at that time, or the government would be placed in an embarrassing and unwinnable position. If it opposed concessions to the catholics the government would become irrevocably alienated from that body, if it supported them it would remove much of the reasoning behind the measure, and thus make it impossible to achieve.[110] Nevertheless the long-term objective for Cornwallis was to secure full rights for the catholics. Likewise Castlereagh was convinced that 'the principle of incorporation is everything'.[111] Influenced by these sentiments Cooke recommended including the catholic question in the union to the king's ministers both before, and after, January 1799.[112] He joined his fellow under-secretary William Elliot in the belief that emancipation must be forthcoming, his colleague being even more certain.

The ambiguity in the castle's dealings with the catholic leadership was mirrored in the hierarchy's attitude to the union. The bishops were always willing to demonstrate their loyalty to the crown, and after being slandered during the late rebellion they were particularly anxious to maintain that appearance. Thus while January 1799 was dominated by parliamentary concerns there also occurred an important set of negotiations with the bishops. On the 17th, 18th and 19th of the month ten leading church figures met to discuss an overture from the castle involving a government stipend for the clergy in exchange for the concession of a veto on the future appointment of bishops, and presumably support for the union. The ten Roman Catholic bishops present at the meeting reluctantly assented to this proposal, including the four archbishops, Richard O'Reilly of Armagh, Edward Dillon of Tuam, Thomas Bray of Cashel, and Troy of Dublin.[113] On 28 January the bishops signed a declaration giving some of their number permission to negotiate with the government, although reactions in Britain quickly made this paper redundant. The catholic bishops soon grew cynical of the castle's manoeuvres and began to rebuff its increasingly clumsy seduction attempts.

Two things saved the government from being forced into making an open stand against the catholics. The first of these was the catholics' decision to remain aloof from the bidding war for their support; they were not forcing a decision, as the lord lieutenant had feared.[114] Instead the catholic leaders chose not to raise the question and thus to avoid embarrassing the government 'for the present'.[115] The second and more crucial factor was that the two main factions against a union, the Ponsonby wing and the Foster wing, were unable to agree on the necessity of enlisting the support of the catholics through promising full relief. It was inimical to Foster even to consider such an alliance. George Canning was justified in his cheerful optimism that government could rely on the strength of Foster's prejudices, and pledges, on the point preventing him from forming a coalition with the catholics.[116] As Bartlett notes, 'if the castle refused to race, so too did the opposition'.[117] When the opponents of the union met, in February 1799, resolutions were passed attacking the lord lieutenant's alleged leniency towards rebels, and espousing high protestant principles.[118]

The attempt by Cornwallis and Castlereagh to solve the difficult tithe problem by introducing a government stipend for the catholic clergy of Ireland did not get far. The king considered the proposal to be 'highly injurious' and 'going far beyond the bounds of justice or policy'.[119] When the question of catholic emancipation was brought before the king by the cabinet, through

Portland, on 31 January, he approved of the decision to inform the lord lieu-tenant that such a policy could not be countenanced. Furthermore the king declared that 'though a strong friend to the union of the two kingdoms, I should become an enemy to the measure if I thought a change of the situation of the Roman Catholics would attend the measure'.[120] George III was starting to become more difficult and vocal on the question of catholic concessions, and Pitt felt it necessary to write to him and 'remonstrate a little against the notions which he seems [to be] forming every day more and more of excluding the catholics in case of a union'.[121] The king's government was decided for the moment. Catholic emancipation would not be bartered to pass the union.

One of the key reasons for the defeat of the union in 1799 was the absence of any proposal for compensating borough owners.[122] The extent of this one issue's influence in determining the opinion of a vast number who opposed, excluding Foster, Parnell, Plunket and the Ponsonbys, was not lost on the chief secretary. He recognised that the country gentlemen were too alarmed by the prospect of the union destroying their seats to consider voting for the measure.[123] Given the temperament of the country Castlereagh did not believe that the union should be attempted again that session. Instead 'private interest' had to be disarmed and the chief secretary threw out a few ideas for compensating borough proprietors depending on the changes made to the seats. If boroughs were combined, either two or three together, the numbers of Irish represen-tatives would have to be increased from 100 to 126 or 141 but the compensation would be easier to handle.[124] Castlereagh again apologised to the home secretary for the defeat of the union, and attempted to reassure him that 'however I may have failed, from inability, in the discharge of the important trust committed to me, I am confident your grace will believe there has been no defect of zeal'.[125]

The union was brought before the British commons on 23 January. As in the Irish parliament the union was not specifically mentioned in the king's address from the throne on the 22nd, but was implied as a necessary policy. Reading the message in the commons Henry Dundas alluded to the settling of 'such a complete and final adjustment as may best tend to impose and perpetuate a connection essential for their common security, and to augment and consolidate the strength, power and resources of the British empire'.[126] The opposition was led by Richard Brinsley Sheridan, who attacked the union in what was believed to be one of his finest speeches, as he moved a very wordy amendment urging the king not to consider a union.[127] Sheridan attempted to remove the ambiguity from the message: 'every one knows that here adjustment means union. Every one knows too that the terms are, to a con-siderable extent, already fixed.'[128] Union, he declared, was 'a plan by which the independence and separate existence of Ireland is to be annihilated'.[129] Suspecting the likely behaviour of government, Sheridan warned that 'a union effected by fraud, by intrigue, by corruption, by intimidation, would ultimately tend to endanger the connection between the two countries'.[130]

This impassioned speech was answered by Canning and then the prime minister. Canning's speech lacked the elegance of that of his rival. He struggled to prove that there was nothing absurd about the union being advantageous to two conflicting groups; both catholics and protestants could gain from the arrangement, 'which would gratify the ambition of one without endangering the safety of the other'.[131] He continued by discussing the conspiracies formed in Ireland that sought neither catholic emancipation nor parliamentary reform but 'the total subversion of all government'.[132] He noted the cynical attitude of those who were now defending the 'final adjustment' of 1782, and who were hailing emancipation and parliamentary reform as the solution to Ireland's problems, because they themselves had not addressed those very points, when in a position to, in 1782.[133]

As the numbers who voted at the debates were to illustrate there was remarkably little interest for the subject in the British commons, although in high society 'nobody talks of anything but Ireland'.[134] Despite this, Pitt used the occasion to place the union in a wider imperial context, and outline some general principles. The prime minister's speeches of 23 and 31 January were hailed as two of his most outstanding, and were certainly highly significant. In the first, Pitt was unaware of what was happening in Ireland. In a sweeping oration he asserted that 'catholic emancipation and parliamentary reform is a phrase made use of by some to cover designs of a very different nature'.[135] A 'calm, dispassionate and sober investigation' revealed, however, that laws would not have the desired effect if the society in which they were implemented was not also changed. Ireland was a 'wretched' country that had become 'retarded by the distractions and divisions of party, by the blind zeal and frenzy of religious prejudices, by old and furious family feuds'.

Ireland could be rescued from a state of poverty only by redistributing wealth and capital. This could not be achieved in a country where 'patriotism amounts to nothing more than an aim at temporary popularity'; a truly impartial legislature was necessary. Somewhat incautiously, the prime minister referred to 'the childish measure of the independence of the parliament of Ireland'. Pitt acknowledged that for the past century Britain had pursued a narrow policy with regards to Ireland, no more so than in the area of commerce. This 'absurd jealousy' was to be buried by the union. 'Good Englishmen and good Irishmen' would be joined, for: 'we must stand or fall together, we should live and die together'.[136] *The Morning Post* reported that Pitt's voice broke after ten minutes, becoming 'shrill, hoarse and irregular', which forced him to adjust his speech and speak lower to regain 'a more firm and stronger sound'.[137] William Wickham recorded, however, that the prime minister's contribution to the debate was 'the *most impressive* and one of the most judicious speeches I ever heard', and was pleased to report that it had decided the union question in Britain.[138]

Sheridan's amendment was defeated without a division, and the motion for the address was put and carried. The hollowness of the victory was revealed a few days later when the government received news of the defeat in the Irish parliament. According to one account, when the dispatches arrived at Windsor for the perusal of the royal family a courtier, Lord Cremorne, was playing cards, and when he saw his nephew and heir's name on the anti–union list he promptly fainted.[139]

Displaying somewhat more character, not to mention self–control, Pitt refused to be discouraged. He was determined to continue with the measure in the British parliament and on 31 January put forward nine propositions for union, which were intended to signal the government's unrelenting commitment. The defeat in Ireland had removed any doubt from Pitt's mind about how to proceed. He informed Cornwallis that

> we have no hesitation *now* in adopting the mode of moving specific resolutions, instead of only proposing to appoint commissioners, because the great object now must clearly be to state distinctly, and to record, the grounds and principles of our measure.[140]

Prone to exaggeration, Auckland considered Pitt's speech on the last day of January to have 'surpassed even the most sanguine expectation of his friends, and perhaps, even any former exhibition of parliamentary eloquence'.[141] A more restrained witness, Canning, believed the speech had shown the Irish 'what we meant for their good' and hoped it would 'set our countrymen on the other side of the channel right. They have been going terribly astray in their notions.'[142] Even the whig MP Charles Grey was forced to admit in parliament that he had been told 'it was as eloquent as any that ever fell from the lips of man'.[143]

This speech was Pitt's statement on the union. It revealed the thinking behind the measure, and the long-term objectives of the policy. From the beginning Pitt asserted that the union had been designed with a view to 'the general welfare of the empire, the immediate interests of both kingdoms, and more particularly to the peace, the tranquillity, and the safety of Ireland'.[144] The defeat in the Irish parliament the prime minister claimed did not worry him. He still felt that the measure should be submitted to the British parliament so that he could explain the grounds for it. The general principle on which the measure was formed was that 'a perpetual connection between Great Britain and Ireland is essential to the interests of both'.[145] The failure of the commercial propositions in 1785 had prevented an attempt to draw the countries closer, and redefine the ambiguous relationship created by the 1782 settlement. The union was an opportunity to present the same advantages to Ireland, and resolve many of the problems facing the empire.

The 1782 settlement was 'imperfect' and the weaknesses created by it had been exploited by the French in the 1790s. Therefore, Pitt argued, it was essential that the empire protected itself by securing its weakest point — Ireland. Pitt's oration was not aimed at the house of commons, but at the nation. It was a statement of his genuine beliefs and convictions. He triumphantly declared that

> this country is at this time engaged in the most important, and momentous conflict that ever occurred in the history of the world; a conflict in which

> Great Britain is distinguished for having made the only manly and successful
> stand against the common enemies of civilised society. We see the point in
> which the enemy thinks us the most assailable. Are we not then bound in
> policy and prudence to strengthen that vulnerable point, involved as we are
> in a contest of liberty against despotism, of property against plunder and
> rapine, of religion and order against impiety and anarchy?[146]

The only way Ireland could achieve a full participation of 'the wealth, the
power, and the stability of the British empire' was through a union. The two
countries, from internal and external forces, were in danger of drifting
permanently apart. The matter could not be discussed, Pitt argued, in any
terms other than how it affected the empire. The prime minister insisted that
a man could not speak as a true Englishman unless he also spoke as a true
Irishman and vice versa.

The question of the religious divisions in Ireland was, Pitt admitted, 'a
dangerous and delicate topic'. But it was one that could be safely addressed in
a united parliament. He hinted that the objections to the catholic emancipation
could be removed 'if the protestant legislature were no longer separate and
local, but general and imperial, and the catholics themselves would at once
feel a mitigation of the most goading and irritating of their present causes of
complaint'.[147] After whatever period of time was thought necessary the
catholics could be safely included amongst the representation of a combined
legislature. That Pitt was prepared to make this assertion, despite all the
opposition to catholic relief in both countries, demonstrated a remarkable
degree of confidence. The position reflected Pitt's growing conviction on the
subject, something that the new strategy in autumn 1799 was to reveal more
clearly, and as he himself was to admit to the king in the lead-up to the events
of 1801.

The question of national pride was one which Pitt dismissed as invalid. The
union did not involve the submission of Ireland, rather it was a voluntary
compact for their mutual benefit, 'in one empire'. Pitt confidently predicted
that the 'free and voluntary association of two great countries' would create
an 'indissoluble connection to render both invincible'.[148] Brougham provides a
splendid contemporary account of Pitt's oratory, no worse for being subjective:

> we even went along with him, and forgot *ourselves*; but we never forgot *him*;
> and while thrilled with the glow which his brilliant words diffused, or trans-
> fixed with wonder at so marvellous a display of skill, we yet felt that it was
> admiration of a consummate artist which filled us, and that after all we were
> present at an exhibition; gazing upon a wonderful performer indeed, but still
> a performer.[149]

The anti-union case was put by Sheridan. In a speech of remarkable prescience he observed that listening to Pitt had made him think that 'a stranger
had got into the house, or that the right honourable gentleman must have
imagined himself in the Irish house of commons and warmly engaged in a

reply to Mr Foster'.[150] This was a shrewd analysis: Pitt had already won the debate in the British commons, he was now attempting to win the debate against the Irish speaker. Sheridan concluded his speech by reading two resolutions, the second being the more significant. It stated that whoever should, in either country, employ the forces of government 'for the purposes of corruption or intimidation, is an enemy to his majesty and to the constitution'.[151] When the commons was asked whether the king's address should be put to the consideration of a committee, the house divided 110 for and 15 against.[152]

Ten thousand copies of Pitt's speech were printed and distributed in Ireland.[153] It is possible that the £5,000 sent in early January was used for this purpose. Earl Stanhope, the relative of one of Pitt's earliest biographers, was once told by the minister that this was one of only three speeches that he had ever revised for publication.[154] The abridged Irish version does indeed show marked differences to that delivered in the commons; some merely stylistic improvements, but others significant alterations to the substance. In the heat of a debate it is not always possible to express ideas as clearly, or as cleverly, as one might like, even for a renowned speaker like Pitt. A textual analysis of the two speeches reveals interesting insights into what Pitt would have liked to have said, and also what modifications he felt were necessary for the Irish audience.[155]

The second version of the speech was occasionally more precise in its language. Unnecessary sentences and phrases, which were perhaps unavoidable in a public oration, were deleted,[156] and more exact terminology was employed. Instead of the 'monied interest' of the first speech there was 'the mercantile and manufacturing interests' of the second.[157] Not all of the changes were salutary. The dramatic, if a touch grandiloquent, 'this country is at this time engaged in the most important, and momentous conflict that ever occurred in the history of the world' was amended to the repetitive 'we are at the moment engaged in the most important and momentous conflict in which this country was ever engaged'. Instead of Britain making the only 'manly and successful stand against the common enemies of civilised society' she was now 'making the only successful stand against the devastations of the common enemy', certainly a more inclusive description. Long and unwieldy passages were rewritten into more eloquent prose. In attempting to elucidate his previous remarks Pitt originally employed the wordy construction:

> long and bitter experience has taught us to feel that it is only the feeble and imperfect representations of those calamities (the result of French principles and French arms), which are every day attested by the wounds of a bleeding world.

This became the more succinct, 'it is now felt to be only a feeble statement of the wounds of a bleeding world, expressed in every part which has fallen under the devastating power of France'.[158]

It was concerning Ireland that the most serious alterations were made. Pitt had been reckless in some of his utterances on the neighbouring kingdom, and had risked offending Irish sensibilities. He was forced to restructure almost all of the Irish sections for the published version. In his attack on revolutionary France Pitt had claimed that 'the avowed enemies of both countries' had been aided by 'internal treason, which ingrafted jacobinism on those diseases which necessarily grew out of the state and condition of Ireland'. To avoid any resentment this was amended to 'internal treason, which grafted jacobinism upon those unfortunate diseases which have so long tended to destroy the tranquillity of Ireland'.[159] The opportunity to correct mistakes enabled Pitt to quote Foster more faithfully. In the commons Pitt had quoted Foster as having said, 'if this infatuated country gives up the present offer, she may look for it again in vain', and followed this by arguing that 'here the honourable gentleman was happily mistaken; Ireland has again the offer of the same advantages, but more complete'.[160] For his Irish audience Pitt made sure his full attack on Foster was reported. Foster's commercial propositions speech was quoted with exactitude: 'if this ill-fated country refuses this offer at present, she may look to it in vain another time. Things cannot remain as they are.' This was followed by a longer rebuttal of the case against the union: 'this was his language shortly after that measure of 1782, which is now, upon his authority, stated to have been a final adjustment, and consequently to render the present measure unnecessary'.[161]

In the commons Pitt's defence of the 'lamentable severities' taken in defence of Ireland was that they were 'unhappily, but unavoidably' taken.[162] And in his critique of the causes of Irish unrest he had made reference to 'the ignorance and want of civilisation, which marks that country more than any other country in Europe'. Again in an attempt to remove remarks that would not engender warmth in Irish readers, towards Pitt or the union, the justification for the extremism was deleted, it was now merely 'called for'; and references to the ignorance of the country were replaced by the insipid phrase, an 'unfortunate degree of want of civilisation'.[163] Ironically, the part of the speech in which Pitt imagined he was speaking to Ireland alone, was changed. Originally, he would have said

> that it would be indispensably necessary for the sake of that country, to compose its present distractions by the adoption of another system. I should say, that the establishment of an imperial legislature was the only means of healing its wounds and of restoring it to tranquillity.[164]

But when he was actually speaking to Ireland, although ostensibly still only imagining that he was, this became: 'I should say that it would be necessary for that country to guard against those distractions which now harm that unhappy country, by the adoption of another system.'[165]

Perhaps unwilling to alienate protestant opinion in Ireland Pitt deleted the reference to the catholics' 'exclusion from the rights and privileges' being a grievance.[166] And he was careful to avoid offence with the statement that 'the subject of religious distinction is a dangerous and delicate topic, especially when applied to a country such as Ireland' by leaving out the second part of

the sentence altogether. The lengthy discussion of the catholic question itself
was rewritten completely. The message was substantially identical, but it was
carefully reworded.[167] Ireland was referred to as 'the sister kingdom' far more
regularly in the Irish version of the speech, and an additional argument was
made about how Yorkshire was no less independent because she was 'subjected
to the general control of the members of England'.[168]

The failure of the union forced a reappraisal of the union strategy. Elliot was
dispatched to England at the close of January to discuss this with ministers.
He arrived at Whitehall on 2 February for a cabinet council on Irish affairs.[169]
This meeting decided that the government was to persevere with its existing
strategy. There was to be no alteration in government policy towards the
catholics. Furthermore the catholic question was to be opposed if brought
forward.[170] It was also decided in cabinet that Elliot should return to Ireland
and instruct Castlereagh and Cornwallis to consult with individuals on the
catholic question but to refrain from holding out any encouragement to the
catholic body until they had reported back to England.[171] These instructions
had been anticipated by the Irish administration. The home secretary had
explained this position to Cornwallis even before the councils. No encouragement was to be given to the catholics regarding any alteration in their situation
for as long as the parliaments of the two countries were separate. Portland was
convinced that catholic emancipation could not be safely granted unless a
union took place; even then, he did not believe that the issue should be one of
the first acts of the united parliament.[172]

The British parliament resumed the debate on the union on 7 February.
Canning light-heartedly admitted that the 'two, if not three, days good debating' would be the 'only good effect that I know of the failure of the union in
Ireland'.[173] He enjoyed nothing better than the cut and thrust of the commons
and even found 'Sheridan's *complimentary abuse* . . . very well done with great
taste and good nature'.[174] The defeat was no more than a temporary set-back,
'it will all be the same this time twelvemonth'. He confidently assured his
Irish mother that 'you will see that we go on here to show them what we
meant for their good'.[175]

Prodigiously talented, and with a vicious tongue that often caused offence,
Canning came up with a cheeky proposal to discredit Foster. William
Wickham was amused by the idea, and Pitt and Grenville agreed that it 'might
be carried into effect with great advantage'.[176] Canning found it 'really too
provoking and too absurd' that the speaker should be allowed to 'make a
market of his patriotism, in order that he may afterwards be enabled to raise
his price upon government when he comes bound (as he must ultimately do)
to favour the union'. To compromise Foster, Canning proposed getting an
Irish MP to suggest a 'pecuniary reward for the discharge of his public duty'.
The speaker had large debts,[177] so this would not seem too strange, and then

> a very *serious* and *imposing* argument might be raised on the impropriety
> of any member of the house of commons, particularly the speaker (whose

purity, *impartiality* etc. etc. ought to be *above all suspicion*) receiving the wages of a party out of doors, for his conduct on any particular question.[178]

Canning discussed this high-spirited scheme with Pitt, who had 'a notion that there could be found no member of the Irish house of commons to exercise so malicious a joke with sufficient gravity'.[179] The idea seems to have gone no further than this theoretical stage, and it is surely no more than a coincidence that a subscription was raised in Dublin, at this time, by the Ponsonby party and the Dublin bankers, which amounted to £16,000. It eventually had to be called off, ensuring, as Malcomson notes, 'that Foster suffered the odium of it, but derived from it no advantage'.[180]

Corruption was the key theme of Sheridan's attack on the union of 7 February. He questioned the legitimacy of government's persistence with the union after it had been rejected by the Irish commons. He asked Pitt if he was not aware that this determination would make the Irish guess how he intended to carry it:

> if he does not succeed on the present occasion, they must be convinced that he only waits for a moment when Ireland shall be more weak to carry his favourite project, and that intimidation and corruption are the engines he proposes to use.[181]

Sheridan constructed an amusing comparison between Pitt and the United Irishmen. Both wished to destroy the existing constitution of Ireland, blamed the parliament for the miseries in the country, and believed that faction had debilitated the parliament; 'they are also agreed as to the remedy: for they both prescribe a revolution'. Pitt had two allies, Sheridan contended, 'corruption and intimidation'; Ireland had 'honour and resolution — honour to resist the corruption and resolution to laugh at the intimidation of the right honourable gentleman'. As in January Sheridan proposed that anyone who used intimidation and corruption to influence the union 'is an enemy to his majesty, and to the constitution of his country'.

The prime minister chose to reply cautiously to these charges. In a short speech he challenged Sheridan's motion for 'insinuating that such conduct has been pursued'.[182] This was denied, and Pitt alluded to the dismissal of Parnell, whom he did not mention by name, as 'the case of a high office in the sister kingdom who has quitted his situation on account of his disagreement with his colleagues in an important fundamental measure of government'. This was stretching things, although Pitt continued by stressing that any resignations or dismissals were not symptomatic of corruption and intimidation. Rather they reflected 'the necessity of a harmony of conduct among the several members of administration'.

As if to prove this point key members of the administration rose to defend the union. Henry Dundas, 'a plain, business-like speaker',[183] delivered a speech that lived up to his reputation. He argued that it was 'a melancholy truth' that there did not exist any confidence in the Irish parliament amongst the majority of the Irish people.[184] This was unavoidable so long as the catholics composed three-quarters of the population, but were excluded from political representation. He claimed that union would see the protestants laying aside their fears and prejudices, convinced in the security of the protestant establishment, and catholics could then 'be admitted into a participation of every privilege and benefit consistent with that connexion'. Union was nothing less than 'a remedy . . . [for] the disease which poisons the peace and happiness of Ireland'. It had not hurt Scotland, indeed she had benefited considerably, and Dundas had no hesitation in 'maintaining that an incorporated parliament, partly English, partly Scotch, and partly Irish, is much better calculated for the management of the affairs of the British empire than separate parliaments'.[185] Through the union of 1707, 'and the cultivation of this waste land, England got also the co-operation of a race of gallant men, who aided her in the most perilous situations, and were frequently the foremost to fight her battles'.[186] 'No sinister arts, as some malignantly insinuate', were to be used to pass the union.[187] Dundas declared that he wished to 'convince, not to intimidate, the people of Ireland'. They would not adopt the rattlesnake tactic of France, who sought first to charm and then to destroy. Union, alone, allowed for a solution to the catholic question and this was the central point for Dundas. The secretary of state for war was genuine in his catholic sentiments, and acutely felt the necessity of the union measure. Although in private he was to concede that 'it will certainly not improve our houses of parliament' he nonetheless believed that

> in all other respects it will answer, and without it, Ireland is a country in which it will be impossible for any civilised being to live, and it will be such a thorn in our sides as to render us forever uncomfortable.[188]

The debate on 12 February witnessed a rare intervention from the speaker of the British house of commons, Henry Addington, who made a substantial contribution.[189] This speech was to be remembered many times afterwards when the catholic question had assumed a much greater significance. Addington discussed the various plans that had been mentioned to restore Ireland to tranquillity. These were catholic emancipation, the complete or partial re-enactment of the penal laws, and a legislative union. The first of these, catholic emancipation, the speaker did not consider an appropriate policy. It would only expose the protestants to danger and place them in a worse position than that of the catholics in the previous century. The second, a re-enactment of the penal laws, would similarly only 'add fuel to the flame, and create new sources of dissension and hostility'. The only viable solution was a union. The speaker denied that such a measure would prohibit any future concessions to the catholics. But on whether such concessions should be granted at a future date he would not comment. He quoted Dr Patrick Duigenan, who was no friend to the catholics, but who was surprisingly said to believe that a union would remove the dangers of giving the catholics full rights.[190] William Molineux's famous *Case for Ireland* . . . was quoted, too, that union was 'a happiness we can scarcely hope for'.[191]

Earlier in the debate Pitt had been cornered into conceding that he once
'went so far as to admit the independence of the Irish parliament', although
he denied ever agreeing 'to any measure that prevented further arrangements'.[192] It had not been a good day for the prime minister. He was forced,
under pressure from Sheridan, to make the bizarre claim that the union
acknowledged legislative independence 'and is a proposal to do something by
no means inconsistent with that independence'.[193] A minor victory had been
won, though, by Pitt's clever rebuttal of persistent calls to introduce catholic
emancipation for Ireland. Affecting bewilderment the prime minister asked
what this could mean only that the opposition expected the parliament of
Britain to legislate for Ireland.[194]

All that was possible was for the government to maintain a steady and consistent line on the union and persist with it until it succeeded. As Grenville
memorably declared, 'if Paddy will set fire to his own house, we must try to
put it out if we can, and if we cannot, we must keep the engine ready to play
upon our own'.[195] The king's government was to display a marked sense of
superiority in its determination to persist with the union, whatever the feeling
in Ireland, until it succeeded. It was aware that it had to win a majority just
one of those times; the opposition had to keep its majority always. Charles
James Fox summed up the position perfectly in a letter to Henry Grattan on
4 February urging vigilance: 'it should be remembered that this is a case
where no number of defeats is final, whereas one victory decides irrevocably
in favour of your enemies'.[196] It was yet to be seen whether Sheridan was naive
in hoping that the honour and resolution of the Irish people could counteract
Pitt's tactics of corruption and intimidation.[197] After defeat in January 1799
the full weight of government power was ready to be brought to bear, and this
time no expense would be spared, to quote Castlereagh, buying out 'the fee-
simple of Irish corruption'. In the chief secretary, the cabinet was to have a
willing instrument for its ruthlessness.

4

Corruption and the catholic question: the union strategy

FEBRUARY 1799–DECEMBER 1799

How shall this bosom multiply and digest
The senate's courtesy? Let deeds express
What's like to be their words: 'we did request it,
We are the greater poll, and in true fear
They gave us our demands.' Thus we debase
The nature of our seats, and make the rabble
Call our cares fears, which will in time break ope
The locks of the senate and bring in the crows
To peck the eagles.
(William Shakespeare, *Coriolanus*, act III, scene i)

When Camden quoted Coriolanus to Pitt in 1793 he was warning against a rash concession of catholic emancipation, fearing that it would only make the catholics more dangerous.[1] Coriolanus, himself, had been standing alone against the people, refusing to supply corn to the starving peasants, arguing that it would only 'nourish disobedience'. Ironically, these two issues, the catholic question and the problem of scarcity, were to affect Camden's successor in 1799. In each case Cornwallis's response displayed a wisdom and compassion that had eluded the doomed Roman leader. Central to both questions for the lord lieutenant was an understanding that loyalty came through generosity, and that securing the support of the people meant that government had to demonstrate it cared about their welfare. A darker, more unattractive side of the administration was evident also. The castle was not just concerned with gaining the help of the country, more importantly it needed a majority in parliament for the union. To win this Cornwallis and Castlereagh ruthlessly brought the full power of government to bear. The seduction of private interests began, as borough compensation was conceded, patronage was widely employed, and every attempt was made to persuade MPs to support the union. Just as the king's government was prepared to stop at nothing in the pursuit of foreign policy objectives, Ireland was to be no different, and legal restrictions were ignored as covert secret service money was transmitted for use in the approaching conflict. Government willed the ends, now it accepted that it must also will the means.

THE PROGRESS OF THE UNION IN IRELAND

Between February and April 1799, it was revealed that while many members in the Irish parliament would oppose the government on the union they were not prepared to join the ranks of opposition permanently. A bill proposed on 26 February 'for the more speedy suppression of the rebellion', authorising joint civilian and martial courts, was passed, and an objection was defeated by 121 votes to 18.[2] This led to a moderate optimism on the government benches but it still cautioned against trying the union again that session.[3] Private interests would first have to be worked upon.[4] Pitt was also unwilling to risk another defeat. He instructed Castlereagh not to attempt the measure unless government were guaranteed a majority of at least 50.[5]

Immediate action was taken on the stumbling block of borough compensation. The castle quickly recommended surrendering the point, suggesting a method for compensating lost seats.[6] John Beresford added his voice to this advice. He blamed the government's stance for many of their difficulties as 'many of the proprietors are very poor, and have lived by the sale' of their seats.[7] He was also quick to castigate Cornwallis for alienating so many influential people. Much offence had been caused by the abandonment of all sorts 'of communication, either convivial or on business, with gentlemen' used to being consulted.[8] Worse, the lord lieutenant had alienated Lords Enniskillen and Kingston, who between them controlled fourteen seats that had opposed the union, and who were still smarting over their treatment by Cornwallis.

In February Castlereagh prepared a paper for London in which he examined the main groups opposed to the union. These were borough proprietors; the primary and secondary interests in the counties; the barristers; purchasers into the present parliament; and individuals concerned with property prices in Dublin.[9] Compensation for the 108 boroughs was estimated at £756,000, while the loss of the 32 seats in the counties was valued at £224,000. The purchase of the 50 barristers' seats would require an expenditure of £200,000, at £4,000 per seat; compensation for purchasers was expected to be £75,000; and Dublin was expected to lose £200,000 in property value. The total expenditure was therefore believed to be around £1,455,000 to facilitate the union.[10] Castlereagh noted that if borough compensation was adopted it could be applied only to the 81 seats that were, strictly speaking, 'property'.[11] The principle of borough compensation was quickly conceded. But, as Malcomson correctly notes, because it was done unwillingly after the January defeat it was seen as bribery and part of government's attempts to buy a majority. Even the following year Cornwallis was to note that some of the compensation remained the most exceptionable part of the whole arrangement.[12] Nevertheless it served to persuade many people to support government and in March Cornwallis was happy to find that partly because of this, public opinion seemed to be changing in favour of the union.[13]

The union was not the only problem for government in the spring of 1799. A spate of cattle houghing in Mayo and Galway and a marked increase in murders and robberies forced Cornwallis to adopt strict martial law.[14] The lower orders were becoming troublesome and matters were not helped by the harsh weather that was affecting crops. Meanwhile Cornwallis was attracting severe criticism for his leniency since his arrival, which prompted a swift denial from the castle. William Wickham, writing from Britain in early March, reported that there was 'a general, I may say universal, persuasion that lenient measures have been carried too far'.[15] The departure from Camden's system was blamed for 'the calamities with which Ireland is now threatened'. Castlereagh was forced to deny the charges in parliament and gave figures for the numbers of rebels executed by Cornwallis.[16] This did not put an end to the 'lies and nonsensical clamour' about his leniency.[17] In a sharp letter to Ross, whom he was annoyed to find believing the allegations, Cornwallis admitted that he had put an end to the burnings, floggings, murders, rapes and robberies that had existed throughout the country and 'if this be a crime I freely acknowledge my guilt'. But he would not accept that he had ever committed 'a single act of improper or impolitic lenity'.

Speaker Foster was to compare his opposition to the union to his actions against the 1793 catholic relief bill, and consistently denied that it was 'general opposition'.[18] This did not prevent him from using every available opportunity to attack the measure in the spring of 1799. Foster's influence was admired by Cooke as 'amazing',[19] and Clare believed that the intensity of the struggle owed much to the part taken by the speaker.[20] Another writer informed Pitt that Foster was a man of 'astonishing weight' in the country and was 'more generally looked up' to than was thought in England.[21] Lord Altamount paid the greatest tribute to the speaker when he observed that he was 'king of Ireland, or may be so when he chooses'.[22] Foster's opposition to the union was determined by his belief that it was neither necessary nor good for Ireland. The intensity of his opposition was decided not by principle but by pride. The behaviour of Cornwallis was an aggravation; the condescension of Pitt was unbearable. To make matters worse, in his speech of 31 January the prime minister had accused Foster of acting inconsistently with his expressed sentiments in 1785 when he seemed to accept that the settlement of 1782 was not final.[23] The charge stung.

Misunderstanding the speaker's intentions in the autumn of 1798, Pitt had believed that Foster would abstain from influencing opinion on the union. The speaker's subsequent opposition was seen as a betrayal, and was bitterly resented. Malcomson states that Pitt's attack on the speaker was 'strong and personal'.[24] No politician wished to be charged with inconsistency, or worse a lack of integrity. This speech spurred Foster into taking a dominant role in the opposition to the union in Ireland. Castlereagh's analysis of the speaker on a separate issue is valid in this case also: he was 'more guided by his passions than by any cool design'.[25] Foster admitted in August 1799 that Pitt's attack had hardened his opposition.[26] He had come to believe that there had been 'a premeditated design to lower him, and run him down'.[27] It was later reported that he would have moderately opposed the measure if he had been shown respect (and no doubt tactfully rewarded), but the offensive way he had been treated demanded that he use his utmost exertions against it.[28]

As the months went by, and Foster avoided replying to Pitt's charges, the speaker's reticence was taken as a sign that he did not wish to pledge himself irrevocably against the union.[29] This cautious optimism started in Dublin, and was quickly passed on to the cabinet as Castlereagh encouraged the belief that the speaker had softened. Meanwhile Pitt was also understood to have mellowed in his feelings towards Foster, and was not inclined 'to be too severe in his conduct towards him'.[30] The hopes for a rapprochement were dashed on 11 April when Foster used the opportunity provided by the regency bill to make his speech on the union. James Fitzgerald, the sacked prime serjeant, had brought forward a bill 'to provide for the administration of the government of Ireland whensoever and as often as it shall be administered by a regent or regency'.[31] When this came before committee Foster elected to state his position. The false confidence was shattered and Castlereagh admitted, now, that the speech had been 'long threatened'.[32] The regency bill was forgotten in an oration that was estimated to have lasted more than four hours.[33] Foster had been infuriated by Pitt's allegations of inconsistency against him, but claimed that he would not have answered them had the charges not been printed and distributed in Ireland. He was to assure Camden at a later date that he had no harsh feelings against Pitt.[34] The speaker refuted the charges levelled against him in England before launching an attack on the commercial points of the union.

The charge of inconsistency was hotly and strenuously denied. If the allegation must be made then he felt it could be better applied to the prime minister, who had not, either in 1785 with his commercial propositions, or three years previously in 1782, said anything to imply that the settlement was anything other than final.[35] Foster charged the minister to 'either retract his new doctrines of 1799 or plead guilty to a shameful and continued dereliction of his duty'. The union was criticised for constitutional and commercial reasons. He threatened that it would damage Irish trade, especially in Dublin and Cork, with no visible benefits. The speaker urged the catholics to join in the struggle to avoid the degradation of their people and their country, from 'an independent kingdom to an abject colony'.[36] Foster's speech was damning to government and made 'a visible impression'.[37]

Responsibility for answering the speaker fell to Castlereagh. He challenged Foster's assertion that Pitt was disturbing Ireland by pressing the union; it was not a state of tranquillity or peace he was affecting, but 'the state of our miseries and distractions to which Mr Pitt was ready to sacrifice his own peace, in the hope of finding a remedy'.[38] Cornwallis was full of praise for his chief secretary, informing the cabinet that he spoke 'with great ability';[39] Cooke was more restrained and testified that he had spoken 'well'.[40] With his speech Foster was seen as having irrevocably aligned himself with opposition: 'he threw away the scabbard'.[41] The only positive outcome of the speech, for the government, was that it had now faced its 'principal adversary, and his arguments will be well understood and answered before the subject comes again into decision'.[42] The chief secretary considered the speech to have been 'that of the able partisan in a bad cause, everything sacrificed to popular impression; but well calculated to impress every class of men with aversion to the measure of union'.[43]

Less than a week after Foster's speech government was embarrassed when Lord Chancellor Clare disdainfully rejected a bill supporting a Roman Catholic seminary at Maynooth.[44] Neither Castlereagh nor Cornwallis had been warned in advance and they had to act quickly to prevent the catholics from becoming alienated from the government. Clare claimed that there had been problems with the bill, and denied being opposed to the seminary itself, and his explanation appears to have been accepted.[45]

SCARCITY AND PARLIAMENTARY CONCERNS

Heavy snow fell in Ulster in April.[46] There was equally harsh weather in the rest of the country throughout the year with serious damage to crops. The extreme conditions were perhaps even more pronounced in Britain where it was reported that 'the weather is severe beyond example, and bears hard on elderly people and young children'.[47] The census of 1851 was to record that 'the latter part of the year 1798 was unusually wet in Ireland, and 1799 was particularly cold; general bad harvest ensued'.[48] Adam Smith had confidently asserted that in corn-producing countries, such as Ireland and Britain, famine was impossible.[49] Ireland was now to see his claims severely tested. When famine is defined as 'enhanced mortality owing to hunger-related diseases' and not deaths through starvation[50] then 1799–1801 can be regarded as, to quote Roger Wells, 'famine conditions and responses'.[51] 'Scarcity' was the preferred term rather than the emotive word 'famine' although one observer in late 1800 in England was to remark that 'in any other country than this . . . [this] would be called famine'.[52]

The Irish parliament met on 15 May as Cornwallis intervened to deal with the threatened scarcity. Castlereagh presented a message from the lord lieu-tenant that began:

> that his excellency having taken into consideration the extraordinary high price of corn in this kingdom for some time past, considerably above that standard which the wisdom of parliament has established as the criterion for opening the ports in the country for the admission of foreign corn . . .[53]

An order was given for the ports to be opened for the admission of foreign corn. Castlereagh explained that this was a precaution 'to guard against the possibility of any scarcity which might arise at a future period in consequence of the lateness of the present season'. An address of thanks moved to Cornwallis was agreed, and there was no recorded dissent in the house. The weather, and possible food shortages, was soon forgotten once the debate proper began. The attack of opposition centred on government's refusal to allow two members, Colonel Galbraith Lowry Cole and William Tighe, to vacate their seats, by accepting a nominal office, to enable anti-unionists to take their seats. The refusal was unheard of, the escheatorships being an established means of vacating seats along the lines of the Chiltern hundreds in Britain. The position of the government was denounced as 'general corruption'.[54] William Plunket delivered a powerful indictment of the administration, and lost no time in taking a personal swipe at Castlereagh, this time for his 'childish hope' in believing that the union would have passed in January.[55] The speech was a precise assessment of government arrogance:

> the noble lord at this moment exhibits a phenomenon unfounded in the history of any free country: after being baffled and disgraced in a vital measure he continues to brave the parliament and the people, and to tell them that that measure shall be carried, no matter by what means.

George Ponsonby dramatically accused those around him of having lost their senses and said that 'I feel it dangerous to trust myself in the house, lest I shall be bitten and go mad myself also.'[56] He dismissed the chief secretary's pledge not to carry the union against the sense of parliament and the country as empty since it suggested that he intended 'either by force or fraud to carry the question of union'. He vindictively asserted that Castlereagh's words were 'hollow and hypocritical, the canting of a mountebank'.[57] The house was reminded that 'the noble lord is at the head of a great army' and that his object was 'to *pack* the parliament for the purpose of carrying a union . . . and to enforce the vote of that *packed* parliament by that army'.

The pettiness of government's refusal to allow Cole and Tighe to vacate their seats under the escheatorship of Munster did nothing to increase its reputation in the country. Even the cabinet was embarrassed by the display and Portland quickly advised Cornwallis to follow the practice of England in future.[58] Nor were matters helped by the persistent deficiencies of Castlereagh and Cornwallis. The chief secretary, while showing improvement as a speaker, 'does not show quite that attention to everyone which the vanity and folly of the Irish world expect'.[59] Worse, the lord lieutenant still 'shows no attention at all'. 'The consequence is unfavourable,' reported Cooke.

There was a gradual realisation of the difficulties involved in gaining a majority in Ireland. Cornwallis warned against any false optimism as 'the people in general here have no fixed principle or design'.[60] He was disgusted by the sham of integrity: 'a man who will acknowledge in the month of April that nothing but a union can save Ireland is very likely to give his vote against it in May'. Cornwallis asked Portland for advice on how to proceed with the question of dismissals. An assertion of authority was necessary if they wanted to weaken their opponents and 'animate our friends'.[61] A general principle was 'critical' for government, any arbitrariness would reflect badly, and any weakness 'could not fail to operate prejudiciously'.[62] Portland recommended taking a strict line towards office holders who opposed union.[63] Three commissioners of revenue, John Wolfe, Thomas Foster and George Knox, were promptly dismissed and three pro-unionists installed in the lucrative £1,000 per annum offices.[64]

Towards the end of May it was estimated that there were 148 definite pro-union MPs in parliament, with 98 against and 54 uncommitted, although Cornwallis believed that many if not all of these undecided would oppose if union was brought forward immediately.[65] Careful management of these members, the lord lieutenant admitted, was the key to securing their support. Public opinion was regarded as important also, and if sentiment in the counties was seen to be in favour of the measure, the task would be made much easier. By June five counties had come forward for the union: Cork, Galway, King's County, Mayo and Kerry. Successful resolutions were also expected from Clare, Derry, Tipperary, Waterford and Wexford. Little unionist sentiment was expected in Carlow, Cavan, Dublin, Fermanagh, Kildare, Louth or Wicklow. The other counties were divided.[66] Fortunately, the temper of the capital was reported to be cooling.[67]

Securing the support of the fickle borough proprietors remained difficult. The concession of borough compensation had an encouraging effect on many; Ely promised general support to Cornwallis in February and vowed to resist any proposition to pledge the house against a union.[68] He declared positively for the union the following month.[69] The lord lieutenant derived little comfort from the assurances and dismissed Ely as 'so weak and corrupt' that his word was meaningless.[70] Downshire was reported to be 'very troublesome and impracticable' in February and it was not expected that he would change from this position.[71] Progress on his sentiments proved bothersome. Nevertheless Downshire's support was considered essential and Cornwallis believed that if it could be obtained then success would be guaranteed in the following session.[72] If he opposed, however, it would raise the price of support amongst those who would then 'insist upon a higher bounty'.[73] The efforts proved unsuccessful and in June the lord lieutenant was informed that Downshire was more hostile to a union than ever, opposed to both the principle and the timing of the measure.[74]

The same month Downshire claimed that his actions had not been motivated by any personal animosity towards the chief secretary.[75] The assertion was dripping with insincerity. Lord Shannon was to note Downshire's intransigence on the union and emphasised that he 'hates Castlereagh'.[76] Castlereagh found Downshire's behaviour perplexing. While claiming to be against a union he was nonetheless engaged in requesting all sorts of favours although 'none perhaps of that magnitude which renders it necessary or polite to bring him to a decided explanation'; the castle found this duplicity 'hardly honourable'.[77] Camden brought the matter before Pitt and suggested generous borough compensation as the best way of guaranteeing the support of Downshire, who was 'not personally corrupt', but could not fail to be influenced by such an offer.[78]

FORGING A MAJORITY: PATRONAGE AND THE UNION

'People are so used to bribes in this country that they will not even do what is right, or their own business, unless they are paid for it.'[79] There was an assumption that Cornwallis and Castlereagh would not have the stomach for gaining an Irish majority by Irish means. Winning a majority was so dependent on private interest that it was feared the union would fail, a second time, unless the battle was won 'out of doors'. The castle, however, was not naive about what was required and it understood that the struggle would involve the use of some highly dubious tactics. The lord lieutenant recoiled at the prospect, enduring 'the shocking task which is imposed upon me' only because he believed that a union was absolutely necessary for the safety of the empire.[80] His chief secretary was to reveal a remarkable perspicacity for the business. In July he admitted that 'nothing but the utmost effort to meet private interest can enable us to buy up the fee-simple of Irish corruption'.[81] Cooke's prediction that the union had to be spoken up and bribed up was now being ruthlessly enshrined as policy. In the game that was being played self-interest dominated and many sought to secure as much personal advantage as possible; it proved difficult to satisfy everyone. Castlereagh warned the king's government that it had to be prepared 'for having the favours and patronage of the crown most deeply engaged to the actors in this contest'.[82] Before the Irish administration embarked on its dangerous course the chief secretary sought an assurance from Pitt that it did so with the full approval of the king's ministers. He wanted a firm commitment on to just 'what lengths he [Pitt] is prepared to go to carry this measure'. The differences between the two countries were defined as such:

> in England a measure may be carried by public opinion against the private inclinations of the parliament, but here not. Besides, we cannot hope that the public will do more than consent. It will ultimately, rely on it, be brought to a private question. Those who thrive by the game of parliament are aggrieved in their hearts against it, and unless connected with their own aggrandisement in some shape, will either oppose it, or give it but a languid support, which encourages opposition in others.[83]

Cornwallis sent a similar analysis to Portland. In Britain the parliament was 'naturally connected' with public opinion, but in Ireland, although it was important, private considerations still dominated.[84]

The lord lieutenant looked with distaste on the full range of government methods that would have to be employed to secure a majority for the union. He understood their necessity but was disgusted that such tactics had to be resorted to to pass a measure so essential for the empire. The 'unpleasant nature' of his job began to weigh on the lord lieutenant, 'negotiating and jobbing with the most corrupt people under heaven. I despise and hate myself for engaging in such dirty work, and am supported only by the reflection that without a union the British empire must be dissolved'.[85] Whenever it proved impossible to satisfy the demands of some politicians Cornwallis would dwell on two lines of Swift, on the viceroy and system of corruption of his time: 'and then at Beelzebub's great hall, complains his budget is too small'.

'AN ACT OF POWER AND CORRUPTION': THE HISTORIOGRAPHY OF THE UNION

The passing of the union has always been steeped in controversy about the extent of the corruption involved. At the time the opposition loudly declaimed that unconstitutional means were being used. It charged government with buying a majority through the indiscriminate dispersal of patronage, peerages, borough compensation, intimidation and bribery. Jonah Barrington levelled the accusation in the commons on 22 January[86] and expanded upon it afterwards in his writings on the union. In his historical memoirs he alleged that Castlereagh had 1.5 million pounds at his disposal and, 'besides, the secret service money of England was at his command'.[87] Barrington's own role in the union negotiations is worthy of further study: vehemently opposed to the measure, he emerges as a heroic tower of integrity in his own writings. Nevertheless he applied for the position of solicitor-general in the autumn of 1799, and had Castlereagh not rejected his application it is unlikely he could have continued in opposition. Allegations also surround him that he acted as an agent of the government in persuading an anti-union MP to vacate his seat and allow a unionist to take his place; what can be proven is that his judicial career was interrupted in the 1810s, and he went into exile in France, after evidence of embezzlement was discovered against him.[88]

The shadowy speculations of Barrington and others were readily believed by Irish nationalists, who were unwilling to accept the destruction of their parliament. The son of Henry Grattan spoke for many when he wrote that 'the union, as regarded by the Irish nation, was an act of power and corruption; the Irish parliament did not consent to its own abolition'.[89] This became a crucial part of the historiography, for if undue and illegal pressure had been placed on the parliament then the union could be dismissed as fraudulent, and an illegal decision. W.E.H. Lecky, in his classic five-volume history of Ireland, asserted that it was 'idle to dispute the essentially corrupt character of the means by which the union was carried'.[90] He readily accepted that 'the virus of corruption extended and descended through every fibre and artery of the political system'.[91] Significantly, he did deny the allegation that secret service funds had been used to assist the measure and concluded that while 'direct money bribes were given' they were not to the extent that nationalists had alleged.[92]

A saintly account of the union by T.D. Ingram in 1887 did little to revise this opinion. He weakly claimed that 'the union was undertaken from the purest motives, that it was carried by fair and constitutional means'.[93] Few were convinced. Even Pitt's sympathetic biographer Lord Rosebery argued that the Irish parliament had been without a mandate to terminate itself. And as for the means employed, 'the corruption was black, hideous, horrible, revolting at any time, atrocious when it is remembered that it was a nation's birthright that was being sold'.[94] Other historians chose to believe the corruption, but dismiss it as unimportant. Charles Petrie in his biography of the second Lord Liverpool managed to be both offensive and racist in his assertion that 'one might as well talk of a negro becoming sunburnt by the English sun' as accuse government of corruption. All that was done was merely the application, on a larger scale, of the 'immemorial methods of obtaining a majority'.[95] A poem written towards the end of the nineteenth century became a nationalist paean to the union, taught in Irish schools, and quoted in every respectable text on the subject:

> How did they pass the union?
> By perjury and fraud;
> By slaves who sold their land for gold,
> As Judas sold his God.[96]

It was not until G.C. Bolton's important study of the union in 1966 that a serious attempt was made to revise the evidence. Bolton played down the use of corruption to pass the union and made a persuasive case that it was the use of generous patronage, borough compensation and the catholic question that secured a majority for the union. He found little evidence to suggest that bribery had been practised and cited as evidence the small number of members who actually changed sides between 1799 and 1800. The most important piece of analysis was that the methods used to secure the government's majority, although cynically regarded now, were seen as an acceptable part of the late eighteenth-century world. Seats were regarded as property and it was only right that they should be compensated; patronage was an inescapable part of political life. 'It is a superficial and exaggerated view to assume that corruption was the main factor that carried the union.'[97] Bolton's work became the key text on the union, and his conclusions influenced how the union was written about over the next thirty years.

Bolton forced a radical reassessment. Previous assumptions about corruption in the period were discarded and even nationalist historians adopted his analysis. Gearóid Ó Tuathaigh, in his study of Ireland before the famine, accepted that while there had been some bribery and a questionable use of patronage, 'such transactions were an accepted part' of the time.[98] The leading work of A.P.W. Malcomson, one of the most pre-eminent historians in the country, did much to make eighteenth-century procedure clearer.[99] The distinguished historian Donal McCartney summed up the shift away from previous interpretations: 'it would be old-fashioned, too nationalistic and much too simplistic to hold that the act of union was carried mainly because of the corrupt methods employed by the government'.[100] McCartney instead argued that the word 'management', rather than 'corruption', described the manipulation involved.

SECRET SERVICE (SS)[101]

The recent discovery of home office secret service accounts has challenged this consensus. In themselves the files are uninteresting, and superficially appear meaningless, but they provide the missing link between the allegations of corruption and government activity during the period. David Wilkinson, of the History of Parliament, assisted in the classification of these documents that were released by the Public Record Office, in Kew, in 1996. Based on his unique access he wrote a paper on the subject that immediately challenged Bolton's conclusions and firmly returned the debate to the question of the legality of the measure.[102]

The civil list act of 1782, which had been applied to Ireland in 1793, declared that only £5,000 of secret service money could be spent in the country, although there was no limit to the amount 'detecting, preventing, or defeating treasonable and other dangerous conspiracies against the state'.[103] This restriction was ignored by the king's government, just as restrictions in Britain were to be circumvented for other activities. In total the figure spent on secret service in Ireland between 1799 and 1800, separate from the regular secret service expenditure that was fully accounted for, came to a final balance of £32,556.6s 11d.[104] This was paid in five instalments, the first being a transmission of £850 on 4 October 1799. It seems that there were three broad purposes for the money: to pay supporters of the union; to purchase seats in parliament; and to discharge any other expenses that were thought necessary during the year.

The importance of the secret service money should not be exaggerated. It alone did not pass the union; it was but one factor amongst many. Nor should there be any false moralising about its use. The king's government was already breaking secret service restrictions in the war against France; it is unreasonable to assume that it was going to shirk from using the funds in Ireland if needed; and ultimately they were very necessary. The castle consistently defined the union question as one of private interests. It understood that people would not view the matter on its merits, but in terms of how it would benefit them. Leaving the union to a free determination would have guaranteed its failure. If the only thing that would work involved making the union palatable to private interests then government had no hesitation about adopting corruption as part of its union strategy. It joined borough compensation, patronage and the catholic question as the 'engines' by which the union would be passed. As Ehrman sagely notes, 'corruption does not exist in a void';[105] what was done in Ireland between 1799 and 1801 reflected Irish habits, and was conformable to government practice elsewhere.

THE COURTING OF THE CATHOLICS

An understanding of opinion on the union outside of Dublin had been lacking in January. In the summer Castlereagh attempted to rectify this by personally gathering intelligence from the countryside.[106] In his three-week mission he was particularly anxious to determine the mood of the catholics. Their position was to vary, or at least the castle's assessment of their position, but at this time they seemed to be sympathetic to a union, although concerned that emancipation should accompany it. As long as this was unclear the support of the catholics would not be forthcoming. The lord lieutenant decided in June 1799 that it was necessary to send Castlereagh to England to report on the state of the parties in Ireland and also to 'ascertain what was likely to be the ultimate decision of his majesty's ministers with respect to the catholics'.[107] Cornwallis was determined to preserve his honour and integrity in his dealings with the catholic body. He would not act in any way towards them that might leave him open to future charges of deception. The chief secretary also wished to return to England for consultation to clarify the government's Irish policy. This request was made, both to Grenville and to Camden, Castlereagh insisting that such a journey was essential for an official definition on the union strategy.[108]

Part of that strategy involved gaining the help of the catholics. Their support had been carefully, and primarily, nurtured by the lord lieutenant. There was a popular belief, shared by Cornwallis and Cooke, that the protestants would not oppose the union if it was pressed by the king's government and the population of Ireland.[109] Securing the support of the catholics was a task that the lord lieutenant could not achieve on his own. Government policy had to change and incorporate their interests. Cooke, for his part, did not see the promise of further concessions to be unreasonable or insufferable, and 'though I do see strong objections, I think they vanish in the superior importance of the question of union'.[110] If the catholic support could be obtained then it was predicted that Dublin might remain quiet, although the opposition would be 'clamorous'. The difficulties would be in parliament.

In August Cornwallis warned the home secretary that the catholics of Dublin and the neighbouring areas would refuse to support the union along its existing lines, and that 'little more is to be expected than neutrality'.[111] The cabinet was left with no choice but to reconsider its exclusionist policy. The ministers faced a stark alternative: either continue with their existing strategy of separating the catholic question and the union, and risk another defeat of the measure, or make an immediate decision on the propriety of conceding emancipation. Pitt, meanwhile, had lost all interest in Ireland. Naval and military matters occupied the greater part of his attentions, as the problems of the neighbouring kingdom became more distant.[112] The pressures of office were beginning to accumulate and his state of mind was not helped by the news that Eleanor Eden, Auckland's daughter, whom he had come close to marrying in 1797, had married Lord Hobart, the former Irish chief secretary.[113]

DEARTH AND DISTRESS

By October it had become clear that there would not be a sufficient food supply in Ireland. As *Barker and Cheyne's report* noted, there were 'continued rains, attended with an unusual degree of cold, [that] occasioned an almost general deficiency in the crops, and a consequent failure of the usual supply of nourishment to the poor, already suffering under many privations'.[114] In Britain a rigid adherence to free trade, and an unwillingness to interfere, allowed the problems to develop into a formidable crisis of government. In Ireland Cornwallis displayed a leadership ability that had been lacking in his political dealings. It was in crises like this that he was at his best, able to solve problems by issuing decisive orders, and not being forced into unwelcome negotiations and compromises. Whereas in Britain the scarcity issue was seen primarily in economic terms Cornwallis chose to regard it as a question of logistics. Instead of supplying troops he applied his military mind to supplying people. His prompt action in May had been valuable, and in the autumn he searched for other ways to avert a famine. An embargo was ordered on all vessels leaving Irish ports with potatoes and the *Hibernian Magazine* reported that 'such measures have been taken to procure a supply of bread corn from the Baltic and America, as will remove every danger of scarcity in this essential article'.[115] One solution, urged by Foster, was stopping the production of spirits in distilleries, who were already doubling their production with a view to exporting it to Britain,[116] and this was eventually carried out.

In Ireland there was 'a ruinous state of the harvest' leading to heavily inflated food prices.[117] Castlereagh advised against shutting down the distilleries believing that it would not be expedient, and might require an act of parliament. Ignoring the perilous state of food supplies in Ireland, and looking only at its own difficulties, the cabinet requested Cornwallis to export spare oats and beans to England.[118] It was an audacious and provocative request. Irish interests, it seemed, were immediately to be subordinated to British demands. Cornwallis was having none of it. It gave him, perhaps, a malicious pleasure to inform Portland politely that it was impossible to meet the request.[119]

Things were no better in November. *Faulkner's Journal* reported that

> the most melancholy accounts of the harvest arrive from all parts of the country; in many places the oats and other late corn remain on the ground not worth the reaping. Great dearth of corn apprehended. The herring fishery very abundant.[120]

In Ulster the baking of anything other than brown bread was prohibited and soldiers were deprived of their hair-powder as this was composed of flour.[121] There was an urgent deficiency of bread in Dublin.[122] The potato crop had failed in England, and the Irish crop suffered similarly. Cornwallis did not wait for instructions from England and acted swiftly, with a decisiveness that was lacking in England. He issued a proclamation on 11 November that placed a bounty on barrels of wheat and flour, to encourage their importation into Ireland. The premium was ten shillings per barrel for the first 40,000 and five shillings for the next 20,000.[123] Portland was quick to rebuke this initiative. He condescendingly informed the lord lieutenant that he was 'probably not aware of the measures which have been taken here upon this subject'.[124] During 'the late period of scarcity' the king's ministers had abstained from 'similar practices' of bounties. It was believed that instead of increasing the quantity of grain imported they would only increase the profit of importers. Portland instructed Cornwallis to follow the policies of England in future, and also told him to make it clear that the bounties did not apply for Great Britain, or to those barrels stored there.[125] The lord lieutenant was forced to comply reluctantly with this order, although both houses of the Irish parliament thanked him for his prompt action.[126]

Cornwallis defended his actions in his response to Portland. He had thought 'it necessary to adopt some measure to quiet the fears of the people in order to counteract the clamour for stopping the distilleries'.[127] This had been seen as unwise by those knowledgeable in revenue matters, who had advised against it. Despite the courageous efforts of the lord lieutenant, by the end of the month it was reported that 'distress had commenced among the poor'.[128]

DEBATING THE CATHOLIC QUESTION

The question of issuing a pledge to the catholics was 'frequently mooted' at cabinet councils in the lead-up to November 1799.[129] No decision was taken. The matter became even more urgent when a rumour was 'industriously propagated' in Ireland that the passing of the union would 'preclude for ever the Roman Catholics of this kingdom from the hopes of further emancipation, that, under the imperial parliament, the junto who opposed them would still prevail, and hold the reins of the government of this country'.[130] In this uncertain atmosphere the chief secretary sailed for England on 13 September.[131] He was to be there until December, his arrival intensifying the debate amongst the king's ministers.

Hobart, who was in Ireland at the time, was kept informed of developments back home in London by his new father-in-law, Auckland. He was anxious that no further concessions were granted to the catholics. He presented his arguments to Pitt 'knowing how much difficulty you must have upon the catholic question'.[132] A government statement on the question he considered neither necessary nor sound policy. The actions of the Irish administration, and a conversation with Castlereagh before he departed, filled him with deep misgivings and he advised Pitt to correct the mistaken beliefs he thought the chief secretary was acting under, fearing otherwise 'a dangerous error' which if not stopped would 'be fatal to the peace of the British empire, and I am persuaded extremely injurious to you personally'. Emancipation, he insisted, had to be avoided. Echoing Camden he argued that the catholics were a 'body of men formidable only in proportion to the way in which they are treated'. Once they recognised that power and prosperity resided with the protestants they could be controlled. The correspondence was motivated by Hobart's horror at the Irish administration seemingly 'in distinct terms telling the catholics that the effect of the union must be to admit them into the state and into parliament'.[133] Such a pledge would be 'an unwarrantable political fraud' that was unacceptable to a man of Hobart's strong opinions. It would lead to a 'total annihilation' of all the benefits of a union and accompany 'the discredit and perhaps the ruin of the administration by which it has been conducted'. These sentiments reflected a sizeable body of opinion in Ireland, and an even greater sentiment in Britain.

Hobart's faith that Pitt would remonstrate with Castlereagh was soon betrayed. His worst fears became adopted as government policy. The strategy to pass the union became broadened to incorporate the definite, eventual, granting of emancipation. This momentous change occurred after deliberations in two cabinet councils, but given the length of time Castlereagh was in London, it is difficult to date the meetings satisfactorily. There is some evidence which suggests they occurred on two consecutive days of the 15, 16 and 17 November.[134] No cabinet minute was taken at either meeting.[135] These would have been avoided because cabinet minutes were only ever taken to send to the king, and this was one discussion that the government wished to keep away from him for as long as possible. The only full account of the meetings was written by Castlereagh, at the start of 1801, to remind Pitt of what had been decided.[136]

The cabinet heard a report from Castlereagh that explained in detail the precarious thread on which the success of the union hung. Castlereagh later recollected that he had outlined how

> we had a majority in parliament composed of very doubtful materials; that the protestant body was divided on the question with the disadvantage of Dublin and the orange societies against us — and that the catholics were holding back under a doubt whether the union would facilitate or impede their object. I stated it as the opinion of the Irish government that circumstances as the parliamentary interests and the protestant feelings then were — the measure could not be carried if the catholics were embarked in an active opposition to it.[137]

The resistance of the catholics would be 'unanimous and zealous' if they believed that the government was continuing with a union similar to that rejected in January. The reticence of the Irish administration, then, had led many catholics to decide that their interests would be better served remaining neutral or even actively resisting the union. Those who did oppose had done so out of a conviction that the union would only serve to 'strengthen the protestant interest and to perpetuate their exclusion'. The integrity of the lord lieutenant, and the honour he felt was due the king's government, would not allow him to hold out false hopes to the catholics to secure their support. Before Cornwallis would 'personally' encourage the catholics, he wished to protect the government from future charges of duplicity, and he himself 'was particularly desirous of being secure against such a risk'.

The cabinet considered this analysis gravely, aware that the success of the union hung in the balance. The chief secretary was invited to attend the second cabinet meeting, at which he was informed that the government had decided to alter its policy towards the catholics. Afterwards Castlereagh was to tell Cornwallis that

> some doubts were entertained as to the possibility of admitting catholics into some of the *higher offices*, and that ministers apprehended considerable repugnance to the measure in many quarters, and particularly in the *highest*, but that as far as the sentiments of the cabinet were concerned, his excellency need not hesitate in calling forth the catholic support in whatever degree he found it practicable to obtain it.

It was understood that the question would not be submitted to the united parliament until a peace. No direct objection was voiced by any minister present. So enamoured did the cabinet appear of the idea that it was even debated whether an immediate pledge to the catholics should not be made public. This was decided against, mainly because of fears that it might alienate protestants in both countries against the union, 'in a greater degree than it was calculated to assist the measure through the catholics'. The lord lieutenant was unambiguously instructed that he was to avoid a pledge to the catholics unless it became absolutely necessary because

> it was not thought expedient at that time to give any direct assurance to the catholics, but that should circumstances so far alter as to induce his excellency to consider such an explanation necessary he was at liberty to state the grounds on which his opinion was formed for the consideration of the cabinet.

Precisely who attended this cabinet is unknown given the absence of any official record. Camden, who attended the first cabinet and almost all of the second, recalled that Portland was present. Loughborough, with his reputation as 'keeper of the king's conscience', was a possible absentee, but it is not clear whether Pitt was aware at this time of the lord chancellor's new religious convictions.[138] Lord Campbell in *The lives of the lord chancellors* contends that Loughborough was not informed of 'the liberal policy' and hypothesises 'the apprehension that he might betray them increased the estrangement between him and the more influential section of the cabinet'.[139] However, from Lord Camden's statement it appears that Loughborough developed his objections only in the summer of 1800, which suggests that he may have been present in 1799 and voiced no objections.[140] The king was not informed of the new policy; Camden later revealed that he 'had never been spoken to with openness and decision, at this time, on this subject by any of his ministers'.[141] Both Pitt and Grenville, on occasion, voiced their personal opinion to the king that catholic emancipation was desirable, but neither gave any hint that it was being planned as a government measure.[142] Henry Dundas went furthest in his conversations with the king. In one famous confrontation, often wrongly attributed to 1801 although it occurred much earlier, George III revealed his concern about the union:

> 'I hope', said the king, 'government is not pledged to anything in favour of the Romanists?' (that was his expression). 'No,' was my answer, 'but it will be a matter for future consideration whether, to render the measure the more efficient, it will not be proper to embrace them in some liberal plan of policy.'[143]

The king was horrified and asked Dundas, 'what say you to my coronation oath?' He was told that this 'can only apply to your majesty, I conceive, in your executive capacity. It does not refer to you as part of the legislature.' This distinction was lost on the king, who remained unconvinced, and replied sharply, 'none of your Scotch metaphysics, Mr Dundas!'[144]

Dundas never wavered in his conviction that the union should accompany full relief for the catholics. It was, he once wrote to Pitt, 'the plainest of all political truths' that something must be done to resolve the catholic question and was a matter that the king had to decide on, 'sooner or later'.[145] Grenville, likewise, was sympathetic to their claims but had become more cautious since the rebellion. The realisation that the catholics' support would be necessary for the union to succeed eased these qualms. His brother, Buckingham, had all along insisted that the catholics were 'the sheet anchor (in this project) with the lower ranks of people, and that every care must be taken to knit them both now and for the future with government'.[146] A key understanding of the foreign secretary's views on religion can be gleaned from a letter to his brother in which he mocked the 'extremely profound politicians' who had discovered that 'the religion of the people has no influence on its morals, or its morals on the prosperity and good government of the state'.[147] Given that he was not opposed to catholic emancipation, as a long-term objective, it is not surprising that he would have approved of the new strategy.

Once more it is Pitt's thinking that is the most difficult to ascertain. Initially, he had been in favour of including emancipation before deciding against it. In November 1798 he had sided with Grenville on separating the issues. Two friends of the prime minister insisted that the catholic question was very important to him. William Wilberforce has a diary entry for 25 January 1799 in which he noted Pitt's confidence that after the union the catholics would quickly obtain political rights and how he was 'resolved to give up [the] plan rather than exclude them'. In this the prime minister was 'as usual more fair and open, and even well-principled than any other person of his class. He is firmly persuaded that the union will open the most promising way by which the Roman Catholics may obtain political power.'[148] John Hookham Frere was even more convinced about the importance of the catholic question for Pitt and ascribed it a prime role in his union thinking. Frere insisted that emancipation was never just an expedient to pass the union; rather, emancipation was the more important measure of the two. Writing many years later Rosebery agreed with Frere that 'the union was to pave the way and conciliate public opinion', for the emancipation which 'he would gladly have carried' at any time.[149] It must be remembered, at the same time, that Frere, in private, did not believe that Pitt's resignation in 1801 was because of the catholic question. Rather he speculated that Pitt had retired to avoid making a peace. Therefore it is not clear just how important he really believed the question was for Pitt.[150] Given that Pitt's position on the union and the scheme to grant emancipation eventually was complex it is certainly plausible that the two men misunderstood, or allowed themselves to mis-interpret, their friend's position.

Pitt was not deeply religious. He had no great faith and it was recognised by many close to him that he was not 'under the influence of a powerful principle of religion'.[151] The desire to include catholics in the political representation was based upon a sense of what was good for the state. In his key speech on the union on 31 January he justified and defended the union in terms of resolving the problematic relationship between the two islands, and providing a solution for many of the internal problems of Ireland. The major internal problem was caused by religious differences. Pitt accepted that emancipation could never be safely conceded as long as Ireland was a separate kingdom. Emancipation could, however, be granted by a united parliament and Pitt recognised publicly that 'many of the objections which at present arise out of their situation would be removed' by union.[152] This was a key advantage of the measure, and in 1799 he insisted that 'if there existed no other I should feel it my duty to submit it to the house'.[153]

It is to misunderstand the character of Pitt to attribute the union policy solely to a desire to solve the catholic question in Ireland. The union was about far more than that. It was, as Pitt was to say in April 1800, 'a measure of great national policy' to counteract the 'restless machinations' of France. The best way of achieving this was to 'calm the sensations, allay the animosities, and dissipate the jealousies which have unfortunately existed'.[154] Catholic emanci-pation was part of the long-term objective for placing 'under one public will the directions of the whole force of the empire'.

The union was considered sound policy by the prime minister, even in the short term without emancipation. Action on the catholic question was always possible once a lasting peace was achieved as there would be time to work on the prejudices of the king. In autumn 1798 Pitt decided to isolate the catholic issue from the larger issue of the union and preserve the religious debate for a later, and safer, period. In autumn 1799 such a separation of policies risked the defeat of one and thus the other. Frere was partially correct in the importance of the catholic question, but perhaps out of a sense of loyalty to his friend wished to protect him from charges of manipulating the support of the catholics for political gain. The catholic question was never the central focus of the union, though it was a focus. When once challenged by his old adver-sary, Tierney, in the house of commons, to state in one sentence without ambiguity the purpose of the war with France, Pitt answered in one word — 'Security.' This was also the objective of the union, the security of the empire, the most important consideration in his life. Security necessitated a union, and a long-term solution to the catholic question: 'We must show that we wish to make the empire more powerful and more secure by making Ireland more free and more happy.'[155] For Pitt this could be achieved only through establishing a harmonious economic and political relationship between the two islands. The aim was to unite them in an indissoluble bond that could resist whatever the enemies of the empire threw at them. Events in Ireland over the previous two decades had convinced Pitt that the country would never be stable or secure unless the people were content; this demanded a solution to the religious divisions in the country. Security was to be achieved through freeing the catholics from their restrictions and allowing Ireland to share the commercial advantages of her sister island.

The shift in policy on the catholic question was welcomed by Cornwallis. He was soon making reference to the privileges 'which have in principle already been conceded' to the catholics.[156] Upon Castlereagh's return to Ireland, in early December, Cornwallis acknowledged to Portland the pleasure he had derived after 'the cabinet ministers had made up their mind on the subject of the future encouragement to be given to the catholics'.[157] The avoidance of any pledge to the catholics upon the point, unless absolutely necessary, was something he fully agreed with, believing that it was better to achieve their support without becoming obligated to them. Emancipation when it came must appear as the gift of the united parliament, not something that had been bartered to secure the union's passage.[158]

The support of the catholics was now possible, and this was helped by the fact that Cornwallis had already gained their 'confidence and goodwill'.[159] Much still depended on the cabinet in London. Cornwallis warned Portland that it would have to stand by him, for if he were to return to 'the ancient system', or if he were revealed to be 'a man of straw, without weight or consideration', then their support would quickly evaporate.[160] In this event resignation would be the only course of action as he would become 'the most improper man to hold my present station'. It was a veiled threat to the cabinet not to force harsh measures on Ireland, or act in any way to undermine his policies.

Pitt and his cabinet determined to keep the new policy regarding the catholic question a secret from the protestants in Ireland, and indeed people in Britain. This did not prevent suspicions being entertained about a shift in government policy especially as things began to change subtly in Ireland, once the lord lieutenant became aware of his freedom to manoeuvre. The rumours of a change in policy were a source of anxiety for some key protestant supporters of the union. They refused to believe that emancipation could be conceded and reminded figures in England that 'numbers vote for the measure to secure themselves against those people'. Beresford, for one, insisted that the 'evil' of emancipation would 'counterbalance all the good of a union, and no power on earth would persuade me to vote for it, as I am strongly convinced that it would end in rebellion, separation and ruin'.[161]

By December it was estimated by Cooke that 148 MPs would favour the union when it was reintroduced. A further 32 members would be added to this number when vacant seats were filled by government supporters. Another 32 were listed as doubtful, with 82 against.[162] Cooke was confident that the game was up for the speaker, who was using the 'most confident language: he has nothing else for it'.[163] Castlereagh predicted that 'the enemy cannot muster above 100' although he was somewhat worried by the likelihood of 30 government absentees on the first day.[164] An encouraging note was sounded when Ely made his terms with government; he would support the union without 'any positive promise as to the marquisate'. This relieved the government 'from much embarrassment'.[165]

THE END OF THE YEAR

As 1799 drew to a close the position of government was considerably brighter than a year previously. The concession of borough compensation, the shift in favour of the catholics, the resources of the treasury, and the willingness to satisfy private interests made the union much more appealing, and supporting government much more enticing. Winning a majority was one thing; the challenge now was to maintain it over the next six months. The seduction of private interests was neither permanent nor complete. Things were made much more difficult by the harsh weather that threatened a famine. Cornwallis's courageous actions had alleviated much of the suffering but not all, and on Christmas eve *Faulkner's Journal* reported that 'the poor of the country, and Dublin in particular, are said to be perishing from the dearness, scarcity, and bad quality of all kinds of provisions, in consequence of the dreary harvest'.[166] In private the castle was less confident about success in the following session. Cornwallis noted pessimistically that 'we have a lukewarm, and in some instances an unwilling majority'; the opposition, meanwhile, had 'a bold and deeply interested minority'.[167] Victory still hung in the balance as the union entered its final stage.

5

The union passes

JANUARY 1800– AUGUST 1800

etween January and June 1800 the Irish parliament once more debated the measure aimed at ending its existence. There were two parts to the work of the castle during this period. The first was the parliamentary struggle; this involved constant attention and vigilance as it worked to steer the union through all the stages, against persistent opposition attempts to defeat it. The fear of failure hung over the castle and made it increasingly anxious to succeed in the second part of its work: winning over the catholics, while at the same time using every means at its disposal to preserve unionist support in parliament. How the government passed the union has been the subject of speculation: eventual success in parliament made these questions assume an even greater importance for the castle as it struggled to honour its commitments. The story of how the union went through parliament, and the methods that sustained its passage, reveals a clear picture of the pressures on government and opposition, and the willingness of both sides to do whatever was necessary for victory.

THE BATTLE IN PARLIAMENT
January 1800 was a stressful time for the castle. Every resource of government was strained in an effort to satisfy its supporters, and it was feared that the inducements would soon run out. Castlereagh wrote to John King, who was now directing the secret service funds from the home office, on 2 January requesting further support: 'we are in great distress and I wish the transmiss was more considerable than the last; it is very important that we should not be destitute of the means by which so much depends'.[1] This application was granted and King quickly forwarded £10,000[2] to the chief secretary, promising that 'the fund was good security for a still further sum'.[3]

The opposition, too, was beginning to show signs of strain. It struggled for unity as various strategies were discussed for attacking government. It had always been difficult to co-ordinate its actions in a way that would be acceptable for its diverse members; now it proved impossible. According to Henry

Grattan's son, who published his father's recollections approximately forty years after the union, some highly unorthodox strategies had been contemplated. While it is impossible to prove the veracity of these stories they have the ring of authenticity. One scheme, suggested by Peter Burrowes, involved the opposition taking the battle out of parliament, and he recommended calling on the yeomanry to uphold their oath to protect the king, lords and commons, and oppose the union by force. Burrowes was convinced that faced with this opposition Cornwallis would back down. William Saurin and John Foster, however, were not prepared to go this far in their actions and the proposal was dropped,[4] although it was unofficially carried out later in the month. Henry Grattan junior was to show no compunction in condoning this violent response: 'unquestionably Lord Clare and Lord Castlereagh deserved to die. The popular execution of these state criminals would have been a national as well as a noble sentence. Some weak old women might have cried out *murder*.'[5]

Three strategies were carefully examined by the opponents of union. The first was to employ the same methods as the government and attempt to buy a majority in parliament. A sum of £100,000 was apparently subscribed for this fund, with Downshire contributing £1,000.[6] The second was to engage in a literary war against the union, but this was seen as coming too late to be effective. The third was an outrageously audacious scheme to stop the government. A pistolling club was to be formed that would duel the castle members, and thus in a gentlemanly way resolve the matter.[7] This too was rejected by the sober minds amongst the opposition. It was believed that Castlereagh was 'rather cold to be a warrior and, according to the language used by his friends, was said *to have a soft hole in him*'.[8]

The Irish parliament opened on 15 January 1800. Unlike the previous year union was not implied in the speech from the throne but was instead kept separate, to be introduced after a three-week adjournment.[9] As Bolton outlines, the union was first to be decided in principle, before the articles would be debated, and subjected to modification by committee. The agreed articles would then be submitted to the British legislature. Hyde suggests that the castle wished to avoid a discussion on the union in January until thirty-nine changes of seats occurred, confidently expecting a majority of these to be filled by government supporters.[10] Perhaps in recognition of this, the opposition decided to attack the union from the outset, a tactic the government was prepared for.

Sir Laurence Parsons moved an amendment to the address, pledging the house to maintain a free and independent parliament. Ireland was already, at least to Parsons, inseparably joined with Britain, and he argued that only an independent legislature could provide the many advantages that should not be discarded willingly. Parsons accused the chief secretary of 'prostituting the prerogative of appointing to places in order to pack a parliament'.[11] It was a fair charge. The place act was the means by which government built its majority. Once a recalcitrant member accepted a nominal place, or a sinecure, his seat became vacant and it was then possible to install a more pliable MP who would vote for the union. The amendment was seconded by one of Downshire's members, Francis Savage. There followed a long debate, 'warm and personal', with the galleries quiet, and the speaker's behaviour, this time, believed to be correct.[12] George Ponsonby delivered a highly ironic critique of the chief secretary's behaviour. It was uncharitable, he said, to accuse him of being 'anxious to put off discussion on the subject of union until he shall be sure of a majority . . . Convinced I am sir that the noble lord has not made undue use of the prerogatives of the crown'.[13] Employing proto-Wagnerian language Ponsonby declared that 'the parliament is to commit suicide upon itself' and he warned that 'the people of Ireland will never consent to the annihilation of their parliament if ever this house shall consent to its own immolation'.[14] William Plunket continued to bait Castlereagh, this time dismissing his 'puny sophistry', and added his voice against the address.[15]

The speeches continued throughout the night and into the morning. As the sun rose on 16 January the house witnessed the dramatic reappearance of a figure from the past. Henry Grattan, who had withdrawn from parliament a few years previously, returned to the house. The union had been weighing heavily on his mind, his wife later reporting that 'he could not bear the idea, or listen to the subject . . . he grew quite wild, and it almost drove him frantic'.[16] He had purchased his seat for £1,200, being elected for the Wicklow borough at midnight. Dressed in his old, blue, volunteer uniform, with its red cuffs and collar, and his cocked hat square to the front, he arrived in the commons at around seven o'clock.[17] In poor health, 'he was so debilitated that he was scarcely able to walk', he was assisted to his seat by two friends. John Egan, the anti-union MP, who was speaking, quickly brought his speech to an end and Grattan requested permission from the house to speak sitting.[18] This was granted, and once the old warrior began his speech his passion dispelled any doubts about his mental abilities. The house heard a two-hour declamation 'in his old, inflammatory, style'.[19] The government was charged with bribery and deceit; 'he, the minister, his budget crammed with corruption, proposes to you to give up the ancient inheritance of your country'.[20] In his peroration Grattan waved an accusatory finger at Castlereagh and asserted that

> the thing which he proposes to buy is what cannot be sold — liberty. He proposes to you to substitute the British parliament in your place, to destroy the body that restored your liberties and restore that body which destroyed them. Against such a proposition, were I expiring on the floor, I should beg to utter my last breath and record my dying testimony.[21]

Grattan was answered by Corry, the chancellor of the exchequer, who questioned the new member's patriotism. The amendment to the address was then put to the house and by eleven o'clock the debate concluded with a victory for the government of 138 votes to 96 against. In his report to Portland Cornwallis expressed a hope that 'this first success will cement our party', noting that 'it is still composed of loose materials, much more intent upon the personal than the public question'.[22] There was a nonchalant acceptance that the government numbers were artificial, neither committed nor enthusiastic about the propriety and necessity of the union. The lord lieutenant was to note cynically, at one point, that half of the government majority would be as delighted as the opposition if the union were defeated.[23]

The melodramatic return of Grattan proved to be of questionable value to the opposition. He was not highly regarded by those who loftily defined themselves as 'loyal anti-unionists', those MPs who were normally supporters of the government. The association with someone they despised as a traitor proved uncomfortable.[24] John Beresford was hugely optimistic about the return. The country gentlemen considered the prodigal member to be 'a rebel', and the speech of 16 January, in which he had argued against the union in terms of the damage it would do to the catholics, had enraged them. While this would not change many votes, the members being committed, it had dampened their enthusiasm for opposition. Beresford promised that little violence would subsequently be spoken against the measure, except from a minority in parliament and the capital city.[25] Where the opposition did gain through the return of Grattan was with respect to the catholics. Although the 'respectable part of the community' believed him to be much 'degraded' he retained great influence over the Roman Catholics of Dublin. They were reported to be feeling alienated from the British government, detesting the imperial connection.[26] This was to prove a significant disadvantage for the government.

Further opposition discomfort, resulting from the return, was caused by the sale of green ribands with the inscription 'Grattan and Foster, the friends of the people'. The speaker was infuriated by the association and it was said that he was 'frantic'.[27] Faced with the might of government arrayed against him, and still feeling an affinity for its benches, he was soon reported to be 'lost and disconcerted'.[28] He again insisted that had he been treated well he would not have opposed so strenuously but that his humiliations at the hands of government had obliged him to use his 'utmost exertions'.[29] The speaker advised the opposition against 'new allies', meaning Grattan and the catholics, and also the danger of 'violence and outrage', which he warned would lose them many supporters, including himself.[30] The moderate language employed afterwards was gladly received by the castle, and Cooke hoped that once the measure of union passed Foster would not attempt to impede it further, and might even be persuaded to facilitate it.

While ostensibly discouraging faction, Downshire directed his energies into opposing the union. He insisted that no offence would be caused to Great Britain by the opposition, a pledge which Cooke dismissed as 'nonsense', but helpful nonetheless.[31] There were still hopes that Downshire could be deflected from the course he had adopted. Cooke 'talked much' with him but to no avail. All that was achieved was a promise that the opposition would avoid 'faction and tumult' and that Downshire would separate from it if the violent language continued. It was believed that a message was sent to the opposition leaders that if the government or Great Britain were attacked

Downshire would leave it, restricting the opposition's freedom to manoeuvre even further.[32]

A meeting was held on 18 January at the house of the young Lord Charlemont, the son of the late volunteer leader, to discuss the anti-union strategy. This was attended by a large number, including Downshire and Foster, and discussed two items. The first was the chief secretary's allegation that they were a faction, an offensive charge they believed slandered them. The second matter was Castlereagh's claim that eighteen or nineteen counties had declared in favour of the union. It was decided that until parliament resumed on 3 February petitions and county meetings should be employed against the union. To placate Downshire the anti-unionist addresses were to be moderate and profess their attachment to the British connection.[33]

In line with this a printed circular letter was distributed on 20 January signed by Downshire, Charlemont and William Ponsonby urging individuals in the counties to secure petitions against the union.[34] The three figures had been chosen carefully. Each represented a different section of the anti-union opposition. Downshire was traditionally a supporter of government and represented the protestant element. Charlemont represented the spirit of his father and was a throwback to a previous time when the volunteers were at their peak and the country had been successfully appealed to. William Ponsonby was the elder brother of George and represented the liberal section that was sympathetic to the catholic claims.[35]

This had effect, greater than Cornwallis anticipated. After the initial show of strength in parliament the government now faced public opinion being mustered against the measure. It was estimated that fifteen counties were now in favour of union: Antrim, Clare, Cork, Derry, Donegal, Galway, Kerry, Leitrim, Limerick, Longford, Mayo, Tipperary, Waterford, Westmeath and Wexford. Nine were divided: Kilkenny, Cavan, Armagh, Queen's County, Sligo, King's County, Meath, Tyrone and Roscommon. Eight counties were opposed to the union: Kildare, Fermanagh, Louth, Monaghan, Wicklow, Down, Carlow and, the most important of all perhaps, Dublin.[36] At the same time inflammatory handbills urged the yeomanry to do whatever was necessary to defend the constitution.[37] The young catholic barrister Daniel O'Connell made a prominent speech at this time in which he claimed that the Roman Catholics would never support the union. He insisted that the people would never sell their country for any price. In a passionate oration O'Connell confidently asserted if an Irish catholic was offered a union

> or the re-enactment of the penal code in all its pristine horrors, that he would prefer without hesitation the latter as the lesser and most sufferable evil; that he would rather confide in the justice of his brethren, the protestants of Ireland, who have already liberated him, than lay his country at the feet of foreigners.[38]

The castle had been defeated once before and would not risk having its overconfidence exposed a second time. Cooke accepted that 'a severe struggle' still lay ahead. The mood of the country was vital, and 'all depends on the tone of the country; if we can keep that right I believe all may do well'.[39] The mood of the people was by no means tranquil. Riots broke out in Dublin and Cornwallis requested military reinforcements.[40] Of the sixty-two who had not voted in the debate, Cooke estimated that fifty would support the government and was confident that 'if no impression of consequence can be made on the country, all is over'.[41] Despite the success of the government in the 16 January division Cornwallis refused to become too sanguine. He suspected, however, that the cabinet would foolishly think the struggle was at an end. Like Cooke, the lord lieutenant was alert to the role public opinion could still play before victory was assured. The belief that a commons majority was sufficient for success was a fallacy, and he feared that the ministers would mistakenly believe that 'a measure so deeply affecting the interests and passions of the nation can be carried against the voice of the people'.[42] Buoyed by the initial parliamentary success Cornwallis delivered a scathing rebuke to Portland. In an astonishing outburst, which revealed the extent of his bitterness, the lord lieutenant assured the home secretary that he would not be idle in his work,

> but my cabinet friends have shown so total a want of confidence in me, and have so eagerly seized every opportunity of reprobating my conduct in severe, if not in acrimonious terms, that I am almost afraid to appeal to the general goodwill of the people at large, which I have the vanity to think I possess.[43]

The opposition tactics proved moderately successful. Cornwallis was forced to accept privately, at the close of the month, that 'the clamour against the union is increasing rapidly, and every degree of violence is to be expected'.[44] The lord lieutenant regretted that he had not been able to 'obtain the smallest degree of favour' from the catholics, who had been more and more alienated by the 'imprudent speeches and the abuse cast upon them by our friends'.[45] In addition to the anti-union petitions, the castle faced the opposition fund that had been established to buy borough seats, with rumours reaching it that £100,000 had been subscribed for the purpose.[46]

Castlereagh's influenza delayed the resumption of parliament for two days. Then, on 5 February, 278 of the 300 MPs attended to hear a message from the lord lieutenant present the union before the house. A partially recovered chief secretary explained the general principle of the union and proposed eight articles as its foundation. At all times the union was presented as a treaty, and therefore its terms were referred to as articles, rather than mere clauses. The first article established that on 1 January 1801 Great Britain and Ireland would be joined in one kingdom with the title the United Kingdom of Great Britain and Ireland. The second concerned the unchanged succession of the imperial crown. The third united the two countries' parliaments into one legislature. The fourth related to Irish representation in the house of lords of the united parliament. The fifth concerned religion and made the continuance of the united protestant episcopal church a fundamental article of the union. The sixth dealt with commerce and gave Ireland what was considered, by Britain, to be a fair share of commercial privileges. The seventh article made each country individually responsible for whatever national debt had occurred up to then, the national expense for the next twenty years being divided between Britain and Ireland in the ratio of 15:2. The eighth article established that the laws and courts of both kingdoms would remain as established, subject to whatever alterations the united parliament saw fit.[47]

'Everyone knows the ignorance of the lower classes in this kingdom.'[48] Castlereagh was uncompromising in his defence of the union and accused the opposition of attempting to mislead the people. He also defended the catholic clergy from the charge that its members had been bribed to support the union: he insisted that the allegation was a smear to lower them in the eyes of their followers. That government was engaged in deceit the chief secretary strenuously denied. The union would not be 'a measure of bribery' and Castlereagh ingeniously argued that

> if bribery and public advantage are synonymous I must readily admit that it is a measure of the most comprehensive bribery that was ever produced: it bribes the whole community of Ireland by offering to embrace them within the pale of the British constitution.[49]

But any illegality was dismissed: 'there are bribes I am not prepared to offer'. Borough compensation was defended, although the delicacy of the subject is highlighted by the fact that this portion of the speech was deleted from one version published by government.[50] The principle of compensation, argued Castlereagh, was 'consonant to the principles of private justice'. The chief secretary ended his oration with the powerful and eloquent assertion that

> if this great work shall be effected and if at any future day the enemies of Great Britain and mankind shall again be let loose upon the social world, I doubt not that Ireland will be in such a situation of unanimity and power as to bear a conspicuous part with Great Britain in the glorious task of again restoring the liberties of Europe.[51]

Another furious debate raged as a motion was made that the house should resolve into a committee and take into consideration the lord lieutenant's message. George Ogle spoke against the union arguing that it would lead to catholic emancipation and reform. Another MP, the larger-than-life John Egan, declared that 'it would be the glory of my life to spill the last drop of blood I have in my veins' to oppose the union.[52] George Ponsonby argued that the effects of the union were clear to see: 'your peerage is to be disgraced, your commons purchased, no additional advantage in commerce'.[53] Henry Grattan again accused Castlereagh of packing the parliament and overturning the liberties of the people.[54] His flowing speech was marked by the usual melodramatic rhetoric. The decision the members had to make was no less than one of

> whether your children shall go to your graves saying a venal, a military court, attacked the liberties of the Irish, and here lies the bones of the honourable

dead men who saved their country. Such an epitaph is a nobility which the king cannot give his slaves; it is a glory which the crown cannot give the king.[55]

Troops were stationed outside the parliament in case of any disturbances.[56] As the debate became more heated Castlereagh threatened to move the proceedings to Cork if there were any serious interruptions. The division revealed a majority for the government of 158 to 115.[57] This fell 21 shorter than Castlereagh had predicted.[58] Twelve supporters of the union deserted the government benches. One, Thomas 'Buck' Whaley, was suspected of having been bought during the debate itself.[59] When Cooke found out he was reported to have offered him, unsuccessfully, 'a *carte blanche*'.[60] Bolton finds evidence for six members, who had supported the government three weeks previously, defecting to the anti-unionist side.[61] Of the twenty-two absentees, four were friendly to the measure but had yet to take their seats: the members for Kerry, Tuam, Maryborough and Donegal.[62] A further MP, being brought in by Lord Llandaff to support the measure, was doubtful. Of the seventeen others, many, it seemed, preferred to remain aloof until their terms were negotiated, by either side it seems.[63] The close of the debate saw 'a little tendency to mobbing' that Cooke dismissed as being of no 'real consequence'.[64]

'Our situation is critical.'[65] Despite some success in parliament the pressure intensified for the castle as it faced the threat of its majority being eroded. The tactics of the opposition created much apprehension. Cornwallis particularly dreaded the use of the 'inflammatory handbills', remembering his experiences in America a couple of decades earlier.[66] Cooke reluctantly accepted that 'the activity, the intimidation, the subscription purse of the enemy has been employed with effect'.[67] The use of 'money and terror' made him fear that there could be further defections from the government camp; 'certainly all our friends are not hearty'.[68] It was a pessimism shared by Castlereagh, who discovered that the opposition was offering as much as £5,000 for a vote against the union. Such an inducement was a potent one and there were many 'timid and lukewarm friends', some of whom were very 'likely to yield to this temptation'.[69]

With the success of the union in the balance, and defeat something that could not be contemplated, the king's ministers moved swiftly. Portland wrote to Cornwallis to stiffen his resolve and persuade him that victory was not to be hazarded at this late stage. Everything was to be wagered in the pursuit of success. The home secretary tacitly informed the lord lieutenant that there were to be no limits or restrictions, reminding him that he 'has been repeatedly and uniformly authorised to give generously to those who might be disposed to support the union'.[70] Nothing was to be reserved in persuading deserters to return, fortifying the resolve of waverers, and maintaining the fickle majority.

In the house of lords the presentation of the union was led by Lord Chancellor Clare. He spoke for four hours on the measure using history to validate his argument, but although the speech had force and 'great effect' it was feared that it was 'rather too anti–catholic'.[71] Clare attacked the bribery policy of the opposition, which was a touch hypocritical, and when Charlemont, 'a foolish boy not removed half a degree from idiocy',[72] asserted that he had never offered a bribe the lord chancellor retorted that he had not claimed such a thing, merely that Charlemont was aware of such transactions. The refutation of these allegations was headed by Downshire, who denied the existence of a fund to promote opposition and proclaimed his loyalty to the king and his government.[73] The division saw a victory of seventy-five for the union, twenty-six against.[74]

While success in the lords had been confidently expected, the majority in the commons was more precarious. The opposition tactics were far-reaching, and morale amongst its members increased when they began to believe that Cornwallis could be driven out of office. The country was regarded as having been won by the unionists, Dublin and the commons presenting the only challenge to the measure. There was 'so much unsteadiness, so much rascality', that Cooke could not guarantee victory.[75] As for the leaders of the opposition, Cooke believed Foster's stance stemmed from hostility towards the administration that had set him aside. Added to this was the speaker's pride, smarting not only against his treatment, but because 'he cannot bear that the union should be carried without him'.[76] Downshire, he believed, had been motivated by pique, Parnell by timidity. The former chancellor of the exchequer, Cooke claimed, was disgusted with opposition but too far pledged to withdraw.[77]

The castle hit upon an inventive scheme to maintain its supporters' morale. When parliament was sitting a lavish dinner was held every day for twenty or thirty members, who could then be whisked to the debating chamber in the event of any emergency. This was not the only advantage, for 'wit and puns began to accompany the bottle'.[78] Cooke, unsurprisingly, was the supervisor of this merriment; and as the alcohol flowed freely, 'with significant nods, and smirking innuendoes [he] began to circulate his official rewards to the company' until eventually, as Barrington memorably described, 'every man became in a prosperous state of official pregnancy'.[79] Afterwards each member left 'fully resolved to eat, drink, speak, and *fight* for Lord Castlereagh' and Barrington was to concede that they showed more personal spirit than the opposition. Confidence was returning to the government benches, as it became clear that their numbers were secure and were not likely to be challenged significantly.

In February the commons debated the merits of the union while procedural motions were being made to form the house into a full committee to discuss the measure. The opposition made attempts to adjourn the house, with some members claiming not to have received the proper papers. This tactic was defeated by 157 to 110 after an earlier attempt had been lost by 123 to 98.[80] Cooke was delighted and noted with pleasure that the government's object had been achieved, namely to show that its support was 'firm and increasing'. Castlereagh then allowed an adjournment to take place, to avoid alienating some undecided members, and allow government an opportunity to conciliate and win over doubters. The compromise involved the opposition agreeing that no further attempt would be made to avoid a discussion of the union question.[81]

Further intrigues against the union were also foiled. Unanimity on a short money bill was not forthcoming. With the delaying tactics proving a failure, and attempts to excite popular resistance defeated, the union appeared secure. Cooke was confident that Dublin would be safe, and free of insurrection.[82] Nevertheless the changeable nature of Irish politics was not lost on the under-secretary.[83] Swift action by the lord lieutenant to reassert the authority of the government contributed to this optimism. Downshire, in a risky attempt to utilise every asset at his disposal, sent an anti-union petition to his militia stationed at Carlow. The 'perennially indiscreet' Jonah Barrington claimed that the regiment was 'determined not to volunteer for service but to remain within the kingdom to resist the measure'.[84] Cornwallis believed that Downshire's behaviour was 'so very criminal'[85] and quickly dispatched his confidant Major-General Sir Charles Ross to investigate the matter in Carlow. His report was not favourable to Downshire.[86] The threat of the militia and orange order forming a powerful conjunction against the union was not one that the lord lieutenant would tolerate. If Downshire was to use every weapon at his disposal then Cornwallis had no qualms in using all of his. Cornwallis had never had any regard for Downshire, considering him 'a proud, ill-tempered fellow',[87] and this time was determined to make an example of him. The king gave his consent on 12 February. Downshire was removed from his command of the militia, from the governorship of the county and from the office of registrar in the court of chancery, and was also stripped of his rank as a privy councillor.[88]

It was a defining moment in the struggle for authority. The lord lieutenant confidently declared that 'by this act of vigour I have saved the country and carried the union'.[89] It was another rare example of where Cornwallis's uncompromising military style of leadership was successful; he was perfectly suited to disciplining unacceptable dissent. The action won approval from the entire spectrum of government supporters. Castlereagh was, of course, delighted by his enemy's humiliation, and even in May it was reported that he was 'in the highest glee on account of his victory in Down'.[90] Cooke applauded the lord lieutenant's 'decisive and prompt conduct' that had raised the spirits of the friends of government. The action, he believed, had been unavoidable, anything less and the administration might have been fatally damaged. Control of the militia and yeomanry was at stake and 'it was considered as the trial of the pulse and nerves of government'.[91] Portland felt Downshire had only himself to blame for his fall and was pleased that 'the dignity of government' had been maintained and its 'character preserved'.[92] Another of Cornwallis's regular critics, Buckingham, shared in the consensus. He had heard that Downshire had insisted on the regiment signing the petition and only regretted that the government had not gone further.[93] Lord

Carysfort was likewise glad that the contagion had been stopped.[94] Clare agreed with the punishment of Downshire but regretted that it had been necessary. He retained sympathy for the man and was saddened to see him subject to 'public degradation, and forfeit all his credit in a momentary fit of passion and folly'.[95] The incident shattered Downshire, who never quite recovered, politically or psychologically, from the blow. Before the month was over he was reported to be 'in low spirits, and quiet, and in no state of exertion'.[96] He roused himself, for the penultimate time, against the union in April 1800, attempting to secure a county petition against the union, but a successful counter-petition by Castlereagh demoralised his adversary even further and Downshire retired to England, where he had not long to live.[97]

On 18 February a lengthy debate, estimated to have lasted between eighteen and twenty hours, culminated in a victory for the government of 161 to 115. The actual vote was on relieving the speaker from the chair; the first proposition, 'that a legislative union of the two kingdoms was desirable', passed without division.[98] The debate was as violent as previous ones and drew blood early on, in a confrontation between Grattan and Isaac Corry. Grattan accused his former friend of misrepresenting and slandering him. The chancellor of the exchequer, in response, delivered a spirited indictment of Grattan's conduct during 'the rebellion from which he fled'. Corry questioned Grattan's right to sit in parliament and called on him to justify his conduct to the world: 'the honourable gentleman is charged with being the associate of traitors; has he denied it? He does not deny it.'[99] Grattan was furious and denounced the charge: 'it was false, it was utterly, totally, and meanly false'. He was unrelenting in his attack on Corry:

> he ought not to have come down to the house with falsities. He would not treat the honourable gentleman like a ruffian. He would not tell the honourable gentleman that he treated him like a coward because the honourable gentleman was a member of parliament.[100]

Grattan accused the 'ministers of the union' of being 'traitors to the constitution' and included another, by now tiresome, reference to laying 'the remains of his constitution on the floor of the house for the welfare of his native land'.[101] Cooke criticised the exchange for being 'abominably personal'[102] and Cornwallis regretted that Corry had 'unwisely' made his strong attack on Grattan.[103] It became a matter of honour for Grattan and Corry, and they resolved to finish it the conventional way. In the duel Corry missed completely, but Grattan's aim was steadier and he hit his opponent in the arm. The seconds then made them fire a second time and Grattan was to claim triumphantly that 'I do not know whether Corry fired at me a second time, I fired above him.'[104] The affair satisfied Grattan no end and he was to boast that he could have killed Corry had he so wanted. After the duel Corry 'gave me his bloody hand; we had formerly been friends'.[105] Beresford did not think the duel of any significance, believing that Grattan had given enough evidence of his treason when he had read extracts from evidence on the rebellion.[106]

Cooke was not so sure. While he shared Beresford's view that Grattan's defence had only damned him further he saw distinct advantages arising from the duel. The wounding of the chancellor gave the victor 'some *éclat*' in a country that was fond of duelling.[107] A few weeks after the incident Cooke was to note with some cynicism the advantages a successful duel had for someone in Ireland.[108]

Back in the debating chamber the speaker attempted to return members' attentions to the union. Foster accused Castlereagh of incredible duplicity, for arguing in 1799 that Ireland needed a union because she was rich and prosperous, and in 1800 saying that the country needed a union because she was poor.[109] The term 'union' was a misnomer, it was 'a word to deceive':[110]

> it is called a union, but it doesn't deserve the name; it is anything you please but what it professes to be; a real union is a full and entire union of the two nations — this is a union of the two parliaments only — there can be no union of the nations while distinct interests exist.[111]

Foster attacked Castlereagh for leaving the section on borough compensation earlier in the month out of the printed version of the speech. Compensation was 'a most monstrous unconstitutional offer', and he challenged the chief secretary to admit publicly that the government considered boroughs to be private property.[112] The government benches were noticeably boisterous during the debate. Towards the end the jeering of one member, James Moore O'Donel, caused him to lose his temper and shout 'is this decency? Is this order? I see a set of men who often cry order and practise disorder; who talk of decorum without knowing how to practise it.'[113]

Whenever the tension became unbearable the castle sought comfort in the secret service fund. On 27 February Castlereagh wrote to John King warning that there was little chance of converting opposition members as they were 'steady to each other'.[114] Money was required, however, to keep the union supporters happy. He warned the paymaster that even a few defections could be disastrous. The message was blunt:

> we require *your assistance* and you *must* be prepared to enable us to fulfil the expectations which it was impossible to avoid creating at the moment of difficulty. You may be sure we have rather erred on the side of moderation.[115]

The castle became even more desperate as its resources were strained even further. Cooke quickly followed up the request to King asking him when it would be possible to send the money promised: 'it is absolutely essential for our demands increase. Pray let Lord Castlereagh know without delay what can be done by you.'[116] The secret service fund was by no means exhausted and £10,000 was promptly dispatched to Ireland. Castlereagh wrote a receipt for this, and the previous sum, on 12 March promising to be accountable for the money.[117]

The increasing government majorities saw the opposition shortly accept that the battle in the commons was lost. Changing tactics, George Ponsonby made an attempt in parliament on 4 March to direct the emphasis towards the country. A motion was moved concerning the sense of the nation. He reasoned that as the king had appealed to that very same notion it was legitimate for the opposition to lay before him all the anti-union petitions to demonstrate that the sense of the people was against the measure. The validity of this new tactic was challenged by Castlereagh, who moved for an adjournment. At half past six in the morning of 5 March the house divided 155 for adjournment and 107 against. The result was a decisive victory for the government, both in terms of recognising its parliamentary strength, and more importantly in terms of morale. The opposition had placed a heavy emphasis on the question and as Cooke recorded 'they made no impression'.[118] Nevertheless when the union resolutions went before the British commons the following month Castlereagh warned the cabinet about the risk of the petitions being used against government and advised that Pitt be briefed about the declarations on both sides.[119] The accuracy of petitions was doubtful. Cornwallis maintained that any man of influence could obtain 'addresses and resolutions on either side';[120] as propaganda, however, they were invaluable. Reports that the opposition fund against the union was running low provided an additional boost, coming so soon after the government fund had been replenished. Cooke was confident that if the public mood could be kept calm then success was assured.[121]

At times it was enough of a challenge keeping the house of commons calm. A steady stream of rumour and speculation ensured that tensions continued to rise, on all sides, with sometimes ludicrous consequences. On 11 March one of the new members, Charles Ball, a vehement opponent of union, entertained his fellow MPs prior to a debate by teasing the pro-union members about possible assassination attempts. His comments produced much mirth in the crowded coffee house as Ball playfully asserted that it required only a few good patriots to save the country: 'it could be easily done by a few hand-grenades or shells thrown from the gallery when you ministerial gentlemen are locked up for a division'. For the benefit of those who were uncomfortable with this banter, Ball concluded with a mock-serious prediction that such a plan was being hatched. Greatly entertained, the house later met and moved to commit the rebellion bill. Foster vacated the chair, but before Cooke could take his place the proceedings were interrupted by a loud cry from the crammed public gallery: 'and now the greatest assassin takes the chair'. In a instant the speculative ramblings of Ball assumed the status of a terrifying prophecy. There was immediate panic in the chamber with members expecting to see shells and hand-grenades fall at any moment; the hysteria translated to the gallery, and in the confusion a number of hats fell over, and were assumed to be bombs by those below. The crisis ended almost as soon as it had begun, however, when it was announced that the interloper had been apprehended in the gallery. Calm was restored, and the pseudo-assassin was brought before the chamber. He was revealed to be a Thomas Sinclair, a struggling barrister, who had been imbued with a moral fervour to speak out against the union after imbibing some 'excellent wine'. Despite being pinioned to the ground, he launched into a furious attack against the measure, as some members, their courage returning, took the opportunity to kick him. The house committed Sinclair to Newgate prison, where he languished for two months.[122]

Occasionally, the tension was dispelled by some of the characters in the commons. A number of anecdotally interesting speeches were made during the union, some of which may or may not be apocryphal. For example, the source of much entertainment in parliament was the notorious blunderer Sir Boyle Roche. According to legend, he had once famously asked, 'Why we should put ourselves out of our way to do anything for *posterity*, for what has *posterity* ever done for us?'[123] An unquestioning supporter of the government, and thus a dedicated proponent of the union, during one debate he caused uproar when he defended 'this most excellent union' by employing his biblical knowledge: 'Sir, there is no Levitical decree between nations, and on this occasion I can see neither sin nor shame in *marrying our own sister*.'[124] Roche's counterpart on the opposition benches was the well-meaning but somewhat ridiculous barrister John Egan, a 'huge, coarse-looking, red-faced, boisterous fellow'.[125] Although he was a skilled duellist, Egan's propensity to self-destruct when speaking made him an easy target for abuse, and he had suffered reputation-damaging humiliations at the hands of Grattan and Barrington. The latter had once provoked Egan's fury by laughing out loud during a speech in which he kept repeating the word 'obdurate'. Furious, Egan enquired if 'the gentleman laughs at my happening to pronounce the word *obdurate* wrong'? Barrington's lethal riposte was that he was only laughing because his colleague had happened to pronounce the word correctly.[126] Incompetent with money, Egan depended financially on the judicial office he had received a few years previously, the chairmanship of Kilmainham. According to nationalist lore Egan was threatened with dismissal unless he supported the union, and during one key debate was seen to be in a state of great anxiety as he weighed up the consequences of his actions. Finally, he rose to his feet and with a thunderous shout declared 'Ireland — Ireland forever! And damn Kilmainham.' Although not deprived of his office he died in poverty in 1810.

Although parliament remained the stage for the most dramatic action, the serious work on the union was still being carried out behind the scenes. It is interesting to note at this time the channel of communication between Cooke and Grenville, used perhaps to supplement the strained line between Cornwallis and Portland. The relationship between lord lieutenant and home secretary was deteriorating rapidly, their letters never missing an opportunity to patronise or disparage the other. Cornwallis was bitter at the 'unkind and mortifying manner in which I have been treated' and resented the knowledge that Pitt had, on occasion, forced the home secretary to modify his criticisms.[127] The lord lieutenant's relationship with Cooke had never been an easy one either, although before the end of the year Cornwallis was to make some con-ciliatory noises. It is also likely that the viceroy was cognisant of Grenville's criticisms. Such an awareness contributed more than any difference of policy to his private outburst in July that Grenville was 'a most dangerous minister', something he had 'long thought', and someone with whom he would rather not share membership of a cabinet.[128]

The constant sniping at Cornwallis did not let up even as the union entered the final stages of completion. Too many people had developed personal grudges against the viceroy and he was not a popular person amongst all of the king's ministers. His predecessor, Camden, regularly encouraged his nephew to join in the criticism, something Castlereagh honourably declined. Cornwallis's suspicions of the yeomanry, a body formed by Camden, hurt, and the cabinet was reported to be in agreement, contrary to Cornwallis, that severe measures against the rebels had been necessary.[129] Only Dundas, it seems, defended the viceroy. Some praise was forthcoming from the military. Colonel Maitland strongly approved of the viceroy's middle line between the extremes of party violence. For him, at least, Cornwallis had acted with common sense and discretion in a difficult situation and the colonel concluded that if his plans were adopted then Ireland would be a jewel; if not, a thorn.[130] Clare was another who praised the lord lieutenant's handling of the union and although he now admitted that he had initially thought him incapable of securing the measure, conceded in April 1800 that he was 'quite satisfied that he has on the whole been the man, of all others, best selected for the crisis'.[131]

The union gathered in momentum as it waited to be debated in committee in March. Foster continued making some noise on commercial points but the remainder of the opposition waited for a popular clamour in the country against the union, reserving themselves for the debate on borough compensation.[132] Cornwallis accepted that the principle of compensation was 'the most exceptionable in the present arrangement'.[133] George Ponsonby gave notice of a motion concerning the issue, and 13 March was set aside for the discussion. This never took place. Ponsonby claimed to be indisposed and Bolton accepts the castle's interpretation that the borough owners had refused their support, necessitating Ponsonby's withdrawal.[134] His place was taken by Parnell, who moved an address to the king calling on him to dissolve the parliament and install a new one before a legislative union would take place.[135] The debate lasted until near four o'clock the following morning and ended with a victory for the government of 150 to 104.[136] During the debate William Saurin, one of the lawyer members of parliament, made an attempt to establish the doctrine of the will of the people, justifying resistance to a law passed contrary to the nation. Castlereagh led the attack on this dangerous principle, which he likened to a jacobin game, and, as Cooke reported, 'he said these doctrines went to excite and justify rebellion'.[137] Grattan refused to get involved in the discussion, which Cooke took as a sign that he was keeping 'strictly constitutional'.[138]

The house of lords posed a threat to the measure in the months of February and March in a rare show of resistance to the will of government. Bolton records the nature of the dispute, noting that the noblemen reacted strongly to the king retaining control over the creation of Irish peerages.[139] A solution was reached only through giving the crown the right of creating one peerage for every three extinctions, until the number was reduced to a figure of one hundred.[140] This protected the Irish peerage from an unacceptably large rise in their numbers and helps explain the increased interest in peerages amongst country gentlemen in 1800.[141]

The full commons met in committee from 14 March with regular reports delivered on the progress to the house. A debate on the commercial points, one of the final articles of union, occurred on that day. Grattan spoke on the matter in a speech of one and three-quarter hours that was reported to have been 'very dull and tedious'.[142] Cooke agreed that the speech was not impressive but wryly noted that the quality did not matter much; Grattan would 'print *editio auctior et emendiatior*'.[143] The debate was noteworthy for the confrontation between Castlereagh and the opponents of the union. Hyde, overly fond of his subject, ignores the affair, which began when, after handling the financial points soundly, the chief secretary launched an intemperate attack on the speaker and those he had allied with. Foster in response affected an ironic style:

> suppose an historian at a future day writing an account of these times and that not having our information he were to judge from appearances only, he might say the sentiments of the nation revolted at the measure and the commons rejected it; the minister however persevered.[144]

This historian, according to the speaker, would see only that forty members had changed sides during two months and speculate that disturbing methods had been used 'as to convert the minority into a majority; that the old rule *divide and conquer* was thoroughly put into practice; that even religion was not held too sacred to be made an engine of'. Protestant had been turned against catholic, catholic against protestant, 'parliament against the people, and the people against parliament'; when Castlereagh had been beaten in the parliament he turned to the other, and when frustrated by people, he returned to the parliament. All the time Ireland was 'covered with unusual military force, far beyond anything ever known', while office holders who opposed were dismissed; all aimed at intimidating the will of parliament and the people, 'such might be the account of the historian, who could judge from appearances only; we who live at the time would be sure to state it otherwise, were we to criticise it'. Grattan was equally scathing and quoted papers of the young Castlereagh (then Robert Stewart) during his membership of the northern whig club. Beresford reported that this made Castlereagh appear 'very foolish'. The more sympathetic Cooke makes no mention of any embarrassment to his friend.[145] The commercial article passed nonetheless and it was decided to bring the resolutions to the house on the Friday.[146]

On 21 March the committee presented a report on the twenty-five resolutions, the union articles, to the commons.[147] Each resolution was read twice before being carried. An amendment was made to the eighteenth resolution dealing with religion where it was made 'an essential and fundamental condition of the treaty of union' that the protestant church would be preserved for ever.[148] The first twenty-four resolutions passed without difficulty, but the last one was recommitted for a further consideration. This was the article that concerned the commercial details of duties and bounties. The committee of the whole house was reconvened to discuss this further. After some debate this resolution was put before the whole house a second time, and carried. The chief secretary was instructed to take the resolutions to the house of lords for their agreement.

By late March Lord Grenville was confident that the union was secure and the labours were drawing to a close. It remained to present the resolutions before the British commons and this was not expected to prove too troublesome, 'speeches and declamations of course, but that artillery has lost its effect'.[149] Praise was forthcoming for Castlereagh, who received letters of congratulation from Camden and Portland, sentiments that he was assured 'conveyed the unanimous opinion of all those who have witnessed the zeal, ability, and spirit' with which he had handled the session. Pitt was also reported to be perfectly satisfied with the chief secretary.[150] The role of the lord lieutenant went largely unnoticed. Cornwallis, however, generously attributed much of the success to 'the character, integrity, and talents of Lord Castlereagh'.[151] The chief secretary was so highly regarded that his presence was requested in London to assist with the resolutions but the lord lieutenant did not feel he could spare him and Cooke was sent in his place.[152]

Despite the consistent government successes there was a pervading sense of unease within the castle. Cornwallis despaired that 'half of our majority would be at least as much delighted as any of our opponents if the measure could be defeated'.[153] Nerves were steadied by the regular supply of covert financial aid from England. A further £5,000 was sent in April, and a similar amount early the following month.[154] This brought the union secret service expenditure to £30,850, a considerable amount considering the patronage that was also at the government's disposal. Henry Grattan junior, again many years after the events, claimed that Castlereagh, 'by means of Mr Cooke', purchased as many anti-union pamphlets, speeches and manuscripts as possible, before taking them to the castle for burning.[155] Cooke was responsible for directing the Irish secret service money,[156] which adds a certain amount of verisimilitude to the allegation, the expenditure being a credible use for some of the money.

There was little trouble passing the union bill in the British commons in April. Bolton pinpoints the main thrust of opposition as coming from two quarters: the whig opposition and the English woollen manufacturers. Both were easily defeated, the former by 133 to 58.[157] One aspect which Bolton ignores is Charles Grey's attempt to make a debate on the catholic question public at this time. He tried to force Pitt into making a declaration that a successful union would require catholic relief to follow. Pitt avoided the matter. Cooke, in England from March, oversaw the final stages of the union there, and made regular reports on the situation for the next six months. He noted that Dundas was not as circumspect as Pitt on the catholic question. The secretary of state for war was prepared to make comparisons with the Scottish union of 1707, which had paved the way for repeal of certain religious laws, and suggested that the Irish union might similarly pave the way for certain things that the Irish parliament would never have passed.[158]

Pitt's speech of 21 April was a notable one. The speech of 31 January 1799 had followed the rejection of the union in the Irish parliament and had been an attempt to remain resolute in the face of defeat. The debate in April 1800 followed success in Ireland and allowed Pitt to provide a firm overview of what 'the important and complicated question' of union would achieve. It was the summation of a policy that had taken almost two years to secure. The union was as important for Britain as it was for Ireland, for it was

> a measure of great national policy, the object of which is effectually to counter-act the restless machinations of an inveterate enemy, who has uniformly and anxiously endeavoured to effect a separation between two countries whose connection is as necessary for the safety of the one as it is for the prosperity of the other.[159]

The union was the culmination of all that Pitt had wished to achieve for Ireland, stretching back to the commercial propositions — a harmonious relationship between the two islands. Union alone could

> calm the dissensions, allay the animosities, and dissipate the jealousies which have unfortunately existed; as a measure whose object is to communicate to the sister kingdom the skill, the capital, and the industry which have raised this country to such a pitch of opulence; to give her a full participation of the commerce and of the constitution of England; to unite the affections and resources of two powerful nations; and to place under one public will the direction of the whole force of the empire.[160]

The address for union was presented by the British commons to the house of lords on 9 May, receiving the king's approval on 12 May. The required documentation arrived in Ireland the same day and immediately messages were sent to both houses of the Irish parliament. Foster read a message in the commons that informed the members that 'his majesty will feel it the proudest day of his reign when he can consider all his subjects as one people, united under the common protection of the same government'.[161] As the matter returned to Ireland for conclusion the country remained quiet and the opposition recognised that its attempts to mobilise a popular clamour had failed.[162] The commons was also becoming bored by the matter, now that its success was assured. A committee, comprising Castlereagh, Corry and some other members, was formed to discuss the resolutions that had been returned from Great Britain.[163] The representation bill was also moved by Castlereagh and, opposed by opposition figures, the house divided 135 for the government and 58 against. This bill went through the committee stage on 17 May. On 20 May the third reading of the representation bill took place, and the measure was carried.[164]

Opposition to the union in parliament had always been composed of two factions: the regular opponents of government; and those who were opposing government only on the union issue. In the final stages of the union, the two groups began to distance further. Recognising defeat, Foster, it was claimed, no longer maintained his intense feelings of opposition and was 'growing more reconciled' to the union and was even 'in tolerably good humour'.[165] This may have been wishful thinking on Cooke's part for the speaker was to demonstrate his feelings on the union very visibly one last time.

The date chosen to bring forward the union bill was 21 May. On that day a motion was successfully made to bring in the bill, and it was read before the house for the first time.[166] The opposition made its final attempt to prevent it, the leaders remaining aloof but 'the dregs' providing 'much abuse and more nonsense'.[167] The house divided at eleven o'clock at night with a victory for the government of 160 to 100.[168] Cooke considered the matter carried and he predicted that there was little likelihood of further debate on the matter.[169] He was wrong. The second reading of the bill took place on 26 May and Grattan was defeated twice: in an attempt to oppose the committal of the bill by 118 to 73;[170] and in an attempt to postpone the second reading until 1 August by 124 to 87.[171] The debate was notable for a particularly fiery exchange between Grattan and Castlereagh. Grattan ended his oration with a stirring attack on the union. Ireland was not lost by the measure:

> I see her in a swoon but she is not dead. Though in her tomb she lies help-less and motionless, still there is on her lips a spirit of life and on her cheek a glow of beauty . . . While a plank of the vessel sticks together I will not leave her. Let the courtier present his flimsy sail and carry the light barge of his faith with every breath of wind. I will remain anchored here, with fidelity to the fortunes of my country, faithful to her freedom, faithful to her fall.[172]

Castlereagh denounced this speech as 'prophetic treason', and charged Grattan with 'inviting future rebellion by cloaking it with the idea of liberty'.[173] The response was immediate and Castlereagh was subjected to a barrage of abuse from different sources. The editor of Plunket's speeches described the chief secretary as responding to Grattan 'with his natural cold-blooded inso-lence'.[174] Castlereagh's response, as Hyde notes, lost nothing for its coolness.[175] He 'called into question the patriotism of those who took every opportunity of inflaming the public mind against such a settlement'[176] and attacked the 'idle parade of parliamentary spirit which led to nothing and which denied in offensive terms what has never been uttered'.[177] According to Cooke 'Lord Castlereagh's reply raised him much in the estimation of the house.'[178] The confrontation almost ended in another duel. The chief secretary, finally beginning to crack under the constant torrent of abuse in parliament, decided to send Grattan a challenge, but was dissuaded by his friends who 'thought he would let himself down by it'.[179] Apparently, Grattan was similarly infuriated. Henry Brougham was later informed by 'a common friend' that a duel between Grattan and Castlereagh had been prevented only by the revelation that the chief secretary had defended the former's honour during the rebellion.[180] If this story is true (and there is no reason to doubt it) then the debate of 26 May is the most likely time for the episode to have occurred.

On Friday, 30 May it was decided by the house to present the bill before a committee of the whole house.[181] The sixth article, dealing with countervailing duties, passed over the next few days. On 5 June a violent opponent of union, James Moore O'Donel again, proposed an amendment in committee urging the people to resist the measure by force.[182] This was withdrawn, after pressure, but the suggestion is indicative of tempers at the time. The next day an address was brought before the house to be sent to the king accusing the Irish ministers of intimidation and corruption and attacking the principle of borough compensation.[183] It was a lengthy document that denounced 'the corrupt and unconstitutional means which have been used', but it was defeated by 135 to 77.[184] The third reading of the bill, on 7 June, saw increasingly desperate efforts against the measure. A motion by O'Donel to burn the bill outside the house created uproar and the galleries were cleared.[185] Some light relief was provided by Francis Dobbs who, obsessed by the millennium, insisted that Ireland's independence 'was written in the immutable records of heaven'[186] and that the country would be both the birthplace of the Antichrist and the kingdom of the Messiah. This speech was received with 'mingled ridicule and horror'.[187] William Plunket began his last attack on the union in the Irish parliament, and levelled the charge of bribery against Castlereagh. The chief secretary was defended by Sir Richard Butler, who was suspected of having been bought with hard cash a month previously.[188] The opposition made one last attempt to prevent the measure; it proposed a postponement of the third reading until 2 January 1801, one day after the union was to come into effect. This too was defeated. The union bill was then successfully read and passed.[189]

Recognising defeat the opposition refused to witness its final humiliation. R.L. Edgeworth led an opposition secession from the house comprising two-thirds of the anti-union MPs. Grattan was to record that 'finding all useless, we retired with safe consciences but with breaking hearts'.[190] It was left to Foster, as speaker, to witness the carrying of the union without a division. In a moment of high emotion he 'flung the bill upon the table with disgust and sunk into his chair with an exhausted spirit'.[191] Henry Grattan junior was to attack bitterly the 'cold-blooded' Castlereagh for his conduct at this time; as the propositions were being read 'at the moment he had no country, no God but his ambition'.[192] With the passing of the union bill in Ireland Cornwallis rejoiced that 'the great work' was completed.[193] At the same time the final bill was carried in the British commons by 208 to 26 and in the lords by 75 to 7.[194] The act of union received the royal assent on 2 July. The king was finally satisfied at the passing of a measure so important for both countries and the wider empire.[195]

The failure of the opposition to nurture and sustain a popular reaction against the union had proved fatal. It severely damaged its morale and at the same time prevented an extra-parliamentary agitation from slowing the passage of the measure. To secure public opinion against the union the support of the catholics, who represented almost nine-tenths of the population, was imperative. The castle was successful in keeping the country tranquil and thus secured a phalanx of strength for the union that the opposition was never able to counter. As July drew to a close Foster began to realise the full extent of what opposition had cost him. He regretted to Camden that he was 'so much out of the political sphere' that he could write nothing 'but conjecture'.[196] Perhaps the biggest blow of all was seeing the union pass with so little bad feeling in the country. Even Cornwallis seemed a little taken aback by the scale of the quiet, even in the capital.[197] A final attempt by Downshire to cause trouble in July proved a failure, and Cornwallis wrote to Dundas about how much the people were indifferent to the union, particularly in the countryside.[198]

When the British parliament rose on 27 July the king expressed his satisfaction, once more, on the passing of the measure. He had long wished the union and it was one he should 'ever consider as the happiest event' of his reign.[199] It would be of great benefit to both countries and 'establish on the most solid foundation, the strength, prosperity, and power of the whole empire'. The close of the Irish parliament, on 2 August, was a more sombre occasion; it was being prorogued permanently. The session ended with Cornwallis formally concluding the work of the houses. He offered his congratulations to the parliament and to the nation for accomplishing the measure:

> the empire is now, through your exertions, so completely united, and by union so strengthened, that it can bid defiance to all the efforts its enemies can make to weaken it by division, or overturn it by force. Under the protection of divine providence, the United Kingdom of Great Britain and Ireland will, I hope, remain in all future ages the fairest monument of his majesty's reign, already distinguished by so many and such various blessings conferred upon every class and description of his subjects.[200]

For the opponents of union the Irish parliament, enshrined by the constitution of 1782, had represented the Irish nation. It had symbolised an ideal, and it was a humiliating experience to find it so easily dismantled and destroyed. Worse, it had been bought out of existence, willingly sold by people they dismissed as misguided or corrupt. Even with the full resources of the king's government arrayed against them it had never appeared inevitable that the union would pass. Ultimately, their prejudiced refusal to include the Irish catholics within their group doomed their struggle to failure. For the proponents of union how the measure was passed was immaterial, it merely reinforced their belief in the essentially corrupt nature of the Irish parliament. They celebrated their victory and looked with confidence to the inauguration of the united kingdom that promised to solve the problems of Ireland and make her an integral part of the empire. Their ruthless determination had withstood all opposition, and had finally triumphed over the many obstacles in their path. In 1782 Grattan announced, or later claimed he had announced, that Ireland had won her nationhood.[201] To him, and his supporters, in 1800 Ireland appeared to have lost everything. The spirit of Pitt, the spirit of Castlereagh, had prevailed: Ireland was no longer a nation.

'PERJURY AND FRAUD'? HOW THE GOVERNMENT PASSED THE UNION

> And thus they passed the union
> By Pitt and Castlereagh:
> Could Satan send for such an end
> More worthy tools than they?[202]

In 1804 Cornwallis, in a letter to his successor, confessed that the union had 'had few sincere friends'.[203] It became a favourite saying of Henry Grattan that 'there were only seven men on the side of government who were not bribed'.[204] The passing of the union was not as corrupt as legend suggests, or as conventional as some historians claim. Success was achieved by three things: the enlistment of the support of the catholics; the legal, if ethically ambiguous, appeal to private interest through borough compensation and patronage; and finally the extra-legal tactics of the government. The opposition was by no means unaware of what was going on, but neither was it naive about the integrity of the average Irish member, and it engaged in similar practices. All it could offer was money; the castle had an extensive range of inducements and the secret service fund was only one part of what was at its disposal.

The question of how far the castle went to enlist the support of the catholics is contentious. Thomas Bartlett asserts that 'the catholic hierarchy and the catholic lords assumed (and may even have received assurances) that emancipation would follow union'.[205] What is clear is that between January and May 1800 the influence of the Roman Catholics was mobilised without any explicit promises made, but with just enough hinted to persuade them to remain aloof from any attempts against the union. At the end of January Cornwallis noted an increasing clamour against the measure and privately regretted that the catholics were joining the ranks of opposition.[206] By April, Troy, the Roman Catholic archbishop for Dublin, in dispatches to Whitehall, was praising Cornwallis for being 'all benevolence, all liberality'.[207]

Care was taken to exclude Lord Chancellor Clare from what was going on. The earl's prejudices on the subject of catholicism were too intense, and the castle had no qualms in betraying his trust, Clare assuming that the union would preclude catholic emancipation for ever. The trial of a man who had murdered a servant of the lord chancellor in autumn 1799 provided one example of the unpleasant state of his mind. Clare raged that it was clear 'that one strong inducement to the murder was that the poor man was an heretic', this deduction giving rise to a critique of any policy beneficial to the catholics. He asked, despairingly, if the king's ministers would ever 'be taught to feel the insanity of letting loose the popish barbarians of Ireland, lay and ecclesiastical, upon the property and respect of the Irish nation'.[208]

Castlereagh and Cooke appear to have revelled in the complex web of secrecy and deceit that shrouded the union business; certainly they proved quite proficient at it. Cornwallis had less stomach for the business. Only his sense of honour and duty compelled him to persist with the work. The welfare of the catholics engaged much of his thoughts although he recognised the obstacles. He had little time for the prejudices of the ascendancy, and their disagreeable attitude partially explains the contempt in which the lord lieutenant held most of them. The ministers in London were not as committed to emancipation and Cornwallis often regretted their disposition to assume that the 'violent and prejudiced party who call themselves friends to England and to the protestant interest' were the people of Ireland.[209] The viceroy was proud of the way he had attempted to satisfy both groups — catholics and protestants. The latter he had 'treated with management and attention' and he felt, perhaps over-optimistically, that he had been 'fortunate as to retain in a great degree their good will'. As important was that by May 1800 he had 'acquired the confidence of the catholics'.[210] This proved decisive.

'No promise of any kind was given to the catholics,' claimed Castlereagh in February 1801.[211] This appears to be true; certainly no explicit promises were given to them. Some confirmation can be found in a memorandum on the question in Pitt's papers which states that 'no favourable assurances or promise were made to them'.[212] In his letter to Pitt at the dawn of the united kingdom Castlereagh insisted that the Irish government had

> omitted no exertion to call forth the catholics in favour of the union. Their efforts were largely successful and the advantage derived from them was highly useful particularly in depriving the opposition of the means they otherwise would have had, in the southern and western counties, of making an impression on the country members.[213]

Avoiding any direct promises to the catholics was fully consistent with Cornwallis's interpretation of what the union should achieve. He repeatedly argued that it would be impolitic to barter emancipation to pass the union; it was an integral part of the success of the overall measure. Promising one to pass the other would only devalue both, making it seem that emancipation was only conceded reluctantly as part of a bargain, rather than something that was an essential component. Cornwallis genuinely believed that 'a gratuitous concession after the measure [w]as infinitely more consistent with the character of government'.[214]

Without any specific promises being made the support of catholics was obtained. It was done by making it implicitly understood that emancipation would follow union at some point, whatever the castle would later claim. The distinction between explicit and implicit assurances is an important one. Cornwallis in 1801 still believed that the granting of emancipation was a point of honour. He was to admit that his influence over the catholic body had been 'considerable'. The union succeeded as a measure in May but the viceroy refused to accept that his work was concluded. He could not, 'either in consideration of my own character or the public safety, leave them [the catholics] as I found them. I have raised no unauthorised expectations, and have acted throughout with the sanction of the cabinet.'[215] The implication is that Cornwallis raised *authorised* expectations that encouraged the Roman Catholics to acquiesce in the union. Bartlett is partially correct when he says that 'the catholics carried the union', but the rest is not mere detail.[216]

With catholic support for the union the country was relatively calm. Now the castle had only to direct its attentions to parliament. The challenge there was to persuade members to vote for the union, or vacate their seats so that a unionist could succeed them, and then maintain their support. G.C. Bolton shows that of all the members who voted against union in 1799 only twelve changed their vote in 1800. Even this, he notes, was partially offset by the defection of three members from the government numbers.[217] According to this interpretation the union involved persuading those MPs who had not voted in 1799, including the eighty-eight new members who had taken seats since the first attempt, to support the bill in 1800. Borough compensation was an important attraction in diluting opposition to the union, but more was being done than just conversion. The eighty-eight new MPs represented a significant number of instances where the outgoing member was persuaded to vacate his seat so that a unionist or anti-unionist could replace him. This was why the opposition was so critical of government for abusing the place act. By its granting of a nominal office to a member who was intractable but was willing to leave his seat for a reward, the seat thus became vacant and the government was able to return one of its own supporters.

The argument of David Wilkinson that there was 'an irresistible stimulus towards corruption'[218] is hyperbole. The opposition also had a considerable fund of money at its disposal, although it is impossible to prove if it actually reached £100,000 as reported. Bolton is correct in highlighting Cornwallis's distaste for payments being used to change a member's vote, quoting the lord lieutenant on the matter: 'if we had the means . . . and were disposed to make such a vile use of them, we dare not trust the credit of government in the hands of such rascals'.[219] In February 1800 Thomas 'Buck' Whaley was converted from a supporter of union by an opposition sum, considered to be £4,000, and at the same time it was reported that the anti-unionists were offering £5,000 per vote.[220] John Bagwell informed Castlereagh on 5 February that he had been promised £9,000 by the anti-unionists for his vote and those of his two sons, and requested £10,000 to remain loyal.[221] He was quickly disabused of his notions, as the castle refused to get involved in unscrupulous auctions. The Bagwells were notable for changing sides *twice* during the union.[222] This is not to deny the role of government funds to maintain loyalty amongst the ranks of government supporters and buy seats that were available. For example, General Gerard Lake, who was not even Irish, was returned to parliament in 1800, purely to vote for the union.[223]

The crucial point is that the purchase of seats was regarded as a normal procedure, and even Grattan bought his Wicklow seat to return to parliament.

Bolton is correct in stating that buying seats, and by extension borough compensation, was acceptable by the conventions of the time, although this was never said publicly. The principle of compensation was used as a weapon to taunt government, who could never admit that it regarded some seats as property. That said, even opponents of the union were compensated for their loss of income, and had no objections to it. The eventual compensation for the boroughs came to £1,260,000.[224] The four proprietors who benefited most were Downshire, Ely, Shannon and Abercorn, the first, a resolute opponent of union, receiving £52,000 for the seven seats he controlled.[225]

On 9 June Cornwallis sent Portland a list of people 'to whom I have ventured to hold out a reasonable expectation that in consequence of their valuable services in the measure' they would be rewarded with peerages.[226] Some of the sixteen recommendations are worthy of examination. Charles Henry Coote, the proprietor of a number of boroughs, had supported an expensive contest to return a pro-union MP.[227] Sir John Blaquiere, a former chief secretary, had 'exerted himself through the whole business of the union in and out of parliament with great zeal'.[228] Two members, Lodge Morris and Sir James Blackwood, controlled a considerable amount of property and their support for the union was deemed very worthy of reward.[229] Sir Richard Quin had bought himself and 'a friend' into parliament with 'the express determination' of supporting the union.[230] John Bingham in Tuam had supporters of the union consistently returned for the seats he controlled,[231] although Barrington alleged that Bingham first 'offered himself for *sale* to the anti-unionists'.[232]

In London, once the union was passed, the king's ministers attempted to distance themselves from the tactics that had been used in Ireland. For a time it appeared that the government was even going to deny all knowledge of what had occurred. It was a harsh lesson in political reality for the castle, which slowly realised that it was expendable now that its work was done. The first hint of the cabinet's embarrassment at what had been done in its name came during the peerages controversy in June 1800. The incident is highly significant, worthy of greater consideration than the summary treatment that Bolton and Hyde have afforded it.[233] It did more than indicate 'the levity and ineptitude with which the home government was prepared to jeopardise relations with the leading Irish'.[234] The matter shook the castle's confidence in the king's government as it began to suspect that it was to be made a scapegoat for any irregularities that were revealed.

The use of peerages as a bargaining tool had greatly assisted the passage of union. Cornwallis and Castlereagh considered it a mere formality to have their work ratified by the king and the government. They were disabused of this notion on 12 and 13 June when Portland, showing deep unease on the subject, suggested delaying some of those on the lord lieutenant's list until after the first election of peers to the united parliament.[235] Blaquiere's peerage was especially unpopular and the home secretary argued that the extensive peerages promised would 'create serious embarrassments for the administration'. The tone of the communications, on these days, gave particular offence to the viceroy and his chief secretary, who rightly guessed that some of their promises were going to be reneged on.

It was a shattering betrayal. Cornwallis was furious and could not emphasise enough to the home secretary the effect of the incident on his 'personal feelings', adding that he had been placed 'in a more distressing situation than I have yet experienced'.[236] It was more than simply securing representative peerages for Sir John Blaquiere and his like. It struck at the heart of all that Cornwallis and Castlereagh had done. They had engaged in long and difficult work to secure the union, work that they had sometimes considered distasteful but had persevered in for the sake of the empire. They had done so confident in the assurances they had received, the most explicit of which being from the home secretary in December 1798 that

> every one of the king's servants, as well as myself, will consider themselves indissolubly obliged to use their best endeavours to fulfil whatever engagements your excellency may find it necessary, or deem it expedient, to enter into.[237]

Now, it seemed, the cabinet was about to repudiate the work of the Irish government in passing the union. There was more than Cornwallis and Castlereagh's integrity at stake.

The lord lieutenant regretted that he was being forced into a situation where he would have to disappoint those to whom he had pledged his word and the word of the king's government. It was very unpleasant, he wrote to Portland on 17 June, to have to 'declare my engagements to be void, because his majesty's ministers have refused to fulfil them'. Delaying the creation of peerages, he accepted, posed little problem to the empire. It did pose a problem to the honour of his government. 'A treacherous delay' was a 'degradation' for the individuals concerned and one the viceroy was not prepared to accept. His feelings had been so hurt that he did not know how to proceed:

> there was no sacrifice that I should not have been happy to make for the service of the king and country, except that of my honour; the mischief, however, will not end with my disgrace, but the confidence of the English government will be shaken, and the ill humour of our disappointed supporters will greatly retard the benefits which might have been expected from the measure.[238]

He would not remain in Ireland to witness this disgrace. The choice for the ministers in London was between honouring the engagements he had entered into on their behalf or his resignation. The king had been served 'honestly and faithfully', and if he would not

> see the necessity of my having entered into embarrassing engagements, according to the various circumstances which occurred during the long and arduous contest; and if any of them should appear so strongly to merit his disapprobation as to induce him to withhold his consent to their being

carried into effect, he will be pleased to allow me retire from a situation which I could no longer hold with honour to myself, or with any prospect of advantage to his service.[239]

Castlereagh's position was no different. In a letter of 18 June he complained to Camden that Portland's tone in the letters had been felt to be 'peculiarly ungracious' by the lord lieutenant and that it conveyed 'a disapprobation of almost the whole of his engagements'.[240] The chief secretary advised that future communications should be 'less unpleasant' and insisted that it would be a disgraceful treatment of the lord lieutenant if the pledges were not honoured. Disgusted, like the viceroy he threatened his resignation. Neither man could remain:

> the moment it is surmised that we have lost the confidence and support of the English government, we shall have every expectant upon our backs, and it will remain a breach of faith, as injurious to the character of government as to our own, having given an assurance which we were not enabled to fulfil.[241]

Cornwallis had cautioned the cabinet a few months previously to endorse his actions or risk making him a 'man of straw'. At the time he had appeared over-anxious, but now his fears were shown to be justified. Castlereagh accepted that 'in *strictness*' Cornwallis had no grounds for complaint as he had never been specifically authorised to grant peerages. Pitt's silence in the recent weeks, however, had been taken as consent on the point.

It was difficult for the Irish ministers to accept that after sending Cornwallis to Ireland at the close of a distinguished political career, they would hazard his reputation 'on a point of patronage after what he has accomplished'.[242] As Hyde writes, Castlereagh considered the whole matter to have been 'a shabby trick' on the part of the cabinet.[243] They were washing their hands of the entire business, keen to avoid tarnishing what had been achieved and offending public sentiment. The cost, as Castlereagh bitterly noted, was 'disappointing their supporters, and . . . disgracing the Irish government'.[244] The chief secretary warned Cooke that schemes to hide unpleasant details of how the union was passed would fail. In a carefully worded threat, which he knew Cooke would pass on to ministers in England, he insisted that 'it will be no secret what has been promised, and by what means the union was achieved. Disappointment will encourage, not prevent disclosure.' The allegations of the anti-unionists would only be assisted by such behaviour, and he warned that it would help proclaim 'the profligacy of the means by which the measure has been accomplished'.[245]

The difficulties involved in securing a peerage for Blaquiere, Castlereagh admitted, had been recognised from the beginning. However, it had been believed that it would be granted out of respect for Cornwallis. It was not acceptable to turn to the supporters of the union and tell them that it was expected 'from their known attachment to the king's government, that they will waive their claims and be perfectly satisfied with whatever the *popular sentiment*

enables his majesty's ministers to do for them'. Cornwallis had been the person
required 'to buy out and secure to the crown for ever the fee-simple of Irish corruption, which has so long enfeebled the powers of government and endangered
the connection'.[246] The treatment of the ministers was unacceptable.

The cabinet were not the only ones beginning to waver. The king was very
reluctant to grant peerages freely. In addition it had not been recognised that
Cornwallis was authorised to offer such privileges. Camden revealed this in a
letter to Castlereagh and assured him that when the peerages issue was
balanced against the respect the ministers had, both for him and for the lord
lieutenant, all attempts would be made 'to overcome the king's prejudices'.[247]
Camden met with Pitt on 22 June and politely insisted, or so he claimed, that
the government should comply with the requests of the castle. This opinion
he also presented to the king 'whenever he has spoken to me on the subject'.[248]
A victory of sorts was achieved by the meeting between Camden and Pitt.
Most of Castlereagh's letter of 18 June was read to the prime minister, who
was very impressed with its 'temperate tone'.[249] Pitt decided to uphold all
pledges that had been made, although some were 'disliked very much',
notably the creation of the new marquisates. The prime minister resolved to
see the king with Portland and secure the promises, with a communication to
follow to Cornwallis.[250] In a letter to Cooke, the same day, Camden repeated
these sentiments but noted that Blaquiere's peerage was 'almost intolerable'.[251]

Cooke forwarded Camden's letter to Castlereagh. The resolution of the
incident, he was able to reveal, had been made possible by the king leaving the
matter in the hands of Pitt and Portland. If he had remained intransigent
there would have been much embarrassment, resignations in Dublin being
especially feared. Leaving the decision to the ministers expedited the concession of everything that had been promised. It was a solution that had left the
king 'not well satisfied',[252] an ominous sign for what was to follow later. The
forthright and uncompromising letter of the lord lieutenant on 17 June had
carried the day. While not having the best of relations with the viceroy, Cooke
nonetheless praised his handling of the matter. He was sure that Cornwallis
had acted correctly 'and it was the only method of carrying the business'.[253]
The difficulty, he claimed, had come from the king, exacerbated by the continuing animosity of Portland towards the lord lieutenant. Pitt had been the
only one who had 'conceived the matter rightly' but even he would have liked
to have avoided Blaquiere's representative peerage. Cooke surveyed the
incident with his customary sharpness and cynicism. He felt Portland had
little cause to be critical of Cornwallis for not communicating with him every
time an engagement was entered into to assist the union. Given the un-
reserved assurances the home secretary had previously given the viceroy,
Cooke could not but ask quizzically, 'What then is a *carte blanche*?'[254]

News of the victory reached Castlereagh on 25 June. It came just as
Cornwallis was beginning to despair about a satisfactory resolution of the
affair. The previous day he had written to Ross about the pessimism he felt,
stating his position to be 'very doubtful'. He did not expect any alteration in

the cabinet's position, certainly not from Portland, who he criticised for his 'harsh and ungracious letter' and for having not lost any opportunity during his viceroyalty of 'reprobating' his conduct.[255] Cornwallis had no personal regrets about leaving Ireland, he had wished to do so for some time, but he was afraid that his leaving in a cloud, with the disapproval of the king's government, would be 'attended with fatal consequences in this country'.[256] The lord lieutenant was aware that he had alienated many people in Britain and he wrote to Dundas, the only minister he trusted, and appealed for him not to give way to the opposition against him in court and cabinet. This letter was written on 26 June, one day after Cornwallis was believed to have received news from his chief secretary about the resolution of the dispute.[257] The incident marked the end of the lord lieutenant's confidence in the king's ministers, with the exception of Dundas. From this point on he had little faith in their assurances, refusing to accept the prime minister's defence that he had not seen Portland's letters: 'this is the more inexcusable in Mr Pitt towards me for he well knows the sort of letters which the D. of P. is apt to write'.[258] He found it 'astonishing that the cabinet should have taken so little concern about the Irish affairs'.[259]

There was considerable relief in the castle when the cabinet finally backed down. Castlereagh was glad to find the honour of the administration upheld, although it pained him that any of their suggestions had been unpleasant to the king and his ministers. Deeper reflection and understanding of the union transactions would, he was convinced, persuade them that it had been passed 'on terms as little injurious either to the character or permanent interests of government as could have been reasonably hoped'.[260] Cornwallis, he revealed, was also inclined to accommodate the ministers now that his engagements, and honour, had been maintained.

The cabinet feigned disapproval for the actions of the castle in making promises without consulting it first. There was a ready answer for this: delay had been considered fatal. While it might have been better if the ministers had been made aware of all engagements at the time of making them, it was conceded, it would have hampered the work in Ireland. It would have shown the castle to be weak and destroyed all confidence between it, the MPs and Whitehall. To have had to report to the cabinet every day on matters of patronage would have been 'injurious' to the attempts to secure a majority for the union. The distances involved ensured that the king's ministers were too far removed from the Irish political scene to allow an effective judgment; the cabinet urging caution when vigour was necessary could have resulted in 'a fruitless expenditure of patronage' and failure for the union.[261] Castlereagh was sure that, although they might have been over-generous dispensing patronage, if the union had failed because of a reluctance to dispense favours he was 'inclined to think we should have met with, and, in fact, deserved, less mercy'. Revealingly, he noted that the success of the measure had been a close-run thing. Many supporters had privately speculated on which side was likely to win, and would have deserted if government had shown signs of indecision and frailty. Things had been so finely balanced that even the defection of 'single individuals' could have had a potentially devastating effect. The union had succeeded and Castlereagh assured Camden that all patronage had not been employed without 'much pain by Lord Cornwallis'.[262]

The same day Castlereagh wrote to Cooke, who was still in England owing to the illness of his sister, to engage him to assist in the reconciliation with the ministers. He regretted Portland's attitude that Cornwallis's silence on the pledges had been a sign of his 'disinclination to confidential communication'.[263] In reality, the silence had been necessitated by the nature of the union negotiations. It would have been 'fatal' to have had any delay in the exercise of patronage:

> government would have had all of the odium and none of the advantages of its favours; while waiting for the sanction of the cabinet, they must have given hopes that it would have been afterwards difficult to disappoint . . . The system which the Irish government acted upon was one of greater responsibility and risk to itself, but for the accomplishment of the object it was indispensable.[264]

Delay would have been read as refusal. The chief secretary was convinced that the union could not have been carried if the lord lieutenant had not had an 'unqualified authority' in the area of patronage. If it had been possible to inform Portland before every decision then it would have been done.

On a separate matter it transpired in June that Pitt once more desired the chief secretary's presence in England. Castlereagh did not believe that he could leave Ireland until after the Irish parliamentary session closed and the election of peers was made. This would delay a journey by up to a month. A postponement was also to be recommended because it would facilitate the completion of all official work, and these papers could be brought with him to London for approval, before being sent to Ireland, for execution in his absence.[265]

Attempts to reconcile the Irish and British administrations were also made by London. Portland wrote to Cornwallis on 27 June to mend relations. He apologised for any hurt caused by his letter of 13 June and assured him that had he been aware of the effect it would produce he would not have written it.[266] He praised the viceroy for his success with the union, 'the greatest and most desirable measure which ever was in contemplation'. Portland maintained that his letters were not meant to be absolute, rather they were intended as an appeal to the lord lieutenant. The king, he revealed, had not wished to create any new peers until the election of the twenty-eight had taken place, but, given the viceroy's pledges on that point, the rest would be confirmed. Still, it was clear that there were some reservations about the liberality of the distribution of the favours of the crown in Ireland: 'his majesty relies upon your excellency's judgment and discretion in preventing any prodigality in the dispensation of the patronage of the crown'.[267]

Castlereagh's father, Lord Londonderry, was entitled to a representative peerage, Portland revealed, but it was hoped that this would be reserved for a later date. A promise was made that at any time Londonderry or his descendants wished to receive the British peerage, it would be granted in honour of 'Lord Castlereagh's most distinguished and meritorious services'.[268] Cooke wrote to Castlereagh on the matter and informed him that he was 'almost persuaded that you will be obliged to postpone your father's peerage'.[269] The arguments were persuasive, and 'no man was ever so flatteringly pressed to decline honours'. It was hoped that Castlereagh would take a lead in the united parliament and not be forced, on the unwelcome demise of his father, into taking a seat in the lords. The same line was taken by Portland in a letter to Castlereagh on 2 July. He praised the chief secretary for the role he had played in the union proceedings and admitted that his 'talents and judgement' had entitled him to many things. The subject of a British peerage for his father was, however, a difficult one. Portland expressed the preference that the peerage be delayed so that Castlereagh could act in the house of commons 'until age, infirmity, or the desire for repose' should make him wish to take up a seat in the lords.[270] This was also reported to be the king's opinion. Whether the reason given may have been just a clever expedient to delay the peerage is unclear. The peerage, at least, was understood to be completely in the hands of Castlereagh.[271]

The same day the chief secretary wrote to Camden having decided his family's position on the question of his father's peerage. The matter had been settled by Portland's dispatch, 'which expresses too strong a wish to allow either my father or myself to hesitate on the subject'.[272] The actual judgment on the matter would have to be taken by the king's government. Although the chief secretary had no qualms about sacrificing all personal considerations, the situation was also one that concerned his father and his children. Lord Londonderry, understanding the situation, chose to decline the honour at that time. He thanked Cornwallis for submitting his name to the king but revealed, at the same time, that he could not avail of the peerage accepting that 'his majesty's interests might best be promoted by his not having that distinction at present conferred upon him'.[273]

It was only a few days after sending this communication that Portland's letter of 2 July arrived. Castlereagh answered on 6 July repeating his earlier statements that he and his father were quite prepared to delay the peerage.[274] In contrast, Cornwallis only got round to answering the home secretary's letters, including that of 27 June, on 7 July. He accepted Portland's explanation that the home secretary would not have included the harsh words in the letter of 13 June if he had known they would have caused offence. The viceroy was genuinely satisfied to find that his engagements would be upheld.[275] As for Londonderry's peerage he accepted the willingness of Castlereagh and his father to delay the offer. He could not, however, be as compromising with the case of the marquess of Drogheda, to whom he had promised a British peerage, as this would not only disappoint a hope, but make him 'guilty of a breach of a positive engagement'.[276] Apart from that, Cornwallis wished to have any unpleasantness between him and Portland done with. He politely assured the home secretary that he should ever set the highest value upon your friendship and esteem, and that I shall endeavour to conduct the public business in which I am engaged in the manner that I think will be most agreeable to the views and wishes of his majesty's ministers.

Drogheda duly received his British peerage when the list was published on 1 August, feigning surprise at the honour.[277]

Some promises the king's government still refused to meet. The castle was forced to tell Sir John Blaquiere that his representative peerage would not be forthcoming. It was a delicate matter but he was persuaded to waive the reward 'for *more substantial* objects'.[278] Castlereagh declined to trouble Cooke with the details. These 'substantial objects' were part of the second strand of government patronage. Peerages were for the proprietors and most important people in the country. Lesser individuals had to be content with financial inducements. The list of these, legal, union engagements is extensive.[279] Blaquiere was given an income of £1,000 per annum for the lives of his wife and daughter, £700 to be put on the pension list from March 1802, and £300 from March 1803. Theobald McKenna, a pamphleteer, was promised £300 a year 'for his literary services'.[280] Faithful Fortescue, MP for Monaghan borough, was to receive £300 a year for himself and his wife to compensate him for the pension he lost on coming into parliament. Cornwallis's successor as lord lieutenant, Hardwicke, discovered that the 'heavy mortgage on the pension list' came to £3,450 from 25 March 1802.[281] He was shocked to report that for the year ending 25 March 1805 there was only £150 of patronage at the disposal of the king's government in Ireland.

The civil engagements of the union were numerous. Twenty-seven members of the Irish parliament were promised various rewards; this was eventually done by securing them sinecures worth between £250 and £800 per year.[282] The law engagements were also considerable. A number of supporters of the union were promised promotion and other judicial rewards for their support.[283] Eleven had been in parliament and had voted for the measure in 1800. Cornwallis considered 'the winding up of the engagements' to be 'more vexatious' than the actual passing of the union.[284] Interestingly, he privately admitted that his military secretary, E.B. Littlehales, had been more valuable than Castlereagh during the measure, having none of the chief secretary's coldness: the 'good humoured and kind attention with which he has treated everybody who has had any business with him has gained the universal esteem and regard of all parties'.[285]

The secret service money provided a means for government to keep its supporters happy until official pensions or sinecures were found for them. This money, which was 'partly supplied from his majesty's privy purse',[286] appears to have been liberally spent on converting members, purchasing seats and preventing defections. It does not appear to have been spent on the government's own propaganda campaign. In October 1801 Cooke was still attempting to discharge the 'pressing' printers' bills of £4,400.[287] An additional sum of £2,400 was also sought, at that time, to pay for two seats that had been purchased the previous year.[288]

The opposition struggled to match the government's benevolence. Patronage provided a legal way for government to reward supporters, and the promises made were considerable, even by the standards of the day. Clare was ready with his praise of Cornwallis for stooping, 'against his nature, to the political traffic imposed upon him'.[289] Castlereagh was to remind Camden in May 1800 that the union had been won on the back of heavy use of patronage. The measure would not have progressed as far as it had 'without the utmost efforts of patronage, and you know, so much of the influence of the crown was anticipated'.[290] When Hardwicke arrived in Ireland to take over as viceroy he discovered 'a heavy mortgage on the patronage of the country'.[291] The list of union engagements took years to fulfil, and even in 1806 Hardwicke was despairing about the difficulties involved.[292] In 1799 the union failed because the nature of the Irish political world had been neither properly understood nor handled with the finesse it demanded. Once this was realised different tactics were adopted; catholic support was obtained, patronage was freely used, every private interest was catered to, and the union passed.

FOLLOWING UP THE UNION

In July 1800 the Roman Catholic bishop of Cork, Dr Moylan, was particularly enthusiastic about the success of the union. He praised the work of Castlereagh, who he felt had shown great ability. The union, he was confident, would 'put an effectual stop to those civil and religious disorders, which have so shamefully disgraced this nation, and which it seems [is] still the inclination of a certain faction to keep up'.[293] This reflected the general optimism, especially amongst the catholics, that the union would herald the start of a new era for them. The next six months would reveal, however, just how strong and resourceful 'a certain faction' actually was.

6

Court and cabinet:
the catholic question in abeyance
SUMMER 1800–JANUARY 1801

In 1800 Pitt struggled to face his greatest crisis. The combination of an unsuccessful war, his own failing health, deteriorating relations with the king and the absence of any consensus on the catholic question became a cascade of pressures that gradually ripped his ministry apart. The union had left many issues unresolved. The most important was the delicate question of catholic emancipation. This one issue would unleash a torrent of opposition that would destroy the already fractured government. Richard Willis believes that 'many of the apparent enigmas of the *crises de régime* of early 1801 dissolve when the issue of catholic emancipation is treated as the catalyst which precipitated a long-impending reaction within the executive'.[1] This is only partially correct. Catholic emancipation was more than the catalyst; it did not just exacerbate existing tensions, it became the divisive issue that challenged Pitt's supremacy within the cabinet, and undermined his relationship with the king. To understand fully the context in which the catholic question was placed in the autumn of 1800 it is necessary to examine the other problems that beset Pitt's administration. While it is misleading to claim that these were the critical issues in the break-up of the government, nevertheless the mounting problems slowly ensnared Pitt in a web from which he found it increasingly difficult to escape. The burden of dealing with scarcity, cabinet dissension, and disagreements with the king, at home, combined with the heavy pressures of an unsuccessful war to tear at the heart of Pitt's ministry. One minor area of foreign policy is particularly significant. In the autumn of 1800 diplomatic relations between Russia and Britain deteriorated almost to the point of open conflict. How the king's government acted to resolve this crisis reveals much about secret service activity in the period and the character of Pitt's administration; it may even be suggested that this was the foreign policy parallel of the Irish act of union. It was into this maelstrom of foreign and domestic policy chaos the catholic question was eventually thrown.

THE DECLINE OF PITT'S MINISTRY

Pitt's health was always a key determinant in the effectiveness of his ministry. When it was poor his control over matters waned, and the work of government suffered. Conversely, when political matters went badly the stress and worry pressed down on his morale and strength. During 1800, and especially in the second half of the year, Pitt's fading health was a major contributant to the gradual fragmentation of the government. The weight of public affairs wore down his spirit and constitution, and served to exacerbate the problems facing an administration grappling with failure. In Pitt's correspondence at this time there is an increased frequency of references to his health.[2] In July, Cooke observed Pitt's 'equivocal' health, which he found particularly worrying given the varying levels of mediocrity of everyone else in the government.[3] Sir Walter Farquhar, Pitt's physician, told George Rose towards the end of that month that Pitt's illness 'arises more from the mind than anything else'.[4] Marquess Wellesley believed that from 1793 on his friend had 'no settled tranquillity of mind'.[5] Keith Feiling concludes that 'in the end his long over-work, at first defied but then intensified by port, made him irritable with lesser men and puny interruption'.[6] After almost seventeen years of governing the country Pitt was burning out, mentally and physically.

With Pitt's weakening capacity for management the problems facing the cabinet were heightened. Richard Pares has noted that 'informality of procedure almost amounted to disintegration in the later years of his long ministry'.[7] This disintegration was assisted, ironically, by the secession of Fox and his followers in 1797. The government were left without any real opposition to direct their energies against, apart from Tierney and Sheridan, and so began to fall out with each other. The dominance of the government in parliament also allowed the king to reassume some of the privileges that he had exercised at the start of the reign, and Pitt began to resent this unwelcome interference in the governing of the country. Willis explains that 'the flux and reflux of political struggle came instead to centre upon the relationships within the cabinet, on those between the government and the court, and especially upon the locus between the prime minister and the monarch'.[8]

The cabinet in 1800 consisted of eleven members. Constitutional historians have categorised them as comprising six efficient officers: Pitt as first lord of the treasury and chancellor of the exchequer, Grenville as foreign secretary, Dundas as secretary of state for war, Portland as home secretary, Earl Spencer as first lord of the admiralty, and William Windham as secretary at war; three ceremonial officers: Lord Chancellor Loughborough, Lord President of the Council Chatham, and Lord Privy Seal Westmorland; one, the earl of Liverpool, who was both, being president of the board of trade, but sitting in cabinet as chancellor of the duchy; and finally Camden, who sat in cabinet as a minister without portfolio.[9] It is debatable, however, whether the office of lord chancellor can justifiably be called merely 'ceremonial'. From 1798 on Dundas and Grenville drew further apart over matters of policy and the relationship became acrimonious in 1799 after the failure of the Holland expedition.[10] Both regularly threatened to resign with Dundas making a genuine attempt to be relieved of his stressful duties in April 1800.[11] He remained in his post purely out of a sense of personal regard towards Pitt, and more importantly because the prime minister would not release him. John Ehrman rightly considers the resignation incident significant, not only for revealing crucial differences on strategy between Dundas and Grenville, but for 'forcing to the surface a growing sense of strain, intellectual but also temperamental, between himself and Grenville; [and] in underlining once more his deep loyalty, both respectful and protective, to Pitt'.[12] Analysing the politicians in July, Cooke regretted that Dundas was 'retiring', Windham 'ingeniously imprudent', and Canning of 'neither rank nor authority' who had 'not yet shown himself a man of business'.[13]

The relationship between Pitt and George III was at the heart of much of the difficulties. The prime minister had come into office as the defender of the king's privileges, not because of any mutual affection. The two men had never experienced a warm personal relationship. Westmorland asserted in 1801 that Pitt had not seen George III in private ten times.[14] Pitt was too cold and aloof for the king, who became increasingly resentful of the minister's arrogant manner. He had lasted as prime minister for seventeen years only out of a recognition of his remarkable abilities, and because the alternative was the unthinkable Charles James Fox. This all changed in the final years of the administration. The prime minister's, and particularly Grenville's, 'authoritative manners' towards the king began to rankle,[15] and he grew to resent Pitt for taking him for granted. For his part, Pitt began to feel that the sovereign was interfering too much in matters of government. He frequently became frustrated by the king's scheming, as in 1799 when an anti-slavery bill introduced in the lords to restrain the slave trade along the Sierra Leone company's coasts was intrigued against. None of the usual anti-abolition arguments had applied, and Pitt detected the cunning hand of the king. He regretted to his elder brother, Chatham, that

> an opposition however has been raised to it, ostensibly by the duke of Clarence, but in fact I am sorry to say by some of the members of the administration, who are supported by a great appearance of court influence.[16]

Lord Holland in his *Memoirs of the whig party* noted the growing divergence between court and cabinet from the Foxite secession to 1801. He recorded that

> it is certain that, during the last three years of Mr Pitt's administration, the court more frequently thwarted the ostensible ministers in small matters, and resorted with greater success to those little arts which had distinguished and disgraced the early part of George III's reign.[17]

Canning told Malmesbury in February 1801 that for the past three years the king had forced numerous concessions from the government and had over-ruled many important measures.[18]

The neglect of the king was further evidence of Pitt's proud and arrogant manner during these years. Willis believes the problem arose from an assumption that he could act as he pleased,[19] a dangerous notion. The problem was added to by Pitt's deteriorating mental and physical condition. His precarious health, coupled with the mounting difficulties in 1800, created a further strain on the relationship, with what Camden records as 'anxiety' and 'fatigue' often preventing the prime minister from communicating with the king, either in writing or in person.[20] Pitt was later to regret that the burdens of office had prevented him paying greater attention to the king. Camden was to note, dis-approvingly, that the prime minister sometimes went six weeks in London without visiting the king at a levee. Whatever the reason, and poor health was hardly enough of a justification, much damage was done to the relationship between king and prime minister. The imperious disregard for normal courtesies, Camden recorded, 'certainly in a degree estranged the king from him [Pitt] and induced him to think of him personally with less interest'.[21]

The 'new fractiousness in the king'[22] created many difficulties. He refused to approve certain military expeditions, and consented to the Holland expe-dition only when the duke of York was appointed as commander-in-chief. In his memorandum on Pitt's resignation, written in 1803 or 1804, Camden was to blame the king for opposing, 'though not openly, yet in such a manner as to defeat by delay', the sending of detachments to assist the Austrians in 1800 that might have turned the crucial battle of Marengo in June. The many examples of the king opposing military expeditions in 1800 provided sufficient evidence for Camden that 'if the king *did consent*, he did so most unwillingly to various measures of his government, during the last two years, and during that period his mind was beginning to be estranged from them'.[23] Piers Mackesy does not blame the king for the failure to send reinforcements in time for Marengo, and also considers the matter to have been beyond the control of the cabinet, but he does find the incident revealing for 'the light it sheds on the war ministry and its mounting problems',[24] the most important being the alienation of the king from his ministers.

In July a unanimous cabinet minute was sent to the king recommending a peace negotiation. George III was uneasy at the note. Agitated, he acquiesced in the proposal on 17 July, but insisted that 'if peace is made it must be permanent'.[25] His disquiet was added to a week later when he discovered that, without his consent sought, military plans were being altered and an expedi-tion for Belle Isle changed to an attack on Ferrol.[26] For the first time in many years the king rejected a cabinet minute when he refused the one noting the change. He explained that he would not consent:

> not having before heard of an expedition against Ferrol and on what grounds
> of supposed success it is to be undertaken, nor what force will remain in this

> country after sending so large a force out of it, I cannot give any answer till I have received the data on which to form an opinion.[27]

Without the king's consent the expedition could not proceed. Five or six valuable days were lost until the matter was resolved. Pitt intervened and skilfully defused the matter before it got out of hand, although Dundas, whose project it was, became bitter. The king eventually relented, and on 31 July orders were sent out approving the Ferrol and Cadiz attacks.[28] Pitt again prevented Dundas from resigning, and placated the king, at least temporarily, but he had not been impressed by George III's behaviour during the affair. Pitt conveyed his displeasure to Grenville, admitting that 'it is really provoking to find a disposition to object to all means of making peace or making war'.[29] Dundas's neglect of form had almost resulted in a serious crisis. Willis is correct in emphasising that the king's objections at this time 'were to men rather than measures, to procedure as much as substance'.[30] The king had acted to reassert his constitutional rights and, as Mackesy notes, demand good manners from his ministers.[31] There was one point on which George III loudly declaimed he would never be 'set aside' — catholic emancipation. In the summer of 1800 he spoke frequently on the subject: 'I am glad of the union as it will take away all pretext for admitting the catholics. What? What?'[32] This seemed to be directed particularly at Windham, a pro–catholic minister, 'who made no reply'.[33]

The king, allegedly, even made a tentative attempt to replace Pitt. In August 1800 he asked Windham and Malmesbury to visit him in Weymouth, apparently with a view towards changing the ministry. At the time, neither man was aware of the king's intention, which Malmesbury learned of only in February 1801 from Pelham. The scheme would have seen Windham become prime minister with Malmesbury as foreign secretary.[34] As Willis explains there were sharp contrasts between the two men: Windham was the disciple of Burke, a supporter of catholic emancipation, and the champion of the Bourbon monarchy; Malmesbury was the negotiator of Lille.[35] The change was as much about replacing personalities as replacing policies.

If, for whatever reason, the king chose not to change the ministry in 1800, it was not because there were no acceptable alternatives to Pitt. Apart from Windham, who shared the king's views on foreign policy, though not on the catholic question, the figure of Henry Addington was also beginning to establish his credentials as a possible replacement. Pitt himself had suggested the speaker as his successor in 1797. When it had appeared that the French government would not make peace with a ministry that had Pitt at its head a suggestion had been put to the king, and apparently accepted, for the prime minister to resign and for Addington to succeed.[36] This had not taken place, but it served to increase the stature and influence of the speaker with the king. In June 1800 the king praised the 'worthy and excellent' Addington for his work as speaker of the house,[37] and it was reported in February 1801 that Addington had enjoyed a free and easy access to the king for some time.[38]

As Pitt's position crumbled he had to face a threat as menacing as war. The problem of scarcity was even more pressing in Britain than in Ireland. In 1800 the country was hit with the problem of dearth which created much distress and unrest. The poor weather almost halved the wheat yield, and stocks of grain and coal were further depleted by the demands of expeditions at war. The government had been divided by foreign problems, it now faced a crisis from within.[39] From autumn 1800 the problem of scarcity became the source of much unrest, exploited by revolutionaries and radicals for their own advantage.[40] It only added to the mounting pressures facing the troubled and war-weary government.

In Ireland the weather also destroyed the grain harvest, and the potato crop suffered with one-quarter destroyed in Ulster.[41] Economic historians like David Dickson and Joel Mokyr have demonstrated the links between food supply crises and birth and death rates. Applying graphs of a parish sample it can be seen that 1800 marked the highest point of burials for fifty years, and also recorded a sharp decline in baptisms.[42] In July Cornwallis noted the distress in Connaught and Leinster and recognised that, but for private sub-scriptions, it could have been much worse in Dublin.[43] Nevertheless he looked with confidence to the harvest, and in his final address to the Irish parliament expressed an optimistic desire that 'under the favour of providence, we may draw a pleasing prospect of future plenty from the present appearance of the harvest'.[44]

John Pollock, Downshire's agent, made some useful suggestions the same month. In a letter to Littlehales he urged swift government action or the scarcity of bread corn would affect the poor considerably, especially as they had exhausted their savings the previous winter.[45] Potatoes were also scarce, little seed had been available, and in any case most of the crop had failed because of the 'uncommonly great drought that has prevailed'.[46] A 'second year of distress to the poor' was predicted. Pollock recommended continuing the ban on the distilleries that had been introduced the previous year and that was praised for preventing an insurrection. Unless action was taken, 'a famine will exist in the country in the ensuing winter'.[47] Cornwallis was 'much struck' by the advice and decided to continue the ban while at the same time importing more grain from America.[48] The drought continued into September and bread prices remained high. The castle was relieved to find that the scarcity was not yet leading to mobs although it 'produces great grumbling here'.[49] As Cornwallis sought the importation of more American Indian corn he was forced to reject more home government requests, this time for all excess rice to be exported to England. The lord lieutenant cautiously decided to keep stores in reserve until 'it be well considered how it could be disposed of here'. Once again Cornwallis was obstinately refusing requests from London as the cabinet became increasingly desperate about its food supplies and the conflict with France.

The war was not going well. After Marengo the complete capitulation of the Austrians seemed only a matter of time. On 29 August the ministry received an ultimatum from the French for a naval armistice. It required an answer before 3 September, although this was soon after extended to 11 September.[50] The king regarded an armistice as impossible, and a peace negotiation as dangerous.[51] In an attempt to assist the Austrians Pitt and Grenville devised a counter-project. They agreed to lift the blockade on French naval ports with certain conditions, and the king reluctantly gave his assent.[52] Dundas had been at Cheltenham recovering his health when he heard the news and postponed his trip to Scotland, rushing back to London. Mackesy highlights this moment as the pivotal one where 'Dundas entered the decisive battle to shape the country's policy: a battle to prevent the naval armistice and to commit Abercromby's army to colonial warfare'.[53] Dundas recorded his dissent from the decision that had been made, noting in private how the offer of an armistice 'put the conduct of both war and negotiation in the hands of the enemy'. Bitter at the actions of his colleagues, particularly Grenville, against whom he was becoming increasingly polarised, he expressed his annoyance that 'I can neither accord with our arrogance and presumption in times of apparent prosperity, nor can I descend to pusillanimity in moments of occasional adversity.'[54]

The importance of the naval armistice negotiation lay not in terms of foreign policy but in its effects at home. Apart from the divisions forming in the cabinet, the king was further estranged from the government. Both Windham and Lord Chancellor Loughborough remained with the king during the discussion of the counter-project, a time when the sovereign was reported to be much 'agitated' by the proposal.[55] Windham shared the king's distress, believing that the French terms should have been rejected out of hand. He had little faith in Pitt, as a leader or as a person. From 1798 on he spoke disparagingly of the prime minister for having 'no distinction of right or wrong'. Deeply disillusioned, he criticised Pitt for being unable 'to consider anything otherwise than as it affected his own situation, confining even that to the mere possession of personal power'.[56] Loughborough stated his approval of the armistice, at least to Pitt, but like Windham shared a growing hostility towards the prime minister. It has been noted that 'not withstanding a display of outward courtesy, there was less and less cordiality between the chancellor and the prime minister . . . By degrees he began privately to speculate — not upon a change of the administration, but of its chief.'[57]

The increasingly erratic behaviour of Tsar Paul I of Russia added a new threat to British security. Paul possessed a violent temper and a rather questionable mental balance.[58] His mother, Catherine the great, had feared his succession, and had unsuccessfully attempted to disinherit him. Once he became tsar, Paul's 'peripatetic fancies' increased.[59] On one occasion he banished a friend for daring to suggest that it might rain when he wanted to go outside. Floggings were routinely administered for any imagined slight. In the spring of 1800 Sir Charles Whitworth, the British ambassador to Russia, was ordered to leave, prompting some candid observations about Paul's sanity: 'the emperor is literally mad'.[60] The expulsion reflected the growing alienation of the tsar from Britain. Russia was an integral part of Britain's wartime strategy against France, and she was encouraged to continue in the coalition by generous subsidies. Paul, however, became increasingly dissatisfied with Britain's behaviour and began speculating on an alliance with Napoleon. India was one target for his designs as the tsar's belligerence towards his supposed ally intensified.[61] Buckingham enquired of Grenville, in May, whether he had any hopes for 'our angry Paul' and speculated that he was 'irrevocably gone'.[62] In the autumn of 1800 English sailors in Russia were arrested and imprisoned in the interior of the country where they faced a bitter winter. Russian historians have been in no doubt that 'this meant war'.[63] One Russian historian, K. Waliszewski, notes that Britain seemed absorbed with France, choosing to ignore Russia, and 'received all this provocation with an admirable, if phlegmatic, determination not to take offence'.[64] The government was aware that a plan had been formed that would take care of its problem for ever.

In the spring of 1800 a conspiracy was devised to overthrow the tsar, organised by Count Nikita Petrovitch Panin, the vice-chancellor. Whitworth was a close friend of Panin[65] and before the ambassador left in May he made a secret payment of 40,000 roubles that was never accounted for.[66] In 1801 a former vice-chancellor, Kochubei, was to write to Vorontsov, the Russian ambassador to Britain, and inform him that 'the English have bought many powerful men among us'.[67] Prince Zubov was a prominent conspirator, and his sister, Whitworth's mistress, was to insist that English gold financed the whole scheme. The conspiracy culminated in the assassination of the tsar on 24 March 1801.[68] *Le Moniteur*, the official gazette in Paris, editorialised that 'it is for history to develop the mystery which surrounds this tragic death, and to declare which cabinet in the world was most clearly interested in bringing about such a catastrophe'.[69] The insinuation was plain. As R.E. McGrew notes, Britain and Russia 'were effectively at war when Paul died'.[70]

It is worth addressing the assassination of Tsar Paul I in this book for two reasons. First, the war with Russia and the actual assassination occurred contemporaneously with the collapse of the ministry, and, while not directly related, should not be ignored. Second, the ruthless attitude that characterised the response mirrored much of the government's work in Ireland. On 2 April 1800 Whitworth wrote to Grenville suggesting that his recall would be temporary, as 'it is perfectly impossible that he [the tsar] can remain long in power, and whatever the change may be it must be favourable to the cause'.[71] He assured the foreign secretary that this would take place, 'one way or another'. Legend in Russia afterwards attributed the assassination to Whitworth and Pitt's gold, viewing them as 'the chief instruments in the crime'.[72] J.J. Kenney, whose study of previously unreleased material in the Kent archive office allowed a re-examination of the evidence, suggests that,

> at the very least, even if the documents do not allow a definite conclusion, the business of Whitworth's disbursement of secret service money in May 1800 provides definite grounds for the charges of 'English gold' so long dismissed by most historians.[73]

Elizabeth Sparrow, the pioneer of alien office research, considers the assassination 'the one great success' of British espionage between 1792 and 1806.[74] For John Ehrman the subversive activities of the secret service 'revealed the determination — ruthlessness — with which Pitt and this small group of colleagues were ready to fight the later stages of a war which he was increasingly anxious to end'.[75] In truth, the secret service were unable to control the conspiracy against the tsar. There is evidence to suggest that assassination was never countenanced by any agent of the alien office. Instead Whitworth financed the initial conspiracy that aimed at either overthrowing the tsar or, more probably, instituting a regency. This was the preference of Panin, who was moderate in his ambitions, but his dismissal and exile in December 1800 effectively ended his control over the plot. Count Peter von der Pahlen replaced Panin as the chief conspirator and added a violent streak to the proceedings. The expulsion of Whitworth and the marginalisation of Panin allowed Pahlen to turn the conspiracy into an assassination plot against the tsar. Yet even in March 1801 many of the conspirators balked at actually killing Paul and clung to a misguided hope that he could be persuaded to abdicate. In the end the tsar was barely given a chance and was savagely assaulted and killed. It is unlikely that the secret service felt any remorse at the death. They probably shared the philosophy of Pahlen on the night of the plot, who, when asked how to proceed if Paul resisted, replied, 'As everybody knows, to eat an omelette requires first breaking the eggs.'[76]

Despite the trouble with Russia, in 1800 the most pressing questions for the king's government remained France, scarcity and the catholic question. The last of these issues completed the division of the cabinet. In the summer of 1800, for what appears to be the first time, Lord Loughborough began to act as the king's conscience on this question in cabinet. He suddenly transformed himself into an opponent of all concessions to the Roman Catholics. These convictions, as applied to the case itself, had not been apparent before that when the lord chancellor had been less dogmatic on the subject. In 1793 he had written to Lord Auckland, who was to become another important figure in the events, on the subject of Fitzgibbon, now the earl of Clare. Loughborough liked the 'manly resolution' of his Irish visitor but regretted that 'his mind is liable to be governed by strong prejudices'. He found it remarkable that Fitzgibbon could consider three-quarters of the population of Ireland as constituting 'a popish faction'. The solution, as Loughborough saw it then, was to unite catholics and protestants 'in the defence of both by securing to them the employment of the benefits of government'.[77]

In 1795 the actions of the then Irish viceroy, Lord Fitzwilliam, in favour of catholic emancipation had prompted the king to examine his conscience on religious issues. Fitzgibbon and Loughborough became joined in intrigue. The former asked John Beresford to remind the latter that by the terms of the union with Scotland 'it is declared to be a fundamental article that the king of Great Britain shall maintain the church of England as by law established in England, Ireland, and Berwick-upon-Tweed'.[78] Loughborough gave the king a paper on the subject in which the above passage was quoted verbatim, the one difference being that it was now 'an essential and fundamental article'.[79] The king, in his response to Pitt on Loughborough's paper, insisted that any indulgences to the Irish catholics would only serve 'sooner or later, to separate the two kingdoms . . . measures to prevent which my family was invited to mount the throne of this kingdom in preference to the house of Savoy'.[80] Most important of all the king made it clear that it was beyond the power of any government to make such a change in policy towards the catholics.

The cabinet faced further division in 1800 by a proposal of Dundas on 18 September to send the major part of the expeditionary forces to Egypt.[81] Grenville believed Portugal should be the destination of the troops, an opinion with a small majority of ministerial support. On 23 September the cabinet gave its assent to give priority to Portugal, with Pitt again siding with his foreign secretary. The only thing that united the old triumvirate of Pitt, Grenville and Dundas was opposition to a scheme from Windham that would have seen the troops return to England.[82] It was an acrimonious meeting. Although Dundas had lost the point in cabinet he would not concede it. According to Mackesy, he alone saw 'that for the sake of a useless gesture to Portugal, Egypt would become French'.[83] Dundas persisted with his Egyptian proposal and turned the cabinet on 30 September, which had been called to discuss emancipation, into one on foreign policy. Circumstances began to favour Dundas, and on 3 October Pitt sided with his secretary of state for war. A majority in cabinet was likewise persuaded, although Lord Liverpool recounted that Pitt presumed to include on his side three members who had not committed themselves: 'he said that Pitt was very ignorant of those subjects'.[84]

FACING THE CATHOLIC QUESTION
In this difficult environment the catholic question struggled to be addressed. The internal and external problems facing the country, the gradual alienation of the king from his government, the disintegration of the cabinet and Pitt's failing health were all key determinants in how the issue of catholic emancipation fared between summer 1800 and January 1801. The discussion on the catholic question only intensified the pressures on a cabinet and a prime minister that were, in all respects, collapsing. Once the union had been carried the cabinet considered it important to decide 'upon the language to be used to the catholics who might forward their claims'. Additional pressure was provided by the fear that the opposition would press the government on the matter once parliament resumed.[85] Preliminary meetings were held in the summer to discuss the matter. There was never a full attendance: Chatham was in Holland, Liverpool was 'frequently indisposed', Dundas was 'often absent' and Westmorland was 'in the country'.[86] The lead proponent of emancipation, according to Camden, was Grenville, who 'always held a firm and decided language upon the necessity of the measure'. Dundas no doubt indicated his support when present, but he seemed preoccupied with military affairs. Pitt

also let it be understood that he too was convinced of the propriety of emancipation but expressed caution about the likely difficulties, notably the king's
opposition to such a proposal. All the ministers were recorded as recognising
this obstacle.[87]

To assist in the deliberations, Castlereagh was summoned to London in
August 1800. He travelled with William Elliot, to brief the ministers, as he
had in late 1798 on the union. All the while, the king was not informed of the
deliberations, Portland telling him only that Castlereagh had been sent for

> in order to consider and prepare the arrangements which the new order of
> things arising out of the happy event of the union will require to be submit-
> ted to your majesty and to receive your majesty's royal sanction in order to
> their being carried into effect.[88]

This, what Willis rightly refers to as 'a curiously phrased statement', was the
only indication the king received at the time.[89] The chief secretary arrived in
London on 19 August and immediately met with Pitt and Portland.[90] Although
the prime minister promised Castlereagh that he would not delay him long in
London, a speedy resolution of the matter was to prove impossible. The visit
was to be a prolonged failure.

While the ministers were preoccupied with other questions of state,
Castlereagh worked to keep their attention on catholic emancipation. He
wrote a memorandum in September 1800 'on the expediency of making
further concessions to the catholics'.[91] This was circulated around cabinet
ministers and presented forceful arguments in favour of emancipation.
Castlereagh contended that,

> if the same internal struggle continues, Great Britain will derive little
> beyond an increase of expense from the union. If she is to govern Ireland
> upon a garrison principle, perhaps in abolishing the separate parliament she
> has parted as well with her most effectual means as with her most perfect
> justification. In uniting with Ireland she has abdicated the colonial relation,
> and, if hereafter that country is to prove a resource rather than a burden to
> Great Britain, an effort must be made to govern it through the public mind.

The central argument was that the union would benefit Ireland only if it
genuinely secured the goodwill of the country. This would be impossible for
as long as emancipation was refused. A half-policy — union without emancipation — was worse than nothing, it provided neither strength nor security.

The king was to be at Weymouth until 7 October. The catholic question
was considered too delicate to broach by a dispatch, and instead Pitt resolved
to speak with him on his return. Until then, the prime minister undertook to
sound 'the opinions of considerable persons in the country and to use every
means in his power to put the question in the best shape'.[92] It is interesting
that Pitt remembered the king's conditions in 1795, and was now endeavouring to meet them:

the subject is beyond the decision of any cabinet of ministers — that, could they form an opinion in favour of such a measure, it would be highly dangerous without previous consultation with the leading men of every order in the state.[93]

A major question for historians of these events has been whether Loughborough revealed the cabinet's scheme for catholic emancipation when he stayed with the king at Weymouth, in September. Loughborough was quite prepared to use the matter for his own benefit, and he wrote a paper in answer to Castlereagh's that was widely distributed.[94] Malmesbury, at the height of the crisis in 1801, judged Loughborough guilty of revealing the scheme to the king at Weymouth.[95] Likewise Camden, writing soon after the events, believed the lord chancellor's behaviour had been deeply suspicious and found it hard to imagine that 'the king's mind was *at least* not less forti-fied in his objections by the company he kept at that place, at this period'.[96] Lord Campbell believed that Loughborough 'behaved disingenuously', and, out of a desire to replace Pitt, resorted to subtle 'arts'.[97] This interpretation has largely been accepted by historians. Hyde argues that Loughborough only showed the king Pitt's introductory letter, which, in itself, was enough to rouse the sovereign's suspicions, and lead to 'a great state of mental agitation', the king becoming 'enraged with Pitt and his other ministers'.[98] Willis shares this analysis, suggesting that Loughborough made it clear that catholic reform was being contemplated in some form but without telling the full story.[99] One biographer of Addington, Philip Ziegler, places the worst possible interpretation on the lord chancellor's conduct, arguing that he showed the king all of Pitt's confidential letters on emancipation, and 'by a few moments' mischief making he transformed Pitt's quiet diplomacy into an explosive clash between prime minister and king'.[100] Ehrman likewise believes that the king's suspicions were alerted by Loughborough, considering the disclosure to have been of a piece with the lord chancellor's past.[101] Given the king's established convictions on the matter Ehrman is wary of overestimating the significance of the intervention. If the lord chancellor did show Pitt's letter George III would have been stunned, and may have considered Pitt's actions a betrayal. The letter revealed that Loughborough's presence was necessary at the cabinet to discuss 'the great question on the general state of the catholics' as well as subsidiary points like tithes.[102]

The evidence in favour of Loughborough informing the king in September is not, however, conclusive. Certainly he was scheming against the measure, more out of a desire to remove Pitt than from any genuine religious principle. That Loughborough was playing his own game is undisputed; after all, he had been the presbyterian in favour of toleration in an earlier incarnation. Subsequent events, most notably the king's apparently genuine shock on hearing of the government's determination, sometime between December and January, make it seem more probable that Loughborough played a closer hand than has generally been accepted. The lord chancellor was content to prime the king, only throwing out half-suggestions, leaving him unaware that catholic emancipation was to be a government measure, so that the king's rage would be all the more intense when the scheme was finally revealed to him. This interpretation explains the confusion of the king when he discovered the scheme a few months later. Loughborough may have realised that were he to inform the king too early his machinations might not succeed with the desired effects. Instead the lord chancellor plotted, and waited patiently.

The crucial cabinet on the catholic question was planned for 30 September. Loughborough returned from Weymouth to attend, his arguments carefully prepared. The meeting allowed for a week's grace, before the king's return, to work on the details. Foreign policy concerns dominated the meeting, and a discussion on the catholic question was postponed to the next day. Dundas took the opportunity to press forcibly his arguments for an Egyptian exped-ition.[103] The troops for Portugal were reduced but he was unable to convince the cabinet to approve his plan for Egypt and 'the response enraged him'.[104] He refused to issue the necessary orders and chose not to attend the council the next day. This cabinet, on the catholic question, included Pitt, Grenville, Loughborough, Chatham, Portland, Spencer, Windham and Camden, with Castlereagh observing. Along with Dundas, Liverpool and Westmorland were also absent.[105] A brief discussion of the need for full catholic relief was inter-rupted by the lord chancellor who delivered a vitriolic attack on the proposals, except for those on the tithe issue.[106] Castlereagh and Pitt were taken aback by this unexpected onslaught. For probably the first time the prime minister realised that he had the difficult task of persuading the king to concede emancipation without having a solid base of support in cabinet to work from. The delicate manoeuvring Pitt had been involved in for the past months suddenly assumed a bleaker, and more ominous, focus. It proved impossible to make a decision on the catholic question at this meeting and the discussion was postponed indefinitely. Other matters assumed a greater importance and Camden was to record that 'with the scarcity which then prevailed and which occupied Mr Pitt almost entirely, and with preparations for the Egyptian expedition, this question was for a time laid aside'.[107]

Addington was to observe that there had never been a more divided ministry.[108] The problem of scarcity became even more threatening in Britain. At the commencement of the harvest torrential rain fell, and bad harvests and rising food prices left the government struggling unsuccessfully for a solu-tion. In September 1800 the problem had intensified to what Roger Wells has described as a 'hypercrisis'.[109] Inflated food prices reduced the real wages of building workers to their lowest point for two hundred years.[110] There were food riots in the midland towns and Bristol, over the increasing price of bread. Public discontent rose alarmingly and there was a popular clamour against Pitt and his ministry, a 'broad-based crisis of confidence'.[111] Political pamphlets became more and more scurrilous and revolutionary. One in Birmingham asked:

will ye English fools have Billy Pitt for a God and starve you in the midst of plenty, can't you smell the fusty bread blood for supper? Damnation, seize Pitt and George, and all in the name of such varmin, down with them.[112]

Two separate attempts had been made to assassinate George III in May 1800.[113] Lord Liverpool, the president of the board of trade, warned in October that 'there will be insurrections of a very serious nature, and that different bodies of yeomanry may possibly fight each other'. The crisis, he said, threatened to 'shake the foundations of the government of Great Britain'.[114] In any other country, it was observed, the problem would be called famine. By the beginning of October 1800 Pitt was facing his greatest test, at a time when he was barely able to cope.[115]

The cabinet was riven by dissension over how to act, so much so that it was 'partially paralysed'.[116] An acrimonious debate split the ministers over whether Adam Smith's free trade policies should be adhered to or abandoned. The chief proponent of non-intervention, Lord Grenville, insisted that private speculations would provide a sufficient supply of food.[117] Lord Liverpool rejected this strategy and urged the immediate importation of corn to prevent further distress. Pitt was torn between ideology and pragmatism and despaired that 'the question of peace or war is not in itself half so formidable as that of scarcity with which it is necessarily combined, and for the evils and growing dangers of which I see no adequate remedy'.[118] The cabinet was polarised, but Pitt decided the matter by siding with Liverpool. Pressured by unrest in the capital, and a petition from London corporation, he ordered the recall of parliament for November to debate the importation of grain. Grenville was furious at Pitt's abandonment of his free trade principles and rebuked him in a strongly worded letter on 24 October:

> we in truth formed our opinions on the subject together and I was not more convinced than you were of the soundness of Adam Smith's principles of political economy until Lord Liverpool lured you from our arms into all the mazes of the old system.[119]

Grenville argued that 'artificial contrivances' would only exacerbate the problem. His conclusion was particularly bitter: 'I detest and abhor as impious and heretical the whole system on which we are now acting on the subject.'[120]

The accumulated stress took its toll on Pitt. He was exhausted, and his fragile constitution was further debilitated by the increasing burden of his responsibilities. Dundas warned the king that the prime minister would not be able to continue throughout the winter without a respite.[121] It was reported that Pitt was suffering from a loss of appetite and vomiting. He was 'a good deal shook; he cannot carry a glass of beer to his mouth without the aid of his second hand'.[122] Pitt was unable to see a solution to the problem of scarcity, and the matter weighed heavily on his spirits. Engaged in 'uncomfortable speculations', in early October, he admitted that he was not 'the better for brooding over them during the confinement and anxiety of some weeks past'.[123] Sir Walter Farquhar anxiously advised Pitt of the necessity of a re-cuperative trip to Cheltenham or Bath. An additional source of worry was the prime minister's straitened finances, as his friends discovered. On 18 October Rose saw a list of debts that 'actually sickened me'.[124] Ziegler remarks that 'physically and mentally Pitt was near to breaking point'.[125] Refusing to go to Bath for his health Pitt instead chose to visit Addington, at his home in Woodley. He stayed for three weeks, and the visit was hailed a success. Addington believed Pitt had improved considerably, and confidently asserted that 'Mr Pitt's health . . . is so well established as to render him fully equal to any exertions that may be required of him.' Pitt was equally optimistic, revealing that he left Woodley on 5 November 'greatly renovated both in health and spirits', having been much 'broken down by anxiety'.[126] Nevertheless he still worried that his strength was not fully restored. The resumption of parliament to discuss the food shortage was less than a week away, and he feared the break had not 'been sufficient to enable me to face the session, and I am not comfortable as to its approaching so near'.[127]

The state of Pitt's health was a cause of great concern, and some innuendo. Opponents of the prime minister, such as Sir Walter Pulteney and the earl of Guilford, claimed that Pitt had gone mad. According to Glenbervie, Dundas believed that Pitt's mind had matured too early, while the same source cited Farquhar as saying that Pitt tried to shirk away from facing the house of commons at this time.[128] Mackesy compares Pitt's condition to that of Lord North in the final stages of his ministry — 'increased symptoms of a breakdown of will and nerve, a growing reluctance to grasp nettles and take decisions'.[129] Keith Feiling believes that at this point Pitt was 'on the verge of a nervous breakdown'.[130]

Summoning every reserve Pitt reluctantly faced the commons on 11 November. The house heard a message from the king which announced that

> my tender concern for the welfare of my subjects, and the sense of the diffi-culties with which the poorer classes particularly have to struggle from the present high price of provisions, have induced me to call you together at an earlier period than I had otherwise intended.[131]

Parliament then debated the 'effects of a dearth' and the danger of 'riot and conflagration'.[132] One member, Richard Robson Bateman, took the opportunity to deliver a damning indictment of the government's foreign policy, blaming Pitt for prolonging the war which prevented 'a free commerce for grain'. The attack was particularly scathing:

> sir, the country, as long as the chancellor of the exchequer remains in office, has no chance of peace. In the hour of success he will not treat. In adversity he will not treat. In God's name, when are we to treat? Is it to be an endless war? Give us peace.[133]

A committee of the whole house was established to consider the importation of corn and other grain. The outlook was not good. Government figures admitted privately that the deficiencies were great, although this could not be admitted publicly for fear of raising prices even further. Unscrupulous merchants had already inflated corn prices leading to the widespread introduction of the use of rice.[134]

The same conditions affected Ireland. The 'unusually hot and dry' summer was followed by 'a wet autumn with deficient crops'.[135] It was later reported that the people were 'in a state of starvation, [and] malignant fever continued from 1798'.[136] The decisive actions of Cornwallis again proved more effective than the dithering in London. Unconcerned with the principles of Adam Smith he willingly interfered in the market whenever he felt it necessary. In September he ordered the importation of more rice to counteract the shortage of bread.[137] The same month the proclamations preventing the exportation of grain expired, and new ones were passed in October.[138] Cornwallis was satisfied that 'our scarcity is not likely to be as great as yours in England'.[139] The failure of the potato crop, however, led him to fear some 'pretty serious distress in the spring'. The home government made further requests for food. At the end of November Portland informed the lord lieutenant that, as wheat and wheat-flour prices were lower in Ireland, a certain amount should be sent over to Britain regularly to furnish the fleet.[140] The home secretary assured him that this would not be violating the corn laws as it would become the Irish fleet, too, from 1 January. Cornwallis hesitated, unwilling to deplete the Irish stocks. He sought advice from Clare on the legality of the request before writing to Portland to refuse.[141] He denied that prices were any lower in real terms once other factors like wages were considered, and a strong case was made that only a small amount could be spared for the navy anyhow.[142] As Cornwallis continually proved recalcitrant the home government engaged Dundas to persuade him, but this manoeuvre also failed.[143]

At this time the fleet was heading for the Baltic, to force Denmark out of the war, and then move on to St Petersburg if necessary. Tsar Paul I was becoming increasingly unpredictable. In December he challenged all of the leaders of Europe, together with their prime ministers, to a duel to settle the fate of the continent. The prospect of George III and Pitt facing up to Napoleon is an intriguing one, but the tsar's proposal was met with ridicule throughout Europe. Paul was obliged to issue a statement insisting that the story was intended as a prank, and it did not enhance his reputation.[144] On 16 December a system of armed neutrality was formed with Russia, Denmark, Sweden and Prussia, and a Russian diplomat was soon on his way to Napoleon to treat for an alliance.[145] In October Grenville had regretted that 'as for Russia . . . we are all but at war with that near and natural ally'.[146] Two months later and it was only the winter season that 'prevented England and Russia from exchanging shots'.[147] The governor of Moscow placed all Englishmen under house arrest,[148] and merchant ships were confiscated as the cold war escalated.[149]

Unable to reach a determination on the catholic question, Castlereagh returned to Ireland. He set out on 3 October, first visiting Mount Stewart, and arrived back in Dublin at the start of December.[150] The lord lieutenant was informed of the difficulties in England, and the uncertainty of ministers. Castlereagh's reports only added to the pessimism that Cornwallis was feeling, and he could not 'help entertaining considerable apprehensions that our cabinet will not have the firmness to adopt such measures as will render the union an efficient advantage to the empire'.[151] He tried to avoid despair, clinging to a fading hope that the ministers would realise that emancipation 'liberally granted' could guarantee the loyalty of the Irish people; no advantage would be derived from the measure if it was forced from government in the future.

The cabinet still wavered on the matter. Cornwallis decided that Castlereagh should return to London in a mission 'to try and persuade the ministers to adopt manfully the only measure which can ever make the mass of the people in Ireland good subjects'.[152] The lord lieutenant was under no illusions about the threat the Irish people posed to the security of the empire unless emancipation was granted. He accepted, unhappily, that government must,

> so long as the present war shall last, feel ourselves under the melancholy necessity of considering the majority of the Irish people as enemies, and employ a large portion of the force, which ought to act against a foreign invader, to keep our own countrymen in subjection.[153]

From what Castlereagh had observed in England, Cornwallis came to realise that the king posed the greatest threat to emancipation. There was 'too much apprehension of giving offence in a certain quarter'.[154] Anxious to end his tenure in Ireland Cornwallis informed the cabinet that he would stay until the summer of 1801, when he wished to be relieved. He believed that this was 'as much as can in reason be asked', the main obstacle to his leaving being the indecision of ministers, who he feared would postpone the catholic question, and make him even 'further pressed'.[155]

The catholic question had become a question of honour for Cornwallis. He refused to abandon the catholics, and worked hard to strengthen the resolve of the ministers in London. He reminded Portland, at the start of December, that the catholics during the union 'certainly had it in their power to have frustrated the views of government, and thrown the country into the utmost confusion'. They had not, and it was up to the king's government to ensure that their loyalty was rewarded. Even if the Roman Catholics were, as the protestants alleged, full 'of obstinate and irreclaimable disaffection', this would be ended once they were 'no longer the objects of suspicion and are relieved from their present mortifying and degrading exclusions'.[156] As far as Cornwallis was concerned the cabinet had to decide whether the catholics could ever be good subjects. If it believed they could then emancipation must logically follow the union. If it did not, if it agreed with 'the hereditary prejudices' of the protestants in Ireland, then the union had been a foolish measure: 'What then have we done? We have united ourselves to a people whom we ought in policy to have destroyed.'[157] The lord lieutenant believed Castlereagh's paper was so clear and well argued on all points that he declined to add to it.

There had been many difficulties within the Irish administration, but now that the union was passed Cornwallis became a little more relaxed in his manner. He and Cooke had rarely agreed on matters of policy, and it was fortunate that Castlereagh, being on good terms with both, had provided a balance. Cooke had bitterly castigated the lord lieutenant after the failure of the union in 1799, and had been critical of him on many other occasions. Cornwallis, for his part, recognised the under-secretary's abilities but found he had 'a narrow minded jealousy which is inexcusable in so clever a fellow'.[158] He was under no illusions about Cooke's contemptuous regard for him. He was also critical of Cooke for being, he wrongly suspected, 'more partial to the old system of government than to the measures which I have introduced'.[159] December 1800 was a particularly difficult month for the two men, especially with Castlereagh's absence in the latter half. The viceroy admitted to Ross that he and Cooke 'had not been in the most pleasant habits', placing the blame on the under-secretary for being for too long connected with Clare and 'the old set of Irish politicians'.[160] For the sake of the administration Cornwallis made an attempt at a reconciliation. He found to his surprise that Cooke was not opposed to catholic emancipation '[n]or disinclined to the line of conduct which I pursue in governing the country'. He was also pleased to find the under-secretary take his side against Clare in a minor disagreement between them.[161]

The rapprochement with Cooke did not distract Cornwallis from his other problems. As the date for the creation of the united kingdom approached, the lord lieutenant became increasingly unhappy with his situation, worsened by the uncertainty surrounding the catholic question. He did not feel that he could abandon his post as long as that question was unresolved. Without emancipation he believed the union would be 'of no avail'.[162] The obstacle to the measure, Cornwallis felt, was not the protestants in Ireland, but figures in England. The main threat came from four sources: the king, the 'cabal of late lord-lieutenants', the 'inferior cabinet on Irish affairs consisting of Lords Hobart, Auckland etc.', and finally 'the timidity of ministers'.[163] To his brother, the bishop of Lichfield and Coventry, Cornwallis wrote that although the union had been passed, 'much remains to be done in order to render [Ireland] a useful appendage to the British empire'.[164]

If emancipation was rejected Cornwallis planned to leave Ireland in June or July 1801. If the 'good genius' of the government prevailed, however, he admitted that he would consider remaining in the country. With Castlereagh once more in London, Cornwallis analysed how the cabinet appeared to be dividing. He correctly believed that Dundas and Grenville were fully in favour of emancipation.[165] The main opponent seemed to be Loughborough. He hoped, however, that the momentum towards emancipation would prove too strong a force for the lord chancellor. Whatever Loughborough's opposition to concession, Cornwallis was convinced that he would 'in a short time, or I am much mistaken, find it still more impracticable to resist'.[166] The lord lieutenant shared the prime minister's outlook on the union — it was about security. With 1 January drawing nearer Cornwallis expressed his one personal wish, in his private statement on the union: 'to leave this country in a state of security, and to have contributed to make the inhabitants of Great Britain and Ireland one people, with a common interest, and a mutual desire to support and assist each other'.[167] The war with France made a solution to Ireland's problems essential. Emancipation was not just a question of benefiting the catholics, it was about helping the empire at war. Cornwallis noted the bleak future facing Britain: 'with almost all Europe leagued against us, we cannot long exist as a divided nation. When Bonaparte has settled matters with the Austrians, which must soon be the case, he will naturally turn his thoughts towards Ireland.'[168] Enlisting the support of the Roman Catholics would help secure the Irish flank, and also provide an important mass of troops for the conflict.[169]

'Lord Loughborough, I find, is our most active and formidable opponent.'[170] Cornwallis's assessment, possibly based upon reports from Dundas, was all too accurate. On 13 December the king had received a paper from the lord chancellor, on what George III referred to as 'the proposal from Ireland of emancipating the Roman Catholics'.[171] The king had been unaware of the moves to make catholic emancipation a proposed measure of government. He knew of Pitt, Dundas and Grenville's personal support for the measure but not, it seems, that they were planning to adopt it in cabinet.[172] Thus as Castlereagh set out for England on 17 December he little realised how dramatically things had changed. The intervention of Loughborough had placed an immense obstacle in the path for securing emancipation.

When Castlereagh called to Whitehall on 28 December he discovered the full extent of what Hyde calls Loughborough's 'poisoned arrows'.[173] Portland revealed that the lord chancellor's arguments had altered his opinion, and presented the chief secretary with a copy of the paper.[174] Castlereagh could only present a résumé of past events to the prime minister, and remind him, in case he was a little unsure, of the commitments that had to be honoured. Castlereagh's letter to Pitt was dated 1 January 1801, a day Hyde believes was chosen as a symbolic reference to the start of the united kingdom. The tone of Castlereagh's letter was uncompromising. Cornwallis, when he had sent the chief secretary over to England, had been prepared

> for some difference of opinion in the cabinet on the principle of the measure itself, and for much confusion on the part of his majesty's ministers in general with respect to the period when they might think themselves justified in prudence in proposing to parliament so important an alteration of the test laws.[175]

He had not been prepared for opposition from sources who, prior to the passing of the union, had not done anything to suggest that their sentiments were adverse to the principle of the measure conceded with the union, much less that they were prepared to oppose the question on its merits and to declare their determination to resist hereafter any further concessions to the catholics.

This was a specific reference to the cabinet councils held in November 1799 at which time, Castlereagh reminded Pitt, no 'direct objection' to emancipation had been stated by the ministers then present. It had even been discussed whether an immediate declaration in favour of the catholics should not be made. Opposition to emancipation had been expected from 'many quarters, and particularly in the highest', but no dissent had been voiced by those who were now leading opposition to the measure. This was an implicit criticism of Portland who had remained silent on those occasions, and perhaps also of Loughborough if he had been present at the deliberations.

Castlereagh informed Pitt that he had been sent to England in the autumn of 1800 to 'recall the attention of his majesty's ministers to the catholic question'. Loughborough had been more vocal in his objections at these councils, Castlereagh reporting back to the lord lieutenant that 'sentiments unfavourable to the concession had been expressed by the highest law authority'.[176] The cabinet in 1800 had refrained from 'a final decision on so momentous a question' in the king's absence. Nevertheless a clear signal had been given by the ministers that the hopes the lord lieutenant had been encouraged to form would not be disappointed. Once again, it seemed to Castlereagh and Cornwallis that they were to be made men of straw. If the ministers in London sided with the opinions in Loughborough's paper they realised that they would be placed in an invidious position with the Irish catholics. The castle had raised expectations and now risked seeing them destroyed, something the meetings in 1799 had specifically been intended to avoid. The support of the catholics had been enlisted to pass the union: the cabinet had understood this, and had endorsed the policy. It was now a point of honour, and resignations were again threatened. If the ministers were suddenly to lessen their determination, Castlereagh informed Pitt of the 'peculiar degree of pain' Cornwallis would feel in being forced to dash the hopes of those that he had been encouraged to secure. The chief secretary made an important distinction regarding the support of the catholics plain to the prime minister: 'Lord Cornwallis is the last person in the world that would wish to consider what has passed on the part of the cabinet as a pledge given to him, though not to the catholics.'

With the United Kingdom of Great Britain and Ireland coming into effect on the first day of the new year the catholic question assumed an even more powerful significance. For Cornwallis the matter rested on the dichotomy between the 'good genius' and the 'evil genius' of the king's government. The catholics remained quiet in expectation of great things. It depended on the courage of the ministers whether their aspirations would be realised.[177] It was seen as vital, by both Cornwallis and Cooke in Dublin, that the catholic question was kept open for discussion and it was part of Castlereagh's mission to ensure that no one prevented this. Cooke was shown Loughborough's paper against emancipation in January, and worked out counter-arguments to assist the chief secretary. A key consideration was that Pitt's speech on the union had committed him to its discussion. The under-secretary felt it would be 'impossible' for Pitt now to 'close the question against the catholics'; he had 'precluded himself from negativing the principle' by what he had said.[178] In any case, circumstances meant the prime minister could not abandon the matter even if he wanted to; the opposition would take it up if he did not. Cooke believed the main threat would come, not from the lord chancellor's arguments, but in the debate 'upon the wisdom, policy, beneficial experience of the test laws, the free principles of the reformation, the freer principles of the revolution, and the conduct and prejudices of two-hundred years'. He warned Castlereagh that if arguments were based upon a defence of the constitution bought with blood, 'the old whig principle may burst out' and assist the prejudices of those 'who dread popery in every shape, and who see anti-Christ in every priest'.[179]

The difficult area of what oaths or tests would be administered in parliament was examined by Cooke, after reports from London emphasised the importance of the question. The plan of the ministers, and Castlereagh, was to introduce a political test that would affirm the catholics' loyalty. Cooke considered it impractical to have two tests, one for catholics and one for protestants, if the one for the latter was to abjure the Pope, and the former was merely to assert political loyalty. Whether the protestants would accept one test remained to be seen and Cooke believed that they may prefer 'the anomaly' of two.[180] One suggestion was to revert to the tests taken by members after the reformation but before catholics were prevented from admission. The problem would be these oaths' vagueness. The best recommendation Cooke could make was that any new law should avoid 'distrust and suspicion'. The tests should serve to include not exclude, 'the less of insinuation and taunt which shall be in the oaths the better'.[181]

Writing from London, Castlereagh was able to offer some reassurance and hope to the castle on 7 January. A successful meeting with Pitt had satisfactorily removed doubts about the prime minister's resolve.[182] In his reply Cornwallis predicted that 'if Mr Pitt is firm, he will meet with no difficulty'. The lord lieutenant foresaw that the difficult circumstances could assist Pitt, the same way 'that the rebellion assisted the union'.[183] It was a shrewd assessment, even if it did ignore some circumstances that would ultimately prove more powerful. Of greater pleasure for the lord lieutenant was the news from Castlereagh that his account of what had passed in the cabinets of November 1799 had been confirmed; the matter was now 'satisfactorily settled'. Cornwallis admitted he had been apprehensive that 'Pitt's recollection was not so clear' as his chief secretary's.[184] The letters from Castlereagh helped to ease Cornwallis's fears. He derived 'real comfort' from their content and was confident that they could now 'turn that great measure of the union to real profit'. Reports from Lord Fingall that many catholics wished to present a petition in favour of emancipation were quickly acted upon. Cornwallis strongly discouraged any such attempt and conveyed similar sentiments to Lord Donoughmore. This was consistent with the lord lieutenant's belief that emancipation should come as a gift, not something that had been unwillingly conceded, or else the entire union strategy would be compromised. Cornwallis was optimistic that finally, after a long struggle, the king's government was on the verge of 'adopting the only means of resisting the hostility of almost all Europe'.[185]

Pitt's management of the catholic question at this time has attracted more criticism than almost any other aspect of his career, apart from his resignation, and that was as a consequence of it. Mackesy alludes to 'the state of the prime minister's mind, and how grotesquely he was mishandling the question'.[186] Even Camden, a friend of Pitt, blamed him for his 'culpable neglect (as I shall always consider it) of not informing the king of the discussions of his cabinet'.[187] The argument, particularly for Mackesy, is that Pitt should have acted on the matter between September and December, and not have given Loughborough room to conspire. In Pitt's defence, his equivocal health from September to November made an adjournment of the discussion unavoidable, while the mounting problems of scarcity and war combined to keep the question in the background. By the end of November, and the start of December, it was too late to stop Loughborough's machinations.

'The cabinet was wearing out.'[188] This was the most important problem for Pitt as he attempted to bring forward emancipation. The disintegration of his ministry destroyed any hope of achieving a consensus on the catholic question. In policy disagreements with the king Pitt derived a position of strength from the backing of cabinet. The clear support of his ministers was usually sufficient to persuade the king to concede on matters that he personally opposed. With the fragmentation of the cabinet went Pitt's greatest weapon. 'Mr Pitt in the course of conversation upon general politics some time before, introduced it [the catholic question]' to the king.[189] Camden's memorandum throws into focus the reasoning behind Pitt's actions. The king was aware of Pitt's feeling on the catholic question, as he was of Dundas's and Grenville's. There was a clear distinction, however, between a private belief, and something that was being pressed as a government measure. 'The king knew his [Pitt's] opinion, but he had never brought it forward as a measure.' Camden reveals that both Pitt and Grenville were aware that 'the king's opinion was always declared to be adverse to it and they both knew that unless they were backed by a majority of the cabinet his majesty was not likely to be moved'.[190] Pitt, Grenville and Dundas met on 10 January to discuss the problem. They were reunited, for one last time, because of the catholic question, convinced that the sacramental test had to be replaced with one that instead asserted political loyalty.[191] The same day Pitt thought deeply about pursuing peace with France. Pitt believed that success in the Baltic and in Egypt would secure a peace on acceptable terms, while in the mean time a fruitless negotiation with France (as it must be) ought not to be declined and I think ought to be sought, though I do not look to its failure with any hope of its leading to a long continuance of the war, for which if the great points I have mentioned [the Baltic and Egypt] can once be well settled, I own I shall have no appetite, and I believe the country will have less patience.[192]

In January 1801 the cabinet effectively splintered over the catholic question. A meeting was held early in the month for 'a preliminary discussion of the matter'. Camden was to record that a number of ministers, including himself, argued that the question was one that had been decided in November 1799, 'and by the conduct of the Irish government', but this did not meet with general agreement.[193] Instead it was decided that the matter was a new one to be settled at that time. Lords Chatham and Liverpool were absent at this cabinet, as they were to be for all councils on the subject in January.[194]

A majority of the cabinet was noted to be in favour of bringing emancipation forward as a government measure. 'There was certainly the strongest ground to suppose that whenever a solemn decision was called for, it would be determined to submit the business to the king for his consideration.'[195] This is a crucial point for understanding the events. Pitt had previously mentioned emancipation to the king as a private belief. There was no need to inform the king that it was being planned as a government measure until the cabinet decided to adopt it. At this preliminary meeting 'the principal opposers' of submitting the question before the king were Loughborough, Westmorland and Portland. Camden also had doubts but believed that, 'with considerable modifications as to the mode of introducing the subject to the king', it should be tried. Even though no formal response was made at the time 'it was not difficult to guess what would be our final decision': catholic emancipation would finally be adopted as a government policy to be submitted before the king.

The united parliament was to sit on 29 January. This created a pressing deadline and a decision became unavoidable. The cabinet had to have an opinion on the catholic question, one way or the other, or risk embarrassment at the hands of opposition, and allow indecisiveness to weaken the ministry further. Although it was not apparent at the time, the meeting of Sunday, 25 January in Lord Grenville's office was to be of great significance. The cabinet had three absentees: Chatham was at Horsham with his regiment; Liverpool was still ill; but the third was the most ominous. Loughborough chose not to attend, now asserting his position outside of cabinet. That the lord chancellor was aware of the purpose of the meeting was something Pitt made repeated reference to, insisting that as Loughborough's 'opinion was known, and was not likely to be changed', they should proceed without him. This sentiment was shared by Grenville. Spencer and Camden disagreed, arguing that although the lord chancellor might be as determined in his beliefs as they were in theirs, they still felt that it was not respectful to him and his office and it did not give us fair ground to state, when the determination of the cabinet was known, that such determination took place in the absence of so important a character, and one who was known to be [*word absent*] to that measure, which would probably [have] carried.

This was probably Loughborough's very intention.

Faced with ministers' reservations Pitt promised to see Loughborough and arrange for another cabinet on the matter the following day. But, as the ministers were assembled, Pitt deviously chose to collect the opinions of those present. He proceeded to do just that, and the matter was not debated. Only Camden contributed anything, saying 'that from everything I had heard of the king's opinion being so decided, from the suspicion I entertained by the law, I thought Mr Pitt should proceed with the utmost caution'.[196] The reason that Camden later gave for why he assented to proceed with the measure is very important. It was because of Pitt's success in softening the king's mind on previous measures, 'and preparing those of others'. Those in favour of adopting emancipation as a government policy were Pitt, Grenville, Dundas, Spencer, Windham and, 'with modifications', Camden. In opposition were Portland and Westmorland. The majority was not as clear as this suggests. Loughborough was vehemently opposed, even though he was not present, and Liverpool and Chatham were also likely to oppose. In real terms then emancipation had a majority of only one — Camden — and he harboured reservations. It is likely that, recognising his importance, Pitt used all of his considerable influence to secure his friend's qualified support. A majority of only one for such a controversial measure was not enough. As with the dispute over the Egyptian expedition it was 'far too shaky to force the hand of the king in a matter of conscience'.[197] Willis, like Mackesy, has been sharply critical of Pitt's behaviour at this time. Not only did Pitt think 'it sufficient to have his decision casually ratified by six members of an eleven-man cabinet', more importantly he was allowing the matter to fall out of his control. Willis finds it difficult

> to avoid the conclusion that the prime minister was behaving like a sleep-walker, that he had been in power so long, and had grown so accustomed to getting the king's reluctant consent to *faits accompli*, that he did not recognise the dangerous difference between royal opposition to peace negotiations, and to catholic emancipation.[198]

The meeting concluded with Spencer and Camden strongly urging that the cabinet should meet again the next day, Monday, 26 January. This was to allow for the lord chancellor to attend if he chose. Camden was to record that 'the impression upon my mind certainly was that we were to meet'. Pitt's understanding was very different. He chose to believe that the cabinet had made its decision, and that he could proceed as he liked; Loughborough was to be given an ultimatum to attend a cabinet on the Monday or have the decision of 25 January taken as final. The lord chancellor refused, making the proposed cabinet irrelevant for Pitt who decided not to hold it. The preliminary decision was taken to represent the opinion of the cabinet. Camden was to regret this as a mistake, and wrote, around 1803 or 1804, that 'it was a great neglect not to summon another meeting after the loose manner in which opinions were collected at the last. None however took place and Mr Pitt certainly imagined our determination to be made on the Sunday.' Pitt's interpretation of what had been decided was, however, maintained by Windham in his diary.[199]

Camden's account clarifies some of the confusion that has existed about the status of these deliberations. Pares has argued that the meeting was one 'whose formal status was never defined because it did not result in an immediate submission to the king'.[200] Willis has refuted this, pointing out that this 'is as much a statement of ordinary cabinet practice in the later 1790s as it is one of unusual behaviour'.[201] Even amongst the ministers there was uncertainty. Grenville believed that the meeting had formal cabinet status, but this was disputed by Loughborough, Portland and Dundas.[202]

A dinner at Camden's residence was held on the evening of Sunday, 25 January. Amongst those in attendance were Pitt, Castlereagh, and the earl of Clare over from Ireland. Pitt had a discussion with the chief secretary in private and informed him that the ministers 'had determined to bring forward the catholic question, with others relative to dissenters, as a government question and authorised him to converse with Lord Clare upon it'.[203] The next day Castlereagh and the Irish lord chancellor set out on a journey to the princess of Wales at Blackheath. It was on this journey that Castlereagh revealed the proposed emancipation policy, news that was 'received by Lord Clare with infinite concern and a declaration of his opposition to it'. Camden was to speculate, again a few years after the events, about the wisdom of informing Clare, given that the king had still not been informed, and particularly as 'discretion of language' was not one of the Irish lord chancellor's distinguishing features.[204]

The crisis worsened. The cabinet was falling apart and Pitt proved incapable of asserting his authority over events. Out of the chaos a momentum was created that destroyed the fragile stability of the ministry. The day before parliament was to meet, all of the private manoeuvring was publicly and embarrassingly revealed. On Wednesday, 28 January what should have been a normal levee became an unpleasant altercation between Dundas, Castlereagh and the king. This started the chain reaction that culminated in the collapse of the ministry. Pitt had clung to the false hope that he had time to gather opinions and support before informing the king that his government was committed to catholic emancipation. The day before parliament was to meet he learned to his cost that the king had discovered the scheme from other sources. What had been considered a difficult but surmountable obstacle had now become an implacable force. The gradual deterioration of relations between the king, his prime minister and his government had been building up to this point. At a time when Pitt was physically and mentally exhausted he had made the most serious miscalculation of his career. He was now to learn just how angry and determined the king could be.

7

The fall of Pitt

28 JANUARY 1801–MARCH 1801

What is the question which you are all about to force upon me? What is this catholic emancipation which this young lord, this Irish secretary has brought over, that you are going to throw at my head? I will tell you, that I shall look on every man as my personal enemy who proposes that question to me.[1]

The levee on 28 January, the day before the united parliament was to meet, was the scene of a dramatic confrontation between George III and Henry Dundas. With one emotional outburst the political situation was changed irrevocably. It was publicly revealed that the king had become aware, through his own sources, of the ministers' proposed policy of catholic emancipation. Any hope of persuading the king to support the measure was dashed, as was any possibility of containing the disagreements to the private sphere. A conflict between prime minister and king became unavoidable, a collision that would reveal much about Pitt, the union, and the nature of royal power, influence and authority.[2]

How the king became aware of the proposed scheme has been a matter for some conjecture. Camden was later to speculate, in his memorandum on the resignations, that once the earl of Clare had been informed of the proposed scheme on 26 January, 'a person who with various endowments and great virtues could not reckon discretion of language amongst his qualifications for great situations', it was not to be wondered 'that the king himself should learn not from channels *most* likely to lead his mind favourably an account of what had been passing'.[3] A powerful conspiracy acted against Pitt, who appears to have been the primary target of its machinations, rather than emancipation itself. A number of individuals are implicated in the affair, with sufficient evidence to suggest that they acted in concert. There were three main figures involved: Lord Chancellor Loughborough, whose role has been examined in an earlier chapter; Lord Auckland, the postmaster-general; and Dr John

Moore, the archbishop of Canterbury. A fourth, Clare, the Irish lord chancellor, seems to have assisted these men somewhat unknowingly. The first two and Clare had a long connection with each other stretching back to 1793,[4] while the archbishop of Canterbury was Auckland's brother-in-law. Richard Willis is somewhat sceptical about the extent of Auckland's involvement, but nonetheless concludes that 'it appears that for all the work done stuffing the powder keg by Loughborough, the explosion itself was touched off by Auckland and Clare in the days immediately before 28 January'.[5] Edward Cooke had spotted the existence of a web of intrigue during his time in London. He grasped that there was always a group

> endeavouring to make him [the king] form opinions of his own, to make arrangements and appointments without the advice of the cabinet, and who used every sinister artifice and low flattery for the purpose. This set must now highly plume themselves upon having fretted his mind at this crisis to take a decision against his ministers.[6]

The catholic question, he said, had been made 'a point on which prejudices in the strongest minds is insurmountable'.

In the aftermath of the resignations Lord Liverpool recounted a number of significant anecdotes about the crisis. In two stories told to Sylvester Douglas, who had just become Lord Glenbervie, the chronology of the events is slightly incorrect, but the first of them, at least, can be verified from other evidence. Liverpool recalled that Westmorland visited the queen's house one night, prior to the levee, and found the archbishop of Canterbury in conference with the king. The importance of this meeting was learned only in February when it was revealed to have been a secret discussion on the catholic question. The archbishop showed the king a letter from Auckland that exposed the extent of the government's activity on the matter. The king was under no illusions about how the letter had come to him; he told the archbishop that 'I suppose I am to consider Lord Auckland's letter to your grace as meant, substantially, to be a letter to me, as he desires you to bring it to me.'[7] After reading the communication the king was urged by the archbishop not to abandon the church. While it is unlikely that this event took place before the cabinet of 25 January, as Liverpool was to suggest, that it did take place is attested to elsewhere. Malmesbury, for example, reported that it was supposed, 'and from good grounds', that in December Auckland had written to his brother-in-law

> stating that he held it his duty to inform him, as head of the church, that a measure was in contemplation, which, if carried into effect, would put the church in danger; that it was resolved on by the leading members of the cabinet, and that he submitted it to the archbishop's judgement whether it would not become him, as metropolitan, etc., to state this danger to the king. Lord Auckland recommended secrecy as to himself.[8]

If this story was true, then Malmesbury believed Auckland had 'made a mockery of religion, and rendered it subservient to the most selfish political ends'. The ministers were not slow to spot the hand of Auckland in the crisis. In February Dundas was reported to be furious with Auckland's behaviour, and he 'complained of his intrigues, but without explaining himself'.[9] In an artful attempt to disengage himself from abuse, Auckland claimed to Pitt on 7 February that he had learned of the proposed measure of catholic emancipation only two weeks previously although, as Willis argues, this still enabled him to play the part described by Glenbervie.[10]

There were numerous reasons behind Auckland's betrayal of Pitt. He had long craved power, not content with the position of postmaster-general, and the other favours that Pitt, out of friendship, had bestowed upon him. Cabinet office was never forthcoming and this created much bitterness as Auckland began imagining himself in high office. In addition Auckland had long advised Pitt against supporting the catholic interest in Ireland. In 1795 he had reminded the prime minister of the coronation oath, and refused to be drawn upon the question of catholic emancipation, 'a point on which I am not yet prepared to form an opinion, and I hope that for some years at least it may remain a question of abstract casuistry'.[11]

There was a yet more serious motive for Auckland's intervention that is frequently ignored. The friendship between Auckland and Pitt reached its zenith at the end of 1796, when the prime minister spent much time amongst Auckland's family at Eden farm. There, he developed an attachment to Auckland's daughter, Eleanor Eden, and it was rumoured that they would soon marry. In January 1797 Pitt abruptly ended the tentative courtship. Philip Ziegler has found it hard to see any difference between Pitt's behaviour at this time and that of 'any other cold, egocentric and, of course, honourable fish'.[12] An even more cynical historian, A.D. Harvey, has scorned Pitt for his innocence with regard to women, an innocence he cites as contributing 'to the suggestion about him of one-sidedness, if not incompleteness and abnormality, and to the view that his talents were entirely verbal, with no real creativity or constructive power',[13] a rather comprehensive deduction. In reality Pitt cared deeply about Eleanor Eden. He admitted as much in a letter to Auckland in 1797, that deserves to be quoted:

> the time I have spent among your family has led to my forming sentiments of very real attachment towards them all, and of much more than attachment towards one whom I need not name . . . whoever may have the good fortune ever to be united with her is destined to more than his share of human happiness. Whether at any rate I could have had any ground to hope that such might have been my lot I am in no degree entitled to guess.[14]

Even as Pitt was terminating the relationship he found it impossible to hide his true feelings. Unfortunately, he found that an attachment was impossible, claiming that the obstacles were 'decisive and insurmountable', but refusing to elaborate. The emotional connection was to remain until his death and was frequently exploited by Auckland.

The whole affair left deep divisions between the Eden family and the prime minister. Auckland informed Pitt that his daughter reciprocated his feelings but to no avail.[15] A further letter from Pitt on the impossibility of the relationship led Auckland to drop the matter.[16] There remained

> the re-establishment of that friendly intercourse which has been in other points of view so pleasant and so valuable to us all. I fear that with regard to other parts of the family that time may be necessary for the purpose.[17]

In response to further communications from Pitt, on the mode of proceeding to avoid any embarrassment for his family, and in particular for the one whom he would not name,[18] Auckland repeated his desire that 'the public' must be made aware 'that there remains an undiminished friendship between us two at least'.[19] In the wreckage of the relationship Auckland saw an opportunity to satisfy his ambition. He applied to Pitt for the vacant cabinet position of lord privy seal: 'to me and to mine it is essential *now*'.[20] The prime minister declined to be manipulated in this way and carefully avoided giving Auckland any cabinet post, although he did make him postmaster-general in 1798, a position outside the cabinet.[21]

A highly devious and complex campaign was waged against emancipation between September 1800 and February 1801. It succeeded in its desired intention of forcing a confrontation between Pitt and the king. Given the intense ambition of Loughborough and Auckland, and their personal animosity towards Pitt, it appears incontrovertible that they were using emancipation to depose the prime minister. By 28 January their machinations had pushed the king into a highly emotional state, on an issue that had always been genuinely important to him. When the king tackled Dundas at the levee it was reported that he did so in 'a loud voice and [an] agitated manner'.[22] Dundas told Glenbervie five minutes after the event that he had apologised for the fact that the king saw the matter in the light he did, adding that he was 'sorry to re-collect that some measures I thought it my duty to propose in 1793 did not entirely accord with your majesty's sentiments'.[23] Camden reported that Dundas was 'naturally astonished' by the king's mode of address and attempted to avoid any conversation and, when this proved impossible,

> attempted to draw his majesty out of the immediate crowd which surrounded them, in order that any conversation which took place should not be over-heard, but in vain, and the king left Mr Dundas with a repetition of his assertion that he should consider every man as his personal enemy who should propose the catholic question to him. Mr Dundas of course combated these observations.[24]

The king's declamation that anyone who proposed emancipation would be considered as his personal enemy drew the short response from Dundas that 'your majesty will find many among those who are friendly to that measure some whom you never supposed to be your enemies'.[25] After this encounter the king entered into excited conversation with a number of people at the levee, and, it was alleged, 'particularly to Lord Auckland and Lord Clare'.[26] Camden did not believe that the king's behaviour to any other minister present was 'marked by any extraordinary expression or manner'.

Glenbervie had an audience with the king at this levee and the discussion is revealing. The king made his observation that 'Mr Pitt was apt to put off laborious or disagreeable business to the last, but then, when forced to it, got through it with extraordinary rapidity', ascribing the reason to the prime minister's ill health.[27] During a discussion about Lady Chatham, the prime minister's mother, the king observed that Pitt did not seem to have inherited the Grenville obstinacy from her, unlike his cousin, Lord Grenville. The king quoted Grenville on the duke of Bedford: 'It is fortunate he is never in the wrong because if he were no power on earth could convince him of it', an analysis that Glenbervie believed was being applied to the foreign secretary. The king also lamented the passing of characters who possessed 'the easy natural flow of good-natured wit', regretting that Pitt had 'nothing of that talent'.[28] Glenbervie, in his turn, criticised the prime minister for having only 'a grave, sarcastic, cutting sort' of wit, and in response the king faulted Pitt for giving too much consequence to bad speakers in parliament so that he could answer them himself.[29] It is further confirmation that the prime minister and the king were not close. Amongst his friends Pitt was renowned for his wit; Wilberforce confirms this, and Pitt, himself, provided examples of his careless humour: 'Don't tell me of a man being able to talk sense; every one can talk sense; can he talk nonsense?'[30]

The events at the levee threw the entire government off balance. Dundas immediately reported the events to Pitt, who, 'upon that communication, abstained from going to court'.[31] A cabinet council was immediately summoned to discuss the changed circumstances, and all the ministers attended. It was decided to postpone the opening of parliament, scheduled for the next day. Camden recorded that

> so extraordinary and so public a declaration upon a measure, which was thus made public, and represented as one decided upon by the government but thus opposed by the king could not fail to make a decided impression upon the minds of all who were parties to it.[32]

It was also resolved that Pitt should

> put on paper the heads of the plan intended to have been communicated to the king and [that he] should after communicating it to the cabinet wait on his majesty with it, and he undertook with Lord Grenville to prepare it by the morrow.

William Windham, the secretary at war, recorded in his diary for the day: 'cabinet, in which discussion of the catholic business, when Pitt declared that he must go out if it was not carried'.[33] Other diarists also recorded their impressions of the day. George Rose wrote that 'on Wednesday, 28 January, Mr Pitt first had distinct and clear proof of the speaker taking an eager and anxious part in influencing persons against the measure of catholic emancipation'.[34] The accuracy of these sources cannot be verified, nor can whether they were actually written on the 28th. Dundas was to tell William Adam, the prince of Wales's attorney-general, that Pitt remonstrated with Loughborough over his paper against the catholics. From the content of the conversation, this is likely to have taken place immediately after the cabinet of 28 January. Pitt blamed the lord chancellor for embarrassing the government to which the lord chancellor replied, 'I shall release you from that difficulty by resigning.'[35]

That evening Loughborough was in communication with the king. He disclosed what had been discussed at the meeting and warned the king that 'very soon a distinct and ample communication of all the considerations' on the catholic question would arrive.[36] Loughborough attempted to evade responsibility for the way the debacle had occurred, begging forgiveness 'for my indiscretion in mentioning a circumstance which may bear an application to that subject, and which at the time I referred to it, I had reason to think your majesty might have heard from the archbishop of Canterbury'. This letter serves to confirm the role of the four individuals in the affair. That Loughborough was aware of the archbishop's intervention suggests that he was in confidential communication with Auckland, who would have been best placed to enlist the support of his brother-in-law.

Pitt was soon aware of Auckland's perfidy. To defuse the tension Auckland sent the prime minister a letter on 31 January in which he attempted to explain and justify his conduct. The editor of Auckland's correspondence has defended his subject from the charge of contributing to the breakdown of the government, and contends that Auckland discovered that emancipation was being contemplated only on 30 January.[37] The evidence against this is compelling. The archbishop of Canterbury was certainly involved, and it is also clear that someone mediated between Loughborough and the archbishop. This figure was probably Auckland, certainly Pitt thought so. After receiving Auckland's letter Pitt wrote to his supposed friend and berated him for 'the failure of friendship, confidence and attention in reference to the business'.[38] Pitt said that he felt this 'so strongly' he could not dwell on it. He concluded, coldly, by saying that 'nothing belonging to this business, painful as it is to my personal feelings with respect to yourself, can make me forget how long, and how sincerely, I have been affectionately yours, W. Pitt'.[39] Responding to this, Auckland set out a detailed criticism of the proposed measure of catholic emancipation. In his conclusion, however, he betrayed that he knew somewhat more about what was going on than he might claim, for he requested that his letter be shown to Addington.[40] It is revealing that Auckland was aware of the speaker's involvement, and his growing importance.

On Thursday, 29 January the summons for a cabinet never came. A visit by the speaker, Henry Addington, halted Pitt and Grenville's attempts to draft a letter to the king on catholic emancipation, and shook the careful strategy Pitt had adopted of communicating the ministers' arguments to the king. Addington divulged that the king had been in communication with him, and had stated his conviction that the government's emancipation proposal was one to which he could never be persuaded to give his consent. In his letter to Addington the king expressed the strong doubts he had about the measure, 'and this by one styling himself a friend to administration, I mean Lord Castlereagh'.[41] The king informed the speaker that 'those best informed' had suggested that Pitt was in favour of placing the catholics on a level of political equality with the protestants. That Grenville and Dundas were also in favour, he had no doubt, 'as they have intimated as much to me', which suggests he was in communication with Grenville at the levee also. He did not disguise his abhorrence of the proposal, nor his belief that it was his duty

> should it ever come forward publicly to express my disapprobation of it, and that no consideration could ever make me give my consent to what I look upon as the destruction of the established church which by the wisdom of the parliament of England I, as well as several of my predecessors, have been obliged to swear the support of at our coronations.

The purpose of the letter, the king revealed, was that he wished the speaker to

> open Mr Pitt's eyes as to the danger arising from the mere agitating [of] so improper a question. That whatever evils have been cured by his manly recantation of his former opinions for parliamentary reform, his showing any countenance to a measure striking our church establishment at the heart, besides unhinging every political tie our forefathers have thought sacred, must affect every man attached to the principles on which our happy constitution is founded. Indeed it is exactly following the steps of the French revolution where every consideration of religion has been destroyed.[42]

At the close of the letter the king expressed his intention that if the measure was still persisted with he would 'set all etiquettes aside and desire the speaker to come to me, as I must know the true sentiments of all those who view this dangerous business in the same light I have uniformly done'. This was an implicit threat that a change of government was being considered. The speaker met with Pitt the same day, probably early on as Camden recorded a few years later, and Addington in his report to the king explained how he 'lost no time' in attempting to prevent the catholic measure being pressed and the king suffering discomfort.[43] The speaker revealed that he had communicated with the prime minister 'in the manner best suited to the occasion' but did not feel comfortable in sending all of the details in a letter. He therefore asked for an audience with the king the following day, or the day after.

Pitt lost any remaining control over events on 30 January. The king granted Addington an audience and the discussion effectively ended Pitt's ministry. Camden provides an accurate account of the meeting in his memorandum, one he claimed Pitt and Addington had verified. The crisis of 1801 has always been perceived as one where Pitt was dominant, and where he was forcing the king to choose between a new ministry or accepting catholic emancipation. In reality the reverse was true. All the time the king was in command and was quite prepared to discard Pitt if emancipation was not dropped; the demand was coming from above. Once Addington was summoned to the king's presence he was asked to form an administration:

> Mr Addington *stated* to his majesty his own unfitness and expressly stated that his majesty must permit him to mention every syllable of what was passing between them to Mr Pitt, without whose concurrence he could not obey his majesty's commands. He strongly advised and anxiously pressed the king not to suffer this matter to come to an extremity, offered his mediation, but if it could not be effected, he gave the king to understand that he would not desert him.[44]

This explains the continued good relations between Addington and Pitt; the speaker could not be held responsible for the king's actions.

The king's ultimatum changed everything. A very unsubtle message was being sent to Pitt: he could continue in office only if he abandoned emancipation. Camden is correct in his assessment that, by enlisting the support of the speaker, the king 'could not but afford to give Mr Pitt great reason to feel himself ill treated'.[45] It was little comfort that the king continually expressed his affection for Pitt while at the same time maintaining the impossibility of ever relenting on the catholic question. The most important short-term effect of the speaker's involvement was that the letter to the king explaining the catholic policy, decided upon at the cabinet of 28 January, was delayed for a number of crucial days. From Thursday, 29 January to Saturday, 31 January Pitt instead communicated to the king through Addington.

Pitt decided on the last day of January to write directly to the king. This letter, which had been in contemplation since the cabinet the previous Wednesday, was finally drafted and sent. It was, as Camden, who was probably shown it at the time, recorded, 'a most masterly exposition of the question itself'.[46] The carefully worded communication does much to defuse criticism of Pitt for assuming that the king could ever be persuaded to grant emancipation. The arguments employed were of such force and brilliance that it is at least possible that they could have had the intended effect but for the interference of certain individuals. Pitt began by asserting that he wished to present to the king points relating to catholics and dissenters that 'must naturally be agitated in consequence of the union'.[47] That the question was one the king would not like to have posed, the prime minister readily acknowledged. It was, he said, 'a painful task' to have to bring it to his attention. It was made more painful by the fact that he had learned from 'some of his colleagues, and from other quarters' the extent of the king's hostility. Nevertheless Pitt disclosed that it was the opinion of a majority of the cabinet that catholics and dissenters should become eligible for offices, and the former to be also eligible for seats in parliament, where the latter were not excluded. Such a scheme was considered 'highly advisable with a point to the tranquillity and improvement of Ireland, and to the general interest of the united kingdom'. No danger would result for the established church; the union had seen to that. Now even if the catholics or dissenters wished to attack the establishment it would prove impossible. The reasons behind the laws of exclusion had 'long been narrowed, and are since the union removed'.

The argument of the prime minister was a powerful one. The laws of exclusion had originated because the lines of division in the country had rested upon questions of religion. In the present age the lines of division were formed, not upon principles of religious belief, but upon principles of political ideology. In these changed circumstances

> a distinct political test pointed against the doctrines of modern jacobinism would be a much more just and a more effectual security than that which now exists, which may operate to the exclusion of conscientious persons well affected to the state.

In addition it would serve the interests of the government to make the catholic clergy in Ireland dependent on the government, as this would allow a measure of control over it. This argument provided a rational basis for solving the tithe problem. As with so many other related aspects for Pitt, security was the most important consideration. With the new religious principles, 'Mr Pitt humbly conceives a new security might be obtained for the civil and ecclesiastical constitution of this country more applicable to the present circumstances, more free from objections, and more effectual in itself than any which now exists.' The inclusion of the catholics would also help to make the mass of the Irish people loyal. It would give proof of the goodwill of the united parliament and 'afford the best chance of giving full effect to the great object of the union, that of tranquillising Ireland and attaching it to this country'.

These sentiments, Pitt insisted, were 'unalterably fixed in his mind. It must therefore ultimately guide his political conduct.' Pitt regretted that the king appeared to be so resolute in his opposition to the proposal. He hoped that the king might yet weigh 'maturely' what he had now submitted, 'and call for any explanation which any part may appear to require'. In the meantime Pitt promised that while the king was considering the matter he would abstain from agitating the subject in parliament, and restrain his friends from doing likewise. If, at the end of such time, the king had not altered his objections then he wished to resign his post as first minister, as 'it must personally be Mr Pitt's first wish to be released from a situation which he is conscious that, under such circumstances, he would not continue to fill but with the greatest disadvantage'. For the first time the question of resignation was brought out into the open. Pitt in the letter added that 'there is no personal difficulty to which he will not rather submit than withdraw himself at such a moment from your majesty's service'. He felt this so strongly that he was prepared to reserve the catholic question for a later discussion, even going so far as to oppose its agitation in the meantime, if this would serve the country. This arrangement, it was to be understood, could last only until a new government was formed. Pitt concluded the letter with a firm instruction. He, 'most respectfully but explicitly', submitted to the king 'the indispensable necessity of effectually discountenancing, in the whole of this interval, all attempts to make use of your majesty's name, or to influence the opinions of any individuals or descriptions of men on any part of this subject'. The message was clear. Pitt would not tolerate the king using his influence to lead an opposition against emancipation, as he had in other instances, like the Sierra Leone slavery bill of 1799. While the matter was under consideration both sides were to refrain from all attempts to rally support.

Pitt already suspected the worst. William Stuart, the archbishop of Armagh, who had been chosen by the king and named without communication with Pitt or Portland, had written to Castlereagh on 30 January, in a communication that betrayed the hand of George III. The problem centred on Isaac Corry, the Irish chancellor of the exchequer, who had been recommended to the seat held by Dr Duigenan. G.C. Bolton is inaccurate when he suggests that the replacement of Duigenan with Corry sparked the king's fury at the levee.[48] The king's anger was triggered by learning that catholic emancipation was being adopted as a government policy; the Corry incident was not significant. What was important was that the primate used the matter of the parliamentary seat to address the catholic question with the chief secretary. In his letter to Castlereagh the primate revealed that

> he understood there was a difference of opinion between the king and his ministers upon a subject, in which the church was concerned. He desired to be informed before he recommended Mr Corry whether he was opposed to the catholic question.[49]

Camden records that 'this reason amongst others induced Mr Pitt to lay a great stress on the king's ceasing to interfere, if he remained in office'. The accuracy of this is verified by Pitt's own notes to his letter of 31 January. For such an important communication Pitt made sketches for the seven main points he wished to make in the letter. The final point was the 'indispensable importance of preventing the king's name being improperly committed in the interval, and of the primate being induced to recall his determination as stated in the l[etter] to Ld C[astlereagh]'.[50]

Following protocol, the letter to the king was written in the third person, but the notes for it were written in the more personal first. Details in these reveal crucial points of emphasis. On the matter of Pitt remaining in office for an interval, there is the significant point that the prime minister considered 'much delay in itself a great evil'. Such a stance was only 'on grounds of present expediency and consistent with my own opinions on principle'. It was, also, only to be for the duration of 'the crisis' (the war) that faced the country, and until a new arrangement could be formed.

The day after sending this letter Pitt wrote to Grenville informing him of the apparent collapse of the ministry. He stated that a communication 'from a quarter which I cannot name and on which I can fully depend', presumably Addington, had left him in no doubt about the 'extent of the king's opinions'.[51] This had persuaded him to write to the king stating his whole intention, 'which you will see I have done on the idea I explained to you, and which is the only one I could bring myself to act upon'. The prime minister was not optimistic as to whether his letter would have the desired effect. He could not shake the feeling that it would prove impossible to persuade the king to relent, and he ended with the ominous remark: 'I have not yet got the king's answer, but I know what it must be.'

The response from the king was as expected. It was sent on 1 February and began pleasantly, expressing 'the cordial affection I have for Mr Pitt as well as high opinion of his talents and integrity'.[52] On the question of catholic emancipation, however, the king became firm. He reminded Pitt of his coronation oath, and that 'this principle of duty must therefore prevent me from discussing any proposition tending to destroy this ground work of our happy constitution'; emancipation would see 'the complete overthrow of the whole fabric'. The king reminded his minister that he had from the beginning insisted that the union should be grounded in a desire to unite the established churches of both kingdoms and 'forever shut the door to any further measures with respect to the Roman Catholics'.

The king accepted Pitt's terms on how to proceed. He pledged to refrain from influencing individuals on the matter, but added that he could not 'help it if others pretend to guess at my opinion which as yet I have never disguised'. However, if those who supported emancipation would allow the matter to rest, the king would 'be silent also'. This would be done purely out of affection for Pitt, and for no other reason; he could not 'sacrifice my duty to any consideration'. The conclusion of the letter made it clear that the king was not prepared to back down on the issue; Pitt had either to relent or to end his political service. The king admitted that he was not optimistic that he could persuade Pitt to adopt the former course. Nevertheless he hoped his prime minister's

> sense of duty will prevent his retiring from his present situation to the end of my life; for I can with great truth assert that I shall, from public as well as private considerations, feel great regret if I shall ever find myself obliged at any time, from a sense of religious and political duty, to yield to his entreaties of retiring from his seat at the board of treasury.

With the receipt of this letter Pitt realised that it was impossible to remain as prime minister. He immediately arranged to meet Grenville the next day and decide their public line. Pitt believed that with the opening of parliament on 2 February difficult and embarrassing questions would be put to the ministers on the matter. Therefore he suggested that

> a few words stating the simple fact that we have found it our duty to resign on a ground which may possibly produce more discussion on some future occasion, will be sufficient. The fact and the cause are in truth both sufficiently known.[53]

Pitt was obliged to help confirm some rumours about the resignations. In order to prevent damaging stories from affecting the stock exchange he had informed the governor of the Bank of England about what was happening. He believed that 'by this step much speculation and some alarm will be prevented'. This was confirmed by a diary entry of Glenbervie which recorded that on 31 January a report, said to have originated from Carlton house, circulated in London that Pitt had resigned, causing stocks to have risen by 2 per cent, from the idea that a change in the ministry would lead to peace with France.[54] Meanwhile, there was little doubt that Addington was to be Pitt's successor. It was evident that the king had made his choice. Pitt was not too worried about the meeting of parliament as he believed a debate could be postponed easily, and a new speaker chosen 'as a preparatory step' to the creation of a new administration.[55] The formal resignations of the ministers could follow the next week.

These sentiments were fully approved by Grenville. The only point on which he differed concerned Pitt's hope that a discussion of the subject might be prevented. Grenville believed that this would prove impossible, 'as *all* that has passed upon it is so publicly and universally known, and is even I believe stated in the newspapers'.[56] There was, however, full agreement between the cousins on the matter of pursuing a common line, as far as was possible, 'without actually doing what I think dishonourable'. The newspapers had indeed been speculating on the possible reasons for the adjournment of parliament, and were to continue to do so. On 2 February *The Times* ascribed it to a dispute over a contentious question of foreign policy. The previous day, Sunday, 1 February, various opposition figures had also been speculating about the rumours. Lord Hamilton wrote to Lord Holland anxious to learn what was happening and disclosing that he, like Grenville, distrusted newspapers. Hamilton's comments are interesting for what they reveal about general whig political opinion at the time:

> that Pitt has been outvoted in the cabinet I can readily conceive — but that he will *therefore* go out, exceeds the limits of my faith — and particularly my faith in his *character*. He would [not] be displaced by so *lenient* a mind, unless he thinks it some way connected with his future prosperity.[57]

On Monday, 2 February Grenville wrote to his brother, Buckingham, about the crisis. He reiterated his belief that

> the union with Ireland would be a measure extremely incomplete and defective as to some of the most material benefits to be expected from it, unless immediate advantage was taken of it to attach the great body of the Irish catholics to the measure itself.[58]

As foreign secretary, Grenville was particularly aware of the strategic importance of keeping Ireland tranquil. The threat of invasion, he felt, made it even more desirable that 'an effort ought to be made to conciliate the affections of the mass of that people'.[59] The idea of a political test, that Pitt had outlined so well in his letter to the king, was one that Grenville and he had long worked at. They had formed 'an extensive arrangement' on the whole subject, replacing the, 'now notoriously evaded and insufficient for any effectual purpose', sacramental test with one directed against jacobin principles. A tithe policy was to have accompanied this, Grenville revealed, and a majority of cabinet members had approved of the scheme, only to find that the king had 'persuaded himself, or has been persuaded by others' that this would subvert his coronation oath. It had reached a point, he regretfully conceded, that 'admits of no compromise'.

The ministers were slow to blame the king. Grenville respected George III's 'conscientious opinion' but hoped that he would likewise recognise that of his ministers. They could not remain in government to see the opposition raise the matter in parliament, and be forced into declaring their opinions. Therefore the king had the choice of softening his objections, or else forming a government composed of those who shared his sentiments. It was a source of great regret that the matter had not been kept private. Grenville was deeply disappointed to find that Pitt's instruction for the king to refrain from agitating the question had not been heeded: 'it is much regretted, that the warmth with which the king feels and expresses himself on this subject, should already have rendered the matter so public'.[60] Worse, Grenville had reason to believe that the king was 'actually engaged in the formation of the new government'. The reply from Buckingham displayed a notable degree of family pride. Persuading the king to approve of emancipation Buckingham had always realised would be a difficult struggle, but he had 'imagined that he [the king] had made up his mind to what was in fact the *avowed* corollary of the union'.[61] It was a matter of great surprise for him that the king wished to change the ministers on the issue; he refused to accept that the king could succeed. Buckingham would not accept that there were suitable materials for a change of ministry, particularly as the issue would cause Ireland to 'run riot'. There was no alternative line of conduct that Buckingham felt Pitt and his brother could pursue,

> for your opinions and your personal credit are at stake on this question; and I should have thought you, under all the circumstances of the union question, the weakest or the wickedest government if you took the contrary line.

When parliament opened on 2 February the king was in dangerously high spirits. It was reported that he 'looked particularly well, and read his speech with particular energy and clearness, much beyond what has been usual with him for the last ten or fifteen years'.[62] It was soon to become apparent that this was just the precursor for a return to the illness that had affected him in 1788. With elements of farce, the king refused to abstain from agitating on the catholic question. Auckland reported a story that occurred when the king was robing in the presence of a number of lords. He discussed with the duke of Norfolk changes the nobleman was making to his castle at Arundel. When the duke acknowledged that he was indeed making 'considerable alterations' the king advised him to take care 'not to meddle with the foundations', all the time 'looking significantly to some of the other lords'.[63]

The king's uncompromising behaviour left no alternative. Pitt was forced to tender his resignation. On 3 February he wrote to the king to inform him that his continuance in office was impossible. Pitt acknowledged the king's motives, which he 'respects and honours', but his

> own unalterable sense of the line which public duty requires from him, must make him consider the moment as now arrived, when on the principle he has already explained, it must be his first wish to be released, as soon as possible, from his present situation.[64]

Pitt did not hide his annoyance at the king's conduct. He felt obliged to

> frankly confess to your majesty that the difficulty even of his temporary continuance must necessarily be increased, and may very shortly become insupportable, from what he conceives to be the import of one passage in your majesty's note, which hardly leaves him room to hope that your majesty thinks that those steps can be taken for effectually discountenancing all attempts to make use of your majesty's name to influence opinions on this subject.

In any case, Pitt had come to realise that it would not be sound policy to remain in office for a short interval, even if the king chose to remain silent. Pitt informed him that a temporary government could only 'produce an effect both at home and abroad which might lead to serious inconvenience'.

Responsibility for the decision now rested with the king. He was faced with the choice of replacing the minister who had served him loyally for seventeen years, or softening his stance on the catholic question. The ministers remained pessimistic about the probable result of the king's deliberations; they accepted they were leaving office. Grenville wrote to his brother on 4 February to reveal that he was sure 'that the resolution is finally taken'.[65] The king's prejudice was considered too strong to 'induce him to depart from it'. Grenville hoped that the king would be able to form a new ministry, and he pledged to support it to 'weather the storm' that it must face at home, and particularly abroad.

There was never any doubt in George III's mind about how he should act. As he was to declare in 1807 'he must be the protestant king of a protestant country, or no king'.[66] It took less than two days for him to send his decision. In his response to Pitt he rebuked him for all his criticisms. He was disappointed to find 'Mr Pitt does not draw the same conclusions' as he had from the letter of 1 February to the minister, when

> I had flattered myself that the strong assurance I gave Mr Pitt of keeping perfectly silent on the subject wherein we entirely differ, provided he on his part kept off any discussion on it for the present, which was the main object of the letter I wrote to him on Sunday, [was enough and] that we both understood our present lines of conduct.[67]

The king noted that he must reluctantly accept Pitt's resignation.

The other ministers who supported emancipation now resigned. The first was Grenville, who sent his letter after finding out the result of the king's communication with Pitt. In an elegant communication the foreign secretary set out 'the warm and dutiful acknowledgments of a grateful heart for all your majesty's uniform goodness and indulgence towards him'.[68] He added that 'his affectionate attachment to your majesty will be the rule of his conduct in all situations and circumstances of his future life'. Nothing would ever give him greater pleasure than 'being able, on every occasion, to contribute by any feeble aid of his, to the ease and honour of your majesty's government'.

A new ministry was already being formed. On Friday, 30 January Addington had stayed with the king for four and a half hours, locked in conference, and it was reported that he was 'very earnest against the catholic question'.[69] By 5 February he had accepted the post of first lord of the treasury, and prepared to resign his post as speaker to make way for the new arrangement.[70] According to one version, Addington initially refused until the king asked him to 'lay your hand upon your heart, and ask yourself where I am to turn for support if *you* do not stand by me'.[71] Lord Granville Leveson-Gower, when handing in his resignation to Addington on 14 February, reported that the former speaker confessed that he was assuming office only 'as a sort of *locum tenens* for Pitt'.[72] This was subsequently denied, ever more strongly as time went on, with the editor of Addington's correspondence claiming that Addington never considered himself a caretaker prime minister.[73] The evidence would seem to justify this. In political circles from 5 February it was widely discussed that the king would form an administration, not from the opposition, but from 'such of Pitt's friends who do not think as he does on this particular point'.[74] The name of the speaker was being mentioned as the most likely successor. It was also reported that 'Lord Auckland *mentions himself*.'[75]

The speculation about the nature of the government continued throughout the week. Malmesbury predicted Addington at its head, with the duke of Portland and Lord Loughborough also expected to remain in office. He considered it strange that Pitt had not written one word to his brother, Chatham, on the subject. The diplomat blamed Pitt for the break-up of the government. He did not believe that Pitt had treated the king with any '*real* respect', and felt that he should have prepared the king's mind gradually with good arguments in favour of a new test. Instead Pitt had allowed himself to be outmanoeuvred by 'Loughborough directly, and . . . Auckland indirectly, through the archbishop of Canterbury and the bishop of London'.[76]

The younger Pitt had, in fact, been in communication with his brother, and had sent him detailed papers on the matter for his deliberation. Chatham, however, was opposed to extending full political rights to the catholics, and on this question sided against his sibling. He returned the papers on 6 February, expressing the 'deep sorrow' his brother's letter had given him.[77] On the measure for catholic emancipation, Chatham wrote that he had 'neither time (nor indeed would it be any use) to say anything at present'. He regretted that he had been absent at the crucial cabinets as he would have attempted to pre-vent the question from being agitated. Despite this, he thought it fortunate that he 'had avoided a discussion which would have been painful to me, in many respects'.[78] Chatham believed that the king could not have chosen a better successor than the speaker. He ended the letter with a hope that

> the good fortune which in so many instances has watched over the affairs of this country, may yet ward off a blow, which I assure you (independent of all private feelings of which I say nothing) I consider as a most serious one indeed.[79]

The third key figure of the government, Henry Dundas, resigned the same day. He informed the king that he did not wish to 'trouble your majesty with any details' of the disagreement, but rather presented his resignation, humbly, to the king and hoped that 'the request will not appear unreasonable at the end of thirty-five years unremittingly and laboriously spent in your majesty's service'.[80] Dundas concluded with the gracious tribute that it would be 'his unceasing prayers to heaven that your majesty in a long, extended reign, may be blessed by the enjoyment of every public and private comfort'. This was followed by the resignation of Camden and the other ministers who had supported emancipation, Windham and Spencer.

There was no hidden motive behind Grenville's resignation. He was genu-ine in his belief that it had been impossible for the ministers to act in any other way without 'agreeing to the disguise or dereliction of one's opinion on one of the most important questions in the whole range of our domestic policy'.[81] He outlined the entire background to the resignations in a letter to the earl of Carysfort, who was on a diplomatic mission to Berlin, that directly followed his letter to the king. In it he revealed that

> the immediate and sole cause of this event is an insurmountable difference of opinion which has arisen between the king and the majority of his present servants on the subject of the measures to be adopted respecting the catholics of Ireland.[82]

Grenville described to Carysfort his long-held belief that the union would not be complete unless it was immediately followed by emancipation. This was also necessary because of the 'general posture of affairs in Europe'. Pitt, 'after much deliberation', had formed the same opinion, as had Dundas, Spencer, Camden and Windham. Therefore 'an extensive plan' had been devised of replacing the religious test with one against jacobin principle. This policy would have produced great advantage from the catholics in Ireland in the first days of the united kingdom. The king's objections, however, had forced the ministers to retire, to be replaced by a government headed by Addington. The ministers could not remain in office and be forced into resisting 'in parlia-ment a measure which we, in our consciences, think so highly expedient, both in itself, and still more particularly with a view to the circumstances of the present moment'.[83]

The foreign secretary hoped that Carysfort, like others uninvolved in the dispute, would remain at his post. It was highly desirable that, at a time when the empire was beset by 'a crisis so very arduous . . . from which the strongest nerves might shrink', the talents of so many different individuals were not removed. Grenville was also aware that Carysfort did not share his views on the catholic question, and he clearly stated that the ministers could not have followed any other line with honour. He remained gloomily apprehensive 'as to the result of all this', but 'it is my duty to submit the event to providence'. The conclusion of the letter was most revealing about Grenville's feelings. To have acted differently 'would have been to do evil that good may come of it'. Grenville would not remain in office in the abstract hope that it might prevent disaster. His sense of duty was unalterable.[84]

The story of the ministers' resignations became openly known on the morning of 7 February. Malmesbury again speculated that Pitt had acted selfishly in the whole affair, playing 'a very criminal part' at a critical time, by attempting to place himself in a position where he could be recalled 'with uncontrolled power'.[85] The diplomat also believed that the prime minister was mistaken in such an assumption. That evening a dinner was held attended by Pitt, Castlereagh, Addington, Dundas and a number of lesser government figures. Dundas informed Alexander Trotter, the paymaster of the navy, that he was leaving office and showed him a copy of his resignation letter. He added that 'he could not walk the streets as a gentleman were he to abandon, what he considered himself pledged to support, the repeal of the test act'.[86] The same day the king answered some of the ministers' resignation letters. In his response to Dundas he threw some light on the background to the events. He claimed that he had learned that the catholic question had been in agitation only 'till within these very few weeks',[87] a claim consistent with the chronology that has been argued here.

The conduct of Dundas was subject to much speculation. Lord Liverpool believed that the reason given by him was not the real one. On 8 February he discussed with Glenbervie what he considered to be at the heart of the problem: that the secretary of state for war was

> apprehensive of enquiry concerning the expeditions, that he has for some time wished to retire from the war department, in order to weaken or avoid any impending blow, and that having hitherto failed in obtaining the king or Pitt's consent to this he has hit on the present mode of obtaining his end.[88]

Glenbervie recorded in his diary that he too entertained these doubts.

The suspicions could not have been more wrong. Far from seeking an excuse to withdraw from office Dundas was actively seeking to prevent the new arrangement, and by the end of the month he would have even concocted a devious scheme to remain in office. His actions were motivated by a conviction that any government formed with Addington at its head would 'crumble to pieces almost as soon as formed'.[89] It was little comfort, for him, that friends of Pitt were remaining on to assist the new administration. They were doing so only with 'the utmost *chagrin* and unwillingness', purely because it was Pitt's wish, but they had no faith in the new ministry. There was a widespread feeling amongst them that they were 'embarking in an administration under a head totally incapable to carry it on and which must, of course, soon be an object of ridicule'. Dundas also disclosed that the aristocracy of the country, who were friendly to government, were shocked that the 'first minister of the country' could be chosen 'from a person of the description of Mr Addington without the slightest pretensions to justify it'. For the sake of the country, and for Addington's reputation, Dundas believed Pitt should intervene. This would not have to involve Pitt's return, but he believed it essential that Pitt persuade Addington to advise the king to choose Portland to head the government.

George Canning was also sharply critical of the new arrangement. He sneered at the choice of Addington, and told Malmesbury that Pitt had 'made him promise *not to* laugh at the speaker's appointment to the treasury'.[90] Canning said that that was all he could 'possibly undertake'. He regarded Addington's decision to accept high office as a joke and a betrayal of his master. Canning revealed that he had urged Pitt not to yield to the king on the catholic question. He was aware that the king, for some three years back, had forced so many concessions, and had overruled so many government measures, that the ministry had been severely weakened. Canning believed that if a stand were not made, 'Pitt would retain only a nominal power, while the real one would pass into the hands of those who influenced the king's mind and opinion out of sight.'[91]

It was revealed on 8 February that Sir John Mitford, the attorney-general, was to succeed Addington as speaker. Mitford, who was later ennobled to become Lord Redesdale, and who was to succeed Clare as lord chancellor of Ireland, reminded Pitt a couple of years later that Pitt himself had urged him to accept the post. Mitford had disapproved of the change of ministers, and felt that the new administration had been 'avowedly formed by your friends'.[92] He had wished to retire from office along with Pitt but remembered that the minister had persuaded him otherwise with the words, 'That you must not do, for my sake.' Lady Stafford expressed her own concern at the change: 'Oh dear! What a sad blow this resignation is! It will destroy us all.'[93]

The fate of the conspirators was instructive. Auckland wrote to his son about the affair and declared his regret at Pitt leaving office:

> I do not think *it* calculated to add lustre to his great character; (it will be thought ill timed and a withdrawing in a crisis of accumulated difficulties) I lament it for my own sake, for despite of our friendly professed intentions these differences on essential points tend to estrange men from each other.[94]

It would soon emerge that these were also Auckland's own feelings; he was to make his views quite public. On the question of the new ministry he attempted to play down the suggestions of his own ambition for high office: 'I have no such views or wishes, *au contraire.*' Nevertheless within a day of this letter Auckland did present his services to Addington:

the respect I owe both to you and myself induces me to say that I shall continue to pursue the line which my sense of duty to the king and of parliament constantly prescribes to me. And in pursuing that line I have no public wish whatsoever but to promote a safe termination of the severe struggles which press upon us, and to preserve the independence, the prosperity, the honour, and the civil and religious constitution of the empire.[95]

Despite this profession of loyalty, no promotion was forthcoming for Auckland. He was forced to remain as postmaster-general 'against his expectation'.[96] It was also speculated that Loughborough would be forced to resign 'against his will' with the resignation he had offered Pitt being taken at its word. Malmesbury believed that both men had '*over-cunning'd* the business', and had not had 'resolution or firmness of character to act openly on what they have combined, I apprehend, secretly'. Dundas was highly critical of Auckland's behaviour in provoking the crisis and in early February spoke of him with 'great acrimony'.[97] His treacherous part was never forgotten; in November 1801 during a disagreement, over whether Pitt would join with Fox, Auckland insisted that Lord Liverpool did not understand the matter as well as he did. Liverpool retorted: 'I certainly do not, my lord, *I have never in my life engaged or meddled in political intrigue*.'[98] It was also noted that both Loughborough and Auckland, and particularly the latter, dreaded a return to power by Pitt for they would 'incur, as they well deserve, his displeasure'. Time would prove the truth of this prediction. One of the first decisions Pitt made when he returned to office in May 1804 was to relieve Auckland of his post of postmaster-general. Pitt was not by nature disposed to forgive conduct that he deemed shabby.

The Times used the opportunity provided by the crisis to turn on Pitt. The paper had been a regular supporter of Pitt's ministry until the prime minister had cut off its official subsidy in 1799. After that its attitude changed with Grenville noting that 'under cover of a pretended support of government [it] is in decided hostility to it'.[99] On 9 February the paper addressed the changes that previously it had only hinted at. The paper believed that Portland was to be prime minister, after an initial plan in favour of Addington had been altered. Addington, it speculated, was instead to become chancellor of the exchequer. On the matter of office for Auckland the paper had a curious message: 'we suppose that Lord Auckland will also fill some high office, as the new arrangements have been principally made under his and Lord Loughborough's direction'.[100] The next day *The Times* divulged that Addington was to be prime minister, as well as chancellor of the exchequer. The paper regretted that George III had not been consulted before promises had been made to the catholics in Ireland, and it praised the virtues and high principles of the king.

In parliament on 10 February Grenville announced that he was leaving office. He informed the lords that some time before, his colleagues in the house, Spencer and Chatham, and other of the king's ministers, had 'thought it expedient that the benefits of the union should be rendered as extensive as possible, by certain disabilities being removed'.[101] As this policy had been rejected by 'his majesty's councils' there had been no alternative but to retire from office. The same day Addington resigned as speaker in the commons. After this, Pitt moved to adjourn the house. On 11 February Mitford was formally chosen as the new speaker.

'The strongest minds', it was soon revealed, had been deeply affected by the stressful events. The manipulation of the king only exacerbated the strain he felt on a matter that he had always considered one of the most important. The problems facing him weighed heavily on his mind and proved an intolerable burden. He found himself unable to control the pressure and as he crumpled there was a return of the condition that had affected him in 1788. This illness was recognised only on 21 February but there are clear indications that it had unbalanced the king's mind much earlier, 11 February being the first evidence of the crisis. This was the date of another levee, the first since the resignations, and it was 'remarkably full'.[102] As soon as Pitt appeared the king made a dash from the people he was with and headed for his minister with, what Pretyman tactfully reported as, 'the most eager graciousness imaginable'. Despite the bishop of Lincoln's discretion the instability of the king's mind was apparent. Finding Pitt he addressed him

> loud enough to be heard at some distance 'Mr Pitt I am glad to see you. I have a great deal to say to you — you have acted throughout the whole business like *yourself*, and more I cannot say.'

Upon hearing this 'Pitt bowed with the greatest respect', attempting to hide his embarrassment at the king's behaviour. Never one for public displays of feeling, Pitt was uncomfortable, and may have guessed that the king was not quite himself. He thanked the king, 'in a way endeavouring to stop the conversation, "your majesty has already said much more than the occasion required"'. The king was not to be stopped:

> 'No no, I must see you presently I have a great deal to say to you — you have done everything you should do — so unlike all your predecessors! I don't care who hears me' (upon Mr Pitt's evident wish to prevent his saying more) 'I must have all the world hear me. I cannot say too much of your conduct.'

After this emotional outburst Pitt went to talk to the king in his closet 'and stayed some time'. It was a moving meeting with the king several times breaking down in tears. The bishop reported that

> the king expressed in the *strongest* terms his *perfect satisfaction*, his *extreme regret*, and his *affectionate attachment* — he was several times *much affected* — expressed an earnest hope that 'though this *unhappy circumstance* in which *both* had acted from a principle of duty had deprived him of Mr Pitt as his *minister* he *might ever consider* him *as his friend*'.

When asked to visit regularly Pitt was forced to disappoint the king. He regretted that if this was not as often as he would like, it would not be out of a lack of affection for the king, rather 'it seemed to him of the highest importance to his majesty's government that it should appear *to stand upon its own bottom*'. When asked many years later if he thought the catholic question was the genuine reason behind Pitt's resignation, Addington insisted that it was 'the real, and he believed the sole cause of Pitt's retirement'.[103] Significantly, Addington was uncomfortable calling it 'retirement'; he said 'the king *positively dismissed him*' when Pitt declared in the closet that he could not back down from proposing catholic emancipation. Addington recollected that 'the king's dismissal of Pitt (though kind in manner) was decisive in tone, and took him [Pitt] quite by surprise'.[104]

The king was not the only one deeply distressed by the meeting. According to Lord Liverpool Pitt 'cried profusely at the audience' and on leaving the closet 'appeared much agitated'.[105] This encouraged Glenbervie to speculate that the resignations resulted, in part, from the excessive psychological strain on Pitt that bordered, perilously, on mental collapse. This, he now believed, had been coming since June 1798 when Pitt had discussed union with him at Holwood, after the duel with Tierney and his illness, and he 'recollected his [Pitt's] faltering, almost intoxicated voice, after a glass or two of wine and water'.[106] Glenbervie had his own reasons to view the resignations in a subjective light. He had received an Irish peerage on the condition that he went to the Cape, as governor, 'under the idea of supporting it with dignity'.[107] The moment Pitt resigned, however, he immediately offered his services to Addington, and received the post of paymaster. Dundas was furious with this duplicity. John Ehrman has rightly labelled Glenbervie a 'capable, unattractive place-hunter'.[108] There is certainly a touch of guilt in Glenbervie's accusations of unscrupulous manoeuvrings. Glenbervie insisted that he was 'quite in the dark' as to the motives of the outgoing ministers,[109] but he refused to accept the reasons given for the change alleging that 'it was supposing men to become fools to act as Pitt, Grenville, etc. had done, on such motives as they *avowed*'. He held Grenville particularly accountable for wanting to 'drive a nail through the king's head'.

The emotionless mask that Pitt had carefully constructed finally collapsed. At the cost of his health the prime minister had weathered an accumulation of pressures between May 1798 and January 1801. Now he was neither physically nor psychologically capable of handling the unrelenting waves of stress. Pitt's nervous state, which had been gradually undermined by the burdens of office, became unbalanced by the turmoil. His resignation was an emotional and deeply upsetting occurrence, made worse by the perceived treachery involved and the hostile attitude of the king. He was reduced to tears on many occasions. On Friday, 6 February he sent for Lord Hawkesbury, Liverpool's son, and persuaded him to remain in office for his sake: 'He was much agitated and cried, but declared that his administration was decidedly at an end.'[110] Glenbervie chose to make a comparison between the prime minister's condition in 1801 and the duke of Marlborough's imbecility, after it was reported that Pitt 'with his intimate friends bursts into tears whenever he spoke of the present explosion'.[111] Canning had always recognised that Pitt was essentially a 'shake-handy' sort of man,[112] but few in public knew the true man, the one who carefully hid his shyness, and shielded his emotions. The prime minister was not an automaton, despite the perception; ultimately he was a very emotional man. He had fought to cope with the tensions of office; he found it initially very difficult to handle the pressures of non-office. The levee with the king would have been deeply disturbing in itself but was made worse by the behaviour of George III that placed severe question marks over *his* mental stability. Seeing the king pushed into a return of his illness would have occasioned an even more emotional response. This reaction determined his conduct over the next month.

The king struggled to face his personal crisis. An example of his troubled state of mind was recounted by Lord Guilford the next month. Guilford had heard that 'a considerable time' ago, roughly around this time in February, the king was out riding with the head of his stables and without warning grabbed the breast of his coat with both hands and told him to 'keep out the pope'. This story was taken as an indication that the illness, or 'madness', was gradually coming on, and was 'of a religious kind'.[113] In a conversation with Portland the king displayed further signs of strain. He told the home secretary that were he to agree to emancipation 'he should betray his trust, and forfeit his crown; that it might bring the framers of it to the gibbet [gallows]'.[114] The duke was convinced that 'the king had rather suffer martyrdom, than submit to this measure'. When out riding with General Garth the king stopped at Kew to examine his coronation oath and despaired that 'I had rather beg my bread from door to door throughout Europe than consent to any such measure' as emancipation.[115]

Friday, 13 February was a fast-day. The king spent a considerable time in church, and as the weather was very snowy, he became 'excessively chilled' on the journey home.[116] Cramps followed and on the next day Addington recommended that the king leave town for a few days. When Addington visited again on the Sunday he found the king with 'a severe cold on him, and almost a total loss of voice'. By Tuesday, 17 February there was still no improvement. Addington reported that the king's manner was 'more hurried, and his countenance more heated than usual'.[117] The next day the prince of Wales saw his father and told the queen that he was heated and feverish. His mother was furious and, protecting her husband, replied 'with warmth': 'He is not. He has not been feverish.'[118]

Although the king held other individuals ultimately responsible for what had happened he resolved, even in his debilitated state, that Pitt would never again be his prime minister. In 1802 the king was reported to have expressed 'his full conviction that *Mr Pitt never would resume office*', and also to have disclosed that he did not believe that the catholic question was responsible for Pitt's resignation but 'that he could not carry on the war, and could not bring his mind to make the peace'.[119] Despite the warm feelings the king expressed for Pitt at the levee of 11 February he was convinced, even then, that Pitt would not return to power. On 18 February the ways and means for the year were passed without debate in parliament, an extraordinary occurrence, and the king wrote to Pitt to express his satisfaction. It seems that the king's undiagnosed illness affected his tone; it did make him irritable and he was to criticise Pitt's conduct to Chatham the next day. The opening was hardly likely to cheer up the outgoing prime minister: 'my dear Pitt as you are closing, much to my sorrow, your political career . . .'[120] As far as the king was concerned Pitt's political service had ended.

There was to be little improvement in the king's condition over the next few days. On 19 February Addington found him 'so much indisposed that he dreaded the effect which the reception of his new ministers in council' the following day might have on his health.[121] Pitt told Rose that the king's 'conduct and conversation' was 'very extravagant', and feared that his mind 'was not in a proper state'.[122] That day, or the next, the king met with Chatham and belligerently informed him that he had 'a bad cold, but it is much the worse for your brother'.[123] In the council of 20 February the king behaved with 'great dignity and calmness'.[124] Glenbervie, who was present, was oblivious to what was going on, and with an unfortunate choice of words said that the king was 'mad with anger against Dundas and Pitt'.[125] He found the king 'quite well', with only a cold affecting him.[126] Malmesbury believed otherwise, considering the king to be 'very bilious'. After the meeting the king gave an audience to Lord Eldon, the incoming lord chancellor, and discussed his previous illness in detail.[127] It was only on Sunday, 22 February that word came from the duke of Cumberland that his father's illness had taken 'an unpleasant turn'.[128] Malmesbury saw the king at twelve o'clock that day and was apprehensive that his bilious state was worsening.[129] The dangerous state of the king's health necessitated the return of Dr John Willis, who had helped assist his father, Francis Willis, in 1788.

The king attempted to hide his illness. On 22 February he wrote to Pitt requesting his presence for a meeting. The subject was 'particular business which cannot be postponed'.[130] The next day any meaningful conversation with the king proved impossible. On Monday, 23 February the king argued with Dr Willis about his competence: 'I am quite well you see — quite well.'[131] Willis was not to be convinced. He told the king that he was 'exceedingly ill', and, refusing to break the king's gaze, bullied his patient into submission. The king dropped his disguise: 'I see I *cannot* deceive you. I have deceived all the rest. They think me well, but I cannot deceive *you*.' After a short pause he broke down 'in an *agony* of tears'. Throwing himself into the doctor's arms he said, 'with an emotion that Willis could not repeat without tears', 'You are right. I *am* ill indeed.' He pleaded with Willis to prevent a regency and guarantee that the doctor's father would not return. The king then cried for a further quarter of an hour before walking around the room with Willis for an hour and a half, 'sometimes agitated, sometimes calm'.

Two sources were blamed by Malmesbury for the king's state. The first was the group of individuals who had, 'secretly and unknown to the ministry, *practised* on the king's *religion* and disposed him to resist the intended measure of catholic emancipation'. The second group was the ministers themselves who had not prepared the king for the measure and had resigned hastily.[132] Within both groups, Malmesbury accepted that some had acted out of principle, but he also maintained that some had acted to gratify private ambition and interest. These he considered 'the most consummate political villains that ever existed'. With the king's condition being ignored, work continued on the formation of the new ministry. Chatham wrote to Addington, after expressing his feelings to his brother, offering his support. The incoming prime minister admitted the letter had given him much 'relief and satisfaction'.[133] Everything, he revealed, was going 'more favourably than I could have supposed'. The following night Addington sent his reply to Chatham after having talked with Pitt until after midnight. Both men were reported as being 'never in their lives so cordial as they are at present'.[134] Some relief was provided by the news that most of the followers of Pitt would support the new arrangement, although there were some exceptions.

It was widely understood that Pitt left office without any hope of returning. He realised this too, and persuaded his supporters to join with Addington rather than risk the country being destroyed by allowing the opposition to govern. Pole certainly believed this interpretation and felt that Pitt would act honourably, convinced that 'he can never agree with the king, or rather never can get the king to agree with him'.[135] It was an important distinction. Pole also believed the new ministry would last despite the doubts expressed by many people. Of the ministers who had left office, Windham was reported to be denying any involvement in the discussion of the catholic question during the union. He apparently found the ministers 'highly blameable' for not making the king aware of what would follow the union. It was also reported that he seemed relieved to be out of office.[136]

Some chose to believe that Dundas and Grenville were also glad to be resigning. General Bude, who was close to George III, reported that the king blamed the foreign secretary for not being straightforward in the business and for secretly wishing to retire.[137] He believed Dundas had acted in a similar way, wishing to 'extricate himself from the difficulties in which the country was involved' without damaging his reputation. Both men were held responsible for forcing Pitt to act as he had. In a letter to Addington the king stated that he felt Pitt had been an unwilling accomplice in their schemes. This was to be a recurring theme for the king, as different individuals at different times were held responsible for the crisis. On 13 February the king was inclined to forgive Dundas and accepted his explanations, instead blaming (although he accepted that it appeared 'extraordinary') Camden, Castlereagh and Canning for persuading 'Mr Pitt to take the rash step he has taken'.[138] Again, he did not hold Pitt responsible for his actions and believed that the minister's 'own good heart' led him to follow the line of support for the new government that he had adopted.

The king was mistaken in his analysis about the ministers leaving. Grenville felt great concern at quitting office at a time 'when the storm appears to augment'.[139] But the outgoing foreign secretary did not accept the criticisms of the change that were being made in public. He had confidence that the houses of parliament had plenty of talented individuals capable of running the government efficiently: nor 'will [there] be any want of great abilities to be called forth by great occasions'. It was not for Grenville to side with 'the vulgar in the present moment'. Glenbervie reported that Grenville appeared very ill at this time.[140] He also noted a startling conversation between the outgoing minister and the king: when Grenville requested an audience, the king snapped and said, 'Well, I am quite ready for you.' The audience was less melodramatic. Grenville asked for, and obtained, a provision for his wife after his death. Far from being angry, the king granted it 'in the handsomest manner, and with an expression of peculiar kindness'.[141]

The junior members of the administration who were devoted to Pitt were devastated by his resignation. Almost en bloc they decided to follow their master into political exile. Canning, Pitt's close friend, was noticeably less composed than Grenville on leaving office. Malmesbury reported that he was 'much out of sorts' and attributed this to his desire to remain.[142] In fact he was deeply unsettled about leaving office, and was ambiguously considering whether he should stay. Writing on 14 February, however, he declared that although Pitt wished him to remain in office he would follow his friend and leader out of it, 'which is rather hard upon me you will say, and so it is perhaps'.[143] His story was a short one: 'Pitt resigns, no matter for what reason, and I feel it right to follow him out of office.' Canning was deeply jealous of his relationship with Pitt and was very anxious to do right by him: 'Others do what they will. I will do what I think right *by Pitt*, even against his own professed opinion and earnest persuasion.'[144] Granville Leveson-Gower, who informed his mother that 'Pitt is the object of my political idolatry', also announced his resignation. He could not serve in an administration that Pitt was not at the head of, and certainly not one led by Addington, because, 'In short, the dregs of government cannot make a respectable administration.'[145] George Rose, likewise, chose not to continue in government unless Pitt was at its head. After seventeen years of service he swore that he would rather consent to the prostitution of his daughter than remain in office without him.[146]

The Times continued with its criticisms of the change. The paper believed that the matter should not have been rushed at a time of 'danger and dismay'.[147] The following day it expressed a hope that the ministers' resignations would not have an effect abroad 'analogous to what we now feel and deplore in our own country'.[148] On the choice of Lord Liverpool's son, Lord Hawkesbury, as foreign secretary, the paper regretted that Auckland had not been chosen. Support was forthcoming for the new administration but its very necessity was regretted. In its editorial comment on 14 February the paper declared that the change of government was one that is 'lamented by every Englishman, and which is calculated to fill the breasts of our enemies with triumph and exultation'. On 16 February it was announced in *The Times* that

Lord Loughborough was to retire from public affairs with a pension of 4,000l a year. The paper continued in its criticisms of the outgoing ministers. It believed that

> whoever considers the perilous moment in which they have quitted the rudder of the state will feel that there must have been another cause to induce men of their high character and spirit to undergo the blame for so questionable a proceeding.

Rumours and doubts about the true cause of the resignations were prevalent. Malmesbury reported the same day that Pitt's conduct was generally criticised and there was 'all sort of idle conjecture as to the *real* cause of his going'.[149] Few figures understood the reasons behind the change. The great adversary of Pitt, Charles James Fox, did not accept the view of some that it was 'a *mere* juggle'.[150] Neither would he accept, though, that Pitt went out '*merely*' because he could not introduce emancipation. As far as the disagreement with the king went, Fox had reason to believe that it had been 'serious, and even warm'.[151] Fox gave a candid assessment of events: 'Pitt was a bad minister; he is out — I am glad.'[152] The wily politician was, however, perplexed as to why the change had occurred. He believed that many aspects of it were 'quite unintelligible' and expressed a hope that 'perhaps time might clear them up'.[153]

Pitt consistently refused to explain the reasons behind his resignation to parliament. When challenged in the commons on 16 February, five days after he had seen the king in his agitated state, Pitt stated that 'opportunities would occur when these [circumstances] would be more properly considered, and he would feel it to be his duty to the house to lay before them that explanation of his conduct which was naturally expected'.[154] This satisfied no one and there were angry calls for a proper explanation. Pitt was forced to speak a second time and skilfully evaded the question with a full display of his debating pyrotechnics. It was, he declared,

> a new and not very constitutional doctrine that a man must not follow his sense of duty — that a man must not, in compliance with the dictates of his conscience, retire from office, without being bound to give to this house and to the public an account of all the circumstances that weigh in his mind and influence his conduct . . . I have never heard that it was a public crime to retire from office without explaining the reason.[155]

With a heavy heart Pitt revealed that there was nothing evil in him relinquishing,

> without assigning the cause, a station that it would be the ambition of my life, and the passion of my heart, to continue to fill, if I could do so with advantage to the country, and consistently with what I conceive to be my duty.

As to the merits of the question that occasioned the resignation Pitt was willing to submit them to the house, although 'I should rather leave it to posterity to judge of my conduct.' Pitt's statement on the ministers' resignations and the line of his own future conduct is worth being quoted in full:

> We did feel it an incumbent duty upon us to propose a measure on the part
> of government, which, under the circumstances of the union so happily
> effected between the two countries, we thought of great public importance,
> and necessary to complete the benefits likely to result from that measure. We
> felt this opinion so strongly, that when we met with circumstances that
> rendered it impossible for us to propose it as a measure of government, we
> equally felt it inconsistent with our duty and our honour any longer to
> remain a part of that government.

The minister then made plain what principles guided his conduct and would
guide his conduct in the future:

> I beg to have it [catholic emancipation] understood to be a measure which, if
> I had remained in government I must have proposed. What my conduct will
> be in a different situation, must be regulated by a mature and impartial
> review of the circumstances of the case. I shall be governed (as it be) only by
> such considerations as I think best to insure the tranquillity, the strength,
> and the happiness of the empire.

The king's illness created an anomalous situation. The outgoing ministers
were technically still in office as the new ministers had not received their seals
of office.[156] Pitt was to retain his seals as head of the treasury and chancellor of
the exchequer for another month. The prince of Wales, sensing an opportunity, attempted to resurrect the plan for a regency that had been abandoned in
1789. He sent for Addington and asked him 'if he was minister'. Addington
admitted that he was not and that Pitt was still prime minister. Upon hearing
this the heir to the throne requested an immediate meeting with Pitt.
Addington hesitated and said that he would have to consult the duke of York.
The prince was not prepared to accept such insolence and haughtily
informed Addington that 'If you decline acceding to my *request*, be so good as
to obey my *commands*.'[157] He did have his meeting with Pitt on Monday, 23
February but it was reported that they did not 'meet, or part, like persons
likely to think the same'.[158] Loughborough also enmeshed himself in the
situation. He too saw the prince of Wales, on Wednesday, 25 February, 'but
rather did harm than good'.[159]

This was not the extent of Loughborough's involvement. On 24 February
he went to the king, in his role as lord chancellor, to receive his signature on
a bill to repeal the brown bread act. This was an emergency measure of the
previous year that all agreed was no longer beneficial.[160] Loughborough was
not allowed into the king's room so he engaged Thomas Willis, a churchman
and brother of Dr John Willis, to secure the signature. Willis hesitated, but
relented when the lord chancellor assumed full responsibility. The king had
no difficulty signing the 'George' but found it impossible to sign the 'R'.
Willis took the paper away for a time and then 'begged him to sign it for the
sake of his people'. On hearing this the king announced that he would 'write
as good an R as ever I did'.[161] MacAlpine and Hunter have argued that

'Nothing more unconstitutional can be imagined.' Dr Willis, someone with-out any office, was the sole witness to a legislative act at a time when the king was not in full command of his senses. Loughborough claimed that the king had believed the bill to be a very good one, and insisted that he had been in full possession of his faculties.[162] In private to Rose he was less confident and confessed that he had not seen the king but that Willis had told him that 'there would be no difficulty in obtaining the royal signature to a dozen papers respecting which no detailed statements were necessary'.[163] That evening the king's pulse was 130. Malmesbury believed his life was in danger and that the fever was responsible for his mental derangement.[164]

The king's illness ensured that Pitt was neither in office nor out of it. There were effectively two cabinets, and both attempted to maintain stability. The intense speculation and uncertainty continued to affect Pitt badly. He was 'very unwell, much shaken, gouty and nervous'.[165] Once the king's condition became known the criticism of his conduct knew no limits. Leading the attack, *The Times* in an editorial of 27 February, out of something 'so different from disrespect', attacked him for resigning given the 'foreseen and unfore-seen calamities' facing the country. The paper also regretted that Pitt remained as de facto prime minister even though the king had nominated his successor. Glenbervie continued to insist that the king had acted unwillingly on the catholic question, out of a sense of duty, and recollected his words on the union: 'I am glad of the union as it will take away all pretext (or ground) for admitting the catholics. What? What?'[166] Lady Malmesbury joined with Glenbervie in the attacks on Pitt and accused him of being 'full of trick, false-hood and inconsistency'. Pitt had 'fine words but no real abilities' and had been found out by the recent events. She did not accept the catholic question as the real cause of the crisis as Pitt had 'all his life governed from circumstances, not on principle', and she claimed to know 'many private instances of his disregard to his honour'.[167]

It was difficult to proceed until the king's health was restored or a regency installed. At the end of February it appeared that the king had made a recovery. There was a relapse on 1 March, and this led to fears for the king's life. The fever broke the next day and it was reported that he was on the way to a com-plete recovery,[168] he awoke refreshed and 'better in every respect'.[169] Attempts were made over the next week to prevent Pitt from withdrawing from office. Canning and Dundas were the chief instigators of different schemes, with the former reported by Malmesbury on 4 March as being 'cool, temperate and uncommunicative; holding new and moderate language; smoothing the way for Pitt's return to power'.[170] Canning regretted that Pitt had 'so much of the milk of human kindness', and was disappointed that his friend would 'never punish those who had now, or at other times, betrayed him'.[171] The Shakespearean reference was an apt one as Canning was doing as much as he could to manipulate Pitt's destiny. Canning left Malmesbury believing that Pitt wished to return to power and that he would do so without Spencer and Grenville.[172] Later that day Malmesbury discussed the matter with Thomas

Pelham, who revealed that Addington would challenge Pitt's return if it was attempted.[173] Addington was not prepared to yield the high office that was within his grasp.

The catholic question was forced to drop until the uncertainty was resolved. Pitt considered giving a pledge never to return to office unless emancipation was granted. This, he thought, might placate the Irish catholics, but Pretyman argued the point with him on 24 February and 'strengthened his doubts' about anything that would bind his future actions.[174] Pretyman pleaded with Pitt to 'leave himself at liberty to act as the situation of the country should demand, that this was true patriotism'. This seems to have eased his mind until the question was unpleasantly brought back to his attention a couple of weeks later. In the first week of March Thomas Willis, a fervent opponent of the proposed catholic emancipation, was requested by the king to send Pitt a letter that made the monarch's feelings clear as to whom he held responsible for his predicament. Willis was instructed to 'Tell him I am now *quite* well, *quite* recovered from my illness; but what has *he* not to answer for, who is the cause of my having been ill at all.'[175] The receipt of this letter was said to have affected Pitt greatly. The welfare of the king and of the empire were entwined in the prime minister's mind. To find that the king held him responsible for his illness was deeply painful. This overrode all other considerations and Pitt believed that there was only one course of action he could adopt. He sent the king, through Willis, a response that was 'most *dutiful*, humble and *contrite*'.[176] In the letter he pledged, as he was to remind the king a few years later and as Glenbervie was to record, 'that not only from regard to his majesty but also from private reasons of his own, he was resolved never again to stir the [catholic] question'.[177] Willis wrote to Pitt that the king exclaimed, upon receiving the promise, 'Now my mind will be at ease.'[178] It is possible that in the king's precarious mental state he forgot the promise for he claimed to be unaware of the pledge until Pitt reminded him of it on a later date.[179]

On 4 March Willis recorded that 'his majesty began to get out of that state' in which he had been.[180] The next day he was able to eat and was capable of holding a cup. Only a 'few exceptions of irritability' were noted. By 7 March the king seemed to be fully recovered 'in mind as well as body'.[181] He enquired of the duke of York if there had been any resignations. When his son informed him that none could take place without the king's permission, George III enquired after the lord chancellor and was told that Loughborough would not resign his seals of office into anyone's hands but those of his king. This seemed to satisfy him, and he ordered Willis to write to Pitt, Addington, Loughborough and Eldon to inform them of his recovery.[182] The king then, it seems, attempted to engage York in a conversation on Pitt's pledge at which his son stopped him, saying that 'since this point, which has given your majesty so much uneasiness is settled, it is better now to forget all that has passed'. The king consented reluctantly and the discussion turned instead to his illness.[183]

From the behaviour of Pitt in dropping the catholic question, 'and from other circumstances and rumours', Malmesbury speculated that the prime minister wished to remain on as head of the government. The pressures of non-office were beginning to affect Addington and he was reported to be 'very unwell'.[184] Malmesbury did not doubt that Pitt could resume control of the government, but he believed that if he did return, would do so 'with less power, but with better and more sane judgement; and the acquiring the last will, in my mind, amply balance the decrease of the first'. The events of the past months, according to Malmesbury, had forced Pitt into some much-needed self-examination. This introspection had apparently revealed 'an overweening ambition, great and opinionative presumption, and, perhaps, not quite correct constitutional ideas with regard to the respect and attention due to the crown'. The cause of these failings, Malmesbury did not necessarily attribute to Pitt's character. They may, he speculated, have resulted from listening to 'bad and silly advisers', and the fact that in his extended tenure as prime minister he had never had 'a single check of adversity'. Whatever the cause, Pitt, he believed, had lost 'much of his popularity, and of the public good opinion'. If he was to remain he would discover that 'his *absolute* power' was at an end. In the place of his presumption might come moderation, 'becoming pliancy, and a right respect to the crown'.

Whether Pitt wished to return or not, plans were formed for his resumption of power. Canning and Dundas, acting separately, developed schemes to save the country from an Addington-led administration that they despised. In a conversation with Malmesbury, Canning disclosed the depth of his feelings on the matter. He blamed Pitt for not making a move towards Addington to persuade him to give up his claim as first minister. As far as Canning was concerned Pitt would not persist with the catholic question, it was 'asleep'. Yet still, bewilderingly, Pitt refused to act unless Addington moved first. He was sure that Addington was fully aware of Pitt's position. Canning was sharply critical of Pitt's successor for not honourably deciding to resign, or going '*voluntarily* to the king to say "now the catholic question is asleep and forgotten, I am ready to resign my office to Mr Pitt"'.[185] The behaviour of Pitt, Canning also believed, was 'to blame, highly to blame, I confess; but he thinks it unbecoming him to take the first step'.[186] Malmesbury told Canning that it was his duty, as 'an independent' and also as a personal friend of Pitt, to persuade him 'to *humble* himself before the king: it will be the most dignified humility ever heard of'. Such a scheme, Malmesbury was convinced, would see Pitt return 'with less power, but *power enough*'.[187] He would have received the lesson of adversity that Malmesbury wished him to have. Malmesbury hoped that Pitt, if it became apparent that certain individuals had 'secretly inflamed' the king's mind, would punish their behaviour 'to preserve power and make it respected'.[188] It was evident that Canning was acting on his own initiative, and had not been directed by Pitt. Canning admitted that he had resolved not to say anything to his friend on the subject as he 'was displeased with Pitt' and much 'out of humour'.[189]

The conversation with Malmesbury persuaded Canning to act. He wrote a letter to Pitt the same day, 8 March, that placed a serious strain on their relationship. Canning revealed that he felt compelled to get involved 'by a sense of what is due to our friendship, to state to you my opinion as to the conduct which the public has a right to expect, and does expect from you, under the present circumstances'.[190] The message in the letter was unequivocal: Canning felt that 'under the present circumstances you ought to withdraw your resignation'. He did not doubt that such an offer would be accepted. The arguments for it were 'all considerations of public honour and public interest: *against* it nothing but miserable, petty, personal consideration'. There were only two difficulties. The first was the catholic question, 'the grounds on which you have given in your resignation'. The second was 'a point of delicacy' towards Addington. These were by no means insurmountable. The first problem he dismissed with ease. He believed that Pitt must accept 'what everybody else takes for granted', that the catholic question was 'disposed of for the present'. What remained, then, was 'purely personal' between Pitt and the king. Nor did he have any compunction about displacing Addington.

At around the same time Dundas produced his own scheme to allow Pitt to remain in office. In his draft ideas for a new cabinet, Pitt was to be restored to the head of the treasury, with Addington as home secretary and war minister, and Grenville as foreign secretary. This suggested cabinet, Dundas argued, would constitute 'the strongest government ever'.[191] The catholic question was to be dropped for the duration of the king's life. Every concession, except seats in parliament and high offices, however, would be given to the catholics. This scheme of Dundas occurred concurrently with Canning's, as shown by a conversation the outgoing war minister had with the duke of York on 8 March. Dundas suggested that Pitt might retain office and still head the government and proposed that the duke suggest this idea to the king. York informed him that he would do whatever was proper to see Pitt return, but wished to discuss the matter with Thomas Pelham before proceeding.[192] The next day Pelham advised the duke to remain aloof from the scheme even though he approved of Pitt remaining in office. Pelham feared that the king might resent York acting as 'a maker of administrations', and certainly the prince of Wales would view the matter of his brother's involvement with displeasure.[193]

The difference between the two schemes was that Pitt was tacitly encouraging Dundas in his manoeuvres. That Canning was not included in the plan was a testament to his volatile temperament, and an indication that there was some estrangement between the men; this could be traced back to his marriage, which had created a coolness. Released, somewhat, from the intolerable pressure, Pitt's constitution slowly recovered. The interregnum provided by the king's illness allowed an invaluable breathing space, and rescued Pitt from the claustrophobic pressures of office. By the beginning of March Sir Walter Farquhar diagnosed that Pitt was 'in high health'.[194] On 9 March the duke of York decided to inform Dundas immediately of his conversation with Pelham and sent his friend out to Dundas's residence at Wimbledon. Pelham was well aware that he would find Pitt there. Pitt agreed with everything Pelham had to say about the proposition and in particular that the duke should not mix himself up in political intrigues and instead consider himself as being independent of all ministers, and belonging only to the king. Pitt examined the question in detail, going through the entire arguments for and against his continuance in office. The main obstacle was considered to be the feelings of Addington. In addition it was not even certain how the king stood on Pitt's retiring from office. Other difficulties were created by the fact that Pitt had other friends to consult on the subject, while not least of his worries was the risk of alienating the Irish catholics. What became apparent from the long discussion was that Pitt 'inclined greatly to return to office, but wished that the *king should move towards him, and Addington spontaneously offer him his place*'. This seems to have been the sticking point; Pitt wished to continue as prime minister but his conception of the role meant that he would not demean himself to do so.

The matter had occupied much of Pitt's thoughts, 'over and over again'. It was Pelham's opinion that Pitt had to act himself, rather than wait for others to take the first step. For Malmesbury it was clear that Pitt wanted to return 'but that his *pride* led him to wish that it should be by *entreaty*'. After speaking to the outgoing prime minister, Pelham went to speak with Dundas who he discovered had 'much less pride, and fewer scruples than Pitt'. Dundas spoke 'decidedly on the subject'.[195] He had firm views as to what Pitt should do, and believed that Addington should be content with a cabinet place and that if this was not sufficient he could be 'overlooked entirely in an arrangement so essential to the public good'. Dundas then made a very revealing comment that Malmesbury believed was made 'very unadvisedly, probably unintentionally', that '*if these new ministers stay in and make peace*, it will *only smooth matters the more for us afterwards*'. This was seen as highly significant and confirmed something Malmesbury had long suspected, that 'Pitt went out because he felt himself incapable either of carrying on the war, or of making peace.'[196]

On 9 March the king requested an audience with Pitt. He did so through the duke of York, who informed Pelham on his return from Wimbledon. Pelham met Pitt accidentally on the way to parliament and the minister told him that he had received a similar request from Willis. Embarrassed, Pitt did not know how to proceed. He did not wish to see the king before anything was determined as this would only create awkwardness. Maintaining a cautious line, in their conversation Pitt said that if he was staying out of office it would be better if Hobart was secretary of state for the colonies, Hawkesbury at foreign affairs and Pelham at the home and war departments. He wished for Cornwallis to remain in Ireland or at the board of control, and to have Chatham at the head of the ordnance. Portland was suggested as president of the council. Malmesbury, however, was in no doubt that this was the talk of a man with little bargaining power and that if Pitt returned a very different cabinet would be formed.[197]

All of these events created a very bad impression on Malmesbury. He believed Pitt and his associates were playing a dangerous game using

Addington to make the peace with France before they returned to office. Either this, or that they were genuinely attempting to be restored to power. If they were returned it was to be because they had forced the king to beg them, and if this did not succeed 'they will gratify their pride another way, by vapouring on the sacrifices they are ready to make for the good of the public'. On the whole it was 'a very sad story — the work of mean and bad passions'. It was nothing more than 'a trial of strength which a great subject presumes to institute with his king, and a king to whom he owes all his greatness'.

Few believed that Pitt was struggling to pursue an honourable line of conduct. His mental equilibrium restored (he had always a remarkable recovery rate), he now had a firm grasp on what was happening and, more importantly, what was required. He wrote to Willis on 9 March regretting that it would not be possible to meet with the king until Addington had seen him first and until his complete recovery could be announced publicly.[198] It was a gracious gesture. Dundas informed Pelham the next day that he did not believe that Addington would voluntarily relinquish office, but that Pitt believed he should. Intervening in the matter the duke of Portland decided to go to Addington and persuade him to tell the king that Pitt had dropped the catholic question and that he (Addington) recommended Pitt remaining on in office. This stratagem, 'the duke said, he could do with perfect consistency as it is conformable to the language he has held all along'.[199] It was vital that the king should see Addington, before Pitt, so that the 'arrangement, whatever it is, should appear to originate with the king, and come from the king to Pitt, and not *vice versa*'. The idea was dropped, however, after Pelham 'injudiciously' informed Dundas of it, and he 'rather unfairly' informed Pitt. Pitt immediately scuppered the scheme, insisting to Portland that he was not to use any influence with Addington to induce him to give way. The prime minister would not depart from the rigorous ethical line he had set for himself. If Addington would not give way '*proprio motu*' he would not be satisfied.[200] Pitt was testing just how deep the ties of friendship and loyalty with Addington really were.

With the government in a state of flux Loughborough once more intervened. The lord chancellor was set to lose his great seal to Eldon in the new arrangement and began scheming once more, this time fantastically, in an attempt to keep Pitt in power. He wrote a letter to the king in which he expressed a wish that 'the incalculable mischief' that would ensue from Pitt's retirement could be averted.[201] The scheme failed, as did an attempt by Addington to make Loughborough president of the council. It was believed that this was due to the dislike felt for him by the king, who was felt to be barring his return to cabinet.[202] In a bizarre twist Loughborough continued to attend cabinet councils, even after Eldon had received the great seal, as if nothing had happened until he was taken to one side and informed that he no longer held office.[203] There is little doubt that the king hated Loughborough, even if he later ennobled him to the earldom of Rosslyn. This was clear by his reaction to the earl's death in 1805. The king interrogated the messenger to prove the veracity of the report as he had recently seen the earl in good health.

Upon having the story of his death confirmed the king exclaimed, 'Then he has not left a greater knave behind him in my dominions!' Brougham quoted George III as having said, 'Then he has not left a worse man behind him,' but admitted that he had taken the liberty of adapting the 'expressive... English of royalty into a phrase more decorous and less unfeeling'.[204]

Meanwhile it was impossible to prevent the question of whether Pitt might remain in office being publicly discussed. It was noted on 10 March that 'the report of Pitt's continuance in office is become so universal as to render it more probable that this discreditable measure is determined on'.[205] Pitt's line of conduct was not as clear to Glenbervie as it was to the prime minister. Aware that Pitt's return would create all sorts of difficulties for himself, Glenbervie speculated that Pitt's plan was 'to gull the country gentlemen by whining declamations'. He regretted that the public might prefer Pitt to Fox, or the inexperienced Addington, and wished there was another alternative. It was the oratorical skills of Pitt alone that Glenbervie believed inspired the country to wish his return, his eloquence was 'so apt to fascinate us all'. He shared the view of Sir Francis Burdett, passed on to him by his wife, that 'There is nothing so pernicious to the commonweal in a free country as eloquence.'

The recovery of the king was welcomed by Portland. He believed that this terminated his relationship with Pitt and he was quite prepared to serve Addington. He found Pitt's behaviour inexplicable, as he understood that he had yielded completely on the catholic question, and had even gone as far as to assert that '*he never will stir it*'.[206] Portland blamed Pitt for much of what had happened, believing that it was 'the most culpable pride possible, if it *was* pride'. He regretted that Addington was not inclined to give way to Pitt, and believed that this was the king's own preference.

On Saturday, 14 March, at three o'clock, Pitt formally resigned. He had a short audience with the king and handed over his seals of office.[207] It was a numbing blow for Canning to accept. Pitt had left his letter of 8 March unanswered for a number of days, responding only on Thursday, 12 March. His reply was short but kind. Pitt expressed his regret that he should differ with Canning on this but '*his mind was quite made up* on the subject'.[208] The two men met the evening after Pitt handed over his seals of office. Canning put two important questions to Pitt that revealed the extent of his ill humour on the matter. He declared that he would 'regulate his conduct by the answers he received, *if* Pitt could, and would, give him the true and real ones'. The first question was whether Pitt and Addington had from the beginning to that day '*acted in concert*', and whether Addington had withheld anything from him, or displayed a desire to assume office himself rather than return it to Pitt. Without any hesitation Pitt replied that Addington could not have behaved any better and that his manner had 'added to his long friendship for him'. Canning's second question, 'and again he appealed to Pitt's sincerity', was whether 'Pitt was *more satisfied* with him for *resigning* office, than with others who *retained* their places'. Pitt's answer eased Canning's worries. He admitted that

> he certainly could not but be pleased with Canning's having resigned office, *taking him in the light of an individual and private friend, but, as a public man*, he very truly and sincerely said, *he was more pleased and obliged to such of his friends who had kept their places.*[209]

This delighted Canning, who recanted all his suspicions, including 'all he really might have said, and all that was attributed to him as having said, with respect to Mr Addington'. Canning sent Addington his resignation with terms of the highest respect, and assurances 'of such support as he could give him'. Addington was received by the king an hour after Pitt, and formally assumed his position at the head of the treasury. Once installed in office he proved even more reluctant to relinquish it. It was reported two days later that he was stiffening against any arrangement that would see him share power with Pitt.[210] Camden had written to him with a proposal for some such arrangement but the new prime minister reacted 'very coldly and formally'. This account from Canning led Malmesbury to feel that 'the whole transaction is enveloped in a thicker cloud than ever'.[211] He found it incomprehensible that Pitt should be acting the way he was, suspecting that there was a hidden meaning behind the events. Malmesbury used an example from the 'Arabian nights' as a metaphor for his argument. In eastern custom when a man divorced his wife, before he could marry her again another man had to marry and divorce her first. This second husband was called a *hullah*. Addington was 'Britannia's *hullah*', according to Malmesbury, and he joked that the former speaker was too safe a choice to follow one trick in the stories and refuse to divorce the wife once married to her.[212] Yet from Addington's unwillingness to return power to Pitt, even before he had assumed it, it is obvious that he had no intention of being anyone's *hullah*, least of all Pitt's.

The resolution of all the ambiguity was greeted with relief by Grenville. He was also happy to find that Carysfort had decided not to resign his diplomatic situation in Berlin. The arguments in favour of the ministers' resignations were as clear to Grenville as they had been a month earlier. It would have been 'unpardonable' to have remained in office as 'the instruments of resisting the measures which are necessary to unite the whole people of Ireland'.[213] Unlike Pitt, Grenville had no inclination to return to office by allowing the catholic question to drop. He agreed with the composition of the new government, happy that it had not gone into the hand of opposition, and his 'most earnest wishes' were with it.[214] What did distress him was that some of his friends were opposing the new arrangement out of a mistaken belief that it was in the country's best interests when in reality it served only Fox. Grenville reluctantly included in this number some of his closest connections.[215] He trusted that he himself would not be suspected of collusion in such ventures, hoping that 'twenty years of public life had established my character above such suspicions'.

Few were convinced by the ministers' explanations and fewer still wanted to be convinced. People preferred to believe the incredible and the unusual over the mundane. Between February and March there was a flurry of rumour and counter-rumour, with every version contributing to the air of confusion that surrounded the resignations. It allowed the opponents of Pitt to place his conduct in the most unfavourable light possible. The most personal attack came during a debate in the house of lords in March. It was from a source who had once been very close to Pitt, and who had not been uninvolved in the events of which he spoke — Lord Auckland. Auckland began his speech regretting the passing of an administration that had for seventeen years 'preserved the British empire from destruction and desolation'.[216] He also regretted the policy that had been determined towards the Roman Catholics of both islands. This enabled him to launch a vicious attack on Pitt, each word carefully chosen to damn the former prime minister:

> I cannot discover a sufficient cause for the unhappy resignations which took place in a moment of accumulated difficulties . . . It is impossible that men of high spirit, and of such fair and well founded ambition, could for a moment be affected by a desire to have less fatigue or less responsibility. It is not in human nature, or in history, that generals, inured to great actions, and born to achieve them, can, without motives of good and superior import, get into their post-chaise and quit their army in the time of action.[217]

Auckland agreed with the sentiments of Lord Carlisle, who had also criticised Pitt, that 'there is in this business a mystery'. He argued convincingly that there was surrounding the events 'a veil through which the eye cannot penetrate. Time and circumstance may remove that veil.'[218] The speech caused an uproar. It was the main topic of conversation at the opera, with much criticism directed at Auckland.[219] Malmesbury could not believe what had induced Auckland to 'be thus imprudent' in 'a most remarkable speech'.[220] It was made worse by the fact that Auckland had 'received from Pitt obligations that no minister but one possessing the power of Pitt could bestow, or any one less eager for office than Lord Auckland ask'.[221] The furore prompted Auckland to send Malmesbury a copy of his speech. Malmesbury believed that

> if *anyone* but he had spoken it, there would have been much to approve in it, and little to censure; but from him it must appear, not as the feelings of an honest, independent mind, but as the action of an *ungrateful* man.[222]

The new government was now in place and not likely to be changed. Pitt was forced to accept his new situation. Entering the commons on 16 March he assumed an unfamiliar position three rows immediately behind the treasury bench.[223] He was joined there, later in the month, by Dundas, Castlereagh and Canning. On 25 March, flanked by those three individuals, Pitt answered Auckland's attack. In a dignified response he pointed out that 'he had lived to very little purpose for the last seventeen years, if it was necessary for him to say that he had not quitted his situation in order to shrink from its difficulties'. For the first time in so many years Pitt had to come to terms with being out of office. His administration, and for all he knew his political career, was over.

8

Ireland, the catholic question and concealment

*We have united ourselves to a people whom we ought in policy
to have destroyed.*
(Lord Cornwallis on the Irish catholics, 1800)

*In 1798 they were charged; in 1799 they were caressed; in 1800
they were cajoled; in 1801 they were discarded.*
(Jonah Barrington on the Irish catholics, 1833)[1]

A high gallows and a windy day, for Billy Pitt and Castlereagh.'[2] Despite
this mischievous song, and the continuing problem of scarcity,
Cornwallis was happy to find that there were 'no symptoms of ill-
humour' in Ireland in January 1801. He was enthusiastic that if the French
were to invade they would meet with few friends. With a cautious optimism
he faced the new year content that 'Nobody would have believed, three years
ago, that union, catholic emancipation, and the restoration of perfect tranquillity, could have taken place in so short a time.'[3] Cornwallis was confident
that most of the one hundred Irish MPs would choose to support catholic
emancipation. He was encouraged in this, somewhat hopeful, assertion, by
signs in favour of the concession from Lords Shannon and Loftus.[4] The
collapse of the ministry in Britain shattered these illusions. Between February
and March 1801 the Irish administration was forced to react, as best it could,
to the changing circumstances in London. Ireland began to exert an influence
over events only when attempts were made to keep the Irish catholics from
causing any unrest over the failure to solve the catholic question. Then in late
March, after the new ministry had formally taken office, Irish affairs once
more assumed a dangerous significance. It appeared that the secret service
funds that had been illegally used to assist the union would be revealed, subjecting the government to much abuse, and threatening to destabilise Ireland

and the union. The stress was too much for Castlereagh, whose peace of mind returned only when a swift cover-up was instituted. In the second half of 1801 the castle, and Cooke in particular, struggled to meet the extensive promises and prevent disclosure of the unsavoury union activities. The threat of exposure faced the government for the next three years until finally the matter was resolved.

THE EFFECTS OF THE COLLAPSE OF THE MINISTRY ON IRELAND

The first indication in Ireland that things were not right in London came from the newspapers. On 3 February Cooke wrote to Castlereagh, who was still in England, to attempt to confirm the stories about the collapse of the government.[5] Despite the many rumours filtering back to Dublin, few chose to believe that Pitt could be leaving office. Lady Kenmare advised people to 'Let what will happen, Mr Pitt will still be minister.'[6] Nor did Cooke accept that Pitt would go, and he told the chief secretary that he could not foresee any changes in the government.[7] The castle remained casually indifferent about what was happening despite increasingly pessimistic news from England. Cooke was curiously nonchalant even though Castlereagh sent a particularly ominous report on 2 February. The under-secretary was confident that, as there was no opposition to be enlisted by the opponents of emancipation, everything would depend only 'on the firmness of the cabinet'.[8]

Soon it was revealed just how much the castle had misjudged the mood in England. With a new government about to be formed Cooke decided that it would be impossible for him to serve in an administration founded on an anti-catholic principle.[9] He shared many of the criticisms of the new ministry that were being expressed in Britain; he did not believe that the government would last, and in any case would not assist its continuance. The choice of Addington as Pitt's successor temporarily deflated Cooke's pessimism. He genuinely believed that the speaker was 'not only the best, but the only man that could be found'.[10] Within a month, however, he was to recant this opinion and scorn Addington for being 'a weak man'.[11] Yet no matter who was chosen to succeed Pitt, Cooke remained reluctant to alter the line of conduct he had set for himself. The peculiar circumstances of the change in ministry made him uneasy; the new government was being formed 'upon a principle, upon which, after long thought, and certainly without necessity, I am known to have committed myself. I do not repent of my decision.'[12] With what he called his 'eagerness and indiscretion' he could not consent to engage in 'mere common drudgery' of work while all the time 'disapproving every measure that is taken by government'. Nor could he serve to counteract a principle, that of catholic emancipation, which he had come to believe was necessary to achieve an imperial security. Cooke was confident that the new government would not dare attempt to punish him for his stance, after his many years of service, and this gave him the boldness to refuse to join an administration 'founded upon one principle alone, which principle, after mature consideration, I think dangerous and untenable'.[13] As far as he was concerned his own political service had ended. If the catholic question was to have 'an extinguisher' put upon it then there was no choice but to leave office; however, if the business was to be postponed, with the principle left open, then he would consider remaining. Cooke wrote to Castlereagh on 11 February and told his friend that he wished to retire when he could be of no further use, although if the new administration followed a moderate line he would 'not absolutely press it', even though it would be his preference.[14]

Pitt was slow to brief the castle about the change. He eventually informed the lord lieutenant about the collapse of his ministry, through Castlereagh. On 9 February the chief secretary wrote to Cornwallis, with Pitt present at the time, revealing that the prime minister,

> from a conviction, I conclude, that the king's mind could not give way, and seeing the danger of the state falling into the hands of opposition, has urged his utmost influence with his friends to lend themselves to the new arrangement.[15]

It was believed, 'but this is merely supposition', that the new government would 'evade rather than negative' the catholic question. Pitt intended, at the 'first opportunity of the question being regularly before the house', to state his opinion on the matter. He did not, however, consider it

> expedient, either with reference to the success of the question itself, or the predicament in which the king stands, for him to press the measure under the present circumstances. The inclination of his mind, after having argued the question, is not to vote at all.

It would be seen by Pitt as a rash, and ultimately dangerous, strategy to press the catholic question in parliament. Even if it succeeded in the commons it would fail in the lords, and agitating it at that time would serve only to 'pledge people against it'. 'A still stronger reason' against pressing the question then, and something that Pitt was particularly anxious for Cornwallis to understand, was that even if the measure passed in both houses of parliament 'it would be deprived of all its benefits, and the king would, at all risks, refuse his assent'. Faced with these considerable obstacles Pitt advised the lord lieutenant on the course of action he should pursue. Cornwallis,

> without bringing forward the king's name, should make the catholics feel that an obstacle, which the king's ministers could not surmount, precluded them from bringing forward the measure whilst in office; that their attachment to the question was such, that they felt it impossible to continue in administration, under the impossibility of proposing it with the necessary concurrence.

It was essential that the catholics should realise that Pitt would not attempt to force the matter. Emancipation could be pressed only when there was a chance of success, and in the meantime Pitt would 'repress . . . any unconstitutional conduct in the catholic body'. He had very little hope that George III could be persuaded to relent, and the death of the king was 'that solution of the difficulty which all parties must equally deprecate'. The 'not very encouraging' prospect, therefore, was that the lord lieutenant must make the catholics realise that *'their* particular interests, as well as their duty, will be best consulted rather by a temperate and loyal conduct, than by giving way to the feelings connected with disappointment and despair'. It was regretted that the changed circumstances would place Cornwallis in a difficult position, although Pitt attempted to reassure the viceroy that his stay in Ireland would be coming to an end. As for Castlereagh himself, the chief secretary informed Cornwallis that he was not prepared 'to remain a single individual on the treasury bench after those with whom we have acted retire from it'. The strategy outlined in the letter was fully endorsed by Cornwallis. He sent an assurance to Pitt that he would not spare any endeavour in attempting to 'tranquillise the public mind, and to avert those evils which the disappointment of the catholics would be so likely to produce'.[16] The conduct of the outgoing ministers was thoroughly praised by the lord lieutenant.[17]

The Irish lord chancellor, the earl of Clare, was in 'a violent mood' over the events.[18] On 8 February 1801 Clare met William Wellesley Pole, the brother of Pitt's friend the Marquess Wellesley, and revealed the extent of his anger. The chance meeting in a London street gave rise to a vicious and personal tirade against the behaviour of the ministers. Clare admitted that he was beginning to think that Pole had been correct about the union, and that he had been 'a damned fool'.[19] When union had been in contemplation, Clare revealed, Cornwallis had asked him to go to England and help negotiate the union. In the course of this conversation Cornwallis had mentioned that catholic emancipation was 'a necessary consequence of the measure', upon which Clare announced that in that case he could neither support the union nor go to England. Faced with this opposition the lord lieutenant reluctantly conceded the point and Clare was told that the idea of emancipation 'was dropped'. After the defeat of the union in January 1799 the debate had arisen a second time. This time Castlereagh went to the lord chancellor and announced that the only chance government had of securing the union was by enlisting the support of the catholics and declaring that emancipation was intended. Clare stated his position in no uncertain terms:

> my lord, if you call in the aid of the catholics, or if it is the intention of your government to grant catholic emancipation, I will oppose this union immediately, and put myself at the head of all the Irish protestants who will do the same.

Once again any talk of emancipation was dropped. From February 1799 to 15 January 1801 Clare insisted that he had never heard one word on the matter until Loughborough asked him if he had seen the papers brought by Castlereagh from Ireland. After this meeting he had learned, from a later conversation with Pitt, that emancipation had been decided upon as a government measure. Upon hearing of the ministers' determination to pursue emancipation Clare angrily insisted that he would never have supported union if he had known that this would have followed, nor would union 'have been tolerated a moment in Ireland'. Clare believed he had been deliberately duped by the castle. He had trusted Castlereagh to be 'a man of honour' only to discover that he was 'base . . . and deserved the execration of every honest man in both countries'. These sentiments were shared by Pole; he had 'long thought Lord Castlereagh the most barefaced rogue that I ever watched in public' and the lord lieutenant no better, for he had 'always been a crooked politician'. Enough evidence had been displayed during the union struggle, Pole felt, to support the belief that Cornwallis 'meant to buy the consequence of the leading men in Ireland and then laugh at them for having sold their birth-rights'.

Cooke wrote to the lord chancellor on 10 February to remonstrate with him for his outspoken criticism of Castlereagh. The chief secretary's conduct was justified on the grounds that he had only recommended policies that had genuinely been seen as the best for Ireland. The proposal to emancipate the catholics Castlereagh 'could only submit to ministers, and he could not disclose it till he had authority from them'.[20] This was cited as the 'true reason' why Clare had not been informed of what had been decided. It was a matter of regret that the lord chancellor differed from the chief secretary 'on a great line of policy, upon which the future security and happiness of the empire rests'. Cooke was glad a 'permanent system' had been brought forward for Ireland, a country that had been governed by expedient, 'the wretched fickleness and versatility of policy', for too long. Union, he revealed, had neutralised the danger of conceding catholic emancipation. Now, it was not only compatible with the security of the empire, but allowed that security to be increased. It would unite the catholics with the protestants and 'disarm their enmity, and may possibly produce their attachment'. Cooke looked upon the union as 'the greatest possible measure for the British empire, because it gave that empire power to satisfy all the fair demands of all its subjects without the slightest danger to its own security'. Emancipation if rejected would only in time serve to alienate the catholics from the state and create dangerous disaffection: 'This makes me tremble.' Cooke concluded by reminding Clare that 'concession risks nothing, and denial risks everything . . . denial can give nothing, and that concession may gain everything'.[21] Significantly, Cooke asked that the letter be shown to Auckland, revealing that the under-secretary was aware of the men's connection. Cooke sought to persuade Auckland, who 'has a friendship for me'. Once ignited, however, Clare's temper was impossible to control, and in the summer he was still raging furiously against Cornwallis, 'that preposterous old mule', whom he accused of having done irreparable damage in Ireland, that would not be corrected even if he lived until 'the end of the new century'.[22]

The change of ministers was regarded by Thomas Conolly, Castlereagh's relative and a distinguished figure in Ireland, as a great loss. He believed the events would tarnish the good work of the union, and weaken the empire: at home the change was not regarded as being real, abroad it was considered a juggle. Discussing the foreign situation, Conolly asserted that enemies attacked 'with tenfold vigour' those whom they despised.[23] The ministers, he believed, had acted badly in making promises to the catholics without first obtaining the approval of the king.

The lord lieutenant acted quickly to prevent the catholics from becoming alienated from the government. Maurice Fitzgerald, the knight of Kerry, and an outgoing, unionist, MP, was enlisted to circulate the administration's position in catholic circles.[24] An official paper was also required, and Cornwallis prepared a statement on the change of ministers, along the lines proposed by Pitt. This done, the lord lieutenant weighed up his own position and found it untenable. For the consistency of his own character he felt obliged to resign. He could not serve for long under men who had come into office 'for the sole purpose of defeating a measure which I consider to be absolutely necessary for the preservation of the empire'.[25] Nor did he have any respect for the new administration and he did not believe that it would survive for long: 'It must very soon be dissolved in its own weakness.' The feelings of the catholics were not helped when Richard Musgrave dedicated his very protestant history of the union to the lord lieutenant. Cooke found this tribute 'amazing', but recognised that Cornwallis could hardly be blamed for what a historian did.[26]

On 16 February Cornwallis sent his resignation to the home secretary. The same day he reflected on the difficult part Pitt would have to play. He believed that it would 'require all his abilities to get through it with credit to himself and utility to the public'.[27] The 'absurd language' of Clare the viceroy contemptuously dismissed. Writing to Castlereagh he explained that he had felt neither 'an inclination nor a right to make any communications on the subject, before the cabinet had formed an opinion', nor had he thought that the chief secretary could have shown Clare his secret correspondence without his permission.[28] The lord lieutenant showed no qualms in having betrayed Clare's vision of the union.

It was soon speculated in Ireland that Pitt was playing 'a double game'.[29] 'The common insinuation' was that the resignations were 'a trick, a German quarrel'. Despite the efforts of Cooke these stories gathered momentum. As for Clare, he remained livid about what he perceived as the treachery of Cornwallis and Castlereagh. Cooke attempted to reassure him that 'no promise of any kind, [n]or hint of a promise had ever been made to the catholics', but to no avail. A more important concern for the castle was the behaviour of the catholics. Cooke believed they would act calmly, from 'a conviction that fairness is intended to them'. Some days later there were still reports that there was 'something ulterior in Mr Pitt's conduct'. The anti-catholic members of the opposition were reported to be 'angry and chagrined' at Pitt's adoption of emancipation. They considered it 'a humbug on his part', speculating that he did 'not fairly mean to do his utmost in the question' and after 'a mock battle' would return to office.[30] It was clear that Pitt's position was going to be a difficult one. 'A refined game' in politics was always a difficult one, Cooke wrote, 'the person who plays it is never understood, and is soon deserted'. Cooke thought it was vital that Pitt should be seen as being sincere on the question. His strategy, the under-secretary believed, should be to 'do his utmost to obtain the most decided expression in favour of concession, and then to press no further at present, but to leave the moment for the concession to be postponed till certain feelings were prepared for it'. The great danger was that 'the common world' would find the outgoing ministers' line of conduct 'perfectly unintelligible'.[31]

A written paper to the catholics seemed necessary to avoid any misconceptions. Two were eventually produced, one based on Pitt's sentiments outlined in the letter of 9 February, and one composed from material in a letter from Dundas.[32] The castle feared that with 'two such prudent leaders' on the protestant side as Clare and Duigenan the calm was not likely to last.[33] Cooke was of the opinion that Castlereagh must speak decidedly on the matter in England, for he had invested his all in the question, and the under-secretary believed his friend must 'show yourself a man, and that you are capable of moving mountains'. The decision to appoint the earl of Hardwicke as Cornwallis's successor was taken at the end of February. At this time Cooke was bemused to discover that he had become 'an object of observation in the new cabinet'.[34] His shadowy influence was being blamed for all that had happened. As he reminded Castlereagh, he had undertaken no communications with the catholics prior to Pitt's announcement of his retirement. The real source of the interference, Cooke shrewdly judged, was the 'little court Windsor party' that had been secretly influencing the king and playing 'an unfair game' against the cabinet.[35]

The catholics' paper urging good conduct, prepared by Pitt, was harshly criticised in Britain. *The Morning Chronicle* led the attack, accusing Pitt of insulting both the country at large and the king.[36] An editorial questioned his request to the catholics to remain aloof from unconstitutional actions: 'Does he wish to amuse the catholics?' Now that Pitt was leaving office the paper felt free to explain how much it despised him. It denounced his communication to the catholics as marking

> a thirst of power unbounded, a spirit of faction and cabal so dangerous, and withal a conduct with regard to the catholic body so delusive, that we cannot think any set of men in the nation can read [it] without indignation. It is equally disgraceful to the man who professes loyalty to his sovereign, affection to his country, and good faith towards those whose confidence he solicits.

William Elliot, in London, informed Malmesbury on 20 February that Cornwallis fully supported the line adopted by the ministers and the necessity of catholic emancipation.[37] Cornwallis, himself, writing to his brother revealed his disappointment that 'an unexpected blast from St James's' had prevented the possibility that the union might make Ireland 'a powerful bulwark for the security of Britain' and had instead 'added grievously to the perils which have of late surrounded us, and threatened to overwhelm us'.[38] It was a bitter blow for the lord lieutenant to accept that after having worked for so long to pass the union, and having united protestants and catholics, unionists and anti-unionists, in goodwill towards the king's government, and into 'surrendering their animosities and prejudices as a sacrifice to the public safety', it should all be ruined by 'a fatal blow' from 'a quarter most interested to avert it'.[39] The chance to augment the security of the empire had been lost, and with it was destroyed the possibility of achieving a genuine union with Ireland: 'Ireland is again to become a millstone about the neck of Britain, and to be plunged into all its former horrors and miseries.'

With the king's illness and the difficulties facing the empire in March, Cornwallis reconsidered his position on the ministers' resignations. He grew sceptical about the position adopted by Pitt and others as it seemed to commit them not to take 'a share in any administration formed under no peculiar exigency of the state, without bringing forward the catholic question'.[40] Much as Cornwallis sympathised with this stance he still maintained that the ultimate security of the empire must take precedence over any other consideration: 'Many circumstances may, and I am sorry to say are, too likely to occur, in which it would be highly criminal in those gentlemen to refuse their services.' Cornwallis shared the opinion of Castlereagh that 'either in the case of a regency or of the king's recovery the [catholic] question must sleep'. Despite his growing doubts the lord lieutenant remained satisfied with Pitt's behaviour for a considerable time. In August 1801 he revealed, in a private correspondence, that he felt the late prime minister had been 'influenced by the purest and most public spirited motives' and regretted that his difficult line was exposing 'his character to much misrepresentation'.[41] Eventually, he too was to become exasperated, and finally disillusioned, by Pitt's behaviour. By February 1804 he had lost all faith in his former head, and criticised his conduct in opposition for being 'very injudicious and highly discreditable'.[42] 'The great Mr Pitt' had fallen far in his estimation.

Anxiously surveying the resignations in March 1801 Castlereagh grew agitated by what was happening. He was even more forthright than Cornwallis on the necessity of the cabinet remaining in office. In that month he wrote a paper on the ministers' resignations that lacked nothing in passion. This monograph acknowledged that Pitt 'and his friends' retired from office because of their firm belief that catholic emancipation was necessary for the empire, and

> under the conviction that they have for the last two years suffered the Irish catholics to form a strong expectation that their hopes . . . would be gratified in contemplation of which the union secured their support and thus made it impossible for the king's ministers [to remain] without being guilty of a breach of faith.[43]

Under the changed circumstances the catholic question, Castlereagh now believed, must be postponed because otherwise the issue would destabilise the government at home and weaken it abroad. Castlereagh believed there were two lines of conduct that Pitt could adopt. The first was to 'profess his adherence to it [the catholic question] as a question upon which his opinion is made up'. The second was to 'give in addition an unmodified pledge that he never will accept office unless he is enabled to propose and carry the question'.[44] There were two grounds for such a pledge: it would put Pitt's motives beyond suspicion, and it would establish an important influence over the catholic body.[45]

The most important issue for Castlereagh was that of Pitt's continuance in office. He believed that Pitt should not 'retire at so very critical a moment from the king's service'. Even 'the most suspicious catholic will hardly suspect him of betraying his cause for that situation which he has resigned rather than abandon it'.[46] A withdrawal was disastrous on all levels, it would destroy 'the public security as well as sacrifice his own power'. Castlereagh, perhaps over-optimistically, refused to accept that anyone could attribute any dishonourable or 'unwarranted' motive to Pitt's continuance in power. He was also convinced that a pledge to the catholics had to be avoided; far from strengthening Pitt's position it would only diminish it. The government could not afford to make themselves the 'slaves rather than directors' of the catholics. A pledge would also be unpopular with the public and thus weaken their cause even further. A greater consideration for Castlereagh than the catholic question was the security of the empire. Pitt could not leave office when his abilities were so necessary, and when 'public danger might be such as to demand his services'.[47] In addition circumstances might change, and if the catholics misbehaved emancipation might become both unattainable and 'inconsistent with the public interest'. The observations concluded with the assertion that if Pitt wanted to adopt the 'best means of carrying the question he must make himself the centre of a party'.[48] Like Canning, the person whose life was to be so inextricably linked to his, Castlereagh made an effort to persuade Pitt to stay, and was very 'eager for his [Pitt's] remaining in office'. The chief secretary informed Pitt that 'if he declined office now, he never could expect to resume it with credit or authority'.[49]

The opinions of Castlereagh, and especially of Cornwallis, carried great weight in London circles and were widely discussed. The lord lieutenant's letter to his chief secretary was seen by a number of political figures, and generally quoted.[50] Dundas, in particular, was 'much pleased' by the communication, and felt that it perfectly expressed his sentiments on the change. This was on 11 March, at a time when Dundas was working to prevent Pitt from retiring from the head of the government. Lord Spencer was even more impressed by the tone of Cornwallis's letter. Pitt, however, was reported as being less enthusiastic, with Malmesbury speculating that he was involved in some secret communication with Grenville.

One story that reached the castle in late March presented a curious interpretation of the events. Carter, the primate's secretary, informed Cooke that Pitt had shown the king all of Castlereagh's papers on the catholic question on 13 September 1800. He had then, apparently, mentioned the subject a second time on 13 December, and a third time on the 18th of the month. On that occasion the king had declared that rather than concede he would prefer to lose his life, 'expressing his strongest regret on Mr Pitt's decision to resign'.[51] This story created doubts in Cooke's mind, and he transmitted the story to Castlereagh in England, recollecting their previous idea that the king had not been consulted before January 1801. Cooke believed that Carter's version explained Loughborough's conversation with the king at Weymouth and his subsequent paper against emancipation. Carter's account appears flawed on a number of counts. If Pitt had made the king aware of the proposed scheme for catholic emancipation in September it contradicts everything else that happened between then and January. The king, himself, after all, informed Pitt in February that the first he had heard of the proposed scheme was 'a few weeks past'.

The weather throughout 1801 remained unhelpful, hot and dry, and 'real distress' was caused by prohibitive food prices.[52] In March Cooke attributed the unrest in the country to the inflated prices rather than any actual scarcity. Charitable relief eased the pressure in Dublin, although the streets were crowded with beggars.[53] Cornwallis purchased a further thousand barrels of Indian meal early in the month, which was retailed at a low cost so the poor could afford it.[54] Even as he prepared to leave office Cornwallis made one last intervention to address the crisis. With the approval of the house of commons[55] he channelled some of the money that had been voted for the Irish administration into purchasing food supplies to assist voluntary subscriptions. The lords of the treasury were sent details on 18 March with Cooke explaining that it had been done to lessen the 'distress of the lower classes of people and the high prices or scarcity of food'.[56] By August observers were predicting a plentiful harvest, although bread prices remained high.[57]

THE ALIEN OFFICE

Another unusual story reached Cooke in February 1801 which he warned Castlereagh never to mention in any conversation in England. Lord Shannon had revealed that a friend of his had received a letter from Vienna that said, 'Before this reaches you Mr Pitt will have resigned.'[58] It was certainly, as Cooke noted, 'an odd coincidence'. William Wickham was at that time temporarily resident in Vienna, and while it is highly unlikely that he would have been so indiscreet, even had he any foreknowledge, the incident reflects the tense and secretive atmosphere that existed. At the beginning of the new year Wickham advised Portland to explain the work of the alien office in detail to Pitt. Although he accepted that the office, in John King's hands, was being excellently managed, he was anxious because so few in the government were aware of its work. He believed that if Pitt spent but half an hour with the secret records and registers 'a mind like his could not fail to see at once' its importance, and how government possessed 'the most powerful means of observation and information, *as far as their objects go*', that had ever existed.[59] It is impossible that Pitt was unaware of the activity of the alien office, but it is interesting that he had chosen not to educate himself about the complex network that had been constructed. Roger Wells has argued, 'There can be no doubt that Wickham played a major role in the genesis of an efficient secret service while working in the alien office between 1794 and 1801,'[60] and that the alien office provided Pitt with a potent form of 'social control' to 'construct some of the machinery of an authoritarian state'.[61] In Wickham's own words the office could provide 'the best system of *preventative* police that ever yet was made use of by any government'.[62]

When the king's government collapsed Wickham was as surprised as anyone. But he thoroughly approved of the 'honourable retreat' that the ministers decided to follow and sought to retire with them.[63] He cautiously admitted to the outgoing foreign secretary that he was not indifferent to any reward that might be bestowed on him, '*as a reward for my past services*', but neither was he afraid to return home and 'live in confined circumstances'. In a delicate reference to his espionage work he revealed that

> too much of the public money has gone through my hands for me ever to wish to be rich, and I had rather leave a good name and a good example to my son than the first fortune in the united kingdom.[64]

Wickham was uncertain how to act if Hawkesbury, the incoming foreign secretary, offered him a position. Grenville believed that he was far too important to be allowed to retire and approved of Hawkesbury's attempts to find a new position for him. Austria was quite specific that it did not want him remaining in Vienna, so America, and Russia, 'when it is open',[65] were considered the two places most suitable for his talents. It was known that Wickham would prefer Russia, but it was not yet clear what the effect would be of the appearance of the fleet in the Baltic, or other activities. It was only in the next month that news arrived of Paul's providential assassination. Cornwallis wrote that his death 'has been a stroke of good fortune that we had no right to expect'.[66] In June Wickham was forced to leave Vienna as a condition of continuing secret peace talks and he refused the American consulate that was offered to him.[67] He held out for a posting to Berlin, but his espionage reputation precluded his appointment. He was made a privy counsellor on his return, and in 1802 became chief secretary of Ireland.

THE RISK OF EXPOSURE

There were many casualties in 1801 who were to prove the truth of Grenville's premonition that it was 'a crisis so very arduous . . . from which the strongest nerves might shrink'. Both George III and Pitt failed to handle the pressures involved, while Viscount Castlereagh was soon to become a further victim. It is surely not a coincidence that of all the politicians it was the two men most adept at hiding their feelings, Castlereagh and Pitt, who suffered the most at this time. With the collapse of the ministry, and the chaos that surrounded the formation of a new one, it appeared that the secret service funds that had been used to assist the union would be exposed.

Revelation risked uproar and humiliation, validating the opposition claims of bribery and corruption and questioning the legality of the entire union. In March a question mark hung over £18,000, probably secret service money, that had to be replaced. The strain was too great for the chief secretary, still in England, and he experienced a mental breakdown similar to the one that was to kill him almost twenty years later. At the end of April Cornwallis was 'under great anxiety' about Castlereagh's health.[68] There was a partial recovery at the beginning of May, but the chief secretary soon relapsed into his fever. The viceroy admitted that he had been, 'and indeed am still, very uneasy about Lord Castlereagh . . . They tell me there is no danger, but I have no idea of a fever of so long continuance without danger.'[69]

The burdens of the job may have been added to by a family weakness; Castlereagh's mother was a Seymour-Conway, and it was said that this blood-line had 'an hereditary taint'.[70] Whether this was the case or not the chief secretary was unable to cope with the risk of exposure. Immediately after Castlereagh's suicide in 1822 Henry Hobhouse recorded the details of the earlier breakdown in 1801. Amongst Castlereagh's biographers only H.M. Hyde, in his account of the death, has mentioned this earlier nervous collapse.[71] The details about £18,000 and secret engagements that had been made in pursuit of the union validate the story. According to Hobhouse, the chief secretary's 'brain fever' lifted only when Addington promised to honour the union commitments: 'This relief operated so powerfully on Lord Castlereagh's mind that he has never ceased to be on the most cordial terms of intimacy with Lord Sidmouth [Henry Addington].'[72] Castlereagh went to Harrogate to convalesce in the summer and by the end of July confessed that he had forgotten politics and had 'grown very fat'.[73]

For his work on the union Castlereagh was obliged to suffer the abuse of generations of Irish people. Daniel O'Connell called him the assassin of his country.[74] Nor was he to be popular in England for his role in Liverpool's (Hawkesbury in 1801) government in the 1810s. When the Cato street conspirators planned to assassinate the cabinet they came to blows over who would get to kill Castlereagh.[75] Speaking in the house of commons in 1817 Castlereagh admitted that 'with respect to Ireland, I know I shall never be forgiven'.[76] But he never regretted having 'incurred the inexpiable guilt of preserving that main branch of the British empire from that separation' which traitors in Ireland and France had intended. He ended his speech with the hope that 'those who are acquainted with me will do me the justice to believe that I never had a cruel or unkind heart'. Close friends and relatives attested to this kindness. Castlereagh's niece insisted that 'The calm dignity of his manner gave an impression that he was cold, but no one who had ever seen his kindly smile, or be[en] greeted by his two hands stretched out in welcome could have thought him so.'[77] Women were by no means put off by his demeanour. Mrs Arbuthnot recorded that with his height, good looks and perfect manners he was 'a great favourite' and even on occasion made his wife jealous.[78] On a rare public visit to Ireland in August 1821, with the new king,

Castlereagh was startled to find himself no longer the subject of widespread hatred. He was nonplussed by this transformation, and with customary dignity was to remark, 'I am grown as popular in 1821 as unpopular formerly, and with as little merit, and of the two, unpopularity is the most convenient and gentlemanlike.'[79]

It was during this visit that King George IV discussed the union with leading Irish figures. He told them that they had 'all committed a great mistake. You should have made terms as the Scotch did, and you could have got any terms.'[80] When one former MP of the old Irish parliament added that the Scottish had made the establishment of their national religion a stipulation, the king replied, 'You are right. They secured that point also.'

In the summer of 1801, although Castlereagh's mind had been eased, the government still faced exposure over its activities during the union. The crisis threatened to reveal the abuse of the secret service funds in Ireland. The problem began when the king lost all recollection of the additional secret service money that had been authorised for use in Ireland upon his recovery from his illness. As Pitt was to explain to Addington, in the autumn of 1800 a saving of £18,000 had been made in the Irish civil list, and the government had decided to apply this money 'to a very important and pressing purpose which was then explained to his majesty and which he was pleased to approve'.[81] The most convenient way of channelling this money was by paying it 'over to his majesty's privy purse, it being understood to be his majesty's gracious intention' that afterwards it would be used to pay John King, Castlereagh or Cooke. This money now had to be accounted for and attempts were made to resolve the embarrassing predicament. Addington felt obliged to write to the king and remind him that the money had been given to John King 'for secret service, to discharge engagements the nature of which Mr Addington understands has been submitted to your majesty'.[82] The king was aghast at what he saw as a cover-up of 'corrupt measures in Ireland' and refused 'to screen those concerned'.[83] The king believed Portland had embezzled the money, and this interpretation has been accepted by Aspinall, although it has now been revealed that the money was part of that used to assist the union. Portland was obliged to remain as home secretary until he was able to replace the missing money, or explain it away. In June he informed Thomas Pelham, who should have replaced him in March, that he could not quit until he had advanced 'between £20,000 and £30,000 at least, out of my own pocket'.[84] Thus there existed the anomalous situation where Portland retained his seals of office long after all the other ministers had resigned, even Loughborough. Malmesbury found it remarkable that Portland had suddenly developed 'a womanish reluctance to quit an office he is grown *at once* so fond of'.[85] It appears that the king was eventually convinced that nothing untoward had occurred, for the matter was soon resolved without any public exposure and it appeared that the events of the union were finally being allowed to rest. In 1802 Pelham approved an entirely fictitious balance of funds in the secret service accounts.[86]

COMPLETING THE COVER-UP

There had been very little doubt in political circles in Britain that generous methods had been used to secure the union. *The Times* wrote on 11 February 1801 that 'It was alleged . . . the lord lieutenant and the minister in Ireland received a *carte blanche* from the confidential servants of the crown.' Few understood how far they had actually gone, least of all many of the members of the new administration. With the resignations of Castlereagh and Cornwallis it was left to Cooke to meet the union engagements without any proper assistance. The new ministry had insisted upon Cooke remaining in office as he was the only member of the Irish administration who understood the full list of union engagements. He had unwillingly consented,[87] but despaired to John King that 'The burden is on my shoulders alone.'[88] The new viceroy, Hardwicke, was little help. He gave a £700 yearly salary to his private secretary when 'two engagements could have been greatly liquidated by a different application of that fund'. Hardwicke found it hard to come to terms with what had been done before his arrival and struggled to fulfil the union promises. Immediately on his arrival he fell out with Cooke, whom he suspected of having embezzled the missing money. After all his service Cooke was furious with being accused and became deeply distressed. Struggling to control his temper he told Hardwicke that 'I have been very unkindly treated in a manner to which I have never been accustomed . . . where no man has greater claims upon government than myself.'[89] It was a stormy meeting and Cooke was in no mood to be conciliatory; he defied 'any person to charge me with an improper act'. Hardwicke was stunned by the outburst and murmured, 'I am sorry, Mr Cooke, to see you so agitated.' Within a matter of days Hardwicke succeeded in alienating Cooke from his new administration, and the remnants of the old castle regime were systematically removed; meanwhile 'the union becomes more unpopular every day'.[90] By the end of September Cooke had been almost completely frozen out of the administration.[91] The only real work he was allowed to do was 'some secret business' in which the new lord lieutenant and chief secretary declined to get involved.[92] This business was the union engagements, 'which were made in the king's name and on the authority of all his late ministry'.[93] Cooke was deeply disillusioned by the treatment he was receiving from Hardwicke, he remained in office shunned and constantly passed over. He had expected some respect: 'I ought to have known better.' Cooke revealed that he had no ambitions to be a minister, but he did want to be able to maintain his honour by fulfilling the union promises. He made a heartfelt plea to Whitehall that 'I feel myself continually in a disgraceful situation, when I am reduced to making shabby and evasive answers without the consciousness that the promises I portend are sacred, will ever be kept . . .'[94] Unless the debts were 'justly paid' he warned that the Irish administration would never be in a state of credit, nor would any servant of it be able to 'look people in the face'.

These debts were becoming pressing. At the beginning of October Cooke was desperate for £6,800, to pay printers' bills of £4,400 and for two seats that had been purchased for £2,400, and requested £14,800 in total from the alien office.[95] Delay was both 'dangerous and discreditable'. The under-secretary was glad to find some sympathy for his predicament in England, and once more regretted that he could not retire until the engagements were fulfilled. The alien office acted quickly to assist Cooke. John King found it impossible to send the £14,800 out of 'the SS fund' as the money that had already been sent had not yet been replaced. The alien office was forced to improvise and King asked the under-secretary to let him know the 'smallest possible sum that will do for the present moment'.[96]

The union engagements were gradually met and Cooke retired with undisguised pleasure. With a palpable relief the government finally believed that the risk of exposure had faded. Between 1802 and 1804 all the old fears were restored when John Foster persisted in searching for evidence to discredit the union. In a commons debate in May 1802 he attacked the measure for having been 'carried by the most improper means'.[97] Castlereagh immediately rejected these 'fallacious insinuations' but Foster would not be stopped. Sensing his opponent's discomfort, he replied with spirit that 'what he had said was not an insinuation but a positive charge of the most corrupt practices which he was ready to prove'. Castlereagh, wisely, chose to remain silent rather than call the former speaker's bluff. Restored to office in May 1804, as chancellor of the Irish exchequer, and first lord of the Irish treasury,[98] Foster continued to investigate the methods that had been used to pass the union. By November he had discovered sufficient proof to cause severe embarrassment and difficulty for the government. He found evidence which contradicted the official secret service accounts that had been supplied by the castle and which revealed that Cooke had not taken the proper oath for this money. Redesdale, the Irish lord chancellor, admitted that 'perhaps he [Cooke] may have been a little irregular'.[99] Foster rejoiced after finally finding the evidence that vindicated his claims of malpractice and corruption, 'he says *it was the price of a union vote*'.[100] Redesdale was certainly convinced: 'I suspect the fact to have been so.' The government began to panic. Redesdale revealed that 'Plenty other things of the same kind have been done and the attorney general is utterly at a loss how to act.' Foster threatened to make the union evidence public and show that it was 'a measure carried by such means that its validity may be questioned'. A.P.W. Malcomson, Foster's excellent biographer, has never been in any doubt as to Foster's 'easy political virtue'.[101] Nowhere was this more evident than here in 1804 when, with all of the evidence in his hands, he refrained from using it. Grattan's prediction in 1799 finally came to pass: 'Foster will be delivered of his religion with as much facility as a lady lying-in, in a hot climate.'[102] Choosing to remain silent, as Redesdale predicted, Foster instead acted to 'make himself the most powerful man' in Ireland and reduce the lord lieutenant to 'a mere cipher'.[103] In December 1804 Foster signed the treasury order approving the secret annuities[104] and Cooke was able to take his secret service oath with 'a full consideration of what the act required'.[105] Alexander Marsden, Cooke's successor, was relieved that finally 'that business is at an end'.[106] After a tense few months the government was able to finalise the concealment of its secret union activity. With Foster's acquiescence there was now no difficulty in producing a fictional set of accounts that would not 'expose anything material'.[107] There was a collective sigh of relief that the truth of how the union had passed would not be revealed. In any case, Marsden concluded, 'I do not, at present, see how any exposure of union jobs can take place. You know we had other courses for satisfying our friends.' With the destruction and disappearance of the evidence there was now no way of convincing people not to believe the lie. The cover-up by the government was complete: it would take its secrets to the grave.

9

The search for character:
interpreting Pitt's resignation

When therefore we contemplate the abilities of Mr Pitt, or recollect the exploits performed under his administration, we may rationally regret his loss . . . But when we turn the tables, and reflect on our own infatuation with him, and his with regard to us, I think it might prompt us to be extremely cautious and modest in our reasonings and decisions concerning him.

(Case of Mr Pitt's late resignation set in a true light, 1761)[1]

In his lifetime he dominated not only the political scene of his own country but also the councils of Europe but subsequently, after the applause had died away and the memory had begun to fade, he appeared more and more a master of sterile expedients, a hollow imitation of a leader, a fake giant surrounded by real pygmies, and deriving his greatness only from the littleness of his admirers.

(A.D. Harvey, *William Pitt the younger, 1759–1806: a bibliography*)[2]

The study of the events of 1801 is the study of Pitt's character.[3] Pitt's resignation has been one of the most widely disputed and misunderstood episodes of his entire career. It was certainly not understood at the time, and amongst historians the only constant has been the absence of consensus. John Ehrman, Pitt's most recent and authoritative biographer, enlisted the earlier analysis of Richard Pares and concluded that 'the occasion has remained one of the "special mysteries" of the age'.[4] The problem that faced the nineteenth-century audience, and was subsequently to face historians, resulted from an inability to understand Pitt's behaviour, stemming in part from a flawed understanding of the Irish dimension, and a faulty comprehension of his character.

Forty years before Pitt's resignation an event occurred that had some influence on the events of 1801. In 1761 William Pitt, the elder, resigned as a minister on the duke of Newcastle's administration 'in order not to remain *responsible* for measures which I was no longer allowed to guide'.[5] The king's rejection of Pitt's 'blue-water war', specifically with regard to war with Spain, induced the minister to leave office rather than remain and implement policies he could not approve.[6] In a direct sense the crisis was different from that his son faced in 1801; the elder Pitt resigned against his colleagues whom the king had sided with on a matter of strategic policy. The two resignations are not connected in a point of substance, the significance lies in how they were presented, and especially in how they were received. The resignation in 1761 divided, and confused, the political nation. A collection of anecdotes on the life of the elder Pitt was published in London in 1796 and recounted how, after the resignation,

> Mr Pitt's character was assailed with the most ardent malignity and savage frenzy that ever disgraced an age or country . . . They branded him with the names of pensioner, apostate, deserter, and with every term of reproach that malice could apply, or depravity suggest.[7]

The importance of the resignation of the elder Pitt was not that it influenced his son; the younger Pitt was nothing if not his own man. But he would have been well aware of the abuse his father, and his reputation, received, and that his resignation might be similarly misunderstood. Historians have also had trouble with the earlier resignation. One biographer, Peter Douglas Brown, has argued that 'only a nervous system strained almost past endurance can explain Pitt's tragic error of judgement'.[8] It is an analysis that has also been used with respect to the younger Pitt's resignation. Robin O'Reilly accounted for the events of 1801 with the 'simple explanation' that Pitt 'had been led by his often untrustworthy optimism into an extraordinary error of judgement'.[9] The elder Pitt's own explanation for his conduct in 1761 was that he could not remain in office for the sake of a false unanimity. The month before he resigned his seals on 5 October he warned that

> he had gone as far as his conscience or even his sleep would permit him, and therefore as he could not execute any orders for making further concessions he must throw himself on the king's generosity for the case of himself and his family.[10]

George III, who had ascended to the throne only in 1760, was never to forgive the elder Pitt for his presumption. Although the king allowed him return to power to direct the government, even as first minister, he never changed his opinion that Pitt was 'the most ungrateful and . . . most dishonourable of men' and 'the blackest of hearts'.[11] In 1778 when the king debated the return of Pitt (who since then had been ennobled to the earldom of Chatham) he still referred to him as 'that perfidious man'.[12] Chatham died on 11 May 1778, after one last dramatic intervention in parliament, when his son had assisted him to the house of lords. In May the same house, under the king's influence, voted by a majority of one that the peers of the realm should not attend the funeral as a body.[13] A monument to Chatham in Westminster Abbey was also opposed by the king as it was a 'rather offensive measure to me personally'.[14] George III's ungracious and antagonistic attitude was not lost on the young William Pitt who was then approaching his nineteenth birthday. Behind his icy reserve, he noted with some bitterness that 'The court did not honour us with their countenance, nor did they suffer the procession to be as magnificent as it ought.'[15]

What Bagehot referred to as the younger Pitt's 'mellifluous abundance of appropriate language' the prime minister always attributed to his father's training.[16] It was often claimed that Chatham had encouraged his precocious child's oratory, using the garden to signify an imaginary house of commons. Henry Addington, years after Pitt's death, occasionally spoke about his late friend. Once, he recounted a somewhat disparaging anecdote from Pitt's childhood when apparently Chatham had been disappointed to find his eldest son, John, debating better than William during one such practice. With a touch of malice Addington revealed that the father 'seemed mortified that his little favourite did not promise to be an orator'.[17]

The younger Pitt grew up on his father's career. When his mother had been ennobled in 1766 to become Baroness Chatham the precocious seven-year-old was reported to have expressed his delight that he was the second son so that he could follow his father into the commons and from there govern the country. There were deep similarities in temperament between father and son. Stanley Ayling has suggested that for all Chatham's 'lordly and overbearing manner he was at many points, mental and physical, a very vulnerable man and his camouflage and smoke screens were sometimes devices to afford a degree of self-protection',[18] a description that could equally apply to his son. As Ehrman has noted, the image Pitt constructed for himself was 'partly an artefact' imposed on himself and on others, that of 'an awkward, reserved personality — "the shyest man alive" — in a world with which in some ways he never felt at ease. He needed to be bold and assertive, and he claimed his position as of right.'[19] But equally, Ehrman also emphasises that Pitt's image was not just a mask adopted to protect himself from being hurt; it was also how he genuinely saw himself:

> an entirely natural leader, from his own point of vantage and in his own dis-
> tinctive way . . . [and] like his father, he gave heart to those who served him
> and to much of the nation at large . . . The image was the ultimate support
> in easing the tensions of which it was itself a part.[20]

The similarities between father and son, and their respective resignations, should not be taken too far. There were crucial differences in the manner of their withdrawals just as their characters were not identical. Ehrman makes a telling point in the conclusion of his three-volume study of Pitt when he argues that 'It would be rash to trace too confidently the psychological springs, in a man long dead and, one would think, not susceptible of easy analysis.'[21] He considers it possible that Pitt owed much to both his hereditary combination of Grenville 'practicality and staying power' with Pitt 'brilliance and extravagance', and the environment in which he grew up. The key difference in character between the two men Ehrman attributes to the son's 'less fissile temperament and an innate hopefulness and resolve', which he believes spared Pitt from the fate of his father, who died an unstable and broken man. Despite the differences it would, nevertheless, be foolish to ignore the correlations. The younger Pitt always felt the weight of the country's destiny on his shoulders. In 1801 this would have been added to by the burden of his family inheritance, and the realisation that his reputation might suffer the way his father's had. Yet in the end he was his own man; he followed the path that he decided was most consistent with his character.

HISTORIANS AND THE RESIGNATION OF PITT

> Mr Dundas said that, from his experience in affairs, he had been taught to have little faith in historians. 'For instance', insisted he, 'the motives I and my colleagues have assigned for our resignation, drawn from the popery question, no historian will believe; and, if any mentions it, he will treat it as a mere pretext to cover the real motive; and he will support his representation by very plausible arguments. Yet nothing can be more true than the reason we assigned was the real one: the king was prepared to oppose us on the popery question.[22]

The finest satirical cartoonist of the day, John Gillray, had no problem, in his drawings, attributing the resignations to the 'justice' of the catholic question, and not to any ulterior motive. His objectivity was no doubt hampered by the fact that he had been in receipt of a pension from Canning since 1797.[23] The doubts surrounding Pitt's resignation were put on record on 20 March 1801 by the earl of Darnley, who used the crisis to make his own point. Moving for the creation of a committee on the state of the nation Darnley was sharply critical of the resignations. He did not believe that the public would view the matter favourably — it was 'a trick, or juggle'. The outgoing ministers had

> found it convenient to retire for a time, in order to resume their situations with more effect hereafter, or that having brought the country, by their misconduct, into a most critical situation, they desert their posts in the hour of danger.[24]

Once more a Pitt was being accused of deserting his country during a crisis. The confusion that surrounded the resignations was reflected in some contemporary accounts. An essay on Henry Addington, written between 1801 and 1802, referred to the prime minister's resignation as 'a measure of a very ambiguous nature', one 'which has never yet been sufficiently explained'.[25] According to this interpretation the change of administration had not been unfavourably received as Pitt's ministry in recent years had 'been supported by the *fears* rather than the *love* of the people'. Upon Pitt's death in 1806 William Hazlitt wrote a scathing attack on the late prime minister. He found it amazing that 'with few talents, and fewer virtues', Pitt had lasted in power with a reputation for 'moral excellence', 'eloquence' and 'wisdom'.[26] The caustic remarks were borrowed largely, as Hazlitt was gracious enough to admit, from a newspaper article by Samuel Taylor Coleridge in *The Morning Post* in 1800.[27] Although for obvious reasons this did not cover his resignation the article contained many observations that influenced how Pitt was later perceived. Coleridge saw the inheritance of Chatham as 'a fact of no ordinary importance in the solution of his character . . . he was cast, rather than grew'.[28] Pitt's oratory was also subjected to some acerbic comments that Hazlitt was also to cite: 'words upon words finely arranged . . . nothing memorable has been said . . . Not a sentence of Mr Pitt's has ever been quoted, or formed the favourite phrase of the day.'[29] The article ended with a swipe at the society and circumstances that had been necessary in order to produce a Pitt.[30] Lord Campbell in the 1840s could shed no light on Pitt's conduct. He speculated that Pitt might have resigned because of peace with France, but concluded that the matter was a mystery, and that even Pitt himself had been guided by forces he did not understand: 'I believe that he never explained his plan to any human being, and that he hardly owned it to himself.'[31]

Of Pitt's main biographers in the nineteenth century Lords Stanhope and Rosebery accepted the catholic question as the only cause of the resignations.[32] Stanhope believed that Pitt had 'fulfilled the duty incumbent on a patriotic minister' and that his conduct in March 1801 was 'free from all ambiguity'.[33] Similarly, towards the end of the century, Lord Ashbourne accepted the stated reason for the resignation as the true one. Ashbourne, however, provided a more critical account of Pitt's behaviour. He hailed the union as 'a great measure — the most important of Pitt's life and policy' but blamed his subject for mishandling the attempt to achieve catholic emancipation.[34] As far as Ashbourne was concerned Pitt had not shown the correct resolve and had been careless in allowing Loughborough to scheme against him. He had pursued emancipation half-heartedly, prepared to accept failure, and Ashbourne believed the king had read this into his letter of 31 January.[35] These arguments summarised an entire body of opinion on the resignations. The catholic question was accepted as the true cause of the government's collapse but Pitt's character was held culpable for allowing the crisis to occur:

> he did not act in the matter like a strong man who meant to effect his purpose, and who would not be denied. His own health was not good; and he had not quite the energy, the decision, or the vigour of early days; and he shrank from taking a resolute stand against the king.[36]

In the nineteenth century Pitt's reputation benefited from an elegant tribute by Lord Macaulay. Macaulay hailed the union as 'a scheme of policy, so grand and so simple, so righteous and so humane, that it would alone entitle him to a high place among statesmen'.[37] The machinations against emancipation, however, had prevented it from becoming 'a union indeed', Macaulay blaming 'traitors' and 'sycophants'.

The nineteenth-century constitutional historian Walter Bagehot replied to Stanhope's biography in 1861, as soon as it was published. The opening of his essay on Pitt was notable for an analysis of the revisionism that was then taking place in historical writing: 'What used to be a sombre and respectable calling, is now an audacious pursuit.'[38] Even 'simple readers' were apparently aware that 'good' historical figures were becoming 'bad', and 'bad' ones 'good'. Bagehot's own position on these developments was ambiguous; he criticised Stanhope for having none of the virtues necessary in 'a great historical writer of the present age . . . he is not anxious to be original'. Bagehot was sympathetic to Pitt's 'overweening' self-confidence and 'presumptuous' energy. These things were failings in 'ordinary men', but not for 'the one exceptional man, who is in his first youth to rule the world'. Such a man 'must be trained not to fear it, but despise it'.[39] On Ireland, Bagehot found Pitt's behaviour far-seeing and just, and regretted that he had not been able to succeed in his proposal for catholic emancipation.[40]

The most compelling attack on Pitt's conduct was made by the respected historian W.E.H. Lecky in the 1890s. In his history of Ireland the worst motives were ascribed to the prime minister, as Lecky continued his cogent case against British misrule. He was convinced that Pitt could have succeeded in carrying emancipation in 1801, had he really wanted. Added to this was the regular opposition's support for emancipation leading to the conclusion that 'If he had persevered he must have triumphed, and the king must have submitted.'[41] Lecky found it significant that Pitt had resigned reluctantly, and speculated that he had been forced into it by Grenville and Canning; there was also the suspicion that peace with France had been an important consideration.[42] The most damning event for Lecky was Pitt's pledge to the king in March 1801 never to raise the catholic question before him again. In his opinion it was 'impossible by any legitimate argument to justify his conduct, and it leaves a deep stain upon his character both as a statesman and as a man'.[43] The illness affecting the king did not strike Lecky as an acceptable justification for Pitt's conduct. An emotional response was impossible for Pitt as 'no English statesman has exhibited during his long career a more austere and rigid self-control; no statesman was less swayed by uncalculating emotion, less likely to be betrayed into unguarded speech or hasty action'.[44] Pitt cared more 'for power than for measures': reluctant to give up his power Pitt abandoned the catholic question so that he could resume his office and face the country's pressing problems. In this interpretation 'the illness of the king gave him an unlooked-for pretext for extricating himself with some colour of magnanimity from his difficulty, and by deserting the catholics he removed the greatest obstacle in his path'.[45]

The publication of books on John Hookham Frere, who had been a friend of Pitt, contributed to the canon of works critical of the prime minister.[46] Gabrielle Festing's study, a year after Ashbourne, contained a letter from George Canning to Frere that blamed Pitt's followers for goading him into resigning.[47] The opinion of Frere himself was also quoted; he had felt that Pitt had pursued his own game in 1801. He had no doubt Pitt foresaw what would happen: 'He did not wish to make the peace which was inevitable, and knew he must come in again soon after it was made.'[48] This echoed Malmesbury and the king's own speculations, but was more damaging coming from one of Pitt's number. The allegation that Pitt went out as a ruse to enable a successful peace with France to take place, and to protect his reputation from having to make it, was to become a popular theme in twentieth-century studies.

John Holland Rose restored some of the lustre of Pitt's reputation in the early part of the century, first with a two-volume life of Pitt in 1923, and then with a short life follow-up two years later.[49] In the second of these, he accepted that when Pitt abandoned the catholic question 'he acted weakly out of regard for the king's temperament'.[50] H. Montgomery Hyde adopted a similar position. He understood why Pitt acted as he did in offering his pledge to the king but regretted 'the unfortunate surrender of ideals which his resigning had commenced . . . The allegiance of a people had been lost at the price of a pacific royal conscience.'[51]

Two biographies of Pitt published in the United States in the 1930s concurred that the catholic question was the sole reason for the resignation. P.W. Wilson mentioned no other issues, while E.K. Chatterton offered other related factors.[52] Despite the somewhat overblown title of Chatterton's work — England's greatest statesman — there were suggestions that Pitt acted as much out of petulance as out of principle. Chatterton argued that the behaviour of the king was taken by Pitt to be 'tantamount to an expression of having lost confidence'.[53] A comparative study of George III and Pitt published by Donald Grove Barnes in 1939 offered 'a new interpretation'.[54] Barnes was sharply critical of Pitt's premiership from 1795 onwards, suggesting that it may have been a greater liability than asset to the country.[55] More important, in terms of his position on the resignation crisis, was Barnes's view that Pitt was not flexible enough to 'serve as a model for other statesmen under a constitutional monarchy'.[56] Pitt's constitutional principles were too much, 'like those of his father', determined 'by his own personality and outstanding ability'. The role of Loughborough in the events of 1801 was dismissed by Barnes who did not accept that there was sufficient evidence that 'he had any real influence in fixing the mind of the king on the question of catholic emancipation'.[57] Barnes does, however, accept that Loughborough 'may have acted in a dishonourable manner in 1806' which was all the more remarkable given that he had passed away the previous year. Accusing Pitt of having deliberately deceived the Irish catholics, Barnes blamed him for being cynically aware 'that he was dangling the prospect of a reward before the eyes of the catholics which he was in no position to honour'.[58] On the resignation issue Barnes adopted a similar position to Chatterton. A blow to his pride, 'personal pique', had induced him to tender his resignation although he was disposed to admit that Pitt had presented a better case than the king on the matter.[59]

In 1953 Richard Pares published his study of George III and the politicians of the period, which remains invaluable. His perspective on the resignation crisis of 1801 is useful, even if he did consider it a 'special mystery'.[60] Pares's insights into cabinet procedure of the time are revealing. A minister 'was bound to propose, and even, perhaps, to insist upon, anything which was, in his opinion, necessary for the king's service; he was not equally bound to insist upon anything which he thought right in itself'.[61] This was held to be highly significant in any attempt to understand why, when Pitt resigned, he did not immediately press the catholic question in parliament. The connections between the resignations of 1761 and 1801 were recognised by Pares. In 1801, once Pitt had become aware 'that the king was not merely neutral but hostile to the measure proposed as necessary for his service, Pitt's position became untenable and he had no choice but to resign, as his father had done'.[62]

G.C. Bolton's authoritative study on the passing of the Irish union, published in 1966, briefly examined the resignation from an Irish perspective. Bolton took issue with the critical interpretation of Lecky and Barnes, which he criticised for underrating the effect of the crisis on Irish politics.[63] The opposition to emancipation of Auckland, Hobart and Westmorland, Bolton believed was 'a determined attempt' to prevent the measure. Adding to the problems the policy faced was the likelihood of its failure in parliament. Only Pitt's small personal following, sixty at best, and 'an unknown number of whigs' would have supported the measure. Faced with this opposition Bolton argues that Pitt's 'decision to dodge the issue in the interest of harmony during war-time becomes more readily explicable'.[64]

Addington's biographer, Philip Ziegler, found Pitt's resignation, 'in sum, as perplexing as any which has disturbed the course of British politics'.[65] Defending the suspicions entertained by contemporaries in 1801, particularly Auckland's 'veil of mystery' hypothesis, Ziegler asserted that

> in the forces, conscious or unconscious, which impelled the various participants along their courses and in the inexplicable mistakes in timing and misjudgements of character which stamped the whole affair, there lies a residue of mystery which no historian can hope entirely to resolve.[66]

While in terms of the Irish dimension, Ziegler accepted the 'excellent reasons' in favour of following up the union with emancipation he failed entirely to see any urgency in pursuing it. Nor was Ziegler sympathetic towards Pitt's pledge to the king in March 1801 never to raise the catholic question before him. This was a further cynical manoeuvre, Pitt could not have felt 'any real responsibility' for the king's mental state, and Ziegler did not believe that Pitt was acting more out of 'a spirit of chivalrous pity than out of deliberate calculation'.[67] Ziegler concluded that although the catholic question was 'the substantive cause' of the resignation it was not the only factor: Pitt was playing his own selfish game, aware that his frail health would not allow him to continue in office, and manipulating the crisis so that Addington would have to make the peace. Pitt wanted out, and 'it is not necessary to believe the wilder stories of his insanity to accept that, after his recent illness, he was still overwrought and conscious that his judgement had lost its clarity'.[68] Ziegler's analysis benefits, on all points, from certain qualifications. He agrees with Malmesbury's interpretation that Pitt went out because he could not make war or peace, arguing that there must have been some truth to this 'even though Pitt may hardly have known it'. Ziegler's conclusion is all the more damning for its pretence at objectivity:

> he [Pitt] did not consciously seek to saddle Addington with all the country's troubles but it was with profound relief that he accepted the change of horses in the middle of one of the most turbulent and treacherous streams which he ever had to cross.[69]

The most important shift in the historiography occurred in 1969. That year John Ehrman published the first volume of his study of Pitt and although it did not cover the resignation it added considerably to the understanding of the prime minister and his character. The same year Richard Willis examined Pitt's resignation in a historiographical and interpretative chapter of his doctoral thesis, 'The politics of parliament', that included Camden's important memorandum, which had previously been unavailable.[70] Two years later the abridged chapter, together with the Camden memorandum, was published in the *Bulletin of the Institute of Historical Research*.[71] The publication of this memorandum, and Willis's own work, were both key contributions to the debate on Pitt's resignation. For Willis the union had been 'an attempt to strengthen a weak strategic flank in the war against revolutionary France'.[72] It had also been a necessary precondition for catholic emancipation 'for both strategic and tactical reasons'. The confusion and suspicions that surrounded the resignation, then and since, Willis believed had 'grown out of an imperfect understanding of the presuppositions of politics at this time'.[73] In this he reflected, and quoted, the opinion of Pares regarding the difference between what a minister thought *right* in itself, and what he thought *necessary* for the king's service.[74] This suggested to Willis a reason why Pitt was, as Ashbourne alleged, negligent on the related questions of tithes and endowment of clergy; it was because they were not as necessary as the broader emancipation question.[75] As for Pitt's refusal to press the catholic question in parliament Willis argued that 'a higher necessity was present in his mind: that of maintaining the stability of government itself'.[76] The pledge to George III given in March 1801 Willis maintained was because of the king's illness 'and not because he resigned on some other provocation, or for some hidden purpose, or because of lack of principle'.[77] The interpretation that Pitt went out to avoid making an unpopular peace with France Willis dismissed as 'an erroneous speculation' taken over from Malmesbury.[78] For Willis 'the contribution of catholic reform to the resignation was essentially a catalytic one'.[79] Pitt went out of office because to have remained would have severely curtailed his effectiveness as a minister.[80] In a later article on cabinet politics Willis argued that 'apart from George III's possible scruples about the coronation oath, the king clearly intended to use the crisis to re-establish his influence within the executive, which Pitt was not prepared to tolerate'.[81] This, for Willis, was the essential point.

This interpretation, and the publication of Camden's memorandum, only reopened the controversy. In 1974 Derek Jarrett published a short biography of Pitt in which he argued that his subject's eyes in 1801 were 'on the future'.[82] The book was memorable for its introduction by A.J.P. Taylor, who used the opportunity to assert that Pitt's was 'a career in which I find much to admire, if, personally, little to like',[83] a criticism that at least answered Coleridge and Hazlitt's charge, that Pitt never said anything memorable, being as it was a paraphrase of something Pitt had said about Edmund Burke.[84] A decade later Piers Mackesy's study of British foreign policy between 1799 and 1802 was subtitled 'the downfall of Pitt'. His position was encapsulated in his chapter on the fall of the ministry, which contained the heading 'the pilot bales out'.[85] The assurances of Dundas and Grenville that the catholic question was the sole reason for the resignations did not convince Mackesy: 'they protested too much'.[86] Nevertheless he did exonerate Pitt from acting 'on a premeditated and logical policy'.[87] The key issue was 'the intolerable pressure of the war on Pitt';[88] other factors such as pride played their part, but it was foreign policy that determined his actions; Pitt would never 'sacrifice power to principle'.[89] The desire to avoid making the peace proved too enticing to resist. Mackesy concluded that 'no single explanation, however, will suffice',[90] encapsulating his argument in the analysis that

> no explanation of Pitt's resignation is complete which ignores his state of mind and health, and the many pressures which had assailed him since the battle of Marengo; disputes over diplomacy, grand strategy and military matters; backbiting in the cabinet; a tired and failing ministry, so divided that it could scarcely make war and could not make peace; conflicts with the king.

He agreed with Willis that the catholic question was merely the catalyst in the reaction. Behind the resignation was a ruthless determination to avoid being cornered as Lord North had been in 1782. Rather than see that happen, Pitt 'allowed himself to become trapped in a matter of principle, between the Irish administration and a large cabinet minority who opposed emancipation. With these stresses he no longer had the resilience to cope.'[91]

An even more critical and cynical interpreter of Pitt's career than Lecky, although with less ability, was A.D. Harvey. He damned the union as 'a belated, and in retrospect very ambiguous instance of Pitt's reformist tendencies'.[92] The innocence of Pitt in the private sphere led him to consider how it 'also contributed to the suggestion about him of one-sidedness, if not incompleteness and abnormality, and to the view that his talents were entirely verbal'. In his short overview of Grenville's career Harvey claimed that the reasons for Pitt's resignation 'remain unclear' although he accepted that Grenville's motives were the stated ones.[93]

Charles John Fedorak continued the discussion in 1992 with an examination that was sharply critical of Willis's interpretation.[94] Fedorak suggested that the matter warranted further study as it was 'illustrative of the way the British political system worked during a period of social, political, and industrial change'.[95] There was no doubt in his mind that Pitt had not gone out on the catholic question. The words of Richard Brinsley Sheridan were quoted approvingly: Pitt 'built a brick wall and then ran his head against it'.[96] The accuracy of Camden's memorandum was also challenged, given that it was written by a friend of Pitt at a time when he was attempting to return to office, even though it was by no means uncritical of Pitt. As for the Irish dimension Fedorak quoted Castlereagh's letter to Pitt in January 1801 in which he stated that no direct promises had been made to the catholics, and concluded from this that 'Pitt was not obliged to honour promises that were not made.'[97] He even suggested that Castlereagh might have been mistaken as to Pitt's position on enlisting the support of the catholics. According to this interpretation 'Pitt was either acting carelessly or trying deliberately to provoke a constitutional crisis.'[98] This was the crux for Fedorak. He refused to believe that Pitt had satisfied honour with regard to the king and the Irish catholics by his 'contradictory gestures' in 1801: it was 'absurd'.[99] The state of the cabinet, he argued, was one of the real reasons for the resignation; the conduct of the war and the question of peace another. Pitt's uncertain health was a final factor: 'Confused and disoriented, Pitt found in the king's outburst of 28 January a means of escape.'[100] Pitt did not plan his resignation, but when the situation arose to withdraw in 1801 he gladly seized it. His reluctance to relinquish office was explained by his 'love of power and devotion to public life'.[101] Pitt used 'the catholic issue for reasons of political expediency' and 'paid the price of acknowledging that the king continued to retain important power over his ministers'.[102]

'Why exactly, it has been asked from that day to this, did Pitt resign?'[103] The question Ehrman posed in the final volume of his study of Pitt was one which he acknowledged contained many problems. He believed that Pitt had acted to introduce emancipation in 1801, rather than leave it for a later and safer period, because of the influence of Cornwallis, Castlereagh, Grenville and Dundas, for 'pragmatic reasons', and because of the recent commitments to the catholics in Ireland.[104] Pitt's letter of 31 January, according to Ehrman, could be read 'almost as an ultimatum rather than a genuine attempt to conciliate or persuade'.[105] For Ehrman the perspective on Pitt's resignation could be framed by three explanations that, perhaps, 'ended at the point of the act': the question of Pitt's health; the dilemma of peace with France; and the problem of maintaining his authority as prime minister.[106] The first of these problems, Ehrman believed, might even have extended to the state of the prime minister's mind; 'The old rumours of madness — Chatham's legacy — revived, and there were also hints that he had burned out.'[107] The second was the possibility that Pitt, in the words of Liverpool, left office because he found it 'impracticable for the ministry to make peace' and because he equally 'found it impracticable to make war'.[108] The final consideration was that the manner in which Pitt had been opposed necessitated a stand against the king, for otherwise he would have remained in office with only a nominal power, one of Canning's myriad interpretations for the resignation.[109] If these three circumstances provided the perspective for Pitt's going then Ehrman believed that they 'had still to be shaped by the point'.[110] This 'point' was the behaviour of the king and the way in which he opposed emancipation, that despite Pitt's insistence the king had continued to canvass opposition to the measure. Where 'the monarch saw an assault on his constitutional duty — on a role which no one else could assume in this instance — the minister saw an assault on the valid process of constitutional advice'.[111] The subsequent behaviour of Pitt, and his apparent desire to remain in office, Ehrman attributed to his changing perspective on the events; his decision on the catholic question, he claimed, had been very recent. Therefore patriotic and other considerations began to take hold during the end of February, accentuated by the king's illness. Ehrman concluded that 'The story of Pitt's retirement is full of loose ends, and motives are seldom unmixed.'[112] The confusion about whether Addington would continue on as prime minister in March 1801 may have pointed Pitt 'towards a decision which in fact he may have preferred'.[113] Ehrman's overview of Pitt's conduct was expansive, but not conclusive. Pitt's attitude

> may be seen as high-minded or less than high-minded depending on one's starting point: as a final evasion, on lines already suggested at his resignation by critics, or on the contrary as embodying the 'character' by which Pitt always set such store. It certainly struck a central chord; it satisfied his conception of himself, and after the hesitations, the weighing of choices and contradictory impulses, it may have come as a relief from the continual compromises of power.[114]

THE CHARACTER OF MR PITT

'My ambition is character, *not office.'*

(Pitt to Canning, 1802)[115]

The most striking traits in his public character are of course too well known to you . . . The vast powers of his mind . . . But it has always been a subject of serious regret to me to observe the little justice which the world has done to his private excellence — for he was as amiable as he was great. He was remarkable for a peculiar sweetness and equanimity of temper, which I never saw ruffled.

(Sketch by W. Dacres Adams, who was Pitt's private secretary, on the late prime minister)[116]

To his friends and admirers Pitt was the noblest and greatest of them all. To his opponents Pitt was proud, selfish, and devoid of any real feeling or emotion. Somewhere between these extremes lies the truth. Dacres Adams's description of Pitt, either deliberately or unintentionally, avoids the complexity and ambiguity that was at the heart of his character. It is absurd to claim that Pitt was never ruffled, that he received the victory of Trafalgar with the same composure as he did the defeat at Austerlitz. The opposite was true, Pitt suffered extremes in mood, 'he was either in a cellar or a garret', and throughout his life struggled to maintain his optimism, which fortunately for him proved resilient. Out of office, but not in opposition, between 1801 and 1804 Pitt refused to act against Addington. His sense of honour again dictated his conduct, and even though it was unintelligible to those around him this mattered little. Pitt consistently refused to flatter any public sentiment; he knew how great he was and that was enough. In one sense, he *was* 'cast, rather than grew'. He had developed his identity early on in his life, and he insisted on being the arbiter of his actions. It was an imposing code he set himself; he admitted to Canning in 1802 that 'I may be overfeeling about *character*.'[117]

'I can say with sincerity, I never had a wish which did not terminate in the dearest interests of the nation.'[118] The outlook of the 23-year-old Pitt in 1783 contained the same guiding principle that was to motivate his conduct at the time of his death. Pitt had no difficulty at that time in explaining the beliefs that constituted his political philosophy. It was a revealing exposition of his character. Ambition was not something he was prepared to hide or deny:

> high situations, and great influence, are desirable objects to most men, and objects which I am not ashamed to pursue, which I am even solicitous to possess, whenever they can be acquired with honour, and retained with dignity. But even these objects I am not beneath relinquishing, the moment my duty to my country, my character, and my friends, renders such a sacrifice indispensable.

Public duty was at the heart of Pitt's character. If it was necessary to give up his 'high situations, and great influence' for the sake of the country, he would do it. For Pitt the constitution, the empire and its welfare was the primary consideration. Any personal feeling was secondary and unimportant. Faced with a choice between private success and public duty he declared in 1783 that he was prepared to sacrifice himself:

> then I hope to retire, not disappointed, but triumphant; triumphant in the conviction that my talents, humble as they are, have been earnestly, zealously, and strenuously, employed to the best of my apprehension, in promoting the truest welfare of my country; and that, however I may stand chargeable with weakness of understanding, or error of judgement, nothing can be imputed to my official capacity which bears the most distant connection with an interested, a corrupt, or a dishonest intention.

The support of Pitt for Addington's administration, his refusal to engage in general opposition for a considerable period, and his unwillingness to form a party around himself as Castlereagh had recommended, attracted considerable criticism. Yet his conduct was to be identical to that he had outlined, with remarkable prescience, in 1783. Then he had declared that, when the time would come for him to leave office, he would not 'mimic the parade of the hon. gentleman in avowing an indiscriminate opposition to whoever may be appointed to succeed'.[119] Instead he would

> march out with no warlike, no hostile, no menacing protestations; but hoping the new administration will have no other object in view than the real

and substantial welfare of the community at large; that they will bring with them into office those truly public and patriotic principles which they formerly held . . . I promise them, before-hand, my uniform and best support on every occasion, where I can honestly and conscientiously assist them.

Although many of these sentiments were common coin with politicians in opposition, Pitt alone actually carried them out in practice. In 1783 he was to follow the line of conduct he had explained to parliament, until he considered it imperative that a change of ministry should occur, and his conduct towards the Addington administration between 1801 and 1804 was to be governed by the same principles.[120]

These beliefs, that revolved around Pitt's love for his country, were at the heart of his character. The inability to understand this, to understand the nature of Pitt the man, generated much of the confusion about his actions in 1801. Pitt was not governed by dogmatic intellectual beliefs in the way he applied his policies; his character was consistent throughout his career, even though his opinion on political matters was not. He saw this as no bad thing. In 1800 he explained to parliament how

all opinions must inevitably be subservient to times and circumstances; and that man who talks of consistency merely because he holds the same opinions for ten or fifteen years, when the circumstances under which it was originally formed are totally changed, is a slave to the most idle vanity.[121]

During a dinner in Downing Street in the spring of 1800, Sir Robert Walpole's favourite maxim, *quieta non movere*, was deliberately introduced into the conversation to determine Pitt's thoughts on political ideology. Involving himself in the discussion the prime minister declared that 'there was no wisdom in establishing general rules or principles in government'.[122] Another indication of his convictions was also noted by Glenbervie during the resignation crisis. When someone, at a dinner at Lord Macartney's in January 1801, had commented that 'the law of nations (where not founded on positive treaty) was deduced from the principle of ethics', Pitt had agreed with a bemused smile, 'Yes, that most certain of all sciences.'[123]

When it came to the constitution Pitt was a conservative; unnecessary tinkering with it could never be recommended. In 1783 he asserted that 'it was not for him, with unhallowed hands, to touch the venerable pile of the constitution'.[124] He was not blind to its flaws, 'to see it stand in need of repair was sufficiently melancholy'; but, six years before revolution in France would prove the danger of excessive change based upon a theory, he warned that when it came to the constitution,

the more he revered it, the more he wished to secure its duration to the latest posterity, the greater he felt the necessity of guarding against its decay. Innovations were at all times dangerous; and should never be attempted but when necessity called for them.

He repeated this in 1800 when he informed parliament that the constitution should not be 'idly and wantonly disturbed from any love of experiment, or any predilection for theory'.[125] Indeed his position on the catholic question in 1801 can best be summarised by his own analysis in 1783 on acceptable changes to the constitution. The objective in altering the test laws, he might well have rationalised, 'was not to innovate, but rather to renew and invigorate the spirit of the constitution, without deviating materially from its present form'. This represents the essence of Pitt's position on both the union and catholic emancipation.

RESOLVING THE MYSTERY
The varying interpretations of Pitt's conduct have proved inconclusive and even internally inconsistent. Criticisms have addressed a number of areas. The prevailing argument has been that Pitt in 1801 was playing his own game, that questions of health, foreign policy and pride induced him to retire from office. One, or more, of these aspects have been enlisted by the historians who have seen hidden motives in the events of 1801. Even admirers of Pitt, such as Ehrman, have not been convinced by his motives and consider it possible that other, less honourable, factors may also have been at work. For Ehrman, in particular, it was a question of emphasis, and he bore in mind that man is not all of one piece. In most of these accounts the catholic question has been dropped, as Dundas so accurately predicted. Fedorak summed up the unimportance of the issue when he argued that Pitt did not have to resign over promises that were never made.

    If few of the interpretations have satisfied it has not been because of a lack of imagination in the hypotheses. 'That Pitt went out because he could not make the peace' and did not want to continue the war has been one of the most popular theories. According to this, one of the earliest explanations, Pitt manipulated the catholic question for the purposes of concealing his true reasons for wanting to retire from office — his desire to avoid responsibility for an unpopular peace with France. Central to the theory, of course, is the belief that he genuinely wished to retire as prime minister. There are two problems with this version. The first stumbling block is that Pitt, strangely, after having manipulated the crisis to allow him to resign, then attempted to remain in office. Such an inconsistency is difficult to reconcile with Pitt's alleged machinations prior to that. Fedorak attempts to explain it with reference to Pitt's love of power, sense of public duty, and the accusation that the prime minister was not acting rationally. The second obstacle to the war hypothesis is the support Pitt subsequently gave to the peace of Amiens with France. If he retired on the catholic pretext to avoid being associated with an unpopular peace it would seem unusual that Pitt should have been so vocal, initially, in its support, even when former colleagues such as Grenville were vehemently opposed. Pitt's health has been another key component in the interpretations. That Pitt was under intense pressure in 1801 is undisputed. It is also clear that this followed a recent period of physical strain, itself partially caused by stress. To deduce from this that Pitt was anxious to retire to regain his strength is mistaken, and the evidence against this is also compelling; Pitt's breakdown in February 1801 was as much caused by having to leave office as anything else, he had no life other than government, and no response to the crisis other than tears. In any case, resilient as ever, his health recovered in March 1801.

Promises *were* made to the Irish catholics. The chief problem of interpretations such as Fedorak's, which ignore the Irish dimension, is that by doing so they fail to place the crisis in its only proper context. It was implicitly understood by the catholics that emancipation would follow the success of the union, and from November 1799 a solution to the catholic question was implicitly a matter of government policy. Castlereagh and Cornwallis both saw it as a question of honour, as they were to remind Pitt. Many historians have failed to understand the urgency of emancipation in 1800 and 1801. Pitt's conception of the union and its value to the empire determined the pace of the measure. If emancipation was to occur then it should complement the union policy, and be seen to do so. It had to be conceded willingly, and generously, to secure the support and goodwill of the Roman Catholics. Postponing it until after peace with France risked alienating the catholics from the union and left the government open to charges of deception. Between September 1800 and January 1801 Pitt acted to secure the support of his cabinet before then attempting to persuade the king and leading public figures of the necessity of catholic emancipation. This was in accordance with the conditions set out by George III in 1795. The process was delayed, perhaps fatally, by the other pressures of government and Pitt's own failing health. In January 1801 Pitt expected difficulty in persuading the king on the point, but he did not expect to find the king's mind secretly influenced against the measure, or find himself surrounded by his enemies waiting to destroy him.

It is indicative of the respect, grudging or otherwise, that historians have afforded Pitt that all have credited him with full control over the events of 1801. In all accounts it was *he* who presented the king with an ultimatum, *he* who threatened his resignation, *he* who chose Addington, and at all times, crucially, it was *he* who commanded his destiny. It is this misconception that, perhaps more than anything, has been responsible for much of the confusion surrounding the crisis. The initiative for what happened between January and March never lay with Pitt; he lost control early on, and spent the remainder of the time struggling unsuccessfully to regain it. Tiring of the prime minister's insufferable arrogance and dismissive treatment, the king, genuinely mortified by the prospect of catholic emancipation, used the opportunity to reassert his own waning privileges. It was the king who selected Addington, and used the speaker, as a pawn, to discipline his proud minister. Pitt reacted to events as they occurred, initially bewildered by what was happening, then demoralised and depressed. Faced with obvious rejection by the king, he became deeply distressed; all semblance of the rigid self-discipline that had masked his physical and mental frailty finally collapsed.

It was not just emancipation that was being undermined: it was Pitt himself. He realised that his ascendancy as the king's prime minister was being eroded from both within and without. The nature of the opposition turned the matter from being a question of government into being a question of character. It was the manner in which Pitt was opposed, 'on the popery question', that determined his conduct. The function of government was to adopt and recommend policies to the king. It was this constitutional role, as much as emancipation, that was under attack in 1801. Other, interested, parties were advising the king, who was prepared to act as he chose. Some have claimed that Pitt in 1801 attempted to assert his supremacy over the king and forced a deliberate confrontation to humiliate his sovereign. The opposite could be argued with more justification. For the last few years of Pitt's administration the king and the government had begun to diverge sharply. The king was not satisfied with his prime minister; 'he had begun to think of him with less interest'.[126] The ministers were happy to refer to themselves as 'the king's government', but by 1801 this had become a polite formality, in all respects it had become Pitt's government. From the infamous outburst at the levee on 28 January onwards it was clear that George III was determined to demonstrate that it was *the king's government*. He was not prepared to listen to the advice of his cabinet; he demanded the surrender of Pitt on the catholic question, and was prepared to sacrifice his minister to assert his own authority.

This was unacceptable to Pitt. The king's conduct struck at the heart of all his constitutional principles. A government had to be free to protect its superior right, when expressed collectively, to submit advice to the king. Emancipation had been adopted as an essential policy by the ministry. On 31 January Pitt informed the king of this fact, the arguments in favour of emancipation, and the importance of the king remaining aloof from unconstitutional attempts at directing an opposition to the measure; this last part was particularly intolerable for the prime minister. It was impossible for him to allow the king to use his influence, or permit his name to be used, against a measure adopted by his government. It was also intolerable that the king should publicly remonstrate with members of that administration. All of this was distinct from the king being personally opposed to the measure. Pitt respected his religious convictions, but he could not permit the manner in which these convictions were being defended. Instead of a constitutional discussion of the matter between king and government Pitt faced a situation where the king was resolutely positioned against his own government, and the person who was at the head of it. When the king continued in his actions against emancipation Pitt was reluctantly forced to accept that the crisis had become a greater one than that of the catholic question alone. It was no longer just about the future political status of the catholics, it had become a question about the future status of the prime minister himself. That Pitt understood the crisis in these terms was demonstrated by a conversation Canning had with Malmesbury in 1802, an interpretation that convinces because it is not one of Canning's own. He revealed that

Mr Pitt told him that he went out, not on the catholic question simply as a measure in which he was opposed, but from the manner in which he was opposed, and to which, if he had assented, he would, as a minister, have been on a footing totally different from what he had ever before been in the cabinet.[127]

Even with his ministry unravelling before his eyes, and his power with it, Pitt refused to yield to the king. In the midst of his ill health and depression Pitt was forced to act instinctively. He tendered his resignation, the most painful decision of his career.

The king's illness changed everything. The emotional turmoil Pitt felt on the thought of leaving office, and leaving the governing of the country to lesser figures,[128] was added to, immeasurably, by the king's return to madness and the prospect of his death. To learn that the king blamed him for his condition was too much for Pitt to bear. Whatever his difficulties with George III, and their relationship had never been close, the figure of the king symbolised everything that Pitt believed in and respected. Pitt responded the only way he knew how, with an emotional pledge to the king never to raise the catholic question with him in or out of government *for as long* as George III lived. The minister had gambled that the weight of arguments in its favour would persuade the king to accept emancipation, as he had relented on other matters of policy. The strategy had failed, and the failure now threatened the welfare of the king and the empire; Pitt could not gamble further. His character was entwined with the interests of the constitution, the country, the empire; the catholic question must rest. Nor did Pitt feel it necessary to engage in a public defence of his actions. His conduct would stand on its own merits; detailed explanation would serve no constructive purpose.[129] Pitt did not abandon the Irish catholics. Through Cornwallis he explained his position to them and the difficulties he had encountered, but he would do no more.

Pitt's hesitancy in leaving office was understandable; he had never wanted to go, and his resignation had been forced by the uncompromising behaviour of the king. Once the catholic question was disposed of for the lifetime of the king there were compelling reasons for remaining. Pitt's natural optimism had recovered during the interregnum provided by the king's illness, and more importantly so too had his mental and physical health. Once the pressure was removed his balance was restored. By the time the king had recovered in March a new Pitt was facing him, much stronger and more determined than the one that had been distraught with overwhelming emotion a month previously; Pitt had been a broken man, now the ruthless tactician was back. Canning and Dundas plotted for his return and even committed proponents of emancipation, like Cornwallis and Castlereagh, believed he should continue for the sake of the empire. Pitt believed so too, but he would not make the first move to the king or Addington, it had to originate with them. In his scheming to keep Pitt in office Canning showed no compunction in having his friend abase himself before the king. For Canning no consideration of pride should prevent Pitt from returning to power, when the country needed him, and when Addington appeared so incapable. Any such humiliation was anathema to Pitt. He would not bargain to remain in power, he would not humble himself before Addington and the king and return as a figurehead, a political nonentity. It was unbecoming behaviour in a prime minister, and certainly unbecoming behaviour in a Pitt. In the last few years of the ministry Pitt was unquestionably guilty of increasing arrogance; the king did have a point. But these feelings were inseparable from the qualities that were responsible for his political genius: his self-confidence; his determination; and his ability to channel his melancholic, almost manic-depressive, energy into politics.

Between February and March 1801 when Pitt's equilibrium was gradually restored, the breathing space also allowed Addington to become entrenched in his new office. The son of Chatham's physician, whom no one had ever predicted great things for, Addington was not prepared to give up high office so lightly. Up until then Pitt had never blamed Addington for his role in the crisis, after all he had been an unknowing pawn of the king, and had he not intervened the country might have been thrown into the hands of the opposition, but from this point on relations gradually deteriorated. As Addington jealously clung, and was to cling even tighter, to his new station Pitt slowly grew to despise him. It was one thing to aspire to being prime minister when there was no acceptable alternative, it was unforgivable to insist upon it when he was waiting. By July 1802 Addington had become, for Pitt, 'the vainest man he had ever met, a man of little mind, of consummate vanity, and very slender abilities'.[130]

At the start of 1801 William Pitt faced the most difficult crisis of his career. He was emotionally and physically drained, and his problems were compounded by a disintegrating ministry, foreign and domestic problems, and a king who was becoming increasingly alienated from his ministers. There could not have been a worse time to address the catholic question. Nevertheless 1801 was the last, best hope to create a real union between Britain and Ireland. The conflict between king and ministers was never just about the catholic question, but it was the issue that unleashed a furious response to the problems that had been slowly fermenting. The crisis was about the nature of the king's government, the constitutional relationship between prime minister and monarch, and the limits of the royal prerogative. Rather than sacrifice his conception of his constitutional role, or his own arrogant nature, Pitt chose to resign and seemingly end his political career. Then, unable to come to terms with the apparent effect of his actions on the king, and faced with further political instability, Pitt acted as his conscience demanded and his character dictated; the catholic question was dropped and he made a genuine effort to remain in power. The empire, characteristically, was put ahead of all public and private considerations. Viewed thus, Pitt's resignation may be found, in retrospect, not to have been a mystery. It was the moment in which, depressed and tormented, Pitt acted instinctively, in the decision that was the culmination of his life, his oratory and his character. Pitt's guiding belief was the empire and he was prepared to risk his reputation, and his career, for what was necessary.

Notes

ABBREVIATIONS

Addington correspondence	George Pellew (ed.), *The life and correspondence of the Rt Hon. Henry Addington, 1st Viscount Sidmouth* (3 vols., London, 1847)
Aspinall, *George III*	*The later correspondence of George III*, ed. Arthur Aspinall. Vol. iii. Cambridge, 1967.
Auckland correspondence	*The journal and correspondence of William, Lord Auckland*, ed. bishop of Bath and Wells. 4 vols. London, 1861–2.
Beresford correspondence	*The correspondence of the Rt Hon. John Beresford*, ed. Lord Beresford. 2 vols. London, 1854.
BL	British Library.
Buckingham, *Courts*	*Memoirs of the courts and cabinets of George the third*, ed. 2nd duke of Buckingham and Chandos. 4 vols. London, 1848.
Campbell, *Lord chancellors*	Lord John Campbell, *The lives of the lord chancellors*. 7 vols. London, 1847.
Castlereagh correspondence	*Memoirs and correspondence of Viscount Castlereagh*, ed. Marquess of Londonderry. 12 vols. London, 1848–53.
Cornwallis correspondence	*The correspondence of Charles, 1st Marquess Cornwallis*, ed. Charles Ross. 3 vols. London, 1859.
CUL	Cambridge University Library.
Ehrman, *Pitt*	John Ehrman, *The younger Pitt*. 3 vols. London, 1969–96.
Glenbervie diaries	*The diaries of Sylvester Douglas, Lord Glenbervie*, ed. Francis Bickley. 2 vols. London, 1928.
Grattan, *Life*	*Memoirs of the life and times of the Rt Hon. Henry Grattan*, ed. Henry Grattan jnr. 5 vols. London, 1839–44.
HMC, *Dropmore papers*	*The manuscripts of J.B. Fortescue, esq., preserved at Dropmore*. 10 vols. HMC, London, 1892–1927.
HO	Home Office, London.
Hyde, *Castlereagh*	H.M. Hyde, *The rise of Castlereagh*. London, 1933.
Lecky, *Ireland*	W.E.H. Lecky, *Ireland in the eighteenth century*. 5 vols. London, 1898.
Malmesbury diaries	*Diaries and correspondence of James Harris, 1st earl of Malmesbury*. 4 vols. London, 1884.
NLI	National Library of Ireland.
PH	*Parliamentary History*.
PRO	Public Record Office, London.
PRONI	Public Record Office Northern Ireland.

Chapter 1 The search for security (pp. 1–24)

1. Philip Stanhope, Lord Mahon (ed.), *Correspondence between the Rt Hon. William Pitt and Charles, duke of Rutland* (London, 1890), p. 19.
2. Lord Ashbourne, *Pitt: some chapters of his life and times* (London, 1898), p. 87.
3. See James Kelly, 'The origins of the act of union' in *Irish Historical Studies*, xxv, no. 99 (May 1987), pp. 236–63.
4. For an analysis of what 'empire' meant at this time see Ehrman, *Pitt*, iii, 159. By applying the term to Great Britain and Ireland alone, Ehrman ignores the conceptual, or

at least rhetorical, significance that was being attached to the word in the 1790s. In debates, for example, Pitt often employed the concept of an 'empire': the union was necessary to 'augment the strength of the empire'; to give Ireland 'a full participation of the wealth, the power, and the stability of the British empire' (*PH*, xxxiv, 267, 269). 'Empire' went beyond Britain and Ireland alone, if not, perhaps, as a geographically recognised entity.

5. This was the thesis of Professor Bartlett's keynote address at the 1798 conference in the University of Luton, July 1998.

6. When it was decided to press, formally, for a union, the government initially referred to itself as 'the English government'; this was immediately amended to 'the king's government'. In this book the term 'king's government' will be used to refer to the general administration; the aptness of the term is demonstrated by the events of 1801. In 1797 Grenville made reference to 'the conduct of the king's government' (17 November 1797, HMC, *Dropmore papers*, iii, 394). Similarly, the term 'prime minister' will be used to refer to Pitt, for the purposes of clarity, even though it was not an official position at the time. Nevertheless it was clear that Pitt was the undisputed head of the ministry and the term 'prime minister' was beginning to be used regularly, for example a diary entry of Sylvester Douglas for 30 December 1798 makes reference to 'Mr Pitt as prime minister of England' (*Glenbervie diaries*, i, 143).

7. George III to Pitt, 13 June 1798 (NLI, MS 886, f. 323).

8. Pitt to Auckland, 28 October 1798 (PRONI, T3229/2/38).

9. Pitt to Rutland, 6 January 1785 (Lord Mahon (ed.), *Correspondence between the Rt Hon. William Pitt and Charles, duke of Rutland*, pp. 58, 65–6).

10. Ehrman, *Pitt*, i, 132; see also idem, iii, 12, where Ehrman shows that despite Pitt's respect for 'that great author' he took from him only what he found suitable.

11. Adam Smith, *An inquiry into the nature and causes of the wealth of nations* (Oxford, 1993), p. 460.

12. Thomas Bartlett, '"A weapon of war yet untried": Irish catholics and the armed forces of the crown, 1760–1830' in T.G. Fraser and Keith Jeffrey (eds.), *Men, women, and war*, Historical Studies, xviii (Dublin, 1993), p. 71.

13. Ibid., p. 67.

14. Cited ibid., p. 73.

15. Oliver MacDonagh, *States of mind: two centuries of Anglo-Irish conflict, 1780–1980* (London, 1983), p. 131.

16. Westmorland to Pitt, 13 November 1792 (CUL, Add. MS 6958, f. 1,145).

17. Pitt to Westmorland, 18 November 1792 (quoted in G.C. Bolton, *The passing of the Irish act of union* (London, 1966), p. 12).

18. Westmorland to Pitt, 10 January 1793 (CUL, Add. MS 6958, f. 1,199).

19. George III to Pitt, 6 February 1795 (CUL, Add. MS 6958, f. 1,631).

20. Bayham (soon to become the second Earl Camden) to Robert Stewart, 4 February 1793 (*Castlereagh correspondence*, i, 156).

21. Ibid., 157.

22. Camden to Grenville, 18 April 1797 (HMC, *Dropmore papers*, iii, 315).

23. Camden to Pitt, 1 June 1797 (CUL, Add. MS 6958, f. 2,166).

24. Thomas Pakenham, *The year of liberty* (London, 1969), preface, p. 13.

25. See Ehrman, *Pitt*, iii, 163.

26. Camden to Pitt, 7 May 1795 (CUL, Add. MS 6958, f. 1,955).

27. Beresford to Auckland, 9 August 1798 (*Beresford correspondence*, ii, 169).

28. Wellesley to Grenville, 21 October 1801 (HMC, *Dropmore papers*, vii, 63). There is a certain ambiguity about whether Wellesley was referring to a union with the catholics or a legislative union; either way it shows concerns with Ireland, and from the evidence of the Smith mission it is likely that the debates were about the latter.

29. Iris Butler, *The eldest brother: the Marquess Wellesley, the duke of Wellington's eldest brother* (London, 1973), p. 98.
30. Valentine Lord Cloncurry, *Personal recollections of the life and times of Valentine Lord Cloncurry* (Dublin, 1849), p. 38.
31. Even Kelly's otherwise comprehensive treatment on the historical background to union makes no mention of the matter ('The origins of the act of union').
32. *DNB*, xviii, 519. On 20 October 1797, soon after he returned from his mission to Ireland, Smith was created Baron Carrington of Upton, Nottinghamshire. Wraxall noted that this was the only instance where George III's objections to giving English peerages to those involved in trade were overcome and alleged that it was in return for financial assistance to Pitt. This was strenuously denied by Smith. In 1802 Carrington's daughter married Pitt's nephew (*DNB*, xviii, 519).
33. Camden to Pitt, 10 October 1797 (CUL, Add. MS 6958, f. 2,245). The letter was mistakenly dated 1799, which is impossible from internal evidence. A.P.W. Malcomson has initialled a correction to the manuscript in the Cambridge University Library collection of Pitt papers, dating it 1797.
34. Ibid.
35. 7 May 1783 (*PH*, xxiii, 829). Pitt was speaking about changes to 'the venerable pile of the constitution'. He admitted that 'to see it stand in need of repair was sufficiently melancholy'.
36. The term 'harmony of interest' is taken from Johan Galtung's structural theory of imperialism which defines it as two parties coupled together so that the living condition gap between them is decreasing. Living condition is itself defined as a combination of factors including income, standard of living, quality of life, and notions of autonomy; see Johan Galtung, 'A structural theory of imperialism' in *Journal of Peace Research*, vol. 13, no. 2 (1971), pp. 81–94.
37. Declan Kiberd, *Inventing Ireland* (London, 1995), p. 251.
38. For Kiberd the psychological rationale of the union could be found in Burke's belief that the English and Irish together had the makings of a whole person (ibid., pp. 19–20). This is overstating the case; rather it was believed that the centre would be strengthened by making Ireland part of it.
39. Patrick O'Farrell, *Ireland's English question* (London, 1971), p. 67; Erich Strauss, *Irish nationalism and British democracy* (London, 1975), p. 65.
40. Thomas Bartlett, *The fall and rise of the Irish nation: the catholic question, 1690–1830* (Dublin, 1992), p. 262. Bartlett is referring to Pitt's manner towards the king but the phrase can also be applied to the ministry in general.
41. See Richard Willis, 'Cabinet politics and executive policy-making procedures, 1794–1801' in *Albion*, vii, no. 1 (1975), p. 8.
42. The essay was entitled 'The right honourable William Pitt' (in *Public characters* (Baltimore, 1803), p. 19).
43. Malmesbury's diary entry for 7 March 1801 (*Malmesbury diaries*, iv, 35). The italics, as with all quotations in this book, follow the emphasis of the original.
44. See Roger Wells, *Insurrection: the British royal experience, 1795–1803* (Gloucester, 1983) for evidence of conspiracies against the state in the period.
45. Elizabeth Sparrow, 'The alien office, 1792–1806' in *The Historical Journal*, no. 33 (1990), pp. 361–84.
46. See Harvey Mitchell, *The underground war against revolutionary France* (Oxford, 1965).
47. See J.J. Kenney, 'Lord Whitworth and the conspiracy against Tsar Paul I: the new evidence of the Kent archive' in *Slavic Review*, vol. 36, no. 2 (June, 1977), p. 209.
48. Ibid., pp. 210, 214.
49. Lord Hawkesbury, quoted in Michael Duffy, 'Pitt, Grenville and the control of British foreign policy in the 1790s' (in Jeremy Black (ed.), *Knights errant and true Englishmen* (Edinburgh, 1989), p. 156).

50. See Wendy Hinde, *George Canning* (London, 1973), p. 55.
51. Quoted in Duffy ('Pitt, Grenville and the control of British foreign policy in the 1790s', p. 164).
52. Lord Henry Brougham, *Historical sketches of statesmen who flourished in the time of George III* (6 vols., London, 1845), i, 207.
53. *PH*, xxxiii, 1,461.
54. Ibid., 1,462.
55. BL, Add. MS 45107E, f. 29.
56. For a full account see Pretyman's version (BL, Add. MS 45107E, f. 29).
57. Lord Stanhope, *Life of the Right Honourable William Pitt* (4 vols., London, 1861–2), iii, 132–3.
58. BL, Add. MS 45107E, f. 29.
59. Pitt to Camden, 28 May 1798 (PRONI, T2627/4/221).
60. George III was commenting during the crisis over the catholic question at the end of January 1801: 'Mr Pitt was apt to put off laborious or disagreeable business to the last, but then, when forced to it, got through it with extraordinary rapidity' (*Glenbervie diaries*, i, 149).
61. See Ehrman, *Pitt*, iii, 456–7.
62. Pitt to Camden, 28 May 1798 (PRONI, T2627/4/221).
63. Lecky, *Ireland*, v, 148.
64. J.H. Rose, *William Pitt and the great war* (London, 1911), p. 391; Bolton, *The passing of the Irish act of union*, p. 54; Bartlett, *Fall and rise*, p. 244; Ehrman, *Pitt*, iii, 170.
65. Pitt to Camden, 8 February 1798 (NLI, MS 886, ff. 217–18).
66. For further information see Michael Lynch, *Scotland* (London, 1992), chapter xviii; or P.W.J. Riley, *The English ministers and Scotland, 1701–27* (London, 1964), chapter i, for a more detailed treatment.
67. The division was carried by four votes. The success of the government was made possible only by the double-cross of the duke of Hamilton, who was well rewarded for his collusion, and who continued afterwards against the union (Lynch, *Scotland*, chapter xviii).
68. Cited in Gordon Donaldson (ed.), *Scottish historical documents* (Edinburgh, 1970), p. 268.
69. Donaldson (ed.), *Scottish historical documents*, p. 275.
70. Pitt wrote to Grenville on either the first or the second of the month inviting him to meet and discuss 'one or two leading points about Ireland' (HMC, *Dropmore papers*, iv, 229).
71. Buckingham to Grenville, 3 June 1798 (HMC, *Dropmore papers*, iv, 227).
72. Pitt to Auckland, 4 June 1798 (*Auckland correspondence*, iv, 2).
73. CUL, Add. MS 6968, f. 3,700; NLI, MS 8056; also printed in J.H. Rose, *Pitt and Napoleon* (London, 1912), pp. 338–41. Ehrman in his chapter on the Irish union revealed that he was unable to find the paper (*Pitt*, iii, 171, fn. 5). 'Points to be considered with a view . . .' is in Grenville's handwriting with notes by Pitt on the margin. Various details help date the paper; the suggestion of 150 Irish MPs in the commons places it at some point before August 1798, while the notes on the catholic question make it even earlier. The most compelling piece of evidence is point six of the paper, which admits that 'the greatest difficulty seems to arise from the impossibility of equalising the systems of commerce and revenue and debts in the two countries'. This was precisely the point of difficulty mentioned by Pitt to Auckland when he requested his assistance on 4 June (Pitt to Auckland, 4 June 1798 (*Auckland correspondence*, iv, 2).
74. CUL, Add. MS 6968, f. 3,700.
75. Elliot to Castlereagh, 24 October 1798 (*Castlereagh correspondence*, i, 404).

76. George III to Pitt, 10 June 1798 (NLI, MS 886, f. 322).
77. Stanhope, *Life*, iii, 135–6; Ehrman, *Pitt*, iii, 82, fn. 1.
78. Lord Rosebery, *Pitt* (London, 1918), p. 139.
79. George III to Pitt, 10 June 1798 (NLI, MS 886, f. 315).
80. Pitt to Hester, countess of Chatham, 9 July 1798 (quoted in Stanhope, *Life*, iii, 138).
81. Pitt to Grenville, 13 August 1798 (HMC, *Dropmore papers*, iv, 280).
82. Auckland to Beresford, 1 August 1798 (quoted in Stanhope, *Life*, iii, 138–9).
83. The opinion of Sir Walter Farquhar, an ex-army surgeon, who first examined Pitt in 1795. He reported that Pitt's health owed much to 'the excess of public business and the unremitting attention upon subjects of anxiety and interest' (Robin O'Reilly, *Pitt the younger* (London, 1978), p. 249).
84. Bartlett, *Fall and rise*, p. 234; Bolton, *The passing of the Irish act of union*, p. 55; Ehrman, *Pitt*, iii, 168–9; Hyde, *Castlereagh*, p. 255.
85. Beresford to Auckland, 1 February 1798 (PRONI, T3229/2/17).
86. Camden to Pitt, 23 March 1798 (NLI, MS 886, f. 258).
87. Camden to Pitt, 26 March 1798 (NLI, MS 886, f. 265).
88. Carlisle to Pitt, March 1798 (PRO, 30/8/121/1, f. 25).
89. R.I. Wilberforce and Samuel Wilberforce, *The life of William Wilberforce* (2 vols., London, 1838), ii, 327. Another example was Pitt's desire to facilitate the defeated rebels by adopting Foster's suggestion of finding employment for the ones who had disbanded (Pitt to Auckland, 28 October 1798 (PRONI, T3229/2/38)).
90. Camden to Pitt, [29 May] 1798 (NLI, MS 886, f. 298).
91. Pitt to Camden, 2 June 1798 (NLI, MS 886, ff. 301–2).
92. Camden to Pitt, 1 June 1798 (CUL, Add. MS 6958, f. 2,166).
93. Camden to Pitt, 6 June 1798 (NLI, MS 886, ff. 307–9).
94. See Michael Fry, *The Dundas despotism* (Edinburgh, 1992), pp. 157–8.
95. See Bolton, *The passing of the Irish act of union*, pp. 25–6. It is likely that the king would have disapproved of the appointment given Cornwallis's sympathy to the catholics. Only the drastic situation in 1798 would have lessened his fears sufficiently for him to approve; see George III to Pitt, 10 June 1798 (NLI, MS 886, ff. 315–22).
96. See Franklin Wickwire and Mary Wickwire, *Cornwallis and the war of independence* (London, 1970), and *Cornwallis: the imperial years* (North Carolina, 1980).
97. Bartlett, *Fall and rise*, p. 246.
98. Elliot to Castlereagh, 24 October 1798: 'Mr Pitt says his judgement is not yet formed on the subject and that some months ago it was favourable to the pretensions of the catholics' (*Castlereagh correspondence*, i, 404).
99. George III to Pitt, 10 June 1798 (NLI, MS 886, f. 322).
100. George III to Pitt, 10 June 1798 (NLI, MS 886, ff. 315–22). There were over one hundred privy councillors in Ireland by 1798. The king was probably referring to a small section of their number, the so-called 'inner cabinet' of Clare, Foster, Agar and Beresford. For details and a list of all the Irish privy councillors see Hyde, *Castlereagh*, pp. 230–32, with a list in appendix two of the book.
101. George III to Pitt, 13 June 1798 (NLI, MS 886, f. 323).
102. Pitt to Grenville, 11 June 1798 (HMC, *Dropmore papers*, iv, 234).
103. Pitt to Camden, 11 June 1798 (Aspinall, *George III*, iii, 78).
104. Lecky, *Ireland*, v, 146–7.
105. The involvement of the British secret service in detecting and arresting the leaders of the United Irishmen in an attempt to prevent the rebellion disproves any far-fetched conspiracy theory; see Sparrow, 'The alien office'.
106. Cornwallis to Castlereagh, 14 January 1801 (*Castlereagh correspondence*, iv, 20).
107. I.R. Christie, *Myth and reality in late eighteenth century politics* (London, 1970), p. 55. Christie was referring to the period before 1790 but it is an equally valid analysis for

the last decade of the century; see also Arthur Aspinall, 'The cabinet council, 1783–1835' (in *Proceedings of the British Academy*, xxxviii (London, 1952), pp. 145–252). Lord Holland revealed much about the informality of procedure in cabinet, 1806–7, in his *Memoirs of the whig party during my time* (2 vols., London, 1852), ii, 84–90. See V.T. Harlow, *The founding of the second British empire, 1763–1793* (2 vols., London, 1964), ii, 234, for analysis of inner cabinet.

108. Quoted in Aspinall, 'The cabinet council', p. 203. It was Spencer Perceval who coined the phrase that Pitt 'was, himself, essentially the government in all its departments'.

109. Ehrman, *Pitt*, iii, 454–5.

110. See Ehrman, *Pitt*, iii, 172. Again this is in line with the earlier analysis of attitudes to cabinet in the period. Pitt would not have shirked from withholding information from the minister with responsibility for the island.

111. Loughborough to Pitt, 13 June 1798 (CUL, Add. MS 6958, f. 2,364).

112. Cornwallis to Portland, 16 September 1798 (*Cornwallis correspondence*, ii, 404).

113. For details of Portland overseeing the collection of information about a union see HMC, *Dropmore papers*, iv, 278.

114. Cornwallis to Portland, 16 September 1798 (*Cornwallis correspondence*, ii, 404).

115. Fry, *The Dundas despotism*, p. 158.

116. William Windham was particularly critical of the infringements upon another minister's jurisdiction. He repeated to Pitt on 13 December 1800 complaints he had made previously about the 'inconveniences that arise from the irregular, and very unceremonious way which the treasury sometimes has of stepping into different departments' (quoted in C.J. Fedorak, 'Catholic emancipation and the resignation of William Pitt' (*Albion*, xxiv, no. 1 (spring 1992), pp. 49–64)).

117. Quoted in K.G. Feiling, *The second tory party, 1714–1832* (London, 1938), p. 166.

118. Portland to Pitt, 12 June 1798 (Aspinall, *George III*, iii, 77).

119. Pitt to Wickham, 12 June 1798 (BL MS 37844, f. 171); see also, for another example, Pitt to Liverpool, 12 June 1798 (*Cornwallis correspondence*, ii, 352).

120. Camden to Elliot, 15 June 1798 (John Gilbert, *Documents relating to Ireland, 1795–1804* (Shannon, 1970), p. 137).

121. Camden to Pelham, 15 June 1798 (Gilbert, *Documents relating to Ireland, 1795–1804*, p. 139).

122. Camden to Pitt, endorsed as received 19 June 1798 (NLI, MS 886, f. 331). It appears to have been written before the letter of 16 June, but after the receipt of Pitt's letter of 11 June.

123. Ibid.

124. Ibid., f. 334. Camden's hurt sensibilities did not show any signs of healing in the following years. In a letter to Castlereagh, in October 1798, he hinted at the pain he had felt on leaving Ireland, his step-nephew knowing, 'as intimately as any one, what I did feel' (Camden to Castlereagh, October 1798 (*Castlereagh correspondence*, i, 391)). After the passing of the union in 1800 he wrote to Pitt acknowledging that he had once had 'the honest and fair ambition of having wished to be the instrument of introducing and carrying the measure of union' (Camden to Pitt, 1 August 1800 (Kent Archives Office, U840/C30/6)).

125. Camden to Pitt, 16 June 1798 (NLI, MS 886, ff. 327–8).

126. Cooke to Pelham, 19 June 1798 (Gilbert, *Documents relating to Ireland, 1795–1804*, p. 142); Castlereagh to Camden, 24 July 1798 (Kent Archives Office, U840/C98/7).

127. Castlereagh to Camden, 24 July 1798 (Kent Archives Office, U840/C98/7).

128. Buckingham to Grenville, 6 July 1798 (HMC, *Dropmore papers*, iv, 245).

129. Cornwallis to Ross, 16 August 1798 (*Cornwallis correspondence*, ii, 387).

130. Foster to Sheffield, 7 July 1798 (PRONI, T2965/158).

131. Foster to Sheffield, 11 September 1798 (PRONI, T2965/163).

132. See Sheffield to Auckland, 12 August 1798 (quoted in Bolton, *The passing of the Irish act of union*, p. 59); and Castlereagh to Camden, 24 July 1799 (PRONI, T2627/4/114).
133. For the importance attached to Clare's intervention see A.P.W. Malcomson, *John Foster: the politics of the Anglo-Irish ascendancy* (Oxford, 1978), p. 75; Bolton, *The passing of the Irish act of union*, p. 59.
134. This is the interpretation of Hereward Senior, *Orangeism in Ireland and Britain, 1795–1836* (London, 1966).
135. See Clare to Auckland, [June] 1798 (*Auckland correspondence*, iv, 8).
136. Buckingham to Grenville, 26 September 1798 (HMC, *Dropmore papers*, iv, 325).
137. For the lord chancellor on Foster's likely opposition see Clare to Auckland, 3 July 1798 (quoted in Bolton, *The passing of the Irish act of union*, p. 60); for the lord chancellor on his support for the union see Clare to Auckland, [June 1798] (*Auckland correspondence*, iv, 8). There is a curious reference in a letter of Sheffield to Auckland in which he refers to the danger for Cornwallis if Clare and Foster 'had continued disgusted with the measures' (quoted in Bolton, *The passing of the Irish act of union*, p. 59).
138. This is revealed by Buckingham's previous comment, and also evident from his correspondence. Senior in his study of orangeism argues unconvincingly that Cornwallis was not sent over with any union instructions and that both he and Castlereagh soon realised it was necessary independently (*Orangeism*, p. 120).
139. Elliot Fitzgibbon, *The earl of Clare: mainspring of the union* (London, 1960).
140. Clare to Auckland, [June 1798] (*Auckland correspondence*, iv, 8). From the internal evidence in Clare's response, Auckland's letter can be dated to June 1798. Clare wrote a second letter to Auckland, on union, on 3 July. These dates are consistent with Buckingham's claim, examined earlier, that Clare was aware of the union before Cornwallis arrived in Ireland.
141. Clare to Auckland, 3 July 1798 (quoted in Bolton, *The passing of the Irish act of union*, p. 60).
142. Camden's praise was in his undated observations on a union (PRONI, T3319/60).
143. In 1797 (quoted in Malcomson, *John Foster*, p. 193).
144. Cooke to Auckland, 27 October 1798 (PRONI, T3229/2/37).
145. Cornwallis to Pitt, 25 October 1798 (NLI, MS 886, f. 403).
146. Cornwallis to Ross, 1 July 1798 (*Cornwallis correspondence*, ii, 357).
147. Ibid., 358. Note the use of the word 'empire' by Cornwallis.
148. Cornwallis to Portland, 8 July 1798 (*Cornwallis correspondence*, ii, 359).
149. See Bartlett, *Fall and rise,* pp. 239–42.
150. See debate on Irish martial law bill in the united parliament in 1801 (*PH*, xxxv, 1,231–8).
151. Cornwallis to Ross, 9 July 1798 (*Cornwallis correspondence*, ii, 362).
152. Cornwallis to General Sir James Steurt, 25 June (*Cornwallis correspondence*, ii, 355).
153. Bartlett, *Fall and rise*, p. 242.
154. Cornwallis to Portland, 28 February 1799 (*Cornwallis correspondence*, iii, 70).
155. *PH*, xxxv, 1,233.
156. Carlisle to Auckland, 30 August 1798 (*Auckland correspondence*, iv, 52).
157. Beresford to Auckland, 9 August 1798 (*Beresford correspondence*, ii, 169).
158. Quoted in P.D. Brown, *William Pitt, earl of Chatham: the great commoner* (London, 1978), p. 340.
159. Grenville to Thomas Grenville, 7 August 1798 (quoted in Feiling, *The second tory party*, p. 220).

Chapter 2 Preparing for a union (pp. 25–53)

1. 20 May 1797 (quoted in Malcomson, *John Foster*, p. 376).
2. PRO, 30/8/330, f. 12.
3. Cornwallis to Portland, 8 July 1798 (*Cornwallis correspondence*, ii, 359).
4. For exceptions to the pardon see Hyde, *Castlereagh*, p. 259, fn. 3.
5. Quoted in Frank Allen, 'The London newspapers and Ireland, 1798–1800' (unpublished MA thesis, UCD, 1994), pp. 46–7.
6. Reported by Clare in 1801 debate (*PH*, xxxv, 1,233).
7. See *Cornwallis correspondence*, ii, 420.
8. Captain Taylor to Lieutenant-General Craig, 18 October 1798 (*Cornwallis correspondence*, ii, 419).
9. Ibid.
10. Elliot to Camden, 28 July 1798 (Gilbert, *Documents relating to Ireland, 1795–1804*, p. 145). Elliot noted, with approval, that Cornwallis displayed a 'sound judgement' on all political points brought before him.
11. Buckingham to Grenville, 23 July 1798 (HMC, *Dropmore papers*, iv, 264).
12. Cornwallis to Ross, 24 July 1798 (*Cornwallis correspondence*, ii, 371).
13. General orders, 31 August 1798 (*Cornwallis correspondence*, ii, 397).
14. Marianne Elliott, *Partners in revolution: the United Irishmen and France* (New Haven, 1982), p. 224.
15. Ibid., pp. 225–30.
16. For a brief account see P.M. Geoghegan, *1798 and the Irish bar* (Dublin, 1998), pp. 21–2.
17. Cornwallis to Portland, 16 September 1798 (*Cornwallis correspondence*, ii, 405).
18. Cornwallis to Ross, 10 August 1798 (*Cornwallis correspondence*, ii, 383).
19. Cornwallis to Portland, 16 September 1798 (*Cornwallis correspondence*, ii, 404).
20. Cornwallis to Pitt, 25 September 1798 (*Cornwallis correspondence*, ii, 414).
21. Cornwallis to Portland, 16 September 1798 (*Cornwallis correspondence*, ii, 405).
22. Cornwallis to Pitt, 20 July 1798 (NLI, MS 886, f. 344).
23. Cornwallis to Portland, 16 September 1798 (*Cornwallis correspondence*, ii, 405).
24. Cornwallis to Pitt, 25 October 1798 (NLI, MS 886, ff. 403–4). Cornwallis had considered the prisoners no more dangerous than 'the general class of American settlers' (quoted in Elliott, *Partners*, p. 251).
25. Pitt to Cornwallis, 17 November 1798 (NLI, MS 886, f. 421).
26. Gilbert Elliot to his wife, 20 December 1798 (quoted in Cyril Matheson, *The life of Henry Dundas* (London, 1933), p. 258).
27. For example see a draft of Portland to Cornwallis, 4 November 1798 (Bolton, *The passing of the Irish act of union*, p. 65).
28. See Gregory Holyoake, *Wellington at Walmer* (Dover, 1996), p. 45.
29. See Marquess Curzon of Kedleston, *The personal history of Walmer castle and its lords warden* (London, 1927), pp. 81, 120–21; see also Simon Schama, *Landscape and memory* (London, 1996) for connections between landscape and character in other periods.
30. Pitt to Grenville, 5 August 1798 (HMC, *Dropmore papers*, iv, 274).
31. Pitt to Auckland, 14 August 1798 (PRONI, T3229/2/35).
32. Sylvester Douglas to Castlereagh, January 1799 (*Castlereagh correspondence*, ii, 125).
33. Pitt to Grenville, 5 August 1798 (HMC, *Dropmore papers*, iv, 274).
34. Pitt to Auckland, 14 August 1798 (PRONI, T3229/2/35).
35. Ibid.
36. See Dáire Keogh, *The French disease: the catholic church and Irish radicalism, 1790–1800* (Dublin, 1993), pp. 62–4.
37. Ibid., 158.
38. Patrick Corish, *Maynooth college, 1795–1995* (Dublin, 1995), p. 20; *Dictionary of Irish Biography* (forthcoming).

39. Quoted in Richard Hayes, *Biographical dictionary of Irishmen in France* (Dublin, 1949), p. 99.
40. Senior, *Orangeism*, p. 108.
41. Castlereagh to Camden, 22 October 1798 (CUL, Add. MS 6958, f. 3,199).
42. Quoted in B.M. Bass (ed.), *Stogdhill's handbook of leadership* (New York, 1981), p. 9.
43. See Portland to Cornwallis, 4 November 1798 (*Cornwallis correspondence*, ii, 430). The draft criticisms were deleted by Pitt.
44. See Buckingham, *Courts*, ii, 408. Buckingham quickly involved Grenville in the affair, who sided with his brother, and became sharply critical of the lord lieutenant.
45. Buckingham to Grenville, 31 August 1798 (HMC, *Dropmore papers*, iv, 296).
46. Buckingham to Grenville, 28 August 1798 (HMC, *Dropmore papers*, iv, 291). This was his second letter of the day to his brother.
47. Buckingham to Grenville, 10 September 1798 (HMC, *Dropmore papers*, iv, 304).
48. Buckingham to Grenville, 15 September 1798 (HMC, *Dropmore papers*, iv, 315).
49. Buckingham to Grenville, 26 September 1798 (HMC, *Dropmore papers*, iv, 324–5).
50. Buckingham to Grenville, 2 October 1798 (HMC, *Dropmore papers*, iv, 331).
51. Buckingham to Grenville, 15 October 1798 (HMC, *Dropmore papers*, iv, 343–4).
52. Buckingham to Grenville, 15 October 1798 (HMC, *Dropmore papers*, iv, 344).
53. Buckingham to Grenville,12 December 1798 (HMC, *Dropmore papers*, iv, 412).
54. Cornwallis to Ross, 8 December 1798 (*Cornwallis correspondence*, iii, 8).
55. Buckingham to Grenville, 15 September 1798 (HMC, *Dropmore papers*, iv, 315); and 2 October 1798 (HMC, *Dropmore papers*, iv, 331). Hobart was a former Irish chief secretary.
56. Cooke to Auckland, 30 October 1798 (PRONI, T3229/2/40).
57. Cooke to Auckland, 2 November 1798 (BL, Add. MS 34455, ff. 26–8).
58. Ibid.
59. Duigenan to Castlereagh, 20 December 1798 (*Castlereagh correspondence*, ii, 53).
60. Castlereagh to Elliot, 9 November 1798 (quoted in Bolton, *The passing of the Irish act of union*, p. 71).
61. Cornwallis to Pitt, 8 August 1798 (NLI, MS 886, f. 347).
62. Cornwallis to Ross, 12 August 1798 (*Cornwallis correspondence*, ii, 381).
63. Castlereagh to Pitt, 7 September (CUL, Add. MS 6958, f. 2,385). The manuscript is not fully dated, but as Castlereagh was in England in September 1799, and it could not have been written in 1800, then it is clear that the letter was written at this time.
64. George III to Pitt, 13 June 1798 (NLI, MS 886, f. 323).
65. Bartlett, *Fall and rise*, p. 247; see also chapter 1 of this book.
66. CUL, Add. MS 6958, f. 3,700.
67. See for example Cornwallis to Ross, 15 November 1798 (*Cornwallis correspondence*, ii, 433).
68. Peter Jupp, *Lord Grenville, 1759–1834* (Oxford, 1985), p. 271.
69. Grenville to Buckingham, 5 November 1798 (Buckingham, *Courts*, ii, 411).
70. See Ehrman, *Pitt*, iii, 456.
71. Cornwallis to Ross, 30 September 1798 (*Cornwallis correspondence*, ii, 414).
72. Ibid.
73. Pelham to Castlereagh, 13 September 1798 (*Castlereagh correspondence*, i, 345).
74. Marshall to Castlereagh, 26 September 1798 (*Castlereagh correspondence*, i, 379).
75. Ibid., 380.
76. Cornwallis to Pitt, 8 October 1798 (NLI, MS 886, ff. 385–6).
77. Ibid.
78. Castlereagh to Camden, 4 October 1798 (Kent Archives Office, U840/C98/3).
79. Buckingham to Grenville, 26 September 1798 (HMC, *Dropmore papers*, iv, 324).
80. See John Derry, *Castlereagh* (London, 1976), p. 60.

81. 16 October 1798 (*Castlereagh correspondence*, i, 393).
82. Clare to Castlereagh, 16 October 1798 (*Castlereagh correspondence*, i, 393).
83. Cornwallis to Pelham, 15 October 1798 (Gilbert, *Documents relating to Ireland, 1795–1804*, p. 193).
84. Cornwallis to Pitt, 17 October 1798 (*Cornwallis correspondence*, ii, 420).
85. Cornwallis to Pitt, 17 October 1798 (NLI, MS 886, ff. 393–4).
86. Ibid.
87. Auckland to Beresford, 17 October 1798 (*Auckland correspondence*, iv, 61).
88. Clare to Auckland, 28 October 1798 (PRONI, T3287/7/22).
89. Canning to Windham, 23 October 1798 (BL, Add. MS 37844, f. 274).
90. Ibid.
91. Ibid.
92. Camden to Castlereagh, 27 October 1798 (*Castlereagh correspondence*, i, 412).
93. Elliot to Castlereagh, 24 October 1798 (*Castlereagh correspondence*, i, 404).
94. Wilberforce to Muncaster, 3 December 1798 (quoted in John Pollock, *Wilberforce* (London, 1977), p. 180).
95. Grenville to Buckingham, 5 November 1798 (Buckingham, *Courts*, ii, 411–12).
96. See Piers Mackesy, *War without victory: the downfall of Pitt, 1799–1802* (Oxford, 1984), pp. 10–11.
97. Quoted ibid., p. 39.
98. Dundas to Pitt, believed to be written in May 1798 (Ehrman, *Pitt*, iii, 175, 176, 521).
99. Cornwallis to Ross, 15 November 1798 (*Cornwallis correspondence*, ii, 433).
100. Elliot to Castlereagh, 9 November 1798 (*Castlereagh correspondence*, i, 431).
101. Ibid.
102. Gilbert Elliot to his wife (quoted in Matheson, *The life of Henry Dundas*, p. 259).
103. Elliot to Castlereagh, 24 October 1798 (*Castlereagh correspondence*, i, 404).
104. Camden to Castlereagh, 27 October 1798 (*Castlereagh correspondence*, i, 412).
105. Pitt to Auckland, 28 October 1798 (PRONI, T3229/2/38).
106. Portland to Cornwallis, 12 November 1798 (*Cornwallis correspondence*, ii, 434).
107. Pitt to Cornwallis, 17 November 1798 (*Cornwallis correspondence*, ii, 440).
108. Cornwallis to Ross, 15 November 1798 (*Cornwallis correspondence*, ii, 434).
109. Ibid., 433–4.
110. Castlereagh to Elliot, 15 November 1798 (PRONI, D3030/347, f. 867).
111. Cornwallis to Ross, 15 November 1798 (*Cornwallis correspondence*, ii, 434); see also Cooke to Castlereagh, 9 November 1798 (*Castlereagh correspondence*, i, 433).
112. Pitt to Cornwallis, 17 November 1798 (NLI, MS 886, f. 420).
113. Pitt to Cornwallis, 17 November 1798 (*Cornwallis correspondence*, ii, 440).
114. Elliot to Castlereagh, 23 November 1798 (*Castlereagh correspondence*, ii, 10).
115. Ibid.
116. Hyde, *Castlereagh*, p. 223.
117. Elliot to Castlereagh, 28 November 1798 (*Castlereagh correspondence*, ii, 29).
118. Ibid.
119. Bartlett, *Fall and rise*, p. 248.
120. Elliot to Castlereagh, 28 November 1798 (*Castlereagh correspondence*, ii, 29). Castlereagh, for his part, considered Elliot's friendship to be 'one of the most fortunate events in my life' (quoted in Hyde, *Castlereagh*, p. 224).
121. Elliot to Castlereagh, 28 November 1798 (*Castlereagh correspondence*, ii, 30).
122. See Hyde, *Castlereagh*, pp. 282–3; Bolton, *The passing of the Irish act of union*, p. 74.
123. Hyde, *Castlereagh*, pp. 282–3, deals with the matter, but only briefly; Lecky also mentions the incident (*Ireland*, v, 203).
124. Castlereagh to Camden, 4 October 1798 (Kent Archives Office, U840/C98/3).

125. Portland to Pitt, 19 October 1798 (NLI, MS 886, f. 395). Robert Marshall referred to this as 'some accident' and reported that Pitt was to write to the speaker on 20 October (Marshall to Castlereagh, 19 October 1798 (PRONI, D3030/298/621).
126. Foster to Pitt, 21 October 1798 (NLI, MS 886, f. 399). The letter to Auckland was written first, which dates Pitt's letter as having arrived on 21 October.
127. Buckingham to Grenville, 5 November 1798 (HMC, *Dropmore papers*, iv, 360).
128. Foster to Auckland, 21 October 1798 (PRONI, T3229/2/36).
129. Ibid.
130. Buckingham to Grenville, 23 October 1798 (HMC, *Dropmore papers*, iv, 351).
131. Buckingham to Grenville, 26 October 1798 (HMC, *Dropmore papers*, iv, 353).
132. Pitt to Auckland, 28 October 1798 (PRONI, T3229/2/38).
133. Cooke to Auckland, 29 October 1798 (PRONI, T3229/2/39).
134. Cooke to Auckland, 12 November 1798 (BL, Add. MS 34455, f. 31).
135. Cooke to Auckland, 6 November 1798 (BL, Add. MS 34455, f. 28).
136. Cornwallis to Pitt, 7 November 1798 (NLI, MS 886, f. 411).
137. Buckingham to Grenville, 10 September 1798 (HMC, *Dropmore papers*, iv, 304).
138. 12 November 1798 (NLI, MS 886, f. 415).
139. Heads of a union with Ireland, November 1798 (HMC, *Dropmore papers*, iv, 397–400).
140. Ibid., 398.
141. Sheffield to Auckland, 13 November 1798 (BL, Add. MS 34455, f. 34).
142. Ibid.
143. Camden to Castlereagh, 16 November 1798 (*Castlereagh correspondence*, i, 450).
144. George III to Pitt, 17 November 1798 (PRO, 30/8/104/2, f. 249).
145. Pitt to Cornwallis, 17 November 1798 (NLI, MS 886, f. 419).
146. Ibid.
147. Ibid.
148. PRONI, T3319/60, and also printed in Rose, *Pitt and Napoleon*, pp. 335–8. I believe Holland Rose is mistaken in attributing the observations to June 1798; they were more likely to have been penned in July or August as the PRONI transcript suggests.
149. Pitt to Cornwallis, 17 November 1798 (NLI, MS 886, f. 419).
150. Elliot to Castlereagh, 23 November 1798 (*Castlereagh correspondence*, iii, 9).
151. Elliot to Castlereagh, 28 November 1798 (*Castlereagh correspondence*, iii, 29).
152. Bartlett, *Fall and rise*, p. 248; Malcomson, *John Foster*, p. 78.
153. Quoted in Malcomson, *John Foster*, p. 432.
154. See Ehrman, *Pitt*, iii, 456.
155. Pitt to Grenville, 16 October 1798 (HMC, *Dropmore papers*, iv, 344).
156. Parnell to Cornwallis, 1 December 1798 (PRONI, D3030/385, f. 1,209).
157. See Malcomson, *John Foster*, p. 78.
158. Ibid.
159. Cornwallis to Pitt, 1 November 1798 (NLI, MS 886, ff. 407–8).
160. Grenville to Buckingham, 5 November 1798 (Buckingham, *Courts*, ii, 411).
161. Ibid.
162. Ibid., 412.
163. Cornwallis to Portland, 5 December 1798 (*Cornwallis correspondence*, iii, 67).
164. Cornwallis to Charles Agar, archbishop of Cashel, 19 November 1798 (*Cornwallis correspondence*, ii, 438).
165. For example Hyde's *Castlereagh* and Derry's *Castlereagh* do not examine the matter. Wendy Hinde's *Castlereagh* (London, 1981), pp. 70–71, does examine the matter, but ignores some of the complexities involved.
166. Beresford to Auckland, 15 March 1798 (PRONI, T3229/2/30); see also Hyde, *Castlereagh*, p. 207.
167. Camden to Pitt, 16 March 1798 (NLI, MS 886, ff. 189–90).
168. Ibid.

169. William Elliot, a Scotsman, had health problems during his residence in Ireland. His sobriquet 'the castle spectre' came from his 'pale and sometimes haggard appearance' (Hyde, *Castlereagh*, p. 224).
170. Portland to George III, 19 March (Aspinall, *George III*, iii, 33). Pitt's doubts at the time were later reported to Castlereagh in a letter from Camden, 31 August 1798 (*Castlereagh correspondence*, i, 325).
171. George III to Pitt, 11 June 1798 (PRO, 30/8/104/2, f. 237).
172. Pitt to Grenville, 12 June 1798 (HMC, *Dropmore papers*, iv, 236).
173. Thomas Grenville to Lord Grenville, 13 June 1798 (HMC, *Dropmore papers*, iv, 236).
174. George III to Pitt, 13 June 1798 (NLI, MS 886, f. 323).
175. Cornwallis to Ross, 6 November 1803 (*Cornwallis correspondence*, iii, 506).
176. Cornwallis to Portland, 8 July 1798 (*Cornwallis correspondence*, ii, 360–61).
177. Cornwallis to Ross, 9 July 1798 (*Cornwallis correspondence*, ii, 363).
178. Buckingham to Grenville, 23 July 1798 (HMC, *Dropmore papers*, iv, 66).
179. Camden to Castlereagh, 31 August 1798 (*Castlereagh correspondence*, i, 325).
180. Pitt to Castlereagh, 1 September 1798 (NLI, MS 886, ff. 367–9).
181. Portland to George III, 4 September 1798 (Aspinall, *George III*, iii, 120).
182. See *Castlereagh correspondence*, i, 325; and also Camden to Castlereagh, 25 September 1798 (*Castlereagh correspondence*, i, 325).
183. Camden to Castlereagh, 25 September 1798 (*Castlereagh correspondence*, i, 325).
184. Robert Marshall to Castlereagh, 26 September 1798 (*Castlereagh correspondence*, i, 378).
185. Castlereagh to Camden, 4 October 1798 (Kent Archives Office, U840/C98/3).
186. Portland to Pitt, 19 October 1798 (NLI, MS 886, f. 393).
187. The views of George III were described in a letter from Portland to Pelham, 1 November 1798 (Aspinall, *George III*, iii, 153).
188. Ibid.
189. Grenville to Buckingham, 5 November 1798 (Buckingham, *Courts*, ii, 411).
190. Ibid.
191. Cornwallis to Pitt, 7 November 1798 (NLI, MS 886, f. 411).
192. Cornwallis to Portland, 7 November 1798 (*Cornwallis correspondence*, ii, 427).
193. See *Cornwallis correspondence*, ii, 430.
194. Camden to Castlereagh, 25 September 1798 (*Castlereagh correspondence*, i, 377); also Camden to Castlereagh, 27 October 1798 (*Castlereagh correspondence*, i, 412).
195. Thomas Grenville to Cornwallis, 27 November 1798 (*Cornwallis correspondence*, iii, 9). Thomas Grenville had refused the job three times previously, in 1782, 1787 and 1795.
196. Cornwallis to Pitt, 7 December 1798 (NLI, MS 886, f. 431).
197. Sheffield to Auckland, 30 December 1798 (BL, Add. MS 34455, f. 59).
198. Cooke to Auckland, January 1799 (BL, Add. MS 34455, f. 154).
199. Buckingham to Grenville, 6 July 1798 (HMC, *Dropmore papers*, iv, 245).
200. Ibid.
201. See Camden to Castlereagh, October 1798 (*Castlereagh correspondence*, i, 391), for details of Pelham's high opinion of the acting chief secretary.
202. Pelham to Castlereagh, 13 September 1798 (*Castlereagh correspondence*, i, 345).
203. Pelham to Castlereagh, 13 September 1798 (*Castlereagh correspondence*, i, 346).
204. Portland to Cornwallis, 25 November 1798 (*Castlereagh correspondence*, ii, 20).
205. All of this was contained in the draft treaty for union (CUL, Add. MS 6958, f. 3,365).
206. Portland to Cornwallis, 25 November 1798 (*Castlereagh correspondence*, ii, 21).
207. Cornwallis to Portland, 7 December 1798 (PRO, HO 100/79, f. 242).
208. Cornwallis sent a letter and paper on representation, via Castlereagh, that the cabinet approved despite reservations from the home secretary (Portland to Cornwallis, 24 December 1798 (*Castlereagh correspondence*, ii, 53–5)).

209. [Edward Cooke] *Arguments for and against an union between Great Britain and Ireland, considered* (Dublin, 1798), p. 9.
210. Ibid., p. 29.
211. Ibid., p. 54.
212. Ibid., p. 62.
213. Buckingham to Grenville, 7 December 1798 (HMC, *Dropmore papers*, iv, 404).
214. *A report of the debate in the Irish bar, 9 December 1798* (Dublin, 1799), p. 7.
215. Cooke to Castlereagh, 10 September 1798 (*Castlereagh correspondence*, i, 343).
216. *A report of the debate in the Irish bar, 9 December 1798*, p. 45. The speaker was Goold.
217. Ibid., p. 55. The speaker was Orr.
218. Cornwallis to Portland, 27 November 1798 (PRO, HO 100/79, f. 181).
219. W.A. Crosbie to the duke of Montrose, 25 December 1798 (HMC, *Dropmore papers*, iv, 423).
220. Ibid.
221. Cornwallis to Portland, 5 December 1798 (*Castlereagh correspondence*, ii, 35); and also Buckingham to Grenville, 7 December 1798 (HMC, *Dropmore papers*, iv, 405).
222. Cornwallis to Portland, 5 December 1798 (*Castlereagh correspondence*, ii, 36).
223. Cornwallis to Ross, 23 November 1798 (*Cornwallis correspondence*, ii, 442).
224. Cornwallis to Pitt, 7 December 1798 (NLI, MS 886, f. 432).
225. Ibid., f. 431.
226. Cornwallis to Ross, 12 December 1798 (*Cornwallis correspondence*, iii, 16).
227. Cornwallis to Portland, 15 December 1798 (*Cornwallis correspondence*, iii, 19).
228. See Hyde, *Castlereagh*, pp. 220–22.
229. Cooke to Auckland, 1 January 1799 (BL, Add. MS 34455, f. 111).
230. Cooke to Auckland, 15 January 1799 (*Auckland correspondence*, iv, 77).
231. Portland to Castlereagh, 26 November 1798 (*Castlereagh correspondence*, ii, 23).
232. See Hyde, *Castlereagh*, p. 287; Ehrman, *Pitt*, iii, 178.
233. Cabinet minute, 21 December 1798 (NLI, MS 8055).
234. Portland to Cornwallis, 24 December 1798 (NLI, MS 886, f. 510).
235. Cornwallis to Portland, [7 December] 1798 (*Cornwallis correspondence*, iii, 7).
236. Buckingham to Grenville, 25 December 1798 (HMC, *Dropmore papers*, iv, 423).
237. Castlereagh to Portland, 2 January 1799 (*Castlereagh correspondence*, ii, 81).
238. Cooke to [Auckland], 6 January 1799 (CUL, Add. MS 6958, f. 2,430).
239. Pollock to Hobart, 26 December 1798 (PRONI, T2627/1/7).
240. Buckingham to Grenville, 11 December 1798 (HMC, *Dropmore papers*, iv, 411).
241. Pollock to Hobart, 26 December 1798 (PRONI, T2627/1/7).
242. Castlereagh to Portland, 9 January 1799 (*Castlereagh correspondence*, ii, 85).
243. Ibid., 82.

Chapter 3 Ruthless inefficiency (pp. 54–76)
1. Mary McNeill (ed.), *The life and times of Mary Ann McCracken* (Dublin, 1960), p. 196.
2. Cornwallis to Portland, 24 December 1798 (*Cornwallis correspondence*, iii, 22).
3. See Bolton, *The passing of the Irish act of union*, p. 92.
4. Dundas was quoted in an undated paper by unknown, written after the peace of Amiens (CUL, Add. MS 6958, f. 3,707).
5. Castlereagh to Portland, 9 January 1799 (*Castlereagh correspondence*, ii, 85).
6. Buckingham to Grenville, 2 January 1799 (HMC, *Dropmore papers*, iv, 435).
7. Ibid.
8. Castlereagh to Portland, 7 January 1799 (*Castlereagh correspondence*, ii, 84).
9. Marsden to William Wickham, 11 January 1799 (Wickham Wickham jnr (ed.), *The correspondence of William Wickham* (2 vols., London, 1870), ii, 88).
10. Cornwallis to Portland, 11 January 1799 (*Castlereagh correspondence*, ii, 91).
11. Ibid., 92.

12. Buckingham to Grenville, 16 January 1799 (HMC, *Dropmore papers*, iv, 442).
13. Buckingham to Grenville, 18 January 1799 (HMC, *Dropmore papers*, iv, 444).
14. Buckingham to Grenville, 16 January 1799 (HMC, *Dropmore papers*, iv, 442).
15. Mary Anne Clarke, *A letter addressed to the Right Honourable William Fitzgerald* (London, 1813), p. 9.
16. Ibid., p. 57.
17. Buckingham to Grenville, 14 January 1799 (HMC, *Dropmore papers*, iv, 441).
18. Percy Bysshe Shelley, 'The masque of anarchy', 1819 (*The works of P.B. Shelley* (Hertfordshire, 1994), p. 341).
19. Buckingham to Grenville, 7 November 1798 (HMC, *Dropmore papers*, iv, 368).
20. The examples of Castlereagh's coldness are numerous, for example R. Griffiths in January 1799 criticised him for being 'cold and distant' (quoted in Hinde, *Castlereagh*, p. 77).
21. Quoted in H.M. Hyde's *The strange death of Lord Castlereagh* (London, 1959), p. 6.
22. Derry, *Castlereagh*, p. 11.
23. Ibid., pp. 7–8.
24. C.J. Bartlett, *Castlereagh* (London, 1964), p. 20.
25. Bolton, *The passing of the Irish act of union*, pp. 72–3.
26. Bartlett, *Fall and rise*, p. 252.
27. Quoted in C.J. Bartlett, *Castlereagh*, p. 29.
28. Charles Greville's profile quoted in Hyde, *The strange death of Lord Castlereagh*, p. 7.
29. Brougham, *Historical sketches*, ii, 121.
30. Ibid., 124–5.
31. Plunket in the debate of 22 January 1799 (*A report of the debate in the house of commons of Ireland on 22 and 23 January 1799* (Dublin, 1799), p. 48).
32. Portland to Cornwallis, 24 December 1798 (NLI, MS 886, f. 510).
33. Cooke to Auckland, 27 October 1798 (PRONI, T3229/2/37).
34. See chapter one and chapter six of this book.
35. See Sparrow, 'The alien office', and Mitchell, *The underground war*.
36. Wells, *Insurrection*, p. 43.
37. Home office to Castlereagh, January 1799 (PRO, HO 100/85, f. 21); Wickham to Castlereagh, 7 January 1799 (*Cornwallis correspondence*, iii, 34).
38. Wickham to Castlereagh, 7 January 1799 (*Cornwallis correspondence*, iii, 34).
39. Castlereagh to Wickham, 10 January 1799 (*Cornwallis correspondence*, iii, 34).
40. Hinde, *Castlereagh*, p. 76.
41. Portland to Cornwallis, 24 December 1798 (NLI, MS 886, f. 510).
42. Buckingham to Grenville, 14 January 1799 (HMC, *Dropmore papers*, iv, 440).
43. Buckingham to Grenville, 16 January 1799 (HMC, *Dropmore papers*, iv, 442).
44. Buckingham to Grenville, 19 January 1799 (HMC, *Dropmore papers*, iv, 445).
45. Castlereagh to Portland, January 1799 (*Castlereagh correspondence*, ii, 143).
46. Downshire to Castlereagh, 30 December 1798 (NLI, MS 886, f. 513).
47. Bolton, *The passing of the Irish act of union*, pp. 6–7.
48. Pitt to Castlereagh, 17 January 1799 (*Castlereagh correspondence*, ii, 116).
49. Ibid.
50. Cornwallis to Portland, 11 January 1799 (*Castlereagh correspondence*, ii, 90).
51. Bolton, *The passing of the Irish act of union*, p. 95.
52. Cornwallis to Portland, 13 January 1799 (PRO, HO 100/85, f. 65).
53. Camden to Castlereagh, 15 January 1799 (*Castlereagh correspondence*, ii, 111).
54. Ibid.
55. Pitt to Castlereagh, 17 January 1799 (*Castlereagh correspondence*, ii, 116).
56. Cornwallis to Ely, 13 January 1799 (*Cornwallis correspondence*, iii, 38).
57. Buckingham to Grenville, 18 January 1799 (HMC, *Dropmore papers*, iv, 445).

58. Buckingham to Grenville, 22 January 1799 (HMC, *Dropmore papers*, iv, 447).
59. December 1798 (HMC, *Dropmore papers*, iv, 432); Portland to Cornwallis, 24 December 1798 (*Castlereagh correspondence*, ii, 59).
60. December 1798 (HMC, *Dropmore papers*, iv, 433).
61. Portland to Cornwallis, 17 January 1799 (*Castlereagh correspondence*, ii, 118).
62. Ibid., 119.
63. Castlereagh to Portland, 9 January 1799 (*Castlereagh correspondence*, ii, 85).
64. Buckingham to Grenville, 16 January 1799 (HMC, *Dropmore papers*, iv, 442).
65. Buckingham to Grenville, 19 January 1799 (HMC, *Dropmore papers*, iv, 445).
66. *A report of the debate . . . on 22 and 23 January 1799*, pp. 1–3.
67. Ibid., p. 14.
68. Beresford to Auckland, 24 January 1799 (*Beresford correspondence*, ii, 194).
69. Jonah Barrington, *Historic memoirs of Ireland* (2 vols., London, 1833), ii, 306.
70. *A report of the debate . . . on 22 and 23 January 1799*, p. 48; J.C. Hoey (ed.), *Speeches at the bar and in the senate by the Rt Hon. William Conyngham, Lord Plunket* (Dublin, 1873), pp. 45–6. In the printed report of the debate the comment is a 'green and limber twig', but Hoey quotes the 'sapless' version and Hyde states that this was generally regarded to be the correct one (*Castlereagh*, p. 298, fn. 1). Emily, Castlereagh's wife, watched all of this from the gallery. The pair remained childless to Castlereagh's death.
71. Hoey (ed.), *Speeches*, p. 42; Barrington, *Historic memoirs*, ii, 309.
72. Hoey (ed.), *Speeches*, p. 30.
73. Carysfort to Grenville, 23 January 1799 (HMC, *Dropmore papers*, iv, 450).
74. Jonah Barrington's black list (NLI, MS 5696).
75. Hyde, *Castlereagh*, p. 299; Jonah Barrington, *The rise and fall of the Irish nation* (Dublin, 1853), pp. 243–4.
76. Barrington, *Historic memoirs*, ii, 299.
77. *A report of the debates in the Irish house of commons on 24, 25, 26, 28 January 1799* (Dublin, 1799), p. 165.
78. January 1799 (Castalia Countess Granville (ed.), *Private correspondence of Lord Granville Leveson-Gower, 1781–1821* (2 vols., London, 1916), i, 239).
79. Crosbie to Wellesley, 31 January 1799 (BL, Add. MS 37416, f. 40).
80. Buckingham to Grenville, 23 January 1799 (HMC, *Dropmore papers*, iv, 451).
81. Cornwallis to Portland, 25 January 1799 (*Castlereagh correspondence*, ii, 131); see also Hyde, *Castlereagh*, p. 301.
82. Castlereagh to Portland, 28 January 1799 (*Castlereagh correspondence*, ii, 143).
83. Castlereagh to Portland (PRO, HO 100/85, f. 136).
84. Buckingham to Grenville, 23 January 1799 (HMC, *Dropmore papers*, iv, 450).
85. Buckingham to Grenville, 25 January 1799 (HMC, *Dropmore papers*, iv, 454).
86. Ibid.
87. *A report of the debates . . . on 24, 25, 26, 28 January 1799*, p. 154.
88. Lecky, *Ireland*, v, 227; Buckingham to Grenville (HMC, *Dropmore papers*, iv, 451–5).
89. Buckingham to Grenville, 23 January 1799 (HMC, *Dropmore papers*, iv, 452).
90. Buckingham to Grenville, 23 and 26 January 1799 (HMC, *Dropmore papers*, iv, 451, 455).
91. Buckingham to Grenville, 24 January 1799 (HMC, *Dropmore papers*, iv, 453).
92. Buckingham to Grenville, 24 January 1799 (HMC, *Dropmore papers*, iv, 453).
93. Buckingham to Grenville, 23 January 1799 (HMC, *Dropmore papers*, iv, 451).
94. Cooke to Auckland, 25 January 1799 (BL, Add. MS 34455, f. 141).
95. Ibid.
96. Cornwallis to Portland, 25 January 1799 (*Castlereagh correspondence*, ii, 131).
97. Pitt to Cornwallis, 26 January 1799 (CUL, Add. MS 6958, f. 2,436).

98. Portland to Cornwallis, 26 January 1799 (*Castlereagh correspondence*, ii, 136).
99. A letter to Auckland, 26 January 1799 (BL, Add. MS 34455, f. 146); Fitzwilliam began the story in October 1798 (see Bolton, *The passing of the Irish act of union*, p. 51).
100. See Bolton, *The passing of the Irish act of union*, pp. 118–19.
101. Cooke to Auckland, January 1799 (BL, Add. MS 34455, ff. 152–3).
102. Grenville to Buckingham, 28 January 1799 (Buckingham, *Courts*, ii, 429).
103. Ibid., 430.
104. Bolton, *The passing of the Irish act of union*, p. 118. Grenville also admitted this.
105. Cornwallis to Ross, 28 January 1799 (*Cornwallis correspondence*, iii, 56).
106. Cornwallis to Portland, 26 January 1799 (*Cornwallis correspondence*, iii, 52).
107. Cornwallis to Portland, 25 January 1799 (*Castlereagh correspondence*, ii, 132); and Cooke to Auckland, 25 January 1799 (BL, Add. MS 34455, f. 144).
108. Buckingham to Grenville, 26 January 1799 (HMC, *Dropmore papers*, iv, 455).
109. Cornwallis to Portland, 28 January 1799 (*Cornwallis correspondence*, iii, 54).
110. Cornwallis to Ross, 28 January 1799 (*Cornwallis correspondence*, iii, 56); Cornwallis and Castlereagh to Portland, 28 January 1799 (*Cornwallis correspondence*, iii, 54, and *Castlereagh correspondence*, ii, 140).
111. Castlereagh to Camden, 22 October 1798 (CUL, Add. MS 6958, f. 3,199); no year is on the manuscript but it can be dated from internal evidence.
112. Cooke to Grenville, 15 January 1799 (HMC, *Dropmore papers*, iv, 442); and Cooke to Auckland late January 1799 (BL, Add. MS 34455, f. 154).
113. Grattan, *Life*, v, 56–8; Keogh, *The French disease*, p. 212.
114. Cornwallis to Portland, 30 January 1799 (*Cornwallis correspondence*, iii, 58).
115. Bishop of Meath to Castlereagh, 31 January 1799 (*Castlereagh correspondence*, ii, 148).
116. Canning to Windham, 4 February 1799 (BL, Add. MS 37844, f. 277).
117. Bartlett, *Fall and rise*, p. 254.
118. Ibid.
119. George III to Pitt, 24 January 1799 (PRONI, T3319/63).
120. Aspinall, *George III*, iii, 186, fn. 2.
121. Pitt to Grenville, 7 February 1799 (HMC, *Dropmore papers*, iv, 468).
122. Beresford to Auckland, 6 February 1799 (*Beresford correspondence*, ii, 209).
123. Castlereagh to Portland, 25 January 1799 (*Castlereagh correspondence*, ii, 133).
124. Castlereagh to Portland, 28 January 1799 (*Castlereagh correspondence*, ii, 144).
125. Ibid., 145.
126. *PH*, xxxiv, 208.
127. Ehrman, *Pitt*, iii, 185; *PH*, xxxiv, 235–6.
128. *PH*, xxxiv, 212.
129. Ibid., 211.
130. Ibid., 213.
131. Ibid., 229.
132. Ibid., 238.
133. Ibid., 240.
134. Lady Bessborough to Granville Leveson-Gower, January 1799 (Granville (ed.), *Private correspondence of Lord Granville Leveson-Gower*, i, 238).
135. *PH*, xxxiv, 247.
136. Ibid., 248–52.
137. Ehrman, *Pitt*, iii, 185, fn. 2.
138. Wickham to Castlereagh, 24 January 1799 (*Cornwallis correspondence*, iii, 53).
139. Bolton, *The passing of the Irish act of union*, p. 158.
140. Pitt to Cornwallis, 26 January 1799 (*Cornwallis correspondence*, iii, 57).
141. *Auckland correspondence*, iv, 87.
142. 1 and 2 February (quoted in Aspinall, *George III*, iii, 186–7, fn. 5); Canning noted a couple of days later that the only positive benefit from the failure of the union in

Ireland was the prospect of 'two, if not three, days good debating' (4 February 1799 (BL, Add. MS 37844, f. 277)).

143. 7 February 1799 (*PH*, xxxiv, 344).
144. *PH*, xxxiv, 254.
145. Ibid., 258.
146. Ibid., 267.
147. Ibid., 272.
148. Ibid., 285.
149. Brougham, *Historical sketches*, i, 204.
150. *PH*, xxxiv, 293.
151. Ibid., 300.
152. Ibid., 321.
153. Hyde, *Castlereagh*, p. 311.
154. Stanhope, *Life*, iii, 172. As far as I am aware Lecky's is the only other account that mentions this fact, although neither he nor Stanhope compares the versions (Lecky, *Ireland*, v, 232).
155. For Pitt's original speech in the commons I have used the *Parliamentary History* account. The version in the *Parliamentary Register* is virtually identical and contains all of the contentious passages altered for the printed version. Any differences in the *PR* transcript will be noted.
156. For example in the commons Pitt referred to the union as 'a question in which an honest, but I must be allowed to say, a mistaken sense of national pride is so likely to operate' (*PH*, xxiv, 256). In the second version this reads, 'a question in which an honest but mistaken sense of national pride is so likely to operate' (*Speech of the Rt Hon. William Pitt* (Dublin, 1799), p. 6).
157. *PH*, xxiv, 256; *Speech*, p. 7. The *PR* account uses the 'mercantile and monied' version so the *PH* version may have been a careless transcription.
158. *PH*, xxxiv, 267; *Speech*, p. 22. The *PR* version is the same as that in the *PH*.
159. *PH*, xxxiv, 259; *Speech*, p. 11. Again the *PR* version is identical to that in the *PH*.
160. *PH*, xxxiv, 263.
161. *Speech*, p. 18. This section was not included in the *PH* but is to be found in the *PR*, vii, 634.
162. *PH*, xxxiv, 270.
163. *Speech*, p. 26.
164. *PH*, xxxiv, 271. Identical in *PR*.
165. *Speech*, p. 22.
166. *PH*, xxxiv, 271; *Speech*, p. 28.
167. *PH*, xxxiv, 272; *Speech*, p. 29.
168. *Speech*, p. 40.
169. Elliot to Castlereagh, 2 February 1799 (*Castlereagh correspondence*, ii, 161).
170. Cabinet minute (quoted in Ehrman, *Pitt*, iii, 190, fn. 3).
171. Minto to Windham, 7 February 1799 (Lewis Melville (ed.), *The Windham papers* (2 vols., London, 1913), ii, 93).
172. Portland to Castlereagh, 29 January 1799 (*Castlereagh correspondence*, ii, 147).
173. Canning to Windham, 4 February 1799 (BL, Add. MS 37844, f. 277).
174. Quoted in Aspinall, *George III*, iii, 187.
175. Canning to his mother, 1 February 1799 (quoted in Aspinall, *George III*, iii, 187). For background to Canning's family see Peter Dixon, *Canning: politician and statesman* (London, 1976), chapter i.
176. For details of this episode see Canning to Wickham, 20 February 1799 (Wickham jnr (ed.), *The correspondence of William Wickham*, ii, 95); this provides a résumé of the scheme, which was probably devised in early February.

177. Malcomson, *John Foster*, p. 82.
178. Canning to Wickham, 20 February 1799 (Wickham jnr (ed.), *The correspondence of William Wickham*, ii, 95).
179. Ibid., 96.
180. Malcomson, *John Foster*, p. 82.
181. 7 February 1799 (*PH*, xxxiv, 322).
182. Ibid., 323–9.
183. Brougham, *Historical sketches*, i, 227.
184. *PH*, xxiv, 348.
185. Ibid., 349.
186. Ibid., 357.
187. Ibid., 367.
188. Dundas to Cornwallis, received 22 March 1799 (*Cornwallis correspondence*, iii, 79).
189. Philip Ziegler, *Addington* (London, 1965), p. 84.
190. *PH*, xxxiv, 461.
191. Ibid., 455.
192. Ibid., 402.
193. Ibid., 393.
194. Ibid., 394.
195. Grenville to Buckingham, 28 January 1799 (Buckingham, *Courts*, ii, 430).
196. Fox to Grattan, 4 February 1799 (Grattan, *Life*, v, 435).
197. *PH*, xxxiv, 324.

Chapter 4 Corruption and the catholic question (pp. 77–96)

1. Quoted by Camden in an important letter to Pitt on the catholic question, in 1793 (CUL, Add. MS 6958, f. 1,212).
2. Bolton, *The passing of the Irish act of union*, p. 122.
3. Castlereagh to Portland, 25 January 1799 (*Castlereagh correspondence*, ii, 133).
4. Cornwallis to Portland, 26 January 1799 (*Cornwallis correspondence*, iii, 52).
5. The source of this information is Barrington, who claimed to have seen the secret communication, which was later lost or destroyed (*Historic memoirs*, ii, 333). I find the story credible, particularly given the detail of the recollection, and while Barrington was not the most reliable of witnesses on certain issues much of his evidence has since been validated (see below).
6. To Portland, 28 January 1799 (*Castlereagh correspondence*, ii, 144, and *Cornwallis correspondence*, iii, 54).
7. Beresford to Auckland, 6 February 1799 (*Beresford correspondence*, ii, 210).
8. Ibid., 209.
9. Castlereagh to Portland, February 1799 (PRO, HO 100/85, f. 199).
10. Ibid., f. 200.
11. Ibid., f. 201.
12. Quoted in Bolton, *The passing of the Irish act of union*, p. 197.
13. Cornwallis to Ross, 28 March 1799 (*Cornwallis correspondence*, iii, 81).
14. Cornwallis to Portland, 23 February 1799 (*Cornwallis correspondence*, iii, 66).
15. Wickham to Castlereagh, 4 March 1799 (*Cornwallis correspondence*, iii, 90).
16. Cornwallis to Portland, 28 February 1799 (*Cornwallis correspondence*, iii, 70).
17. Cornwallis to Ross, 15 April 1799 (*Cornwallis correspondence*, iii, 89).
18. Bolton, *The passing of the Irish act of union*, p. 81; and as Castlereagh said to Camden in the summer.
19. Cooke to Auckland, 7 May 1799 (Kent Archives Office, U840/081/3).
20. Bolton, *The passing of the Irish act of union*, p. 83.
21. Morton Pitt to William Pitt, 16 September 1799 (CUL, Add. MS 6958, f. 2,524).

22. Altamount to Gosford, 9 February 1799 (PRONI, D1606/1/1/203d).
23. *PH*, xxxiv, 263–4.
24. Malcomson, *John Foster*, p. 80.
25. Castlereagh to Camden, 24 July 1799 (PRONI, T2627/4/114); the chief secretary was discussing the speaker's opposition to Cornwallis, in the early days of his viceroyalty, on the state prisoners issue.
26. Foster to Camden, 3 August 1799 (PRONI, T2627/4/116).
27. Cooke to Camden, 7 May 1799 (Kent Archives Office, U840/081/3).
28. Cooke to Auckland, 20 January 1800 (PRONI, T3229/2/52).
29. Camden to Castlereagh, March 1799 (PRONI, D3030/692/38).
30. Camden to Castlereagh, 25 March 1799 (PRONI, D3030/699/71).
31. Quoted in Bolton, *The passing of the Irish act of union*, p. 121.
32. Castlereagh to Portland, 12 April 1799 (*Castlereagh correspondence*, ii, 269).
33. Buckingham to Grenville, 12 April 1799 (HMC, *Dropmore papers*, v, 11); and Castlereagh to Portland, 12 April 1799 (*Castlereagh correspondence*, ii, 270).
34. Foster to Camden, 3 August 1799 (PRONI, T2627/4/116).
35. *The speech of the Rt Hon. John Foster* (London, 1799), p. 27.
36. Ibid., p. 110.
37. Castlereagh to Portland, 14 April 1799 (*Castlereagh correspondence*, ii, 274).
38. Reply of Castlereagh (*The speech of the Rt Hon. John Foster*, p. 16).
39. Cornwallis to Portland, 13 April 1799 (*Cornwallis correspondence*, iii, 87).
40. Cooke to Wickham, 12 April 1799 (*Cornwallis correspondence*, iii, 86).
41. Ibid.; PRO, HO 100/86, f. 262.
42. Castlereagh to Portland, 12 April 1799 (*Castlereagh correspondence*, ii, 270).
43. Ibid.
44. Cornwallis to Portland, 18 April 1799 (*Cornwallis correspondence*, iii, 91).
45. Clare to Cornwallis, 18 April 1799 (*Castlereagh correspondence*, ii, 277); Cornwallis to Clare, 18 April 1799 (*Castlereagh correspondence*, ii, 278).
46. McNeill (ed.), *The life and times of Mary Ann McCracken*, p. 196.
47. Auckland to Beresford, 7 February 1799 (*Beresford correspondence*, ii, 212).
48. Quoted in George O'Brien, *The economic history of Ireland from the union to the famine* (New Jersey, 1972), p. 226.
49. See Roger Wells, *Wretched faces: famine in wartime England, 1793–1801* (Gloucester, 1988), p. 35.
50. Used by Wells, *Wretched faces*, p. 2.
51. Ibid., p. 1.
52. Ibid., Colonel Clinton, p. 35.
53. *Debate in the house of commons of Ireland* (Dublin, 1799), p. 3.
54. Ibid., pp. 14–15.
55. Ibid., p. 15.
56. Ibid., p. 25.
57. Ibid., p. 33.
58. May 1799 (*Cornwallis correspondence*, iii, 100).
59. Cooke to Camden, 7 May 1799 (Kent Archives Office, U840/081/3).
60. Cornwallis to Ross, 15 April 1799 (*Cornwallis correspondence*, iii, 89).
61. Cornwallis to Portland, 24 May 1799 (PRO, HO 100/86, f. 425).
62. Ibid., f. 429.
63. Portland to Cornwallis, 30 May 1799 (PRO, HO 100/86, f. 439).
64. Cornwallis to Portland, 26 June 1799 (PRO, HO 100/87, f. 21).
65. Cornwallis to Portland, 24 May 1799 (PRO, HO 100/86, f. 428).
66. Cornwallis to Portland, 22 June 1799 (PRO, HO 100/87, f. 16).
67. Ibid., f. 17.

68. Cornwallis to Dundas, 8 February 1799 (Aspinall, *George III*, iii, 186).
69. Castlereagh to Portland, 27 March 1799 (*Castlereagh correspondence*, ii, 421).
70. Cornwallis to Dundas, 8 February 1799 (Aspinall, *George III*, iii, 186).
71. Ibid.
72. Cornwallis to Portland, 22 June 1799 (*Castlereagh correspondence*, ii, 337).
73. Cornwallis to Ross, 19 June 1799 (*Cornwallis correspondence*, iii, 104).
74. Cornwallis to Portland, 22 June 1799 (*Castlereagh correspondence*, ii, 337).
75. Castlereagh to Camden, 20 and 28 June 1799 (Kent Archives Office, U840/C98/5).
76. Shannon to Boyle, 5 July 1799 (PRONI, D2707/A3/3/166).
77. Castlereagh to Camden, 17 July 1799 (PRONI, T2627/4/112C).
78. Camden to Pitt, 11 August 1799 (CUL, Add. MS 6958, f. 2,509).
79. [Unknown] to General Abercromby, 12 June 1799 (NLI, MS 55, f. 172).
80. Cornwallis to Ross, 19 June 1799 (*Cornwallis correspondence*, iii, 104).
81. Castlereagh to Camden, 24 July 1799 (PRONI, T2627/4/114).
82. Castlereagh to Camden, 17 July 1799 (PRONI, T2627/4/111–12C).
83. Ibid.
84. Cornwallis to Portland, 13 August 1799 (PRO, HO 100/87, f. 111).
85. Cornwallis to Ross, 8 June 1799 (*Cornwallis correspondence*, iii, 102).
86. See Bolton, *The passing of the Irish act of union*, p. 100.
87. *Historic memoirs*, ii, 354.
88. J.R. O'Flanagan, *The Irish bar* (London, 1879), p. 108; the charge of acting as a government agent is made in the old *Dictionary of National Biography*, and is also in the forthcoming *Dictionary of Irish Biography*.
89. Grattan, *Life*, v, 8.
90. Lecky, *Ireland*, v, 289.
91. Ibid., 303.
92. Ibid., 304–9.
93. T.D. Ingram, *A history of the legislative union of Great Britain and Ireland* (London, 1887), preface, p. vii.
94. Rosebery, *Pitt*, p. 189.
95. Charles Petrie, *Lord Liverpool and his times* (London, 1954), p. 55.
96. See James McGuire's analysis, 'The act of union' (in Liam de Paor (ed.), *Milestones in Irish history* (Cork, 1986), pp. 72–3). The poem is attributed to John O'Hagan.
97. Bolton, *The passing of the Irish act of union*, pp. 51, 181–2.
98. Gearóid Ó Tuathaigh, *Ireland before the famine, 1798–1848* (Dublin, 1972), p. 32.
99. See, for example, his 'The parliamentary traffic of this country' (in Thomas Bartlett and D.W. Hayton (eds.), *Penal era and golden age* (Belfast, 1979), pp. 137–61).
100. Donal McCartney, *The dawning of democracy* (Dublin, 1987), p. 12.
101. The money was usually accounted as being for 'the purposes of S.S.' (PRO, HO 387).
102. 'How did they pass the union? Secret service expenditure', *History*, 82, no. 266 (April 1997), pp. 223–51.
103. Oath for secretary of state, *Statutes*, 171. When money was requested it was stated to be 'for the purposes of S.S.' (PRO, HO 387).
104. PRO, HO 387.
105. Ehrman, *Pitt*, iii, 187.
106. Castlereagh to primate of Ireland, 16 July 1799 (*Castlereagh correspondence*, ii, 352).
107. This was recollected by Castlereagh in a crucial letter to Pitt, 1 January 1801 (CUL, Add. MS 6958, f. 2,827).
108. Castlereagh to Grenville, 26 June 1799 (HMC, *Dropmore papers*, v, 107); Castlereagh to Camden, 17 July 1799 (PRONI, T2627/4/112C).
109. Cooke to Camden, 14 August 1799 (CUL, Add. MS 6958, f. 2,513).

110. Ibid.
111. Cornwallis to Portland, 24 August 1799 (*Cornwallis correspondence*, iii, 128).
112. Auckland to Beresford, 23 August 1799 (*Beresford correspondence*, ii, 223).
113. Pitt to Auckland, [April/May] 1799 (*Auckland correspondence*, iv, 96). Pitt gave his congratulations and admitted that it was not an occasion 'where I feel sentiment the least'.
114. Quoted in 'William Wilde's table of Irish famines, 900–1850' (in E.M. Crauford (ed.), *Famine: the Irish experience, 900–1900* (Edinburgh, 1989), p. 15).
115. Ibid., pp. 15–16.
116. Marsden to Castlereagh, 14 October 1799 (*Castlereagh correspondence*, ii, 427); Cornwallis to Portland, 20 November 1799 (PRO, HO 100/87, f. 252).
117. Ibid., 427.
118. Ibid., 431.
119. Ibid.; Marsden informed Castlereagh that the request 'has been civilly refused by his excellency'.
120. Quoted in 'William Wilde's table of Irish famines, 900–1850', p. 16.
121. McNeill (ed.), *The life and times of Mary Ann McCracken*, p. 196.
122. Cornwallis to Portland, 20 November 1799 (PRO, HO 100/87, f. 252).
123. PRO, HO 100/87, f. 254.
124. Portland to Cornwallis, 14 November 1799 (PRO, HO 100/89, f. 278).
125. Ibid., f. 280.
126. See Wickwire and Wickwire, *Cornwallis: the imperial years*, pp. 230–31.
127. Cornwallis to Portland, 20 November 1799 (PRO, HO 100/87, f. 252).
128. *Faulkner's Journal* (quoted in 'William Wilde's table of Irish famines, 900–1850', p. 16).
129. This was the recollection of Camden approximately four years later ('Memorandum on Pitt's retirement' (printed in *Bulletin of the Institute of Historical Research*, vol. xliv, no. 110 (1971), pp. 247–57)).
130. Moylan to Hippesley, 14 September 1799 (*Castlereagh correspondence*, ii, 400).
131. Ibid., 401.
132. Hobart to Pitt, 2 November 1799 (CUL, Add. MS 6958. f. 2,540).
133. Hobart to Auckland, 7 November 1799 (PRONI, T3229/2/43).
134. This is not certain although there are various pieces of evidence to support such a hypothesis. Camden in his 'Memorandum' noted that the 'two cabinet councils were held on two succeeding days'. *The Times* on 18 November reported that two cabinet meetings were held on the two previous days, the first of which was said to have been on Irish affairs. The same newspaper on 16 November revealed that a cabinet had also been held the previous day. A final piece of evidence is that five days after 17 November, Cornwallis, in a letter to the home secretary, revealed that he was aware of the cabinet's deliberations, during a discussion of the question of catholic peers in the lords, when he mentioned the 'mortifying and provoking' circumstances that would arise if government denied the catholics the 'full enjoyment of those privileges which have in principle already been conceded to them' (22 November 1799 (*Cornwallis correspondence*, iii, 141)).
135. Camden, 'Memorandum', pp. 247–57.
136. Castlereagh to Pitt, 1 January 1801 (CUL, Add. MS 6958, f. 2,827).
137. Ibid.
138. The reference to Loughborough was by Pitt in October 1798 (HMC, *Dropmore papers*, iv, 337).
139. Campbell, *Lord chancellors*, vi, 294.
140. Camden, 'Memorandum', pp. 247–57.
141. Ibid., p. 249.
142. Ibid., pp. 250–52.

143. This was recounted afterwards to James Mackintosh, who put it in his memoirs (R.J. Mackintosh (ed.), *Memoirs of the Rt Hon. Sir James Mackintosh* (2 vols., London, 1835), i, 170).
144. Ibid., 171. George Pellew, when he edited Addington's correspondence, attributed the conversation to February 1801 and most historians have been content to follow this dating (*Addington correspondence*, i, 298).
145. Dundas to Pitt, [believed to be May 1798] (Ehrman, *Pitt*, iii, 521, fn. 2, and 173, fn. 3).
146. Buckingham to Grenville, 17 November 1799 (HMC, *Dropmore papers*, vi, 27).
147. Grenville to Buckingham, 6 November 1799 (HMC, *Dropmore papers*, vi, 11).
148. Wilberforce and Wilberforce, *The life of William Wilberforce*, ii, 324–5.
149. Rosebery, *Pitt*, p. 198. Frere was a friend of George Canning since their time at Eton and had run the *Anti-Jacobin* with him (see Ehrman, *Pitt*, iii, 111).
150. Gabrielle Festing, *John Hookham Frere and his friends* (London, 1899), p. 44.
151. Wilberforce (quoted in Ehrman, *Pitt*, iii, 827); see also pp. 827–8 for a brief analysis of Pitt and religion; although he did attend services regularly according to witnesses at Walmer.
152. *PH*, xxxiv, 272.
153. Ibid., 273.
154. Speech in the commons, 21 April 1800 (quoted in Rose, *Pitt and Napoleon*, p. 17).
155. Ibid., p. 18.
156. Cornwallis to Portland, 22 November 1799 (*Cornwallis correspondence*, iii, 141).
157. Cornwallis to Portland, 9 December 1799 (BL, Add. MS 35919, f. 194).
158. Ibid.
159. Cornwallis to Portland, 22 November 1799 (PRO, HO 100/87, f. 259).
160. Ibid.
161. Beresford to Auckland, 18 December 1799 (PRONI, T3229/2/46).
162. Cooke to Auckland, 12 December 1799 (PRONI, T3229/2/44).
163. Ibid.
164. Castlereagh to Auckland, 13 December 1799 (PRONI, T3229/2/4).
165. Castlereagh to Portland, 11 December 1799 (PRO, HO 100/87, f. 276).
166. Quoted in 'William Wilde's table of Irish famines, 900–1850', p. 16.
167. Cornwallis to Ross, 28 December 1799 (*Cornwallis correspondence*, iii, 153).

Chapter 5 The union passes (pp. 97–129)
1. Castlereagh to John King, 2 January 1800 (*Cornwallis correspondence*, ii, 156); PRO, HO 100/93, f. 2.
2. PRO, HO 387/2; a receipt for the ten £1,000 notes is included in PRO, HO 387/4/4, f. 3.
3. *Cornwallis correspondence*, iii, 156.
4. Recounted in Grattan, *Life*, v, 67–8.
5. Ibid., 68.
6. Ibid., 70.
7. Ibid., 74.
8. Ibid.
9. Bolton, *The passing of the Irish act of union*, p. 186.
10. Hyde, *Castlereagh*, p. 341.
11. *A report of the debate in the house of commons of Ireland on 15 January 1800* (Dublin, 1800), p. 8.
12. Cooke to Grenville, 16 January 1800 (HMC, *Dropmore papers*, vi, 105).
13. *A report of the debate . . . on 15 January 1800*, p. 35.
14. Ibid., p. 36.
15. Ibid., p. 90.

16. Quoted in Grattan, *Life*, v, 77.
17. Grattan, *Life*, v, 89; Hyde, *Castlereagh*, p. 343; and Cooke to Grenville, 16 January 1800 (HMC, *Dropmore papers*, vi, 105).
18. Grattan, *Life*, v, 88.
19. Cooke to Auckland, 16 January 1800 (PRONI, T3228/2/50).
20. *A report of the debate . . . on 15 January 1800*, p. 136.
21. Ibid., p. 137.
22. Cornwallis to Portland, 16 January 1800 (*Cornwallis correspondence*, iii, 163).
23. *Cornwallis correspondence*, iii, 228.
24. Cooke to Auckland, 18 January 1800 (PRONI, T3229/2/51).
25. Beresford to Auckland, 20 January 1800 (PRONI, T3229/2/53).
26. Cornwallis to Ross, 21 January 1800 (*Cornwallis correspondence*, iii, 167).
27. Cooke to Auckland, 20 January 1800 (PRONI, T3229/2/52).
28. Cooke to Auckland, 18 January 1800 (PRONI, T3229/2/51).
29. Cooke to Auckland, 20 January 1800 (PRONI, T3229/2/52).
30. Beresford to Auckland, 20 January 1800 (PRONI, T3229/2/53).
31. Cooke to Auckland, 18 January 1800 (PRONI, T3229/2/51).
32. Cooke to Auckland, 20 January 1800 (PRONI, T3229/2/52).
33. Cooke to Auckland, 20 January 1800 (PRONI, T3229/2/52).
34. PRONI, D207/10/6.
35. This is the analysis attached to the transcript (ibid.).
36. Cooke to Auckland, 20 January 1800 (PRONI, T3229/2/52).
37. Cornwallis to Ross, 21 January 1800 (*Cornwallis correspondence*, iii, 167).
38. Quoted in Grattan, *Life*, v, 62.
39. Cooke to Grenville, 16 January 1800 (HMC, *Dropmore papers*, vi, 105).
40. Cornwallis to Portland, 18 January 1800 (*Cornwallis correspondence*, iii, 165).
41. Cooke to Auckland, 18 January 1800 (PRONI, T3229/2/51).
42. Cornwallis to Ross, 21 January 1800 (*Cornwallis correspondence*, iii, 167).
43. Cornwallis to Portland, 21 January 1800 (*Cornwallis correspondence*, iii, 167).
44. Cornwallis to Portland, 31 January 1800 (*Cornwallis correspondence*, iii, 175).
45. Cornwallis to Ross, 31 January 1800 (*Cornwallis correspondence*, iii, 174).
46. Castlereagh to John King, 25 January 1800 (*Cornwallis correspondence*, iii, 170).
47. *Castlereagh correspondence*, iii, 211–12.
48. *A report of the debate in the house of commons of Ireland on 5 and 6 February 1800* (Dublin, 1800), p. 7.
49. Ibid., p. 37.
50. Ibid., p. 41.
51. Ibid., p. 44.
52. Ibid., p. 14.
53. Ibid., p. 46.
54. Ibid., p. 62.
55. Ibid., p. 65.
56. Barrington, *Historic memoirs*, ii, 354.
57. *Journal of the house of commons of the kingdom of Ireland* (Dublin, 1800), p. 29.
58. Bolton, *The passing of the Irish act of union*, p. 190, fn. 1.
59. Cornwallis to bishop of Lichfield and Coventry, 8 February 1800 (*Cornwallis correspondence*, iii, 183).
60. Grattan, *Life*, v, 71.
61. Bolton, *The passing of the Irish act of union*, p. 190.
62. Carysfort to Grenville, 6 February 1800 (HMC, *Dropmore papers*, vi, 118).
63. Ibid.
64. Cooke to Grenville, 6 February 1800 (HMC, *Dropmore papers*, vi, 118).

65. Cornwallis to bishop of Lichfield and Coventry, 8 February 1800 (*Cornwallis correspondence*, iii, 183).
66. Bolton, *The passing of the Irish act of union*, p. 189.
67. Cooke to Grenville, 6 February 1800 (HMC, *Dropmore papers*, vi, 117).
68. Ibid., 118.
69. Castlereagh to Portland, 7 February 1800 (*Cornwallis correspondence*, iii, 182).
70. Portland to Cornwallis, 9 February 1800 (*Cornwallis correspondence*, iii, 188).
71. Cooke to Grenville, 10 February 1800 (HMC, *Dropmore papers*, vi, 121).
72. Clare to Wellesley, 9 March 1800 (PRONI, T3287/5).
73. Cooke to Grenville, 10 February 1800 (HMC, *Dropmore papers*, vi, 121).
74. Cornwallis to Portland, 11 February 1800 (*Cornwallis correspondence*, iii, 184).
75. Cooke to Grenville, 10 February 1800 (HMC, *Dropmore papers*, vi, 122).
76. Cooke to Grenville, 14 February 1800 (HMC, *Dropmore papers*, vi, 128).
77. Cooke to Grenville, 10 February 1800 (HMC, *Dropmore papers*, vi, 122).
78. Barrington, *Historic memoirs*, ii, 335. This is the only source for the story, but it strikes me as authentic, and appears unlikely to have been invented.
79. Ibid., 336.
80. Cooke to Grenville, 14 February 1800 (HMC, *Dropmore papers*, vi, 126–7).
81. Ibid., 127.
82. Ibid.
83. Ibid., 128.
84. Bolton, *The passing of the Irish act of union*, p. 189.
85. Cornwallis to Portland, 7 February 1800 (PRO, HO 100/95, f. 88).
86. Bolton, *The passing of the Irish act of union*, pp. 191–2.
87. Cornwallis to Ross, 19 June 1799 (*Cornwallis correspondence*, iii, 104).
88. See *Castlereagh correspondence*, iii, 241, fn. 1.
89. Cornwallis to Ross, 13 February 1800 (*Cornwallis correspondence*, iii, 189).
90. Shannon to Boyle, 2 May 1800 (PRONI, D2707/A3/3/181).
91. Cooke to Grenville, 14 February 1800 (HMC, *Dropmore papers*, vi, 127).
92. Portland to Cornwallis, 17 February 1800 (*Castlereagh correspondence*, iii, 241).
93. Buckingham to Grenville, 21 February 1800 (HMC, *Dropmore papers*, vi, 138).
94. Carysfort to Grenville, 17 February 1800 (HMC, *Dropmore papers*, vi, 134).
95. Clare to Wellesley, 9 March 1800 (PRONI, T3287/5).
96. Cooke to Grenville, 29 February 1800 (HMC, *Dropmore papers*, vi, 149).
97. Hyde, *Castlereagh*, pp. 354–5.
98. Cooke to Grenville, 18 February 1800 (HMC, *Dropmore papers*, vi, 136); Cornwallis to Ross, 18 February 1800 (*Cornwallis correspondence*, iii, 196).
99. *A report of the debate in the Irish house of commons on 18 February 1800* (Dublin, 1800), p. 19.
100. Ibid.
101. Ibid., p. 21.
102. Cooke to Grenville, 18 February 1800 (HMC, *Dropmore papers*, vi, 136).
103. Cornwallis to Ross, 18 February 1800 (*Cornwallis correspondence*, iii, 196).
104. Grattan, *Life*, v, 108.
105. Ibid., 109.
106. Beresford to Auckland, 18 February 1800 (PRONI, T3229/2/59).
107. Cooke to Grenville, 29 February 1800 (HMC, *Dropmore papers*, vi, 150).
108. Cooke to Grenville, 1 March 1800 (HMC, *Dropmore papers*, vi, 150). In 1807 two prospective parliamentary candidates duelled, with one fatality. Wellington recorded that it was 'reckoned fair in Ireland' (quoted in Christopher Hibbert, *Wellington: a personal history* (London, 1997), p. 62).
109. *A report of the debate . . . on 18 February 1800*, p. 34.

110. Ibid., p. 36.
111. Ibid., p. 34.
112. Ibid., p. 40.
113. Ibid., p. 82. There is some confusion about the spelling of this member's name. He is variously referred to as Donnell, O'Donel, O'Donnel, etc. For convenience I have consistently used O'Donel.
114. Castlereagh to John King, 27 February 1800 (*Cornwallis correspondence*, iii, 200).
115. Ibid., 201.
116. Cooke to John King, 1 March 1800 (*Cornwallis correspondence*, iii, 202).
117. 'Received from John King two sums of £10,000 each, for which I promise to be accountable, Castlereagh' (PRO, HO 387/4/4, f. 2).
118. Cooke to Grenville, 5 March 1800 (HMC, *Dropmore papers*, vi, 152).
119. Castlereagh to John King, 2 April 1800 (*Cornwallis correspondence*, iii, 224).
120. Cornwallis to bishop of Lichfield and Coventry, 24 January 1800 (*Cornwallis correspondence*, iii, 169).
121. Castlereagh to John King, 2 April 1800 (*Cornwallis correspondence*, iii, 224).
122. *Dublin Evening Post*, 13 March 1800; *Journal of the house of commons of the kingdom of Ireland* (1800), pp. 94, 127; Barrington, *Historic memoirs*, ii, 364–6.
123. Barrington, *Personal sketches*, i, 215.
124. Ibid.
125. Ibid., 216.
126. For further details about Egan's career see the forthcoming *Dictionary of Irish Biography*.
127. Cornwallis to Ross, 13 February 1800 (*Cornwallis correspondence*, iii, 189).
128. Cornwallis to Ross, 3 July 1800 (*Cornwallis correspondence*, iii, 270).
129. Camden to Castlereagh, 11 April 1800 (*Castlereagh correspondence*, iii, 273).
130. Colonel Maitland to William Huskisson, 14 May 1800 (*Cornwallis correspondence*, iii, 236).
131. Clare to [Auckland], 2 April 1800 (PRONI, T3456/1).
132. Cooke to Grenville, 10 March 1800 (HMC, *Dropmore papers*, vi, 159).
133. Cornwallis to Portland, 11 March 1800 (PRO, HO 100/87); Bolton, *The passing of the Irish act of union*, p. 197.
134. Cooke to Grenville, 14 March 1800 (HMC, *Dropmore papers*, vi, 162); Bolton, *The passing of the Irish act of union*, p. 197.
135. *Journal of the house of commons of the kingdom of Ireland* (1800), p. 97.
136. Ibid.
137. Cooke to Grenville, 14 March 1800 (HMC, *Dropmore papers*, vi, 162).
138. Ibid., 163.
139. Bolton, *The passing of the Irish act of union*, pp. 197–8; Cooke to Grenville, 15 March 1800 (HMC, *Dropmore papers*, vi, 163).
140. Cooke to Grenville, 24 March 1800 (HMC, *Dropmore papers*, vi, 173).
141. Bolton, *The passing of the Irish act of union*, p. 198.
142. Beresford to Auckland, 19 March 1800 (PRONI, T3229/2/60).
143. Cooke to Grenville, 21 March 1800 (HMC, *Dropmore papers*, vi, 171).
144. *A report of the debate in the Irish house of commons on 14 March 1800* (Dublin, 1800), p. 25.
145. Beresford to Auckland, 19 March 1800 (PRONI, T3229/2/60); Cooke to Grenville, 21 March 1800 (HMC, *Dropmore papers*, vi, 171).
146. Cooke to Grenville, 21 March 1800 (HMC, *Dropmore papers*, vi, 171).
147. *Journal of the house of commons of the kingdom of Ireland* (1800), pp. 108–11.
148. Ibid., p. 112.
149. Grenville to Wickham, 28 March 1800 (HMC, *Dropmore papers*, vi, 186).

150. Camden to Castlereagh, 23 March 1800 (*Castlereagh correspondence*, iii, 258).
151. Cornwallis to Portland, 11 April 1800 (PRO, HO 100/86, f. 70).
152. Cornwallis to Portland, 29 March 1800 (*Cornwallis correspondence*, iii, 223).
153. Cornwallis to Ross, 18 April 1800 (*Cornwallis correspondence*, iii, 228).
154. PRO, HO 387/4/4, f. 4.
155. The allegation is recounted in Grattan, *Life*, v, 180.
156. See Gilbert, *Documents relating to Ireland, 1795–1804*; the secret service accounts in this book represent the official funds, and do not include the extra money that was transmitted.
157. Bolton, *The passing of the Irish act of union*, pp. 200–1.
158. Cooke to Cornwallis, 22 April 1800 (*Castlereagh correspondence*, iii, 286).
159. *PH*, xxxv, 39–40.
160. Ibid.
161. PRO, HO 100/96, f. 152.
162. Cornwallis to Portland, 3 May 1800 (*Cornwallis correspondence*, iii, 233); see also Bolton, *The passing of the Irish act of union*, pp. 203–4.
163. *Journal of the house of commons of the kingdom of Ireland* (Dublin, 1800), p. 127.
164. Ibid., p. 138.
165. Cooke to Grenville, 17 May 1800 (HMC, *Dropmore papers*, vi, 230).
166. *Journal of the house of commons of the kingdom of Ireland* (1800), p. 141.
167. Cooke to Grenville, 22 May 1800 (HMC, *Dropmore papers*, vi, 238).
168. *Journal of the house of commons of the kingdom of Ireland* (1800), p. 141.
169. Cooke to Grenville, 22 May 1800 (HMC, *Dropmore papers*, vi, 238).
170. *Cornwallis correspondence*, iii, 242; PRO, HO 100/96, f. 295.
171. *Journal of the house of commons of the kingdom of Ireland* (1800), p. 153; Grattan, *Life*, v, 174–5.
172. Grattan, *Life*, v, 176. As Koebner's work on Grattan's early speeches reveals, and as Cooke noted, Grattan was fond of editing his speeches before publication (see Richard Koebner, 'The early speeches of Henry Grattan', in *IHR Bull.*, xxx (1957), pp. 102–14). Most of Grattan's speeches quoted here are based on accurate accounts of the time, and the general accuracy of the speeches in May 1800 can be deduced from contemporary correspondence and other accounts.
173. Cornwallis to Portland, 27 May 1800 (PRO, HO 100/96, f. 293).
174. Hoey (ed.), *Speeches*, p. 76.
175. Hyde, *Castlereagh*, p. 357.
176. Hoey (ed.), *Speeches*, p. 76.
177. Cooke to John King, 27 May 1800 (*Cornwallis correspondence*, iii, 242).
178. Ibid.
179. Ibid.
180. Brougham, *Historical sketches*, ii, 126.
181. *Journal of the house of commons of the kingdom of Ireland* (1800), p. 156.
182. Hoey (ed.), *Speeches*, p. 79.
183. PRO, HO 100/96, f. 459.
184. *Journal of the house of commons of the kingdom of Ireland* (1800), pp. 173–8.
185. Cornwallis to Portland, 7 June 1800 (*Cornwallis correspondence*, iii, 248).
186. Quoted in Lecky, *Ireland*, v, 416.
187. Hoey (ed.), *Speeches*, p. 79.
188. Ibid., p. 81.
189. *Journal of the house of commons of the kingdom of Ireland* (1800), p. 184.
190. Grattan, *Life*, v, 178.
191. Barrington, *Historic memoirs*, ii, 367.
192. Ibid., 368.

193. Cornwallis to Portland, 9 June 1800 (*Cornwallis correspondence*, iii, 251).
194. *Castlereagh correspondence*, iii, 219.
195. Portland to Cornwallis, 2 July 1800 (*Castlereagh correspondence*, iii, 346).
196. Foster to Camden, 28 July 1800 (PRONI, T2627/4/120).
197. Cornwallis to Portland, 17 June 1800 (*Cornwallis correspondence*, iii, 262).
198. Cornwallis to Dundas, 1 July 1800 (*Cornwallis correspondence*, iii, 110).
199. *Castlereagh correspondence*, iii, 220; *London Gazette*, 29 July 1800.
200. *London Gazette*, 29 July 1800.
201. Some doubt has been put over the accuracy of Grattan's early published speeches by Koebner ('The early speeches of Henry Grattan'); and bear in mind Cooke's witty rejoinder that Grattan would 'print *editio auctior et emendiatior*'.
202. The poem 'How did they pass the union' (quoted in McGuire 'The act of union').
203. Cornwallis to Hardwicke, 29 September 1804 (quoted in Michael MacDonagh, *The viceroy's post-bag* (London, 1904), p. 205).
204. Quoted in Grattan, *Life*, v, 113.
205. Bartlett, *Fall and rise*, p. 261.
206. Cornwallis to Ross, 31 January 1800 (*Cornwallis correspondence*, iii, 175).
207. Troy to home office, 26 April 1800 (NLI, MS 5027).
208. Clare to [Auckland], 2 April 1800 (PRONI, T3456/1).
209. Cornwallis to Ross, 21 May 1800 (*Cornwallis correspondence*, iii, 237).
210. Ibid.
211. Castlereagh to Thomas Conolly, late February 1801 (quoted in Hinde, *Castlereagh*, p. 50).
212. *Cornwallis correspondence*, iii, 344.
213. Castlereagh to Pitt, 1 January 1801 (CUL, Add. MS 6958, f. 2,827).
214. *Cornwallis correspondence*, iii, 344.
215. Cornwallis to Ross, 21 May 1800 (*Cornwallis correspondence*, iii, 238).
216. Bartlett, *Fall and rise*, p. 259.
217. Bolton, *The passing of the Irish act of union*, pp. 169–70.
218. Wilkinson, 'How did they pass the union?'
219. Bolton, *The passing of the Irish act of union*, pp. 166–7; Cornwallis to bishop of Lichfield and Coventry, 8 February 1800 (*Cornwallis correspondence*, iii, 184).
220. Cornwallis to bishop of Lichfield and Coventry, 8 February 1800 (*Cornwallis correspondence*, iii, 183).
221. Wilkinson, 'How did they pass the union?', p. 35.
222. See Barrington's black list (Grattan, *Life*, v, 193).
223. Ibid., 194.
224. *Cornwallis correspondence*, iii, 321–3.
225. Ely had six seats, Shannon and Abercorn controlled four each.
226. Cornwallis to Portland, 9 June 1800 (PRO, HO 100/96, f. 457).
227. Ibid., for list see f. 463.
228. Ibid., f. 464.
229. Ibid., f. 465.
230. Ibid., f. 467.
231. Ibid., f. 469.
232. Black list (Grattan, *Life*, v, 192).
233. Bolton, *The passing of the Irish act of union*, pp. 205–7; Hyde, *Castlereagh*, pp. 363–4.
234. Bolton, *The passing of the Irish act of union*, p. 206.
235. Portland to Cornwallis, 12 June 1800 (*Castlereagh correspondence*, iii, 321); 13 June 1800 (*Cornwallis correspondence*, iii, 258).
236. *Castlereagh correspondence*, iii, 324.
237. Portland to Cornwallis, 24 December 1798 (NLI, MS 886, f. 510).

238. *Castlereagh correspondence*, iii, 325.
239. Ibid., 326.
240. *Castlereagh correspondence*, iii, 326.
241. Ibid., 327.
242. Castlereagh to Cooke, 21 June 1800 (*Castlereagh correspondence*, iii, 330).
243. Hyde, *Castlereagh*, p. 363.
244. *Castlereagh correspondence*, iii, 330–31.
245. Ibid., 331.
246. Ibid., 333.
247. Camden to Castlereagh, 21 June 1800 (*Castlereagh correspondence*, iii, 333).
248. Ibid., 334.
249. Camden to Castlereagh, 22 June 1800 (*Castlereagh correspondence*, iii, 334).
250. Ibid.
251. Camden to Cooke, 22 June 1800 (*Castlereagh correspondence*, iii, 334).
252. Cooke to Castlereagh, 22 June 1800 (*Castlereagh correspondence*, iii, 325).
253. Cooke to Castlereagh, 23 June 1800 (*Castlereagh correspondence*, iii, 336).
254. Ibid.
255. Cornwallis to Ross, 24 June 1800 (*Cornwallis correspondence*, iii, 268).
256. Ibid., 269.
257. Cornwallis to Dundas, 26 June 1800 (quoted in Richard Willis, 'The politics of parliament, 1800–6' (Ph.D. thesis, University of Stanford, 1969), p. 74).
258. Cornwallis to Ross, 11 July 1800 (*Cornwallis correspondence*, iii, 277).
259. Ibid., 276.
260. Castlereagh to Camden, 25 June 1800 (*Castlereagh correspondence*, iii, 339).
261. Ibid., 340.
262. Ibid., 341.
263. Castlereagh to Cooke, 25 June 1800 (*Castlereagh correspondence*, iii, 336).
264. Ibid., 337.
265. Ibid., 338.
266. *Castlereagh correspondence*, iii, 344.
267. Ibid., 346.
268. Ibid.
269. 2 July 1800 (*Castlereagh correspondence*, iii, 350).
270. *Castlereagh correspondence*, iii, 348.
271. Ibid., 349.
272. Castlereagh to Camden, 2 July 1800 (*Castlereagh correspondence*, iii, 351).
273. Ibid., Castlereagh was quoting his father.
274. *Castlereagh correspondence*, iii, 357.
275. *Castlereagh correspondence*, iii, 359.
276. Ibid.
277. Altamount to Gosford, 1 August 1800 (PRONI, D1601/1/1/230).
278. Castlereagh to Cooke, 12 July 1800 (*Cornwallis correspondence*, iii, 278).
279. PRO, HO 100/103 ff. 101–8; also printed in MacDonagh, *The viceroy's post-bag*, pp. 43–53.
280. PRO, HO 100/103, f. 101.
281. MacDonagh, *The viceroy's post-bag*, p. 53. The total comes to £2,800 in the list in PRO, HO 100/103 as three of the pensions are not included.
282. Ibid., pp. 46–50.
283. Ibid., p. 51.
284. Cornwallis to Ross, 3 July 1800 (*Cornwallis correspondence*, iii, 269).
285. Ibid., 270.
286. Hardwicke to Hawkesbury, 26 September 1804 (BL, Add. MS 35709, f. 128).

287. Cooke to George Shee, 4 October 1801 (PRO, HO 100/104, f. 141).
288. Ibid.
289. Clare to [Auckland], 2 April 1800 (PRONI, T3456/1).
290. Castlereagh to Camden, 10 May 1800 (CUL, Add. MS 6958, f. 2,628).
291. MacDonagh, *The viceroy's post-bag*, p. 36.
292. For the list see MacDonagh, *The viceroy's post-bag*, pp. 43–53; Hardwicke to Grenville, 12 March 1806 (ibid.), p. 250.
293. Moylan to Marshall, 26 July 1800 (*Castlereagh correspondence*, iii, 364).

Chapter 6 Court and cabinet (pp. 130–55)
1. Willis in 'Cabinet politics'.
2. Introductory note to PRO, 30/8 series for 1799–1800.
3. Cooke to Castlereagh, 2 July 1800 (*Castlereagh correspondence*, iii, 350).
4. Quoted in Mackesy, *War without victory*, p. 168.
5. Quoted in Curzon, *The personal history of Walmer castle and its lords warden*, p. 132.
6. Feiling, *The second tory party*, p. 165.
7. Richard Pares, *George III and the politicians* (Oxford, 1953), p. 155.
8. Willis, 'Cabinet politics', p. 8.
9. Ibid., p. 9; see also A. Aspinall, 'The cabinet council', pp. 145–7. George Canning's wife called the ceremonial officers the 'sleeping partners of the firm' (Aspinall, p. 151).
10. Mackesy, *War without victory*, pp. 14–16.
11. Dundas to Pitt, 14 April 1800 (PRO 30/8/157).
12. Quoted in Ehrman, *Pitt*, iii, 358. See also Mackesy, *War without victory*, pp. 92–3.
13. Cooke to Castlereagh, 2 July 1800 (*Castlereagh correspondence*, iii, 350).
14. 2 February 1801 (*Glenbervie diaries*, i, 124).
15. The king's opinion recorded by Malmesbury on 27 February 1801, after having been told by Pelham that George III had been dissatisfied with Pitt for 'a long time since' (*Malmesbury diaries*, iv, 22).
16. Pitt to Chatham, 29 May 1799 (PRO 30/8/101, f. 144).
17. Lord Holland, *Memoirs of the whig party*, ii, 92–3.
18. 8 February 1801 (*Malmesbury diaries*, iv, 4).
19. Willis, 'Cabinet politics', p. 14.
20. Camden, 'Memorandum', p. 255.
21. Ibid., p. 256.
22. Feiling, *The second tory party*, p. 214.
23. Camden, 'Memorandum', p. 256.
24. Mackesy, *War without victory*, p. 112.
25. Aspinall, *George III*, iii, 356.
26. Mackesy, *War without victory*, p. 127.
27. Quoted ibid., pp. 127–8.
28. Ibid., pp. 128–31.
29. Pitt to Grenville, 26 July 1800 (HMC, *Dropmore papers*, vi, 279).
30. Willis, 'Cabinet politics', p. 15.
31. Mackesy, *War without victory*, p. 131.
32. 28 February 1801 (*Glenbervie diaries*, i, 183).
33. 2 February 1801 (*Glenbervie diaries*, i, 152).
34. 27 February 1801 (*Malmesbury diaries*, iv, 22).
35. Willis, 'Cabinet politics', p. 11.
36. See Ehrman, *Pitt*, iii, 46–7, for details of the scheme.
37. George III to Pitt, 18 June 1800 (PRO 30/8/104, f. 285).
38. Lord Bruce to George Rose, 25 February 1801 (L. Vernon-Harcourt (ed.), *Diary and correspondence of George Rose* (2 vols., London, 1860), i, 318).

39. Mackesy, *War without victory*, p. 49; and see Ehrman, *Pitt*, iii, chapter x.
40. Ehrman, *Pitt*, iii, 307.
41. Wickwire and Wickwire, *Cornwallis: the imperial years*, p. 231.
42. David Dickson, 'The Irish experience, 900–1900' (in Crauford (ed.), *Famine: the Irish experience, 900–1900*, p. 103). Mokyr's research is taken from Dickson.
43. Cornwallis to Portland, 28 July 1800 (*Cornwallis correspondence*, iii, 283).
44. Cornwallis's speech of 2 August 1800 (*Union tracts*, ix, 5).
45. Pollock to Littlehales, 16 August 1800 (PRO, HO 100/97, ff. 134–5).
46. Ibid., f. 133.
47. Ibid., f. 137.
48. Littlehales to Castlereagh, 23 August 1800 (PRO, HO 100/97, f. 141); Marsden to Castlereagh, 25 August 1800 (*Castlereagh correspondence*, iii, 372). Agar also recommended the ban to Cornwallis, 26 August 1800 (*Cornwallis correspondence*, iii, 289).
49. Marsden to Castlereagh, 17 September 1800 (*Castlereagh correspondence*, iii, 383).
50. Mackesy, *War without victory*, p. 138.
51. Ibid., p. 139.
52. Ibid., p. 140; Ehrman, *Pitt*, iii, 385–6.
53. Mackesy, *War without victory*, p. 141.
54. Ibid., p. 141.
55. Loughborough to Dundas, 17 September 1800 (Campbell, *Lord chancellors*, vi, 304).
56. Windham to Lady Anne Barnard, 20 April 1798 (Mackesy, *War without victory*, p. 167, fn. 11).
57. Campbell, *Lord chancellors*, vi, 292.
58. K. Waliszewski, *Paul the first of Russia, the son of Catherine the great* (London, 1969), p. 45.
59. Talleyrand's description (quoted in Waliszewski, *Paul the first*, p. 196).
60. Waliszewski, *Paul the first*, p. 379.
61. Ibid., p. 371.
62. Buckingham to Grenville, 11 May 1800 (HMC, *Dropmore papers*, vi, 221).
63. Waliszewski, *Paul the first*, p. 337.
64. Ibid.
65. Kenney, 'Lord Whitworth and the conspiracy against Tsar Paul I', p. 206.
66. Ibid., p. 214.
67. Ibid., p. 205.
68. All dates are given in the new style.
69. Kenney, p. 205.
70. R.E. McGrew, *Paul I of Russia, 1754–1801* (Oxford, 1992), p. 308.
71. Kenney, 'Lord Whitworth and the conspiracy against Tsar Paul I', p. 213.
72. Waliszewski, *Paul the first*, p. 414.
73. Kenney, 'Lord Whitworth and the conspiracy against Tsar Paul I', p. 219.
74. Sparrow, 'The alien office', p. 384.
75. Ehrman, *Pitt*, iii, 471.
76. Quoted in McGrew, *Paul I of Russia*, p. 331.
77. Loughborough to Auckland, 1793 (BL, Add. MS 29475, ff. 35–6).
78. Fitzgibbon to Beresford, 2 March 1795 (*Beresford correspondence*, ii, 75).
79. Campbell, *Lord chancellors*, vi, 298.
80. George III to Pitt, 1795 (Campbell, *Lord chancellors*, vi, 171).
81. Mackesy, *War without victory*, p. 151.
82. Ibid., p. 153.
83. Ibid., p. 154.
84. 9 February 1801 (*Glenbervie diaries*, i, 159–60); see also Ehrman, *Pitt*, iii, 409–10.
85. Camden, 'Memorandum', p. 249.

86. Ibid., p. 250.
87. Ibid.
88. Portland to George III, 5 August 1800 (Aspinall, *George III*, iii, 390–91).
89. Willis, 'Cabinet politics', p. 19.
90. Hyde, *Castlereagh*, p. 374.
91. *Castlereagh correspondence*, iv, 392–400.
92. Camden, 'Memorandum', p. 250.
93. Ibid., 300.
94. This can be found in an appendix to *Addington correspondence*.
95. 26 February 1801 (*Malmesbury diaries*, iv, 20–21).
96. Camden, 'Memorandum', p. 250.
97. Campbell, *Lord chancellors*, vi, 306–7.
98. Hyde, *Castlereagh*, pp. 384–5.
99. Richard Willis, 'The politics of parliament', pp. 86–7.
100. Ziegler, *Addington*, p. 91.
101. Ehrman, *Pitt*, iii, 498.
102. Pitt to Loughborough, 25 September 1800 (Campbell, *Lord chancellors*, vi, 306).
103. Mackesy, *War without victory*, pp. 156–7.
104. Ehrman, *Pitt*, iii, 409.
105. Hyde, *Castlereagh*, p. 382.
106. Ibid.
107. Camden, 'Memorandum', p. 250.
108. *Glenbervie diaries*, i, 160.
109. Wells, *Wretched faces*, p. 120.
110. Ibid., p. 1.
111. Ibid., p. 221.
112. Quoted in Wells, *Wretched faces*, p. 144.
113. Wells, *Wretched faces*, p. 146.
114. Ibid., p. 1.
115. Mackesy, *War without victory*, p. 173.
116. Ibid., p. 221.
117. Stanhope, *Life*, iii, 220.
118. Pitt to Addington, 8 October 1800 (quoted in Stanhope, *Life*, iii, 244).
119. Quoted in Stanhope, *Life*, iii, 248.
120. Ibid., 249.
121. Mackesy, *War without victory*, p. 174; Aspinall, *George III*, iii, 428.
122. Mackesy, *War without victory*, p. 175.
123. Pitt to Addington, 8 October 1800 (quoted in Stanhope, *Life*, iii, 244).
124. Mackesy, *War without victory*, p. 174.
125. Ziegler, *Addington*, p. 89.
126. *Addington correspondence*, i, 267.
127. Quoted in Mackesy, *War without victory*, p. 175.
128. *Glenbervie diaries*, i, 167, 169, 174–5, 180.
129. Mackesy, *War without victory*, p. 176.
130. Feiling, *The second tory party*, p. 221.
131. *PH*, xxxv, 495.
132. Ibid., 498, 500.
133. Ibid., 522.
134. Auckland to Beresford, 18 November 1800 (*Beresford correspondence*, ii, 254).
135. *Corrigan's fever and famine* (quoted in 'William Wilde's table of Irish famines, 900–1850'), p. 16.
136. Ibid.

137. Marsden to John King (PRO, HO 100/94, f. 171).
138. *Castlereagh correspondence*, iii, 392.
139. Cornwallis to Ross, 24 October 1800 (*Cornwallis correspondence*, iii, 295).
140. Portland to Cornwallis, 28 November 1800 (PRO, HO 100/94, f. 235).
141. Cornwallis to Portland, 3 December 1800 (PRO, HO 100/94, f. 257).
142. Ibid., f. 259.
143. Cooke to Castlereagh, 6 January 1801 (*Castlereagh correspondence*, iv, 15).
144. Waliszewski, *Paul the first*, pp. 375–6.
145. Ehrman, *Pitt*, iii, 397.
146. Ibid.
147. Waliszewski, *Paul the first*, p. 334.
148. Ibid., p. 333.
149. Kenney, 'Lord Whitworth and the conspiracy against Tsar Paul I', p. 205.
150. Hyde, *Castlereagh*, pp. 387–9.
151. Cornwallis to Ross, 8 October 1800 (*Cornwallis correspondence*, iii, 294).
152. Cornwallis to Ross, 24 October 1800 (*Cornwallis correspondence*, iii, 296).
153. Cornwallis to Portland, [early September] 1800 (*Castlereagh correspondence*, iii, 374–5).
154. Cornwallis to Ross, 24 October 1800 (*Cornwallis correspondence*, iii, 296).
155. Ibid.
156. Cornwallis to Portland, 1 December 1800 (*Cornwallis correspondence*, iii, 307).
157. Ibid.
158. Cornwallis to Ross, 25 December 1800 (*Cornwallis correspondence*, iii, 315).
159. Cornwallis to Ross, 12 December 1800 (*Cornwallis correspondence*, iii, 310).
160. Cornwallis to Ross, 18 December 1800 (*Cornwallis correspondence*, iii, 313).
161. Cornwallis to Ross, 25 December 1800 (*Cornwallis correspondence*, iii, 315).
162. Cornwallis to Ross, 18 December 1800 (*Cornwallis correspondence*, iii, 313).
163. Ibid.
164. Cornwallis to bishop of Lichfield and Coventry, 22 December 1800 (*Cornwallis correspondence*, iii, 314).
165. Cornwallis to Ross, 25 December 1800 (*Cornwallis correspondence*, iii, 316).
166. Cornwallis to Castlereagh, 29 December 1800 (*Castlereagh correspondence*, iii, 418).
167. Cornwallis to Ross, 30 December 1800 (*Cornwallis correspondence*, iii, 317).
168. Ibid.
169. See Bartlett, 'A weapon of war yet untried'.
170. Cornwallis to Ross, 30 December 1800 (*Cornwallis correspondence*, iii, 317).
171. Campbell, *Lord chancellors*, vi, 308.
172. Camden, 'Memorandum'.
173. Hyde, *Castlereagh*, p. 391.
174. Ibid.
175. Castlereagh to Pitt, 1 January 1801 (CUL, Add. MS 6958, f. 2,827).
176. Ibid.
177. See earlier for 'good genius' reference; for 'evil genius' see Cornwallis to Castlereagh, 2 January 1801 (*Castlereagh correspondence*, iv, 13).
178. Cooke to Castlereagh, 9 January 1801 (*Castlereagh correspondence*, iv, 17).
179. Ibid.
180. Cooke to Castlereagh, 11 January 1801 (*Castlereagh correspondence*, iv, 18–19).
181. Ibid., 19–20.
182. Taken from Cornwallis's response, 14 January 1801 (*Castlereagh correspondence*, iv, 20).
183. Ibid., 20.
184. Ibid., 21.
185. Cornwallis to Castlereagh, 22 January 1801 (*Castlereagh correspondence*, iv, 21).

186. Mackesy, *War without victory*, pp. 186–7.
187. Camden, 'Memorandum', p. 251.
188. Feiling, *The second tory party*, p. 213.
189. Camden, 'Memorandum', p. 251. Charles Fedorak has questioned the objectivity of the Camden memorandum ('Catholic emancipation and the resignation of William Pitt', p. 51), but as Ehrman has pointed out Camden's account is by no means uncritical of Pitt (*Pitt*, iii, chapter xv).
190. Camden, 'Memorandum', p. 251.
191. Mackesy, *War without victory*, p. 187.
192. Pitt to Canning, 10 January 1801 (Willis, 'The politics of parliament', p. 69).
193. Camden, 'Memorandum', p. 250.
194. Ibid., p. 251.
195. Ibid.
196. Ibid., p. 252.
197. Mackesy, *War without victory*, p. 188.
198. Willis, 'Cabinet politics', p. 21.
199. See Ehrman, *Pitt*, iii, 503, fn. 1.
200. Pares, *George III and the politicians*, p. 156, fn. 1.
201. Willis, 'Cabinet politics', p. 21.
202. Pares, *George III and the politicians*, p. 156, fn. 1.
203. Camden, 'Memorandum', p. 252.
204. Ibid.

Chapter 7 The fall of Pitt (pp. 156–91)
  1. Camden, 'Memorandum', p. 252.
  2. This historiography of the crisis will be dealt with in the final chapter. As there are so many conflicting interpretations about what actually occurred, I think it is necessary to provide my own chronology and narrative of events, as they inevitably determine the conclusions that are drawn.
  3. Camden, 'Memorandum', p. 252.
  4. BL, Add. MS 29475, f. 35.
  5. Willis, 'The politics of parliament', pp. 87 and 92.
  6. Ibid., p. 64.
  7. 14 February 1801 (*Glenbervie diaries*, i, 168).
  8. 24 February 1801 (*Malmesbury diaries*, iv, 16).
  9. 9 February 1801 (*Glenbervie diaries*, i, 158).
 10. Willis, 'The politics of parliament', p. 88.
 11. Auckland to Pitt, 16 March 1795 (CUL, Add. MS 6958, f. 1,681).
 12. Ziegler, *Addington*, p. 84.
 13. A.D. Harvey, *William Pitt the younger, 1759–1806: a bibliography* (London, 1989), introduction.
 14. Pitt to Auckland, 20 January 1797 (BL, Add. MS 46491, ff. 164–5).
 15. Auckland to Pitt, 21 January 1797 (BL, Add. MS 46491, f. 167).
 16. Pitt to Auckland, 22 January 1797 (BL, Add. MS 59704, f. 11).
 17. Auckland to Pitt, 22 January 1797 (BL, Add. MS 46491, f. 170).
 18. Pitt to Auckland, 23 January 1797 (BL, Add. MS 46491, ff. 172–3).
 19. Auckland to Pitt, 23 January 1797 (BL, Add. MS 59704, f. 20).
 20. Ibid.
 21. See Ehrman, *Pitt*, iii, chapter iii for some speculations about the matter. In 1799 Eleanor Eden married Lord Hobart, the former Irish chief secretary. When Pitt found out he wrote to Auckland expressing that 'there could be no event interesting to any part of your family which would not be so to me, and certainly this is not the

instance where I feel sentiment the least. I congratulate you and all around you with the most cordial good wishes' (*Auckland correspondence*, iv, 96).

22. Camden, 'Memorandum', p. 252.
23. 29 January 1801 (*Glenbervie diaries*, i, 147).
24. Camden, 'Memorandum', pp. 252–3.
25. Quoted in Mackesy, *War without victory*, p. 189, fn. 11.
26. Camden, 'Memorandum', p. 253. Camden had been unable to authenticate this story.
27. 29 January 1801 (*Glenbervie diaries*, i, 149).
28. Ibid.
29. Ibid., 150.
30. Quoted by Walter Bagehot, 'William Pitt' (in Norman St John-Stevans (ed.), *Bagehot's historical essays* (New York, 1966), pp. 49–50).
31. Camden, 'Memorandum', p. 253.
32. Ibid.
33. Quoted in Aspinall, *George III*, iii, 475.
34. Ibid.
35. 16 March 1801 (*Glenbervie diaries*, i, 200). The story would appear to have some basis in truth given that Addington, when he formed his ministry, appears to have been of the opinion that Loughborough had resigned.
36. Loughborough to George III, 28 January 1801 (Aspinall, *George III*, iii, 475).
37. *Auckland correspondence*, iv, 114.
38. Pitt to Auckland, 31 January 1801 (BL, Add. MS 34455, f. 370).
39. Ibid., f. 371.
40. Auckland to Pitt, 31 January 1801 (Aspinall, *George III*, iii, 481).
41. George III to Addington, 29 January 1801 (Aspinall, *George III*, iii, 476).
42. Ibid., 477.
43. Addington to George III, 29 January 1801 (Aspinall, *George III*, iii, 477).
44. Camden, 'Memorandum', pp. 253–4.
45. Ibid., p. 254.
46. Ibid.
47. Pitt to George III, 31 January 1801 (CUL, Add. MS 6958, f. 2,836).
48. Bolton, *The passing of the Irish act of union*, pp. 210–11. Bolton's error comes from reading out of context two letters of George III and Loughborough.
49. Quoted in Camden, 'Memorandum', p. 255.
50. CUL, Add. MS 6958, f. 2,836.
51. Pitt to Grenville, 1 February 1801 (HMC, *Dropmore papers*, vi, 434).
52. George III to Pitt, 1 February 1801 (CUL, Add. MS 6958, f. 2,837).
53. Pitt to Grenville, 1 February 1801 (HMC, *Dropmore papers*, vi, 434).
54. 2 February 1801 (*Glenbervie diaries*, i, 151).
55. Pitt to Grenville, 1 February 1801 (HMC, *Dropmore papers*, vi, 434).
56. Grenville to Pitt, 1 February 1801 (CUL, Add. MS 6958, f. 2,838).
57. Hamilton to Holland, 1 February 1801 (BL, Add. MS 51570, f. 71).
58. Grenville to Buckingham, 2 February 1801 (Buckingham, *Courts*, iii, 128).
59. Ibid., 129.
60. Ibid., 131.
61. Buckingham to Grenville, 3 February 1801 (HMC, *Dropmore papers*, vi, 435).
62. 3 February 1801 (*Glenbervie diaries*, i, 153).
63. Ibid.
64. Pitt to George III, 3 February 1801 (CUL, Add. MS 6958, f. 2,841).
65. Grenville to Buckingham, 4 February 1801 (Buckingham, *Courts*, iii, 136).
66. Quoted in I.R. Christie, *Wars and revolutions: Britain 1760–1815* (London, 1982), p. 388.

67. George III to Pitt, 5 February 1801 (CUL, Add. MS 6958, f. 2,842).
68. Grenville to George III, 5 February 1801 (CUL, Add. MS 6958, f. 2,843).
69. 2 February 1801 (*Glenbervie diaries*, i, 152).
70. Ehrman, *Pitt*, iii, 509.
71. Quoted in *Addington correspondence*, i, 287.
72. 14 February 1801 (*Malmesbury diaries*, iv, 8).
73. *Addington correspondence*, i, 340–41.
74. 5 February 1801 (*Malmesbury diaries*, iv, 2).
75. Ibid.
76. 6 February 1801 (*Malmesbury diaries*, iv, 3).
77. PRO, 30/8/122/2, f. 151.
78. Ibid., f. 152.
79. Ibid. John Ehrman has speculated that Chatham was jealous of his younger brother. Certainly a strain had been placed on the relationship in 1795 when Pitt had been forced to reshuffle his brother from the admiralty because of his inadequacy (CUL, Add. MS 6958, ff. 1,537, 1,558, 1,564, 1,565, 1,566). In 1803 Chatham was reported to be complaining 'loudly' about his brother's conduct (HMC, *Dropmore papers*, vii, 195).
80. Dundas to George III, 6 February 1801 (CUL, Add. MS 6958, f. 2,844).
81. Grenville to Lord Minto, 13 February 1801 (HMC, *Dropmore papers*, vi, 445).
82. Grenville to Carysfort, 6 February 1801 (HMC, *Dropmore papers*, vi, 435).
83. Ibid., 436.
84. The years would not see any alteration in this line of conduct. In 1809 Grenville revealed that he was convinced that 'every public man is bound, especially in those awful times in which our lot has been cast, to labour to the utmost of his power for the union and harmony of a people having the same interests to defend, and the same dangers to fear' (Grenville to the earl of Fingall, 4 January 1809 (HMC, *Dropmore papers*, ix, 255)). Grenville's beliefs on the catholic question were not just determined by a sense of what was right. They were also grounded in the very real sense of what was best for the empire. Emancipation would serve to join the catholics in Ireland in a union of interest and affection with the protestants in Britain. Therefore securing emancipation Grenville considered to be 'numbered among the most important services that can be rendered to the British empire' (ibid.). Grenville, in a letter in the same year to Dr Hodson, the principal of Brasenose College, Oxford, revealed that he had opposed catholic concessions after 1793. It was only through the union that he and Pitt had believed they could be safely conceded, 'accompanied always by such securities and safeguards for the interests of the church as might remove all apprehensions for that object, to which no public men ever were more sincerely attached' (Grenville to Hodson, 2 November 1809 (HMC, *Dropmore papers*, ix, 360)).
85. 7 February 1801 (*Malmesbury diaries*, iv, 4).
86. 8 February 1801 (*Glenbervie diaries*, i, 156).
87. 7 February 1801 (*Cornwallis correspondence*, iii, 333).
88. 9 February 1801 (*Glenbervie diaries*, i, 156–7).
89. Dundas to Pitt, 7 February 1801 (CUL, Add. MS 6958, f. 2,845).
90. 10 February 1801 (*Malmesbury diaries*, iv, 5).
91. Malmesbury paraphrased the conversation, 8 February 1801 (*Malmesbury diaries*, iv, 4).
92. Redesdale to Pitt, 16 April 1803 (PRO, 30/8/170/2, f. 204).
93. Lady Stafford to Granville Leveson-Gower, 8 February 1801 (Granville (ed.), *Private correspondence of Lord Granville Leveson-Gower*, i, 291).
94. Auckland to William Eden, 8 February 1801 (BL, Add. MS 34455, f. 372).
95. Auckland to Addington, 9 February 1801 (BL, Add. MS 34455, f. 373).

96. 10 February 1801 (*Malmesbury diaries*, iv, 5).
97. 9 February 1801 (*Glenbervie diaries*, i, 158).
98. 15 November 1801 (*Glenbervie diaries*, i, 284).
99. Quoted in Ziegler, *Addington*, p. 131.
100. *The Times*, 9 February 1801.
101. *PH*, xxxv, 945.
102. The report was by Pretyman, who was present (CUL, Add. MS 6968, f. 2,847*).
103. Told to Croker (in L.J. Jennings (ed.), *The Croker papers: the correspondence and diaries of the late Right Honourable John Wilson Croker* (2 vols., London, 1884), ii, 340).
104. Ibid.
105. 15 February 1801 (*Glenbervie diaries*, i, 169).
106. 14 February 1801 (*Glenbervie diaries*, i, 167).
107. 7 and 12 February 1801 (*Malmesbury diaries*, iv, 7, 9).
108. Ehrman, *Pitt*, iii, 514, fn. 4.
109. 21 February 1801 (*Malmesbury diaries*, iv, 14).
110. 9 February 1801 (*Glenbervie diaries*, i, 158); Norman Gash, *Lord Liverpool* (London, 1984), p. 38.
111. 14 February 1801 (*Glenbervie diaries*, i, 167).
112. Hinde, *George Canning*, p. 81.
113. 3 March 1801 (*Glenbervie diaries*, i, 186).
114. 12 March 1801 (*Malmesbury diaries*, iv, 44).
115. *Addington correspondence*, i, 286.
116. Reported by Fitzharris, 4 March 1801 (*Malmesbury diaries*, iv, 27).
117. Ibid.
118. 19 February 1801 (*Glenbervie diaries*, i, 173).
119. Buckingham to Grenville, 26 September 1802 (HMC, *Dropmore papers*, vii, 111).
120. George III to Pitt, 18 February 1801 (CUL, Add. MS 6958, f. 2,849).
121. Quoted in Ida MacAlpine and Richard Hunter, *George III and the mad business* (London, 1969), p. 112.
122. Ibid.
123. 24 February 1801 (*Glenbervie diaries*, i, 180).
124. 4 March 1801 (*Malmesbury diaries*, iv, 27).
125. 19 February 1801 (*Glenbervie diaries*, i, 173). But from the reference to the council must have occurred on 20 February.
126. 21 February 1801 (*Malmesbury diaries*, iv, 14).
127. MacAlpine and Hunter, *George III and the mad business*, p. 112.
128. 4 March 1801 (*Malmesbury diaries*, iv, 27).
129. 22 February 1801 (*Malmesbury diaries*, iv, 14).
130. George III to Pitt, 22 February 1801 (CUL, Add. MS 6958, f. 2,851).
131. Notes taken on 23 February 1801 (CUL, Add. MS 6958, f. 2,851*).
132. 22 February 1801 (*Malmesbury diaries*, iv, 15).
133. Addington to Chatham, 9 February 1801 (PRO, 30/70/227/G10).
134. Pole to Wellesley, 10 February 1801 (BL, Add. MS 37416, f. 74).
135. Ibid.
136. 12 February 1801 (*Malmesbury diaries*, iv, 7).
137. 14 February 1801 (*Malmesbury diaries*, iv, 7).
138. George III to Addington, 13 February 1801 (Aspinall, *George III*, iii, 409).
139. Grenville to Rufus King, 13 February 1801 (HMC, *Dropmore papers*, vi, 447).
140. 19 February 1801 (*Glenbervie diaries*, i, 176). But from the reference to the council must have occurred on 20 February.
141. Grenville to Buckingham, 20 February 1801 (Buckingham, *Courts*, iii, 139).
142. 14 February 1801 (*Malmesbury diaries*, iv, 8).

143. Canning to Sneyd, 14 February 1801 (Josceline Bagot (ed.), *George Canning and his friends* (2 vols., London, 1909), i, 180).
144. Quoted in Hinde, *George Canning*, p. 94.
145. Leveson-Gower to his mother, 7 February 1801 (Granville (ed.), *Private correspondence of Lord Granville Leveson-Gower*, i, 290).
146. 17 February 1801 (*Glenbervie diaries*, i, 171).
147. *The Times*, 12 February 1801.
148. *The Times*, 13 February 1801.
149. 16 February 1801 (*Malmesbury diaries*, iv, 9).
150. Fox to Denis O'Brien, 16 February 1801 (BL, Add. MS 47566, f. 72).
151. Ibid., f. 73.
152. Quoted by Edward Lascelles, *The life of Charles James Fox* (New York, 1970), p. 290.
153. Fox to Denis O'Brien, 16 February 1801 (BL, Add. MS 47566, f. 73).
154. 16 February 1801 (*PH*, xxxv, 958).
155. Ibid., 970.
156. The exceptions were at the admiralty and foreign office, see Grenville to Minto, 6 March 1801 (HMC, *Dropmore papers*, vi, 462).
157. 27 February 1801 (*Malmesbury diaries*, iv, 24).
158. 25 February 1801 (*Malmesbury diaries*, iv, 16).
159. Ibid., 17.
160. MacAlpine and Hunter, *George III and the mad business*, p. 116.
161. Quoted ibid.
162. 24 and 26 February 1801 (*Malmesbury diaries*, iv, 16 and 17).
163. Quoted in MacAlpine and Hunter, *George III and the mad business*, p. 116.
164. 26 February 1801 (*Malmesbury diaries*, iv, 17).
165. 26 February 1801 (*Malmesbury diaries*, iv, 17).
166. 28 February 1801 (*Glenbervie diaries*, i, 183).
167. Ibid., 184.
168. Grenville to Carysfort, 2 March 1801 (HMC, *Dropmore papers*, vi, 459).
169. 2 and 3 March 1801 (*Malmesbury diaries*, iv, 23).
170. *Malmesbury diaries*, iv, 26.
171. Ibid.
172. Ibid., 27.
173. Ibid., 28.
174. Pretyman to his wife, 25 February 1801, *English historical documents*, p. 164; in *EHD* it is wrongly attributed to George Rose but John Ehrman has corrected this mistake (*Pitt*, iii, 530). I disagree with Ehrman that Pitt thought the cabinets on emancipation 'hasty'; this appears to have been Pretyman's own interpretation.
175. 7 March 1801 (*Malmesbury diaries*, iv, 31).
176. Ibid.
177. 19 August 1804 (*Glenbervie diaries*, i, 389).
178. See Stanhope, *Life*, iii, 304–5, and Ehrman, *Pitt*, iii, 528, fn. 5.
179. The countess of Carysfort in a letter to Grenville in 1803 revealed that Pitt had 'made Dr Thomas Willis the channel of a promise which he made to the king never to bring forward the Roman Catholic question' (HMC, *Dropmore papers*, vii, 195). The countess speculated that 'the promise *did never actually* reach' George III. George Rose repeated the pledge to the king in August 1801 in Pitt's name (Ehrman, *Pitt*, iii, 528).
180. Quoted in MacAlpine and Hunter, *George III and the mad business*, p. 118.
181. Ibid., p. 119.
182. 7 March 1801 (*Malmesbury diaries*, iv, 31).
183. Ibid., 32.
184. Ibid., 33.
185. 8 March 1801 (*Malmesbury diaries*, iv, 36).

186. Ibid., 35.
187. Ibid., 36.
188. Ibid., 37.
189. Ibid., 35.
190. CUL, Add. MS 6958, f. 2,859.
191. Dundas's draft of a new cabinet, 1801 (BL, Add. MS 40102, ff. 94–5).
192. 9 March 1801 (*Malmesbury diaries*, iv, 37).
193. Ibid., 38.
194. 11 March 1801 (*Malmesbury diaries*, iv, 42).
195. 9 March 1801 (*Malmesbury diaries*, iv, 39).
196. Ibid. Note the similarities between this statement and the king's opinion quoted by Buckingham.
197. Ibid., 40.
198. Pitt to Willis, 9 March 1801 (BL, Add. MS 41694, f. 66).
199. 10 March 1801 (*Malmesbury diaries*, iv, 41–2).
200. Ibid., 42.
201. Loughborough to George III, March 1801 (Campbell, *Lord chancellors*, vi, 317).
202. Campbell, *Lord chancellors*, vi, 319.
203. He apparently attended four cabinets after he had formally handed over his great seal, until Addington wrote to him on 25 April 1801 informing him that 'much as I should feel personally gratified in having the benefit of your lordship's counsel and assistance', his presence was no longer required or wanted (*English historical documents*, p. 87).
204. Campbell, *Lord chancellors*, vi, 334). Brougham, *Historical sketches*, ii, 107.
205. *Glenbervie diaries*, i, 196.
206. 12 March 1801 (*Malmesbury diaries*, iv, 43).
207. 14 March 1801 (*Malmesbury diaries*, iv, 45).
208. 17 March 1801 (*Malmesbury diaries*, iv, 46).
209. Ibid., 47.
210. 16 March 1801 (*Malmesbury diaries*, iv, 45).
211. 17 March 1801 (*Malmesbury diaries*, iv, 47).
212. Original note to *Malmesbury diaries*, iv, 47.
213. Grenville to Carysfort, 16 March 1801 (HMC, *Dropmore papers*, vi, 473).
214. Grenville to Carysfort, 24 March 1801 (HMC, *Dropmore papers*, vi, 474).
215. Ibid., 475.
216. 20 March 1801 (*PH*, xxxv, 1,200).
217. Ibid., 1,201.
218. Ibid., 1,202.
219. 22 March 1801 (*Malmesbury diaries*, iv, 50).
220. 21 March 1801 (*Malmesbury diaries*, iv, 49).
221. Ibid., 50.
222. 24 March 1801 (*Malmesbury diaries*, iv, 51).
223. Ehrman, *Pitt*, iii, 552; and see 25 March, *Glenbervie diaries*, i, 205.

Chapter 8 Ireland, the catholic question and concealment (pp. 192–207)
1. Barrington, *Historic memoirs*, ii, 332.
2. Quoted by Cooke to Castlereagh, 29 January 1801 (*Castlereagh correspondence*, iv, 24).
3. Cornwallis to Castlereagh, 2 February 1801 (*Castlereagh correspondence*, iv, 25).
4. Ibid., 24.
5. *Castlereagh correspondence*, iv, 26.
6. Cooke to Castlereagh, 5 February 1801 (*Castlereagh correspondence*, iv, 26).
7. Ibid.

8. Cooke to Castlereagh, 6 February 1801 (*Castlereagh correspondence*, iv, 26).
9. Ibid., 27.
10. Cooke to Castlereagh, 9 February 1801 (*Castlereagh correspondence*, iv, 28).
11. Cooke to Castlereagh, 7 March 1801 (*Castlereagh correspondence*, iv, 78).
12. Cooke to Castlereagh, 9 February 1801 (*Castlereagh correspondence*, iv, 28).
13. Ibid., 29.
14. *Castlereagh correspondence*, iv, 47.
15. CUL, Add. MS 6958, f. 2,847.
16. Cornwallis to Castlereagh, 12 February 1801 (*Castlereagh correspondence*, iv, 48).
17. Ibid., 47.
18. Cooke to Castlereagh, 11 February 1801 (*Castlereagh correspondence*, iv, 47).
19. Pole to Marquess Wellesley, 10 February 1801 (BL, Add. MS 37416, f. 75).
20. *Castlereagh correspondence*, iv, 41.
21. Ibid., 46.
22. Quoted in A.C. Kavanaugh, *John Fitzgibbon, earl of Clare* (Dublin, 1997), p. 369.
23. Conolly to Castlereagh, 13 February 1801 (*Castlereagh correspondence*, iv, 48).
24. R.G. Thorne (ed.), *The commons, 1790–1820* (London, 1986), iii, 752.
25. Cornwallis to Castlereagh, 14 February 1801 (*Castlereagh correspondence*, iv, 50).
26. Cooke to Castlereagh, 3 March 1801 (*Castlereagh correspondence*, iv, 70).
27. Cornwallis to Castlereagh, 16 February 1801 (*Castlereagh correspondence*, iv, 50).
28. Ibid.
29. Cooke to Castlereagh, 16 February 1801 (*Castlereagh correspondence*, iv, 51).
30. Cooke to Castlereagh, 23 February 1801 (*Castlereagh correspondence*, iv, 60).
31. Ibid., 61.
32. Cooke to Castlereagh, 25 February 1801 (*Castlereagh correspondence*, iv, 62).
33. Ibid.
34. Cooke to Castlereagh, 27 February 1801 (*Castlereagh correspondence*, iv, 63).
35. Ibid., 64.
36. *The Morning Chronicle*, 12 March 1801.
37. *Malmesbury diaries*, iv, 13.
38. Cornwallis to bishop of Lichfield and Coventry, 17 February 1801 (*Cornwallis correspondence*, iii, 338).
39. Cornwallis to Ross, 26 February 1801 (*Cornwallis correspondence*, iii, 340).
40. Cornwallis to Castlereagh, 7 March 1801 (NLI, MS 55, f. 202).
41. Cornwallis to Ross, 4 August 1801 (*Cornwallis correspondence*, iii, 38).
42. Cornwallis to Ross, 13 February 1804 (*Cornwallis correspondence*, iii, 511).
43. Castlereagh's draft observations on the change of ministers (PRONI, D3030/1678A, f. 713). The original of the paper is in the PRONI with a transcript in the Castlereagh correspondence. A close examination of the original document reveals, however, that the folios were numbered incorrectly and the transcript follows this error. From the quality of the ink, and also internal evidence, the paper was actually written with ff. 717–20 coming after ff. 721–4.
44. Ibid., f. 721.
45. Ibid., f. 722.
46. Ibid., f. 724.
47. Ibid., f. 717. Note how this section logically follows on from f. 724.
48. Ibid., f. 719.
49. Ibid.
50. 11 March 1801 (*Malmesbury diaries*, iv, 42).
51. Cooke to Castlereagh, 23 March 1801 (*Castlereagh correspondence*, iv, 83).
52. Census of 1851 (quoted extensively in O'Brien, *The economic history of Ireland from the union to the famine*, p. 226); Cooke to Castlereagh, 7 March 1801 (*Castlereagh correspondence*, iv, 78).

53. Cooke to Castlereagh, 7 March 1801 (*Castlereagh correspondence*, iv, 78).
54. Ibid., 79.
55. Resolution of the house of commons, 27 February 1801 (*Castlereagh correspondence*, iv, 69).
56. Cooke to the treasury, 18 March 1801 (BL, Add. MS 40204, f. 343).
57. Beresford to Auckland, 1 August 1801 (*Beresford correspondence*, ii, 257).
58. Cooke to Castlereagh, 18 February 1801 (*Castlereagh correspondence*, iv, 53).
59. Wickham to Portland, 3 January 1801 (BL, Add. MS 33107, ff. 1–2).
60. Wells, *Insurrection*, p. 31.
61. Wells, *Wretched faces*, p. 285.
62. Quoted in Wells, *Insurrection*, p. 30.
63. Wickham to Grenville, 7 March 1801 (HMC, *Dropmore papers*, vi, 467).
64. Ibid., 466–7.
65. Hawkesbury to Grenville, 18 March 1801 (HMC, *Dropmore papers*, vi, 474).
66. Cornwallis to Ross, 18 April 1801 (*Cornwallis correspondence*, iii, 356).
67. Wells, *Insurrection*, p. 31.
68. Cornwallis to Ross, 22 April 1801 (*Cornwallis correspondence*, iii, 357).
69. Cornwallis to Ross, 7 May 1801 (*Cornwallis correspondence*, iii, 359).
70. 22 August 1822 (in A. Aspinall (ed.), *The diary of Henry Hobhouse, 1820–1827* (London, 1947), p. 93).
71. Hyde, *The strange death of Lord Castlereagh*.
72. Aspinall (ed.), *The diary of Henry Hobhouse*, p. 93.
73. Ibid., p. 166.
74. C.L. Falkiner, *Studies in Irish history and biography* (London, 1902), p. 181.
75. Hyde, *The strange death of Lord Castlereagh*, p. 84.
76. Ibid., p. 154.
77. Ibid., p. 77.
78. Ibid., pp. 101–2.
79. Ibid., p. 147.
80. Ibid., p. 145.
81. Pitt to Addington, 26 June 1801 (Aspinall, *George III*, iii, 565).
82. Addington to George III, 11 May 1801 (Aspinall, *George III*, iii, 535).
83. George III to Addington (Aspinall, *George III*, iii, 535).
84. Portland to Pelham, 11 June 1801 (Aspinall, *George III*, iii, 564–5).
85. Aspinall, *George III*, iii, xxi.
86. PRO, HO 387.
87. Cooke to Auckland, 8 October 1801 (PRONI, T3229/2/65).
88. Cooke to John King, 28 August 1801 (BL, Add. MS 60338, f. 78).
89. Conversation on 31 August 1801 (BL, Add. MS 35730, f. 233).
90. Beresford to Auckland, 5 September 1801 (PRONI, 99T3229/2/63).
91. Cooke to Auckland, 25 September 1801 (PRONI, T3229/2/64).
92. Cooke to Auckland, 8 October 1801 (PRONI, T3229/2/65).
93. Ibid.
94. Ibid.
95. Cooke to George Shee, 4 October 1801 (PRO, HO 100/104, f. 141). Aspinall has claimed that the details of how government controlled the press 'will probably never be revealed' but the evidence of the secret service papers provides a likely answer (Arthur Aspinall, *Politics and the press*, 1780–1850 (London, 1949), p. 114).
96. John King to Cooke, 10 October 1801 (BL, Add. MS 60338, f. 80).
97. *PH*, xxxvi, 651.
98. Malcomson, *John Foster*, p. 94.
99. Redesdale to Perceval, 5 November 1804 (BL, Add. MS 49188, f. 179).

100. Ibid., f. 180.
101. Malcomson, *John Foster*, p. 413.
102. Ibid., p. 81.
103. Redesdale to Perceval, 5 November 1804 (BL, Add. MS 49188, f. 179).
104. Marsden to Redesdale, 10 December 1804 (BL, Add. MS 35725, f. 104).
105. Marsden to Hardwicke, 7 December 1804 (BL, Add. MS 35725, f. 100).
106. Marsden to Redesdale, 10 December 1804 (BL, Add. MS 35725, f. 104).
107. Marsden to Redesdale, [December 1804] (BL, Add. MS 35725, f. 132).

Chapter 9 The search for character (pp. 208–26)
   1. London, 1761.
   2. Introduction.
   3. I would like to thank John Ehrman for his kind assistance with my Ph.D. thesis, which was the basis of this book. The title of this chapter is itself a reference to chapter xvii of the final volume of his biography of Pitt, entitled 'In pursuit of character'. That chapter dealt with the interlude after Pitt's retirement from office, but throughout the book the sense of 'character' is crucial in the examination of his life.
   4. Ehrman, *Pitt*, iii, 509; Pares's quote is from the first page of his *George III and the politicians*.
   5. Pitt's letter to the town's clerk of the city of London, 15 October 1761 (*Case of Mr Pitt's late resignation set in a true light, 1761*, p. 6).
   6. See Brown, *William Pitt, earl of Chatham*, p. 256.
   7. *Anecdotes of the life of the Right Honourable William Pitt, earl of Chatham* (2 vols., London, 1796), i, 371.
   8. Brown, *William Pitt, earl of Chatham*, p. 251.
   9. O'Reilly, *Pitt the younger*, p. 304.
  10. Pitt to Bute (quoted in Brown, *William Pitt, earl of Chatham*, p. 242).
  11. Quoted in Erich Eyck, *Pitt versus Fox: father and son, 1735–1806* (London, 1950), p. 94.
  12. Ibid., p. 215.
  13. Brown, *William Pitt, earl of Chatham*, p. 394.
  14. Eyck, *Pitt versus Fox*, p. 219.
  15. Ehrman, *Pitt*, i, 65, fn. 2.
  16. Bagehot, 'William Pitt' in St John-Stevans (ed.), *Bagehot's historical essays*, p. 51.
  17. Jennings (ed.), *The Croker papers*, ii, 340.
  18. Stanley Ayling, *The elder Pitt: earl of Chatham* (London, 1976), p. 10.
  19. Ehrman, *Pitt*, iii, 851.
  20. Ibid., 851–2.
  21. Ibid., 853.
  22. Mackintosh (ed.), *Memoirs of the Rt Hon. Sir James Mackintosh*, i, 170.
  23. Kenneth Baker, *The prime ministers: an irreverent political history in cartoons* (Slovenia, 1995), pp. 63–4.
  24. 20 March 1801 (*PH*, xxxvi, 1, 178).
  25. *Public characters* (Baltimore, 1803), p. 288.
  26. William Hazlitt, 'Character of Mr Pitt, 1806' (in A.R. Waller and Arnold Glover (eds.), *The collected works of William Hazlitt* (London, 1902), p. 346).
  27. Although the article is included in Hazlitt's collection of essays so the authorship may have been shared or it may even have been completely written by Hazlitt.
  28. *The Morning Post*, 19 March 1800 (in Waller and Glover (eds.), *The collected works of William Hazlitt*, p. 351).
  29. Ibid., p. 355.

30. Ibid., p. 356.
31. Campbell, *Lord chancellors*, vi, 296.
32. Stanhope, *Life*, iii, 266–75; Rosebery, *Pitt*, pp. 222–31.
33. Stanhope, *Life*, iii, 310–13.
34. Ashbourne, *Pitt: some chapters of his life and times*, p. 301.
35. Ibid., p. 308.
36. Ibid., p. 303.
37. Lord Macaulay, *William Pitt* (London, 1904), p. 54.
38. Bagehot, 'William Pitt' (St John-Stevans (ed.), *Bagehot's historical essays*, p. 44).
39. Ibid., p. 49.
40. Ibid., pp. 70–71.
41. Lecky, *Ireland*, v, 442.
42. Ibid., 444–5.
43. Ibid., 456.
44. Ibid., 457–8.
45. Ibid., 458–9.
46. B.W. Pickering (ed.), *The works of the Right Honourable John Hookham Frere in verse and prose* (London, 1874); Festing, *John Hookham Frere and his friends*.
47. Festing, *John Hookham Frere and his friends*, p. 82.
48. Ibid., p. 44.
49. J.H. Rose, *Life of William Pitt* (London, 1923); *A short life of William Pitt* (London, 1925).
50. Rose, *A short life of William Pitt*, p. 181.
51. Hyde, *Castlereagh*, p. 398.
52. P.W. Wilson, *William Pitt the younger* (New York, 1933), pp. 292–6; E.K. Chatterton, *England's greatest statesman: a life of William Pitt, 1759–1806* (Indianapolis, 1930).
53. Chatterton, *England's greatest statesman*, p. 315.
54. D.G. Barnes, *George III and William Pitt, 1783–1806: a new interpretation based upon a study of their unpublished correspondence* (New York, 1965).
55. Ibid., p. 326.
56. Ibid., preface, p. ix.
57. Ibid., p. 351.
58. Ibid., p. 368.
59. Ibid., pp. 379–80.
60. Pares, *George III and the politicians*, p. 1.
61. Ibid., pp. 163–4.
62. Ibid., p. 180.
63. Bolton, *The passing of the Irish act of union*, p. 212.
64. Ibid., p. 214.
65. Ziegler, *Addington*, p. 90.
66. Ibid.
67. Ibid., p. 105. Ziegler agrees with Lecky's assertion that Pitt's actions could not 'unfairly' be called 'a gross breach of faith with the catholics'.
68. Ibid., pp. 107–8.
69. Ibid., p. 109.
70. Willis, 'The politics of parliament'.
71. Richard Willis, 'William Pitt's resignation in 1801: re-examination and document' in *Bulletin of the Institute of Historical Research*, xliv, no. 110 (1971), pp. 239–57.
72. Willis, 'The politics of parliament', p. 80.
73. Ibid., p. 99.
74. Ibid., pp. 99–100.
75. Ibid., p. 101.
76. Willis, 'William Pitt's resignation in 1801', p. 246.

77. Ibid.
78. Ibid., p. 240.
79. Ibid., p. 243.
80. Willis, 'The politics of parliament', p. 73.
81. Willis, 'Cabinet politics', p. 22.
82. Derek Jarrett, *Pitt the younger* (London, 1974), p. 199.
83. Ibid., A.J.P. Taylor's introduction, p. 10.
84. Pitt said there was much to admire in Burke's French writings and nothing to agree with (Ehrman, *Pitt*, ii, 80).
85. Mackesy, *War without victory*, chapter ix, p. 185.
86. Ibid., p. 193.
87. Ibid., p. 195.
88. Ibid., p. 200.
89. Ibid., p. 199.
90. Ibid., p. 200.
91. Ibid., p. 201.
92. Harvey, *William Pitt the younger, 1759–1806: a bibliography*.
93. A.D. Harvey, *Lord Grenville, 1759–1834: a bibliography* (London, 1989).
94. Fedorak, 'Catholic emancipation and the resignation of William Pitt'.
95. Ibid., pp. 49–50.
96. Ibid., p. 50.
97. Ibid., p. 53.
98. Ibid., p. 55.
99. Ibid., p. 58.
100. Ibid., p. 61.
101. Ibid., p. 62.
102. Ibid., p. 63.
103. Ehrman, *Pitt*, iii, 509.
104. Ibid., 510–11.
105. Ibid., 512.
106. Ibid., 517.
107. Ibid., 515.
108. Ibid., 516.
109. Ibid.
110. Ibid., 520.
111. Ibid., 521.
112. Ibid., 530.
113. Ibid., 532.
114. Ibid., 533.
115. Quoted 20 October 1802 (*Malmesbury diaries*, iv, 78).
116. To John Gifford, 11 December 1808 (in *English historical documents*, p. 126).
117. *Malmesbury diaries*, iv, 78.
118. *PH*, xxiii, 553.
119. Ibid., 554.
120. As John Ehrman has written to me: 'After all, Pitt (uniquely in the century?) did not go into opposition for some three years.'
121. 21 April 1800 (*PH*, xxxv, 46).
122. 2 February 1801 (*Glenbervie diaries*, 152). Bagehot elaborates on the maxim in his essay on Pitt: 'to deal shrewdly and adroitly with what must be dealt with; to leave alone what must be left alone' ('William Pitt' in St John-Stevans (ed.), *Bagehot's historical essays*, p. 71).
123. *Glenbervie diaries*, 153.

124. *PH*, xxiii, 829.
125. 21 April 1800 (*PH*, xxxv, 47).
126. Camden, 'Memorandum'.
127. 20 October 1802 (*Malmesbury diaries*, iv, 75).
128. Pitt's father in 1756 had revealed, 'I know that I can save the country and that no one else can' (quoted in Brown, *William Pitt, earl of Chatham*, p. 131); while the younger Pitt was never as direct it was clear that he held a similar, perhaps justified, opinion of his own importance.
129. 'No pressure of public accusation, nor heat of innocence in its own defence, shall ever tempt me to disclose a single circumstance which may tend to humiliate my country' (21 February 1783, *PH*, xxiii, 547).
130. Comments of Pitt quoted in Curzon, *The personal history of Walmer castle and its lords warden*, p. 41, fn. 2.

Bibliography

PRIMARY SOURCES

A. Manuscript Sources

Public Record Office Northern Ireland (Belfast)

D1606	Gosford MSS
D2707	Shannon MSS
D3030	Castlereagh papers
T2519	Foster papers
T2627/1	Hobart papers
T2627/4	Camden papers
T2965	Sheffield papers
T3228	Harrowby papers
T3229	Fitzgibbon papers
T3287	Sneyd (Fitzgibbon) papers
T3319	Additional Pitt papers
T3456/1	Dacres Adams [Pitt] papers

Cambridge University Library
Add. MS 6958 William Pitt correspondence (17 boxes)

National Library of Ireland (Dublin)

MSS 54–5	Melville papers
MSS 886–7	Lord lieutenants' correspondence, 1786–1804
MS 4155	Tracts on the union
MS 5027	Hippisley correspondence
MS 5696	Jonah Barrington's 'black' list
MS 8055	Cabinet minute 'to press for a union', 1798
MS 8056	'Points to be considered . . .'

British Library (London)

Add. MS 29475	Auckland papers
Add. MS 33107	Pelham papers
Add. MS 33130	Pelham papers
Add. MSS 34453–5	Auckland papers
Add. MS 34523	Mackintosh collection
Add. MS 35709	Hardwicke papers
Add. MS 35725	Hardwicke papers
Add. MS 35730	Hardwicke papers
Add. MS 35766	Hardwicke papers
Add. MS 35919	Hardwicke papers
Add. MS 35933	Hardwicke papers
Add. MS 37416	Wellesley papers
Add. MS 37844	Windham papers

Add. MS 37923	Windham papers
Add. MS 38192	Liverpool papers
Add. MS 38736	Huskisson papers
Add. MS 40102	Melville papers
Add. MS 40204	Peel papers
Add. MS 41694	Willis papers
Add. MSS 45107 A–J	Pretyman papers
Add. MS 46491	Auckland papers
Add. MS 46519	Auckland papers
Add. MS 47566	Fox papers
Add. MS 49188	Spencer Perceval papers
Add. MS 51570	Holland house papers
Add. MSS 58908–9	Dropmore papers
Add. MS 58972	Dropmore papers
Add. MS 59407A	Dropmore papers
Add. MS 59704	Pitt papers
Add. MS 60338	Shee papers

Public Record Office (London)

AO1 2122/7	Secret service accounts
PRO	Chatham papers, 30/8/100–331
PRO 30/70	Pitt papers
HO 36, 40	Additional secret service papers
HO 100/79–104	Home office papers for Ireland
HO 387	Secret service papers

Kent Archives Office (Maidstone)
U840 Pratt [Camden] papers

B.   Printed Sources

I.   Parliamentary Records
(a) Statutes etc.
The statutes at large of England and Great Britain. Ed. Danerby Pickering. 46 vols. Cambridge, 1761–1807.
The statutes at large passed in the parliaments held in Ireland . . . Vols. iii–xx. Dublin, 1786–1801.
The statutes revised edition. Vol. iii. London, 1872.

(b) Journals
Journal of the house of commons [of England, Great Britain, and the United Kingdom]. Vols. x–lv.
Journals of the house of commons of the kingdom of Ireland. 3rd ed. Vols ii–xx. Dublin, 1796–1800.

(c) Debates
Debate in the house of commons of Ireland. Dublin, 1799.
Parliamentary History, 1778, 1783, 1798–1802
The parliamentary register, 1798–1801
A report of the debate in the house of commons in Ireland on 22 and 23 January 1799. Dublin, 1799.

A report of the debates in the Irish house of commons on 24, 25, 26, 28 January 1799. Dublin, 1799.

A report of the debate in the house of commons in Ireland on 15 January 1800. Dublin, 1800.

A report of the debate in the house of commons in Ireland on 5 and 6 February 1800. Dublin, 1800.

A report of the debate in the Irish house of commons on 18 February 1800. Dublin, 1800.

A report of the debate in the Irish house of commons on 14 March 1800. Dublin, 1800.

Speeches at the bar and in the senate by the Rt Hon. William Conyngham, Lord Plunket. Ed. J.C. Hoey. Dublin, 1873.

Speeches of the Rt Hon. Henry Grattan. Ed. D.O. Madden. London, 1874.

Speeches of the Rt Hon. William Pitt. Ed. W.S. Hataway. 4 vols. London, 1806.

Union tracts. 9 vols. Dublin, 1799–1800. [The reports for the Irish parliamentary debates are all contained in this collection.]

II. Pamphlets

An impartial account of the life and death of the Rt Hon. William Pitt. Leeds, 1806.

Billy Pitt and the union. Dublin, 1798.

Case of Mr Pitt's late resignation set in a true light. London, 1761.

Conspiracy of Pitt and co. detected. Dublin, 1799.

[Cooke, Edward.] *Arguments for and against an union between Great Britain and Ireland, considered*. Dublin, 1798.

III. Newspapers

Annual Register

The Courier

Dublin Evening Post

The Morning Chronicle

The Morning Post

The Times

IV. Diaries, Memoirs and Correspondence

ABBOT. *Diary and correspondence of Charles Abbot, Lord Colchester*. Ed. Lord Colchester. 3 vols. London, 1861.

ADDINGTON. *The life and correspondence of the Rt Hon. Henry Addington, 1st Viscount Sidmouth*. Ed. George Pellew. 3 vols. London, 1847.

AUCKLAND. *The journal and correspondence of William, Lord Auckland*. Ed. bishop of Bath and Wells. 4 vols. London, 1861–2.

BERESFORD. *The correspondence of the Rt Hon. John Beresford*. Ed. Lord Beresford. 2 vols. London, 1854.

BUCKINGHAM. *Memoirs of the courts and cabinets of George the third*. Ed. 2nd duke of Buckingham and Chandos. 4 vols. London, 1848.

CASTLEREAGH. *Memoirs and correspondence of Viscount Castlereagh*. Ed. Marquess of Londonderry. 12 vols. London, 1848–53.

CORNWALLIS. *The correspondence of Charles, 1st Marquess Cornwallis*. Ed. Charles Ross. 3 vols. London, 1859.

CROKER. *The Croker papers: the correspondence and diaries of the late Right Honourable John Wilson Croker*. Ed. L.J. Jennings. 2 vols. London, 1884.

ELLIOT. *Life and letters of Sir Gilbert Elliot, first earl of Minto*. Ed. Countess of Minto. 2 vols. London, 1874.

FOSTER. *An Anglo-Irish dialogue: a calendar of the correspondence between John Foster and Lord Sheffield*. Belfast, 1975.

GEORGE III. *The later correspondence of George III*. Ed. Arthur Aspinall. Vol. iii. Cambridge, 1967.

GLENBERVIE. *The diaries of Sylvester Douglas, Lord Glenbervie.* Ed. Francis Bickley. 2 vols. London, 1928.

GRATTAN. *Memoirs of the life and times of the Rt Hon. Henry Grattan.* Ed. Henry Grattan jnr. 5 vols. London, 1839–44.

GRENVILLE. *The manuscripts of J.B. Fortescue, esq., preserved at Dropmore.* 10 vols. HMC, London, 1892–1927.

HOBHOUSE. *The diary of Henry Hobhouse, 1820–1827.* Ed. A. Aspinall. London, 1947.

HOLLAND. *Memoirs of the whig party during my time, by Henry Richard Lord Holland.* Ed. Henry Richard Lord Holland jnr. 2 vols. London, 1852.

LEVESON-GOWER. *Private correspondence of Lord Granville Leveson-Gower, 1781–1821.* Ed. Castalia Countess Granville. 2 vols. London, 1916.

McCRACKEN. *The life and times of Mary Ann McCracken.* Ed. Mary McNeill. Dublin, 1960.

MACKINTOSH. *Memoirs of the Rt Hon. Sir James Mackintosh.* Ed. R.J. Mackintosh. 2 vols. London, 1835.

MALMESBURY. *Diaries and correspondence of James Harris, 1st earl of Malmesbury.* 4 vols. London, 1884.

PITT. *Correspondence between the Rt Hon. William Pitt and Charles, duke of Rutland.* Ed. Philip Stanhope, Lord Mahon. London, 1890.

ROSE. *Diary and correspondence of George Rose.* Ed. L. Vernon-Harcourt. 2 vols. London, 1860.

SHANNON. *Lord Shannon's letters to his son: a calendar of the letters written by the 2nd earl of Shannon to his son, Viscount Boyle, 1790–1801.* Ed. Ester Hewitt. Belfast, 1982.

TONE. *The writings of Theobald Wolfe Tone, 1763–98.* Eds. T.W. Moody, R.B. McDowell and C.J. Woods. Vol. i. Oxford, 1998.

WICKHAM. *The correspondence of the Rt Hon. William Wickham.* Ed. William Wickham jnr. 2 vols. London, 1870.

WINDHAM. *The diary of the Rt Hon. William Windham, 1784–1810.* Ed. C.A. Baring. London, 1866.

___ *The Windham papers.* Ed. Lewis Melville. 2 vols. London, 1913.

V. Collections of Documents

Aspinall, A. and Smith, E.A. (eds.). *English historical documents, 1783–1832.* London, 1959.

Curtis, Edmund and McDowell, R.B. (eds.). *Irish historical documents, 1172–1922.* London, 1977.

Donaldson, Gordon (ed.). *Scottish historical documents.* Edinburgh, 1970.

VI. Contemporary and Near-contemporary Works and Descriptions

Anonymous. *Anecdotes of the life of the Right Honourable William Pitt, earl of Chatham.* 2 vols. London, 1796.

___ *Memoirs of nine illustrious characters.* Dublin, 1799.

___ *Public characters.* Baltimore, 1803.

Barrington, Jonah. *Historic memoirs of Ireland.* 2 vols. London, 1833.

___ *The rise and fall of the Irish nation.* Dublin, 1853.

Brougham, Henry Lord. *Historical sketches of statesmen who flourished in the time of George III.* 6 vols. London, 1845.

Campbell, John Lord. *The lives of the lord chancellors.* 7 vols. London, 1847.

Clarke, Mary Anne. *A letter addressed to the Right Honourable William Fitzgerald.* London, 1813.

Cloncurry, Valentine Lord. *Personal recollections of the life and times of Valentine Lord Cloncurry.* Dublin, 1849.

De Mezilliac, Gilbert. *Essai comparatif entre le cardinal-duc de Richelieu et M. William Pitt.* Paris, 1816.

Gifford, John. *A history of the political life of the Right Honourable William Pitt.* 3 vols. London, 1809.

Hazlitt. *The collected works of William Hazlitt.* Ed. A.R. Waller and Arnold Glover. London, 1902.

MacNeven, *Pieces of Irish history.* New York, 1807.

Smith, Adam. *An inquiry into the nature and causes of the wealth of nations.* Oxford, 1993. [London, 1776]

Wilberforce, R.I. and Wilberforce, Samuel. *The life of William Wilberforce.* 2 vols. London, 1838.

SECONDARY SOURCES

Allen, Frank. The London newspapers and Ireland, 1798–1800 (MA minor thesis, NUI (UCD), 1994).

Ashbourne, Lord. *Pitt: some chapters of his life and times.* London, 1898.

Aspinall, Arthur. *Politics and the press, 1780–1850.* London, 1949.

____ The cabinet council, 1783–1835. In *Proceedings of the British Academy,* xxxviii (London, 1952), pp. 145–252.

Ayling, Stanley. *George the third.* London, 1972.

____ *The elder Pitt: earl of Chatham.* London, 1976.

Bagot, Josceline (ed.). *George Canning and his friends.* 2 vols. London, 1909.

Baker, Kenneth. *The prime ministers: an irreverent political history in cartoons.* Slovenia, 1995.

Barnes, D.G. *George III and William Pitt, 1783–1806: a new interpretation based upon a study of their unpublished correspondence.* New York, 1965.

Bartlett, C.J. *Castlereagh.* London, 1964.

Bartlett, Thomas. *The fall and rise of the Irish nation: the catholic question, 1690–1830.* Dublin, 1992.

____ 'A weapon of war yet untried': Irish catholics and the armed forces of the crown, 1760–1830. In T.G. Fraser and Keith Jeffrey (eds.), *Men, women, and war. Historical studies,* xviii (Dublin, 1993).

Bass, B.M. (ed.). *Stogdhill's handbook of leadership.* New York, 1981.

Beckett, J.C. *The Anglo-Irish tradition.* London, 1976.

Bolton, G.C. *The passing of the Irish act of union.* Oxford, 1966.

Brooke, John. *King George III.* London, 1972.

Brown, P.D. *William Pitt, earl of Chatham: the great commoner.* London, 1978.

Butler, Iris. *The eldest brother: the Marquess Wellesley, the duke of Wellington's eldest brother.* London, 1973.

Chatterton, E.K. *England's greatest statesman: a life of William Pitt, 1759–1806.* Indianapolis, 1930.

Christie, I.R. *Myth and reality in late eighteenth century politics.* London, 1970.

____ *Wars and revolutions: Britain 1760–1815.* London, 1982.

Colley, Linda. *Britons: forging the nation, 1707–1837.* Yale, 1992.

Corish, Patrick. *Maynooth college, 1795–1995.* Dublin, 1995.

Crauford, E.M. William Wilde's table of Irish famines, 900–1850. In E.M. Crauford (ed.), *Famine: the Irish experience, 900–1900.* Edinburgh, 1989.

Curzon, Marquess of Kedleston. *The personal history of Walmer castle and its lords warden.* London, 1927.

Derry, John. *William Pitt.* London, 1962.

____ *Charles James Fox.* Gateshead, 1972.

____ *Castlereagh.* London, 1976.

Dickson, David. The Irish experience, 900–1900. In E.M. Crauford (ed.), *Famine: the Irish experience, 900–1900*. Edinburgh, 1989.

Dixon, Peter. *Canning: politician and statesman*. London, 1976.

Duffy, Michael. Pitt, Grenville and the control of British foreign policy in the 1790s. In Jeremy Black (ed.), *Knights errant and true Englishmen*. Edinburgh, 1989.

Ehrman, John. *The younger Pitt*. 3 vols. London, 1969–1996.

Elliott, Marianne. *Partners in revolution: the United Irishmen and France*. New Haven, 1982.

Eyck, Erich. *Pitt versus Fox: father and son, 1735–1806*. London, 1950.

Falkiner, C.L. *Studies in Irish history and biography*. London, 1902.

Fedorak, C.J. Catholic emancipation and the resignation of William Pitt. In *Albion*, xxiv, no. 1 (spring 1992), pp. 49–64.

Feiling, K.G. *The second tory party, 1714–1832*. London, 1938.

Festing, Gabrielle. *John Hookham Frere and his friends*. London, 1899.

Fitzgibbon, Elliot. *The earl of Clare: mainspring of the union*. London, 1960.

Foster, R.F. *Modern Ireland, 1600–1972*. London, 1988.

Froude, J.A. *The English in Ireland in the eighteenth century*. 3 vols. London, 1874.

Fry, Michael. *The Dundas despotism*. Edinburgh, 1992.

Galtung, Johan. A structural theory of imperialism. In *Journal of Peace Research*, vol. 13, no. 2 (1971), pp. 81–94.

Gash, Norman. *Lord Liverpool*. London, 1984.

Geoghegan, P.M. *1798 and the Irish bar*. Dublin, 1998.

Gilbert, John. *Documents relating to Ireland, 1795–1804*. Shannon, 1970.

Harlow, V.T. *The founding of the second British empire, 1763–1793*. 2 vols. London, 1964.

Harvey, A.D. *William Pitt the younger, 1759–1806: a bibliography*. London, 1989.

___ *Lord Grenville, 1759–1834: a bibliography*. London, 1989.

Hayes, Richard. *Biographical dictionary of Irishmen in France*. Dublin, 1949.

Hibbert, Christopher. *Wellington: a personal history*. London, 1997.

Hinde, Wendy. *George Canning*. London, 1973.

___ *Castlereagh*. London, 1981.

Holyoake, Gregory. *Wellington at Walmer*. Dover, 1996.

Hyde, H.M. *The rise of Castlereagh*. London, 1933.

___ *The strange death of Lord Castlereagh*. London, 1959.

Ingram, T.D. *A history of the legislative union of Great Britain and Ireland*. London, 1887.

Jarrett, Derek. *Pitt the younger*. London, 1974.

Johnston, E.M. *Great Britain and Ireland, 1760–1800*. Edinburgh, 1963.

Jupp, Peter. *Lord Grenville, 1759–1834*. Oxford, 1985.

Kavanaugh, A.C. *John Fitzgibbon, earl of Clare*. Dublin, 1997.

Kelly, James. The origins of the act of union. In *Irish Historical Studies*, xxv, no. 99 (May 1987), pp. 236–63.

Kenney, J.J., jnr. Lord Whitworth and the conspiracy against Tsar Paul I: the new evidence of the Kent archive. In *Slavic Review*, vol. 36, no. 2 (June 1977), pp. 205–19.

Keogh, Dáire. *The French disease: The catholic church and Irish radicalism, 1790–1800*. Dublin, 1993.

Kiberd, Declan. *Inventing Ireland*. London, 1995.

Koebner, Richard. The early speeches of Henry Grattan. In *IHR Bull.*, xxx (1957), pp. 102–14.

Lascelles, Edward. *The life of Charles James Fox*. New York, 1970.

Lecky, W.E.H. *Ireland in the eighteenth century*. 5 vols. London, 1898.

Lynch, Michael. *Scotland*. London, 1992.

MacAlpine, Ida and Hunter, Richard. *George III and the mad business*. London, 1969.

Macaulay, Lord. *William Pitt*. London, 1904.

McCartney, Donal. *The dawning of democracy*. Dublin, 1987.

MacDonagh, Michael. *The viceroy's post-bag*. London, 1904.

MacDonagh, Oliver. *Ireland: the union and its aftermath*. London, 1977.

___ *States of mind: two centuries of Anglo-Irish conflict, 1780–1980*. London, 1983.

McDowell, R.B. *Ireland in the age of imperialism and revolution, 1760–1801*. Oxford, 1979.

MacGregor Burns, James. *Leadership*. New York, 1978.

McGrew, R.E. *Paul I of Russia, 1754–1801*. Oxford, 1992.

McGuire, James. The act of union. In Liam de Paor (ed.), *Milestones in Irish history*. Cork, 1986.

Mackesy, Piers. *War without victory: the downfall of Pitt, 1799–1802*. Oxford, 1984.

McNally, V.J. *Reform, revolution and reaction: Archbishop John Thomas Troy and the catholic church in Ireland, 1787–1817*. Dublin, 1995.

MacNeill, J.G. Swift. *The constitutional and parliamentary history of Ireland 'till the union*. Dublin and London, 1917.

Malcomson, A.P.W. *John Foster: the politics of the Anglo-Irish ascendancy*. Oxford, 1978.

___ 'The parliamentary traffic of this country'. In Thomas Bartlett and D.W. Hayton (eds.), *Penal era and golden age*. Belfast, 1979.

Marshall, Dorothy. *The rise of George Canning*. London, 1938.

Matheson, Cyril. *The life of Henry Dundas*. London, 1933.

Mitchell, Harvey. *The underground war against revolutionary France*. Oxford, 1965.

Moody, T.W. and Vaughan, W.E. (eds.). *A new history of Ireland, 1691–1800*. Oxford, 1986.

O'Brien, George. *The economic history of Ireland from the union to the famine*. New Jersey, 1972. [London, 1921]

O'Farrell, Patrick. *Ireland's English question*. London, 1971.

O'Flanagan, J.R. *The Irish bar*. London, 1879.

O'Reilly, Robin. *Pitt the younger*. London, 1978.

Ó Tuathaigh, Gearóid. *Ireland before the famine, 1798–1848*. Dublin, 1972.

Pakenham, Thomas. *The year of liberty*. London, 1969.

Pares, Richard. *George III and the politicians*. Oxford, 1953.

Petrie, Charles. *Lord Liverpool and his times*. London, 1954.

Pickering, B.W. (ed.). *The works of the Right Honourable John Hookham Frere in verse and prose*. London, 1874.

Pollock, John. *Wilberforce*. London, 1977.

Riley, P.W.J. *The English ministers and Scotland, 1701–27*. London, 1964.

Rose, J.H. *William Pitt and the great war*. London, 1911.

___ *Pitt and Napoleon*. London, 1912.

___ *Life of William Pitt*. London, 1923.

___ *A short life of William Pitt*. London, 1925.

Rosebery, Lord. *Pitt*. London, 1918.

Schama, Simon. *Landscape and memory*. London, 1996.

Senior, Hereward. *Orangeism in Ireland and Britain, 1795–1836*. London, 1966.

Sergeant, Lewis. *William Pitt*. London, 1882.

Sparrow, Elizabeth. The alien office, 1792–1806. In *The Historical Journal*, no. 33, 2 (1990), pp. 361–84.

Stanhope, Lord. *Life of the Right Honourable William Pitt*. 4 vols. London, 1861–2.

St John-Stevans, Norman (ed.). *Bagehot's historical essays*. New York, 1966.

Strauss, Erich. *Irish nationalism and British democracy*. London, 1975.

Temperley, H.W.V. *Life of Canning*. Connecticut, 1970.

Waliszewski, K. *Paul the first of Russia, the son of Catherine the great*. London, 1913. [1969 edition]

Watson, J.S. *The reign of George III*. Oxford, 1960.

Wells, Roger. *Insurrection: the British royal experience, 1795–1803*. Gloucester, 1983.

___ *Wretched faces: famine in wartime England, 1793–1801*. Gloucester, 1988.

Wickwire, Franklin and Wickwire, Mary. *Cornwallis and the war of independence.* London, 1970.

___ *Cornwallis: the imperial years.* North Carolina, 1980.

Wilkinson, David. The Fitzwilliam episode. In *Irish Historical Studies*, xxix, no. 115 (May 1995), pp. 315–39.

___ 'How did they pass the union? Secret service expenditure', in *History*, 82, no. 266 (April 1997), pp. 223–51.

Willis, Richard. The politics of parliament, 1800–6 (Ph.D. thesis, University of Stanford, 1969).

___ William Pitt's resignation in 1801: re-examination and document. In *Bulletin of the Institute of Historical Research*, xliv, no. 110 (1971), pp. 239–57.

___ Cabinet politics and executive policy-making procedures, 1794–1801. In *Albion*, vii, no. 1 (1975), pp. 1–22.

Wilson, P.W. *William Pitt the younger.* New York, 1933.

Ziegler, Philip. *Addington.* London, 1965.

Dictionaries and Reference Works

Dictionary of Irish Biography. Royal Irish Academy. Forthcoming.

Dictionary of National Biography. 22 vols. Rev. ed., London, 1908–9.

Thorne, R.G. (ed.). *The commons, 1790–1820.* 5 vols. London, 1986.

Index